T0351905

Investing in Place

Sean Markey, Greg Halseth,
and Don Manson

Investing in Place
Economic Renewal in Northern British Columbia

UBCPress · Vancouver · Toronto

21 20 19 18 17 16 15 14 13 12   5 4 3 2 1

Printed in Canada on FSC-certified ancient-forest-free paper (100% postconsumer recycled) that is processed chlorine- and acid-free.

Library and Archives Canada Cataloguing in Publication

Markey, Sean Patrick

Investing in place : economic renewal in northern British Columbia / Sean Markey, Greg Halseth, and Don Manson.

Includes bibliographical references and index.
Issued also in electronic format.
ISBN 978-0-7748-2291-6

1. Economic development – British Columbia, Northern. 2. Rural renewal – British Columbia, Northern. 3. British Columbia, Northern – Economic conditions. I. Halseth, Greg, 1960- II. Manson, Don, 1961- III. Title.

HC117.B8M37 2012   338.9711'8   C2012-901116-9

Canada

UBC Press gratefully acknowledges the financial support for our publishing program of the Government of Canada (through the Canada Book Fund), the Canada Council for the Arts, and the British Columbia Arts Council.

The authors gratefully acknowledge the publication grants provided for this book from the University of Northern British Columbia and Simon Fraser University.

UBC Press
The University of British Columbia
2029 West Mall
Vancouver, BC V6T 1Z2
www.ubcpress.ca

Contents

Figures and Tables

Figures

Tables

Acknowledgments

This book, and our understanding of the community and economic development of northern BC, is the product of a very long and rewarding engagement with many people and communities. We thank them all for their patient contributions to our work and we hope that this book repays at least some of the confidence they have shown in us.

Much of the work shared in this book comes from various research projects, so our first thanks go to all of the people and organizations who over the years have taken time to meet with us, to participate in our projects, to provide information, to attend workshops or roundtables, or to be interviewed.

These projects would not have been possible without funding support, and we wish to acknowledge support from the Social Sciences and Humanities Research Council of Canada (through their Standard Research Grants, Social Cohesion Program, Insight Development Grants, Knowledge Impact in Society Program, and Initiative on the New Economy Program), and the Canadian Institutes for Health Research. Specific project support also came from organizations such as Indian and Northern Affairs Canada – Office of the Federal Interlocutor and Economic Development Branch, and Industry Canada. We would like to acknowledge the publication fund assistance provided by the University of Northern BC (UNBC) and Simon Fraser University (SFU).

We also acknowledge support from Western Economic Diversification Canada for specific projects such as: Northern BC Economic Development Vision & Strategy Project; Terrace Economic Development Project; the 2005 and 2006 Northern BC Economic Forums; the innovative "From Space to Place" conference where we were able to bring in eighteen speakers from nine OECD countries to talk about the "next" rural economies. Through WED Canada we have benefitted from assistance over the years from Garth Stiller, Greg De Bloeme, Curtis Johnston, and Wendy Rogers, as well as support from Gerry Salembier, assistant deputy minister, Western Economic Diversification Canada.

Support from Service Canada, especially the offices in Prince George and Terrace, assisted with the Old Massett Five Year Human Resources Development Strategy and the Northern BC Service Sector Project. We thank Louise Côté Madill, Andrea Robertson, and Agnes J. Pindera for their assistance.

Specific work on community transition and future forest- and fibre-use projects were supported by the federal government's Community Economic Development Initiative, the Omineca Beetle Action Coalition, and the BC Ministry of Community Services. Advice and assistance from Fred Banham, Brent Mueller, Elizabeth Andersen, Sharon Tower, Herb Langin, Sarah Fraser, Keith Storey, Bill Reimer, David Bruce, Derek Wilkinson, Frank Caffrey and Denis Pelletier of Timberline Natural Resources Group, and Ashley Kearns are greatly appreciated. Our thanks also to Leslie Lax for his direct research contributions and helpful reviews of our manuscript.

Greg Halseth also wishes to acknowledge the support he received through the Canada Research Chairs program and the associated support of the Canadian Foundation for Innovation.

A number of other groups and individuals have provided project support over the years. These include former Community Futures Development Corporation managers Don Zurowski (Fraser Fort George) and Roger Leclerc (16/37), Andrew Webber at the Regional District of Kitimat Stikine, John Disney in the economic development office in the Village of Old Massett, and Ted Richardson, Cheryl Thomas, and Leslie Groulx in Clearwater; also, Marc von der Gonna, Rick Thompson, Ken Starchuk, Ray Gerow, Veronica Creyke, Stephanie Killam, Mark Fercho, Sylvia Arduini, Susan Garland, Charles Helm, Mike Caisley, George Hartford, Clay Iles, Margaret Warcup, Kathy Bedard, Bernice Magee, Chris Bone, Lori Ackerman, Alice Maitland, Don Basserman, Mike Frazier, Sarah Cunningham, and Trevor Williams. In addition, we thank George Holman and Nan Love from Atlin, Ted Staffen (former speaker of Yukon assembly), Valoree Walker (Northern Research Institute, Yukon College), Len Fox (former mayor Vanderhoof), and Cacilia Honisch and Carolyn Hesseltine on Haida Gwaii.

Within our own institutions we have had great support. At UNBC this includes Max Blouw (former vice president of research, now president of Wilfred Laurier University); the current vice president of research, Gail Fondahl; long-time UNBC president Charles Jago; recent past-president Don Cozzetto; current president George Iwama; UNBC's Community Development Institute, and internal funding for key research such as the Tourism Development Foundations Project, as well as ongoing and strong support for the idea that UNBC was created to address the information and research needs of northern BC's communities.

Greg Halseth would like to thank the wonderful staff and colleagues at UNBC with whom he works, especially those whose work on projects connected with this book, including Annie Booth, Neil Hanlon, Catherine Nolin, Rob Budde, Dave Snadden, Glen Schmidt, Ramona Rose, Gail Curry, Anne Hardy, and Tracy Summerville.

At SFU we have received tremendous support through the Centre for Sustainable Community Development, the Department of Geography, and the Explorations Program in Arts and Social Sciences. Our specific thanks go to John Pierce, dean of the Faculty of Environment, Mark Roseland, director of the Centre for Sustainable Community Development (CSCD), and colleagues Ted Hicken, Roger Hayter, Robert Anderson, Peter Hall, Stephen Ameyaw, Heather Dawkins, Paul Matthew St. Pierre, and Kelly Vodden at Memorial University. We would also like to acknowledge the wonderful support from staff in Explorations, the CSCD, and the Faculty of Environment.

Perhaps most importantly, our work has been tirelessly supported by the students and staff who over the years have formed the Rural and Small Town Studies team at UNBC. At its heart, this team includes Laura Ryser and Lana Sullivan – as much a part of the family as anything else. Also valued members of our team are Rosemary Raygada Watanabe, Julia Schwamborn, and Kyle Kusch. Into this team we also had the pleasure to welcome for a time Deborah Thein as a postdoctoral research fellow. Graduate researchers at SFU who have contributed greatly to our research include Karen Heisler and Sean Connelly.

One of the great pleasures of university-based research is the opportunity to involve undergraduate and graduate students. So many of these students have gone on to pursue graduate studies or other research careers. Some have become recognized researchers in their own right. It has been an honour and pleasure to have worked with them all. This wonderful group includes Alex Martin, Allison Matte, Amy Gondak, Anisa Zehtab-Martin, Anne Hogan, Ashley Kearns, Brendan Bonfield, Brian Stauffer, Carla Seguin, Catherine Fraser, Charlene Ponto, Chelan Zirul, Christine Creyke, Colin Macleod, Courtney LeBourdais, David Angus, Eric Kopetski, Gretchen Hernandez, James McNish, Jamie Reschny, Jennifer Crain, Jennifer Herkes, Jenny Lo, Jessica Rayner, Joanne Doddridge, Kelly Giesbrecht, Laurel van de Keere, Lila Bonnardel, Liz O'Connor, Marc Steynen, Marisa MacDonald, Melinda Worfolk, Melissa Zacharatos, Michelle White, Mollie Cudmore, Nora King, Onkar Buttar, Pam Tobin, Paul Pan, Petter Jacobsen, Priscilla Johnson, Rachael Clasby, Rebecca Goodenough, Rheanna Robinson, Rosalynd Curry, Sarah Quinn, Sarena Talbot, Shawn Rennebohn, Shiloh Durkee, Tobi Araki, and Virginia Pow.

We have received tremendous support from the broader academic community for our work. This includes contributions from various journals (and their numerous reviewers) where our work has appeared. Adapted excerpts from these writings appear throughout this volume, so our thanks and acknowledgements go to the *Canadian Geographer,* the *Journal of Rural Studies,* the *Canadian Journal of Regional Science,* the *Journal of Rural and Community Development, International Planning Studies,* the *International Journal of Urban and Regional Research, Planning Practice and Research,* the *Community Development Journal,* and *Local Environment.*

Finally, our sincere thanks to the outstanding publishing team at UBC Press, including specific thanks to Randy Schmidt and Anna Eberhard Friedlander. It has been a pleasure to work with you on this volume and your contributions to its betterment are greatly appreciated. We also received excellent feedback from the anonymous reviewers selected by UBC Press for this work. Thanks also to Kathy Plett at the College of New Caledonia, for her invaluable work on the index.

In closing, our greatest thanks go to our families for their ongoing support of our research journeys.

Sean Markey Greg Halseth Don Manson

With ice cream cones, on the patio of the Mt. Robson Café

2011

Part 1
Introduction

1
Introduction: Foundations for Renewal

> A British Columbia Parable:
>
> In the early 1950s, the WAC Bennett government bought a shiny new truck. With that truck, the province was able to get to work and do all the things it needed and wanted to do. That truck ran really well for nearly thirty years. After 1980, however, the truck was worn out and didn't fit well with the new jobs now being asked of it. Instead of looking around, kicking tires, and deciding to buy a new hybrid economy car with lots of interior space and good gas mileage, successive provincial governments have tried to keep that old truck running. They have tinkered here, and have added parts there. But the fact is that the truck's useful life is long since finished. It is time to invest in a new vehicle to carry us into the future.

This book is about creating the foundations for renewing northern British Columbia's rural and small-town economy as we move into the twenty-first century. It is about creating the foundations of renewal so that we can employ our place-based assets to take advantage of rapidly emerging and changing opportunities within local, regional, national, and global economies. Here, through eleven chapters, we will explore (1) how northern BC's economy developed over time, (2) the disjunctures rooted in global and technological changes not yet fully incorporated into regional development, and (3) opportunities for taking proactive action – at all levels – to better equip and situate our rural and small-town places to be competitive in the new economy.

As we conceptualize it, the key to renewal is not based in nostalgia. It is not about returning to the economies and political structures of the past. It is not about seeking some kind of mythical rural idyll. Renewal entails building a pragmatic vision for development that proactively addresses the realities and opportunities of the new economy by finding a balance between economic, community, environmental, and cultural issues. Renewal is about finding a way forward that is grounded in tested practices and with a solid understanding of how development happens, how to mobilize action for change, and how to respond to the ongoing processes of change that define the global economy.

Our approach to writing this book rests on research that has sought to understand development practices throughout northern British Columbia. Our knowledge of the north is deeply rooted in an appreciation for the historical context and development pathways that have created the province that we see around us today. These perspectives will reveal themselves in the following chapters in our attempt to bring readers along the same conceptual journey, arriving at our core argument in favour of a place-based approach to economic renewal. Our treatment of these issues combines a variety of "voices," including scholarly research, summaries of best practice for policy makers, and practical stories and case studies that we hope will resonate with communities across northern British Columbia and in other rural and small-town settings – in Canada and internationally. Our own research has benefitted greatly by balancing and infusing our scholarly work with involvement in policy processes and tangible development projects. We have traversed the northern landscape many times over to capture stories, learn from people, and participate in the discussions and projects that are actively shaping the north.

Readers will detect a tone of advocacy surrounding our treatment of the principles and practices of place-based development. There are two reasons for this. First, our research in northern British Columbia, combined with research from other jurisdictions, tells us very clearly that the foundation for successful rural development is in the context of place. We must work to understand how to employ all of our place-based assets to create viable communities that are economically robust, socially resilient, and environmentally sustainable. Place-based development is a collaborative and co-constructed approach that requires the active participation and engagement of all levels of government and communities; it is not passive in any direction: either waiting for the market, for government direction, or community action. Second, place-based development is a completely underutilized and generally unfamiliar approach to development in northern BC. We will work, in the following chapters, to define the concept of place-based development, illustrate how to use it in communities, and identify some of its main challenges. In the final chapters, we will step out of our academic research voice to present a vision for how this form of development may be constructed and what its impact might have been in twenty years time. In essence, place-based development asks us to consider what development would look like in northern BC if we were building communities and regional economies of permanence – and not simply treating the region as a resource frontier.

The purpose of this introductory chapter is to begin to outline an argument for renewal and to present the framework of this book. The chapter opens with some key messages that underscore the importance of renewal for northern BC's rural and small-town economy. These messages include the following: rural and small-town BC has long been set within a global economy, and recent changes in that global economy now require more attention to "place-specific" assets and attributes. We outline how there will be no hope for rural and small-town renewal if the various senior governments continue to off-load their responsibilities for providing coordination, infrastructure, and vital services, and there will not be successful renewal if rural and small-town residents and decision makers look only to senior governments for support and a vision for the future. Top-down and bottom-up supports and engagement must co-create solutions. The future of rural and small-town British Columbia is one that includes and involves all of our peoples, both Aboriginal and non-Aboriginal. The next section draws on our research in which we asked people across northern BC how they would renew their community and economic foundations. This section describes a vision built on lifestyles, assets, and strategic investments in infrastructure that link people and places with economic opportunity. Finally, we close with an outline of the remaining chapters of this book.

Locating Northern BC

Before outlining our key messages, it is important to offer a quick reference to our definition of northern BC. Describing or defining regions across the large and varied physical landscape of British Columbia is always a challenge. When done, there are always those who would argue for a different alignment, a different location for "edges," and even different nomenclature. There are the challenges of edge communities' feeling more closely linked to places outside of any supposed region versus feeling intensely linked to the "core" of the designated region. We do not argue with any such challenges and recognize that defining a region is fraught with complications.

For the purposes of this book, northern BC includes everything from 100 Mile House north to the Yukon, and from Alberta to Haida Gwaii (see Figure 1). In many ways, this region is a wonderful exemplar of resource-dependent rural and small-town regions across Canada and in other member countries of the Organization for Economic Co-operation and Development (OECD) that display a variety of common characteristics. Economic development since the Second World War has remained focused on resource-extractive industries, with population growth and decline being linked to international market demands and prices for resources. Control of industries

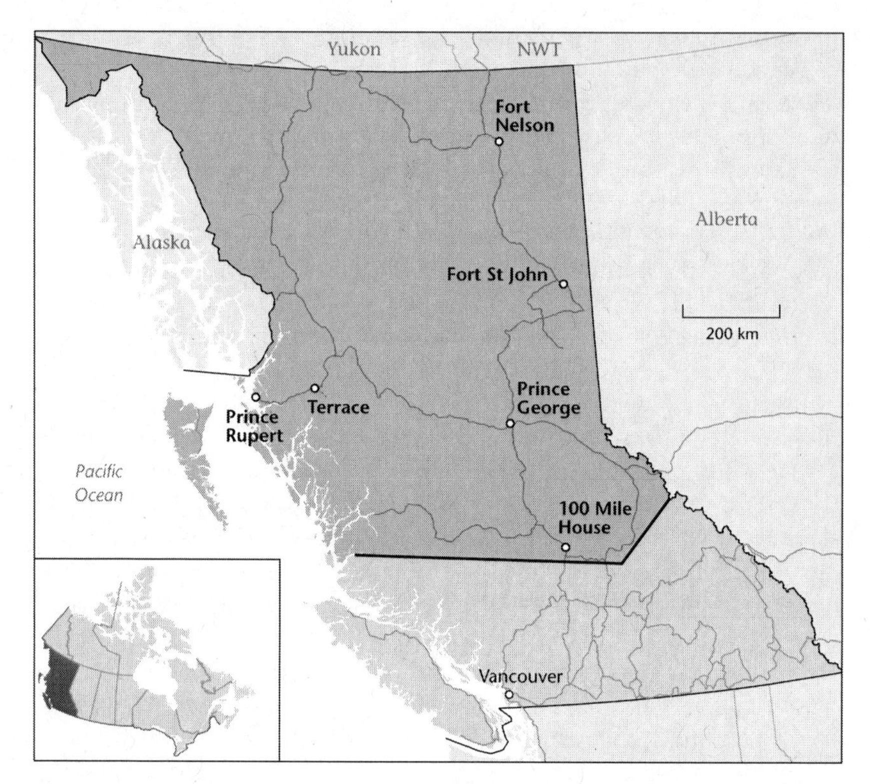

Figure 1 Northern British Columbia. *Source*: K. Kusch, UNBC Community Development Institute.

and state-delivered services is external (multinational capital and metropolitan core regions respectively). The existing economic infrastructure is aging, there has been an extended extraction of wealth with limited reinvestment, the working population is aging-in-place, there has been an out-migration of youth, and many available services are being closed and consolidated. In a dispersed settlement landscape, long distances and few local economic options exist when industrial closure is threatened. We must realize, in looking to the future, that our competition in the global economy is other countries and that to be successful, northern BC (and the province as a whole) needs to work collectively.

Our research adopted a regional approach for a variety of reasons. First, BC's economic competitors across Canada and in other industrialized parts of the world have scaled up from local to regional approaches. This means that for northern BC to remain economically competitive in a global marketplace, we need to start working more collaboratively. Second, other jurisdictions have shifted from sectoral to "place-based" policies in their efforts to direct and conduct development in their rural regions. We have much to learn from the successes and challenges of using this approach to understand communities and the regions in which they are situated. Third, in the context of our current political and economic realities, limited funds for infrastructure and services need to be wisely invested, and this can only be accomplished by taking a wider view of costs and benefits across the region as a whole. Finally, and perhaps most importantly, a regional, collective voice has a greater impact on public policy debates and on seeking changes and enhanced benefits from the corporate sector. Through the early stages of our research on regional development, people would inevitably start the conversation with "it seems a good idea, but our area is so unique that it has little in common with the rest of northern BC." However, once they talked through how linkages exist in political relationships, economic flows, infrastructure and service needs, attention to lifestyle and the environment, and a host of other factors, they came to value the opportunities inherent in thinking about their community as part of a much larger and wider northern BC.

A Rationale for Renewal

Over the past 200 years, the social, economic, cultural, and political landscape of northern BC has undergone considerable transformation. The pace of change has accelerated over recent decades, and communities, industries, businesses, and decision makers recognize that this creates both new challenges and new opportunities (Hayter 2000; Hutton 2002; Morford and Kahlke 2004). Against this backdrop of accelerating change, there is an emerging recognition from within all sectors of the need for a new vision to guide community and economic revitalization.

To illustrate the need for a renewed vision we can look just about anywhere across northern BC. The past decade has seen some areas enjoy substantial benefits from a significant resource economy boom. The demand for oil and gas buoyed provincial coffers with healthy surpluses. The demand for minerals, spurred by China's rapidly growing industrial base, boosted prices and led to a resurgence of mining across BC. Meanwhile, the US housing market consumed all that interior forestry mills could put out as they ran at full capacity – supported as well by an "uplift" of wood supply as the province sought to recover economic value from forests infested by the mountain pine beetle.

Certainly, the boom of 2004-2007 created social and economic benefits for both the province and those areas of northern BC where the resources were located. This time, however, things were different. First, there were not as many new jobs created as had happened in past booms. Second, there was no preparation in the service sector to cope with the new demands. Third, there were critical skills shortages across a range of sectors; and fourth, the places that were bearing the costs of these developments within their community and environment were not seeing the benefits they had anticipated. A report by the North Peace Economic Development Commission, for example, pointed out that the region was realizing only about 10 percent of the employment and economic benefits of the oil and gas boom (Nicol 2003). While the Commission's report may overestimate the benefits that could reasonably come to the region, the social and infrastructure costs were so pressing on the communities that, in the elections of 2005, municipal voters in both Dawson Creek and Fort St. John replaced almost their entire city councils. Concerns about water, housing, conservation, and community quality of life are suddenly as important as concerns for jobs.

Following the boom was the bust, a pattern that has repeated itself at important junctures throughout BC's postwar history. Beginning in 2007, with the collapse of the US housing and credit markets, the economic downturn became global through a parallel implosion of banks and other financial organizations, sovereign debt, and a much wider slowing of consumer demand and resulting slowdowns in manufacturing. The key point that BC and Canada must take away from the recent downturn is the following: no matter how much decision makers and the popular press may have become convinced that cities are our economic engines, it has, in fact, been the collapse of the resource commodities (wood, pulp, paper, oil, gas, minerals, coal) produced in our rural and small-town communites that resulted in Canada recording its first export deficit in approximately thirty years and in BC's provincial government revenue flows dropping precipitously. Moreover, because of this persisting economic dependency, the recession hit rural and small-town communities particularly hard.[1]

In light of our most recent boom-bust experience, the challenge for renewal is clear. (1) We must invest in BC's rural and small-town communities so that we are ready to take full advantage of future economic upswings (across a wide range of economic opportunities) as they unfold, instead of playing catch-up because of a lack of preparation. (2) We must keep more of the benefits of any upswing in the north and invest them wisely into development decisions to support more economically diversified and socially resilient rural and small-town places.

Addressing this challenge serves as the core purpose of this book. To identify an appropriate approach to rural and small-town renewal in northern BC, we will be drawing from and adapting the lessons of the WAC Bennett era of "province building" and merging them with specific insights offered by the increasing recognition of the significance of place in social and economic development. This synthesis exposes troubling gaps in our current development approach.

To start our discussion, in the next section, we offer a thumbnail portrait of the argument and approach that we will expand in the chapters that follow. Central to the future of rural and small-town BC is divining the roles of small places within the global economy. The messages are relatively simple in this regard. First, the global economy itself is not anything new, and therefore, we should not approach it with fear or apprehension. Second, the value of small places is increasing because, as space is becoming relatively less important in the global economy, place is becoming more important. Both of these messages reinforce an older understanding in BC: that our rural and urban places are closely interconnected and that the economy of the province as a whole depends on the participation and strength of both partners.

A Global Economy

The past twenty-five years have witnessed rising discussion and recognition around rural and small-town BC that we live in a global economy. Drawing on work from the United States, Fitchen (1991) offers an interesting perspective on change, and how it affects our sense of the past, present, and future. She warns that only when one is immersed in change does "the past appear [to one as] stable and unchanging by contrast" (259). It is only through today's heated media and public discussions about the impacts and consequences of change in the global economy that we forget how BC's economy has long been both changing and globally organized.

Since time immemorial, northern BC has been a trading economy (see Northwest Tribal Treaty Nations [NWTT] 2004). The quality of life for First Nations people and communities has for a long time been intimately linked to the natural resource base of the lands and waters and to the organization of those resources so that they can fulfil community needs and aspirations. We know a great deal about how different First Nations traded goods across the BC landscape. They traded seafood (especially the prized oolichan grease), cedar, shells, and a host of other products from the coast with people living across the interior. In turn, people living on the interior plateau traded goods not available on the coast. These trading networks rested on principles of commodity exchange in order to obtain goods not available locally. They also created a dense network of trade routes and exchange sites across the landscape. Volume 1 from the magnificent Historical Atlas of Canada series contains a number of map plates describing the complexity and extensiveness of these trade networks at local, regional, and continental scales (Harris and Matthews 1987). The national historic site at Fort Kitwanga marks the location of one especially strategic crossroads point in the trading trails of northwestern BC. Alexander Mackenzie, on his famous crossing of North America to the Pacific in 1793, made a hard right turn near Alexandra Ferry to go overland to Bella Coola. This would seem quite remarkable for a man who had previously gone everywhere by river, when in fact, he was simply following the well-worn and locally known grease trail to the coast that provided a safe and certain path to his goal.

The European fur trade followed Mackenzie into the interior of northern BC. With it, the economic future and fortunes of the region became increasingly determined by industries and governments located outside of the region (Harris 2002). When the Hudson's Bay Company factor at Fort St. James (then the capital of New Caledonia) wanted to make decisions, he would write to headquarters. The message would go by canoe eastward to Montreal and by ship across the Atlantic to company offices in London, where meetings would be held, decisions made, and instructions put together. The reply would then retrace the journey back to Fort St. James the following year. Although the process was slower than today's electronic communication systems, the process was, nevertheless, still very much the same – a branch manager would contact headquarters for instructions and then act once those instructions were received. The purpose of the factor or branch manager was to ensure that raw materials from the resource-producing region got into the production chain of the larger company for processing into finished products for later sale via global marketing networks. We should not underestimate the success of this older and slower version of the system, as Fort St. James functioned successfully as a focal point for the Hudson's Bay Company's fur trade empire in northern BC for nearly a hundred and fifty years. Globalization, in this sense, is not a new phenomenon to northern BC's rural and small-town places.

What is new about the global economy is that the pace of change has accelerated. We are now much more connected and influenced by affairs in distant places and by how our markets in those distant places perceive affairs in BC. In 2003 alone, examples such as the SARS epidemic and the Okanagan/Clearwater forest fires, which had a significant and immediate downward impact on BC's tourism industry, illustrate just how quickly events can change the economics of entire industries. The economic crisis that accelerated during the autumn of 2008 is, of course, a very dramatic symbol of the pace and interconnectedness of this global economic system: "Today's world changes even faster, and even more profoundly. There is a lot more to understand and a much more pressing need to get it right. Look around in today's business environment and you can see the companies that are good at market intelligence; the reason you can't see the others that didn't get it right is because they no longer exist" (Apsey 2006: 48).

The rapid pace at which change occurs has several implications. To start, actions in BC have consequences. For example, as wealthy tourists approach wilderness adventures with an increasingly well-informed environmental mindset, perceptions about BC's environmental protection regulations and policies, and even our standing in the global community in terms of such indicators as energy consumption per capita, will colour their mindset. A more direct consequence is that the pace of such change challenges the responsiveness of large institutions like the provincial government. Large governments simply cannot respond in a nimble manner to rapidly changing opportunities and crises. Small-town places across northern BC must be prepared and equipped so that they can be flexible and responsive to opportunities as they arise, not to mention robust in responding to economic cycles of boom and bust – because there is no way that the provincial government can facilitate the take-up of such opportunities from a purely reactionary position.

At the start of the twenty-first century, the rural and small-town places of northern BC are home to a vibrant set of cultures within a diverse physical landscape. It remains a place with rich resource endowments, with one of the key resources being the people who live in, and have made a commitment to, these places (BC Progress Board 2002). Its assets and resources remain in great demand within the global economy – resources that now include much more than simply fish, fur, timber, agricultural products, minerals, and oil and natural gas. Renewal is about moving forward to transform existing resource development strength into a diversified economic strength founded on rich resource assets and amenities.[2] Renewal is about diversifying within existing economic sectors, and growing new economic sectors that complement both our "place-based" assets and our aspirations.

From Space to Place

If a global economy itself is not new, what facets are new with respect to reconsidering the role of small places in the economy? Two are important here. The first has to do with the application of technologies that allow real-time production management at a global scale. Consider the computer on your desk as an illustration. Likely the headquarters of the company that manufactures it are in the United States or Japan. The telephone order to procure it goes through a call centre in southern Asia. The various component parts of your computer come from many locations around the world, and your order is finally assembled in yet another country. Then it goes out to you via a courier company, the headquarters of which are in yet another country (perhaps an island resort nation with favourable corporate tax regimes). All of this happens in a matter of days.

In today's technologically connected world, geographic space (raw distance, even if measured in terms of time or financial transfer costs) is declining in importance. But if capital can locate anywhere, the question becomes why is it that capital locates in the places that it does? The characteristics of places in terms of regulations, connectivity to the world economy, available labour supply, supportive industries and skills, quality-of-life services and amenities, natural environment, safety, political stability, and a host of other inputs to the production and decision-making systems mean that differences between places will guide the investment decisions of capital. In others words, as space is becoming less important in the global economy, place is becoming more important.

Porter (2004) identifies the increasingly important role that "traded industries" play in the global economy. These industries are not resource dependent; instead, they sell products and services locally, regionally, and internationally. They can be located anywhere, and thus factors affecting the competitiveness of places are key to decisions concerning location. Renewal, as argued by Porter, will involve the evolution of rural economies. Inherited endowments such as location and natural resources are important, but even more so are the choices made by local leadership to understand and mobilize rural assets in order to be more competitive.

Approaches to regional development in a space-based economy have tended to focus on economic issues. These have included regulatory changes and transportation investments to reduce the costs of production to capital. Part of the sequence has been for governments to reduce tax burdens on capital – with resulting (and increasing) gaps in our ability to maintain local services and community infrastructure. What is becoming increasingly the case, however, is that the lack of attention to key infrastructure and quality-of-life investments that result from a continued policy focus on tax cuts is costing industry and economic development interests much more than the savings they gained through the cuts (Lee 2003). To be clear, there is no suggestion here to decrease the competitiveness of northern BC's rural and small-town places with a taxation regime that is above the norm for OECD countries. Rather, the point is that a simplistic focus on tax cuts, in fact, leaves the state less and less able to support business and industry with a competitive investment environment. Recent announcements by the BC provincial government regarding massive infrastructure investments in various "gateway" transportation initiatives, for example, are all justified on the basis that the savings to small and large businesses and industries from an improved transportation system far outweigh the expenditure of public monies. This being the case, the real question is why we are lagging so severely in our rural infrastructure investments – if it does cost our businesses and industries in their economic bottom line, then we should have been using taxation reinvestments in services, workforce training, and infrastructure efficiently so as to boost the economy as a whole.

Yet, such an approach to space-based economies and reducing business and industrial tax burdens misses the opportunities embodied within a place-based development approach. Focusing on a "race to the bottom" in economic development supports misses, and even harms, opportunities in other sectors of the new economy. Put in more colloquial terms, focusing on only 20 to 25 percent of the economic options possible within our rural and small-town places means that we miss realizing the 75 to 80 percent of possible opportunities bound up within these places. A place-based economy is about finding and supporting opportunities across the whole economy, something we will be referring to throughout the text as the four bottom lines: economic, environmental, cultural, and community.[3] Each supports the other and each provides new opportunities for investment, development, and diversification on its own.

Another way to understand the shift from a space-based economy to a place-based economy is from the perspective of moving from comparative to competitive advantage. At its root, comparative advantage involves the principle whereby territories "produce those goods or services for which they have the greatest cost or efficiency advantage over others, or for which they have the least disadvantage" (Gregory et al. 2009: 105). The principle helps to explain, in part, patterns of regional specialization (i.e., mining, forestry, fishing) witnessed across a resource periphery like British Columbia. In contrast, Kitson et al. (2004: 992) provide a straightforward definition of territorial competitiveness "as the success with which regions and cities compete with one another in some way – over market share or capital and workers." Competitiveness may be, in part, an outcome resulting from a region's comparative advantages; however, it refers specifically to an outcome of intentional human intervention. Malecki (2004) refers to this complexity when stating that regional competitiveness is multidimensional, mixing traditional factors of infrastructure with attributes like social capital.[4] Over the past twenty years, comparative advantage has declined in primary significance in successfully reorganizing the dimensions of a staples or commodity trading economy in order to increase local benefit (Henderson and Novack 2003). Instead, a focus on competitive advantage may be more useful in describing how regions compete with one another globally over market share, capital, and workers.

Seeking Renewal

Our approach to rural and small-town renewal across northern BC is a pragmatic one. It is rooted in the new economy with attention to the economic, environmental, cultural, and community dimensions of places. Renewal is about strong community development foundations to support flexibility in economic development, flexibility that is so critical to keeping up with the pace of global economic change.[5]

Complaints that the global economy is too complicated, and that we should do nothing to intervene in the marketplace, must not derail attention to renewal. The period immediately after the Second World War was in many ways more complex and uncertain. Today, many of the fundamentals of global political and economic organization have been in place for more than thirty years. Attention to renewal must not be derailed by simplistic renderings that urban centres are the focus of the new economy and that rural or regional decline is inevitable. BC's economy is one in which urban and rural are intimately interlinked. BC's 2004-2006 economic upswing was bolstered by resource revenues from nonmetropolitan BC and investment spending leading up to and surrounding the 2010 Olympics in metropolitan BC. The current downswing is the result of declining global market demands for resource commodities. For both of these concerns, attention to renewal must be about outlining opportunities in the global economy and mobilizing a reimagined and rebundled set of nonmetropolitan assets so as to build on our competitive (as opposed to comparative) advantages.

Our starting point in looking forward to renewal is the Northern BC Economic Development Vision and Strategy Project (NEV). Started in 2003, the NEV was designed to find out what ideas northerners themselves had for improving economic and community development opportunities where they live. The project sought to answer a simple question (Halseth et al. 2007): If people in northern BC were going to devise a vision and plan for economic renewal, and a structure to manage that renewal, how would they do it?

Development processes or plans have too often been imposed from outside the region, with people in northern BC participating only to have key recommendations or outcomes changed or rejected (Halseth and Booth 2003; Mascarenhas and Scarce 2004). This legacy has created a good deal of skepticism about regional economic planning in the north. Current economic challenges (during both booms and busts) have created a great impatience to get on with the task of creating a plan to renew the economic strength and resiliency of our communities. Through the NEV, people spoke of a willingness to set aside the skepticism and to "roll up their sleeves" to get on with the job of creating a "made in the north" approach to renewal.

Collectively, the NEV provided a catalyst for the exchange of local economic information and ideas between government, industry, labour, small business, First Nations, economic development organizations, and community groups. Importantly, for our work, the project set the foundation for a longer-term research relationship with many of these communities. Since that time, we have engaged in a large number of projects with communities throughout northern BC, using a range of methods to explore issues such as housing, community transition, rural health, economic competitiveness, the service economy, Aboriginal community development, industry relations, and others.

Messages from Northern BC

Three opening messages derived from our cumulative research throughout rural and northern BC serve as core principles for the remainder of this book. The first is a clear recognition that northern BC's rural and small-town community and economic futures are connected. This connectivity extends to the infrastructure and technology that increasingly binds and facilitates interaction, community development, and economic vitality, and to the natural resources and environments that have long supported the economy and local quality of life. Regional discussions on the strategic options for deploying these assets will benefit and support local economic and community development.

Regional development, defined by varying dimensions of connectivity, has become a popular tool in other jurisdictions (Savoie 1997; Storper 1997; Fairbairn 1998; Polèse 1999; Australian Government 2002; Canada, Secretary of State for Rural Development 2002; Drabenstott and Sheaff 2002a; Welsh Development Agency 2002). Recently formed economic strategy groups in northern BC are aware of these trends and have increasingly been placing attention to a coordinated regional approach at the top of their planning agenda (Cariboo-Chilcotin Beetle Action Coalition 2008; Omineca Beetle Action Coalition 2009). Importantly, a regional approach to tackling issues of restructuring and change must develop and/or adapt models that address the particular circumstances of the particular places (Jones 2001; Macleod 2001a, 2001b; Natcher et al. 2003; O'Brien et al. 2004).

The second message is that rural and small-town northern BC is demanding the tools and resources necessary to coordinate the future development of its community and economy. There is a keen recognition that resource wealth has long supported the development of the province; yet, fewer benefits stay reinvested in our rural and small-town places. Throughout this book, we will be referring to this phenomenon as the resource bank approach to development – where metropolitan decision makers view northern and hinterland regions as places rich in resource assets that can be exploited or "withdrawn" when needed to fund metropolitan investments, but without making adequate return deposits.

The third, and perhaps most important, message is that the economic future of northern BC's rural and small-town regions must include everyone. The future must respect the quality of life and environmental foundations of all of our people, places, and cultures. Building on these messages, suggestions for enhancing community and economic strength will build on a foundation of core components for renewal, including the following: (1) a comprehensive vision, (2) recognition and celebration of the quality of life in the north, (3) identification of strategic assets for development, and (4) reinvestment in an integrated blend of development infrastructures.

Vision: Moving from Strength to Strength

Rural and small-town futures across northern BC involve moving from strength to strength. This means moving from a resource economy strength to a renewed strength that is inclusive of a resource economy foundation, adds diversified community and economic development opportunities, and retains more of the economic and social value and benefits from these developments within our communities.

Rural and Small-Town Lifestyle

An affordable lifestyle and quality of life form the foundational assets for new economic development. In the new economy, quality of life and many of the other characteristics that have long described rural and small-town places form crucial economic development assets (Canada West Foundation 2001; Rural Secretariat 2001; Canada, Industry Canada 2004). For example, an outdoor lifestyle and wilderness setting creates opportunities in both tourism and resource development. The small-town characteristics of safe and familiar communities provide an ideal setting for recruiting both young families and retirees (Beesley et al. 1997).

Rural and small-town places in northern BC are affordable and connected places for living and doing business. With the connectivity of the "information age," these places are attractive economic and quality-of-life destinations for companies and government agencies seeking to relocate from expensive and congested metropolitan areas while at the same time staying connected to the global economy (Doloreux et al. 2004). Our northern quality of life, while becoming an attribute of competition between similar communities, can be a foundation for both economic and community development.

To be competitive in the global economy involves not only the broad foundational supports noted above but also competing for the talent needed to ensure that opportunities can be realized (Scott 2009). This competition for talent first received attention in Florida's (2002) work on the "creative class" within the new generation of workers. To take advantage of new economic opportunity, places have to attract workers – and achieving the right mix of educated workers and new economic drivers emerges as one of the keys to successful engagement in the knowledge-based global economy. The rural and regional development research literature has identified how this same process applies as well to nonmetropolitan places. Rural and small-town places need to "get into the game" of attracting and retaining talent. To do this, rural communities need to know something about this new workforce (Gamu 2008; Rye 2006; Barcus 2004). For one thing, these workers will be able to exercise considerable bargaining power. As a result, workers in the new economy have the option to find work where they want to live. Beyond salary rates these demands will include matters such as living in a clean environment, having access to a reasonable level of services, having a safe and healthy place in which to raise a family, achieving a balance in work/life relationships, and enjoying a strong sense of community while still maintaining global connectivity. These attributes are fully compatible with the potential of rural and small-town places (Halseth 2010).

The message from our interactions with people across northern BC is very clear: people want economic development that not only creates jobs for residents, but that also respects people, the environment, and the quality of life that defines the rural and small-town lifestyle. Economic development that depends on fly-in employees, where most of the social and economic benefits flow out of the region, and where the region is left only with the social or environmental "costs" of this new activity, does not fit well with this message. Places need to be equipped to take advantage of new opportunities and residents to fill the jobs that such opportunities create (Barry and Associates Consulting 2003; Donaldson and Docharty 2004; Tahltan First Nation and International Institute for Sustainable Development 2004).

Strategic Assets

To create benefits for rural and small-town places, we must rebundle our assets to create new strategic opportunities and advantages.

The old economy focused on economic assets and costs versus benefits, and in doing so, it was missing opportunities embodied within three-quarters (environmental, cultural, and community) of the available place-based assets. Renewal of the new economy means finding creative and innovative ways to rebundle these economic, environmental, cultural, and community assets to create opportunities that fit with local aspirations. To do this, there are challenges to overcome. For example, there is the argument that if you focus on these other dimensions of the new economy you will be harming our economic competitiveness in traditional resource sectors. Given, however, that we are always adjusting our comparative advantage to remain competitive in the old economy, additional adjustments need not privilege one over the other. In a place-based economy, each of the four assets – economic, environmental, cultural, and community – enhance competitiveness and build resiliency and diversity, which are key features needed in today's fast-paced and rapidly changing global economy. The vision is to use the strengths of the resource sector while setting a foundation for other economic activities and sectors.

Infrastructures

We will realize renewal through investments in physical infrastructure, human resource infrastructure, community capacity infrastructure, and economic and business infrastructure.

To support economic renewal by moving from strength to strength, we must reinvest in four critical areas of infrastructure. During BC's 1950s-1970s development era, decision makers clearly understood that strategic investments would pay dividends for a long time. At the start of the twenty-first century, our myopic focus on cutting taxes and showing results that fit with government election cycles or corporate quarterly reports to shareholders now sees such investments only as expenses (this occurs despite a provincial debt that has climbed significantly since 1980). We have to change this thinking. In the following chapters, we outline an argument for why we need to reinvest in our province's physical infrastructure, human resource infrastructure, community capacity infrastructure, and economic and business infrastructure. We provide stories from across northern BC of places that are making these investments in highly successful ways.

Physical infrastructure investments were a cornerstone of earlier province-building policies, but this infrastructure needs updating to meet the needs of a new economy (Harvey 2004). This includes transportation, communications, and local civic infrastructure, all of which are key economic development assets. Transportation infrastructure includes road, rail, and air transport facilities. Communications infrastructure includes the critical connecting technologies that drive the speed of the global economy. While some places in northern BC still rely on radio-phones, it is not enough to just get Internet – reliable, high-speed Internet is needed. Civic infrastructure includes recreation and amenity facilities that are central to recruiting and retaining both residents and businesses. It is necessary to make investments in both the "old" and "new" economy infrastructures.

Human capacity infrastructure concerns education and training, both for youth and for an established workforce seeking to compete in new economic sectors. In a flexible and dynamic new economy, human resource development will be a crucial support to regional diversification. It will demand enhanced access to a range of educational facilities at all levels.

We need to renew and diversify our community capacity. This includes the need to provide health care, education, and social support services in ways that recognize the realities of rural and small-town life (including enhancing support to the voluntary sector, which provides so much of rural and small-town BC's community capacity). Building community capacity entails support for and attention to community leadership and planning processes that guide the making of local and regional decisions.

Finally, regional development and renewal must include our economic and business support and training services, and increasing access to capital and business development advice, especially for small and emerging businesses. Some support agencies already exist, but their roles need to be strengthened, coordinated, and refined to fit a place-based economy. One area for increased support concerns the development of more social economy enterprises (e.g., for health care and service delivery) that operate within the framework of business but are designed to channel their activities or profits towards addressing community needs and goals.

Book Outline

Renewal of both communities and economies across northern BC is about moving from strength to strength. Renewal is about building on our community and natural resource assets creatively to take advantage of opportunities as the global economy moves from a space-organized economy to a place-organized economy. Part 1 of this book provides a conceptual and contextual foundation for understanding this transition. This introductory chapter outlines some of our key concepts and provides a rationale for renewal based on the voices and realities of northern BC. Chapter 2 offers an overview of the general development and settlement patterns that have shaped northern BC into its current condition. This includes a review of basic socio-economic profile information and demographic trends across the north.

Chapter 3 details a rationale about the need for, and opportunity of, the renewal imperative. It starts with a description of the whole community approach to renewal – an approach that understands that economic development rests on a solid foundation of community development, especially important as we seek sustainable options within the fast-paced, changing, and flexible global economy. An enhanced description of the foundations for renewal, including a delineation of the meaning of space-based and place-based economies, and the impact of change on mobilizing for community and economic development follows. These building blocks are supported by a series of vision and strategy statements, as outlined by the residents of northern BC and collected through our research, that give direction to guide renewal.

Part 2 comprises three chapters that complete our look at the creation of a space-based resource-extraction economy in northern BC. Chapter 4 provides an historical summary of the evolution of a space-based economy in rural and small-town BC. It starts with a description of the First Nations foundations of a trading economy dependent on the exchange of resources. Attention then turns to the Post-War Rehabilitation Council and its recommendations for a proactive approach to exercising BC's resource-based comparative advantages in the emerging global industrial complex after the Second World War. WAC Bennett's government adopted the Council's outline, and this set in place a foundation of economic and community infrastructure that sustained BC for more than thirty years.

Chapter 5 probes some of the issues that caused the breakdown of the space-based economy. Under a succession of crises to the Fordist regime of production, industry began to adopt flexible production systems that have since become associated with deep restructuring and change across BC's resource industries. The provincial government followed suit by undertaking a series of refocusing and retrenchment actions commensurate with trends predominant during an era of neoliberalism. Against this tide of industrial and state "pull-back," local governments and communities were obliged to respond to economic change with a shrinking set of tools. The chapter outlines the erosion of some of these fundamental tools, but finishes with a description of recent economic renewal exercises.

Chapter 6 is about transitions from a development approach founded on a hinterland resource bank towards one driven by place-based opportunities, assets, and aspirations. It describes in detail some of the macro- and micro-responses to restructuring. At the macro-level, these include the creation of regional development agencies, action towards treaty settlement, and the success of initiatives such as the establishment of regional trusts. At the micro-level, however, the story is one of local actions being "stuck in the middle." Economic and community development, as played out over the past twenty years, has too often lacked a firm grounding in the unique characteristics and assets of places and regions and, similarly, has not been supported by aggressive programs of implementation. Without these two bookends, suggestions for economic opportunities remain stuck in the middle.

The three chapters in Part 3 describe the importance of reimagining a place-based economy and of exercising competitive (rather than comparative) advantages in renewing the economies of northern BC. Chapter 7 examines the forces of renewal now permeating rural and small-town BC. Critical here is the ascendancy of place as a new context for rural and small-town renewal. Issues central to place mobilization are postproductivism and economic competitiveness. In this chapter, we examine these concepts and trends using a rural lens.

Chapter 8 delves into some of the dynamic tensions surrounding rural and small-town renewal. These include many of the actors identified in earlier chapters as crucial to northern BC's mobilizing for change: business, industry, labour, communities, nongovernmental organizations (NGO's), local/band/tribal council government, civil society, and a host of others. The transition from a space-based to a place-based economy will be difficult, and recognition of potential barriers can assist with the transition.

Chapter 9 explores some immediate directions and actions for transforming northern BC into a more competitive place-based economy that is responsive to shifts and opportunities in the global economy. Using a vision of northern BC "in twenty years" as its starting point, the chapter then describes sets of actions and opportunities for a host of players in the public, private, and civil society sectors.

The last part of this book (Part 4) consists of two chapters. Chapter 10 examines issues central to intervention. As noted for the 1960s-1970s development period in British Columbia, state investment and intervention was critical to realizing a successful vision of community and economic development. Following a neoliberal-led policy and investment withdrawal from northern BC's rural and small-town places, this chapter enunciates the argument for a return to forms of intervention that fit with the renewal approach and ethos.

Our concluding chapter summarizes the core issues from our detailed analysis of the development trajectories and potential of northern BC. Aside from the many recommendations and case examples that follow, one central lesson is critical: it is important to take action. As will be discussed, a laissez-faire approach to regional development is just too unpredictable and reactionary to stake our futures on. Doing things matters; not doing things has consequences.

The renewal of northern BC's rural and small-town communities and economies looks like a big task, and what will make it possible is doing a great number of little things. If you have a strategic plan to guide renewal, small coordinated actions become cumulative. Renewal is about building and implementing that strategic plan. Renewal is about providing a framework so that groups, individuals, governments, and economic partners will all see steps they can take to better situate their place in the global economy.

2
The Development of Northern British Columbia: General Processes and Specific Circumstances

> Variety should not be seen as a deviation from the expected; nor should uniqueness be seen as a problem. General processes never work themselves out in pure form. There are always specific circumstances, a particular history, a particular place or location. What is at issue – and to put it in geographical terms – is the articulation of the general with the local (the particular) to produce qualitatively different outcomes in different localities.
> (Massey 1984: 9)

The purpose of this chapter is to orient readers to the development processes and the local and regional patterns that have emerged to shape BC's resource hinterland. We begin with a basic socio-economic overview of northern BC. Then we provide a profile of the changing demography of the province highlighting the emergence of different development regions, each with unique population and economic trajectories. Next, we offer a review of the shifting age structure within northern communities, including demographic trends in First Nations communities. Combined, these sections examine the general trends shaping northern BC, and at the same time, illustrate some of the considerable variability across the region – variability that, as later will be seen, influences development possibilities and trajectories. As this chapter's opening quote indicates, combinations of assets, populations, histories, and local circumstances mean that general processes are modified by the matrix of place. Viewing these general trends across northern BC will allow us to view places with a more informed perspective of the broader structural forces that influence, shape, and – perhaps – react to the dynamics of place.

The profile information that follows reveals considerable unevenness in the settlement patterns and socio-economic conditions of rural and urban BC. In the final section of this chapter, we address this divide – in its conceptual and practical forms. An important ingredient related to the emergence of place as a key development factor is the functional interrelationships between rural and urban BC. In moving towards renewal, we must recognize that we do this together. There is no artificial divide in BC between urban and rural economies, between north and south, or Aboriginal and non-Aboriginal communities – they are all interwoven. The rural-urban divide is a challenge in British Columbia, and all of Canada as, through an emergent "city" agenda, the argument is made that urbanization is inevitable and that our cities drive the new economy. Evidence cited for this often includes that our older resource towns in remote and rural regions are declining in population and that measures such as GDP show increasing concentrations of activity in urban centres. These positions, unfortunately, are built from deficient understandings of provincial economies.

A Profile of Northern British Columbia

As stated in the introduction, for the purposes of our research, northern BC includes the area from 100 Mile House north to the Yukon Territory, and from the Alberta border to Haida Gwaii. This space may be called a region to the extent that it exhibits common patterns of historical development and present-day socio-economic characteristics. In a Canadian context, it is a classic rural and small-town region. There is a single hub city of 70,000 people: Prince George. The small towns typically range from 5,000 to 20,000 people, while the rural areas comprise small settlements of less than 1,000 people. Because of the mountainous terrain, a limited transportation network links such places. The region is culturally complex, inclusive of thirty-four municipalities and approximately sixty-two First Nations. A large share of the region's population lives in the rural countryside. See Table 1 for an overview of population levels, and Figure 2 for the corresponding regional districts.

The economy of northern BC is similar to other northern economies, being heavily dependent on forestry, mining, power generation, and tourism (BC Progress Board 2002; Horne 2004). There is a robust second economy of hunting, fishing, and trapping. Structural economic change has been slow across northern BC. A study by Nelson and MacKinnon (2004) notes that although some other regions in nonmetropolitan BC may be diversifying away from a staples-based economy, northern BC remains dependent on traditional staples. The resource-dependent nature of the northern BC economy is illustrated in Tables 2 and 3.

Finally, socio-economic indicators show the north to be performing at comparatively lower levels than the provincial average (see Table 4). Income levels are moderately lower, education completion rates are lower, and health indicators are lower. Across the northern landscape, these patterns vary in magnitude; however, as a generalization, socio-economic performance tends to decrease as the distance from metropolitan areas increases. Socio-economic

Table 1

Population of Northern BC, Southern BC, and all of BC, 2001 and 2006

	Northern BC[a]	Southern BC[b]	All of BC
Total population in 2001	330,298	3,577,440	3,907,738
Total population in 2006	319,069	3,794,418	4,113,487
Change 2001-06 (%)	-3.4	6.1	5.3
Males (%)	50.8	48.8	49.1
Females (%)	49.2	51.2	50.9
Aboriginal identity (%)	17.8	3.7	4.8
All visible minorities (%)	4.1	26.2	24.5
Age distribution (% of population)			
0-4	6.0	4.8	4.9
5-14	14.2	11.4	11.6
15-19	7.8	6.6	6.7
20-24	6.4	6.5	6.5
25-44	26.9	27.4	27.4
45-54	16.7	16.1	16.1
5-64	11.9	12.3	12.3
65-74	6.3	7.7	7.6
75-84	3.1	5.3	5.1
85 and over	0.8	1.9	1.8

Source: Statistics Canada, *Census of Canada*, 2001 and 2006.

a For our purposes, northern BC encompasses eight regional districts: Bulkley-Nechako Regional District, Cariboo Regional District, Central Coast Regional District, Fraser Fort George Regional District, Kitimat-Stikine Regional District, Northern Rockies Regional District, Peace River Regional District, and Skeena-Queen Charlotte Regional District; as well as the unincorporated Stikine Region.

b Southern BC encompasses nineteen regional districts: Alberni-Clayoquot Regional District, Capital Regional District; Central Kootenay Regional District; Central Okanagan Regional District; Columbia-Shuswap Regional District; Comox-Strathcona Regional District; Cowichan Valley Regional District; East Kootenay Regional District; Fraser Valley Regional District; Greater Vancouver Regional District; Kootenay Boundary Regional District; Mount Waddington Regional District; North Okanagan Regional District; Nanaimo Regional District; Okanagan-Similkameen Regional District; Powell River Regional District; Squamish-Lillooet Regional District; Sunshine Coast Regional District; and Thompson-Nicola Regional District.

indicators are particularly poor in Aboriginal communities, where a legacy of colonialism, dispossession, resettlement, cultural and territorial loss, residential schools, and a lack of treaties combines with contemporary outcomes from poverty, long-term lack of employment opportunities, and a host of other issues to create and reinforce multiple barriers to social and economic development.

The specifics of place are particularly important to remember when viewing standard statistical evidence for northern BC. These indicators and their

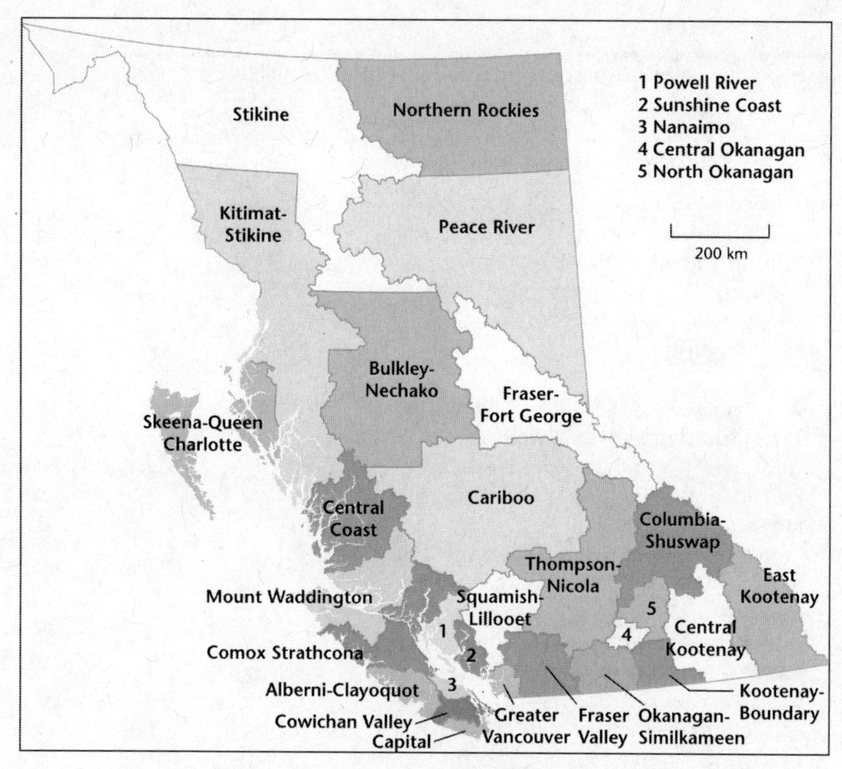

Figure 2 Regional districts of British Columbia. *Source*: BC Stats.

trends provide important information and speak to a need for new strategies of development and policy intervention. However, while the region may compare less favourably with the province as a whole (statistically dominated by the Lower Mainland and Capital Region metropolitan areas), the diversity of the north means that there is every socio-economic condition imaginable across the region. Pockets of tremendous wealth highlight the richness of the resource sector. Similarly, certain communities pride themselves on their outstanding education levels. In the following sections, we narrow our profile lens to view changes within the north and to explain the development patterns and structural forces that have contributed to northern BC's current status.

An Overview of Regional Change

During the 1950s and 1960s, the drive to develop BC's resource industries transformed the interior and northern regions of the province. New roads and rail lines helped established settlements to boom with new growth, and the push for resource industrial development led to the creation of entire

Table 2

Structure of labour force, Northern BC and all of BC, 2006

	Northern BC	All of BC
Total experienced labour force by industry[a]	177,945	2,226,380
Labour force by industry (%)[b]		
Agriculture, forestry, fishing, and hunting	9.1	3.4
Mining and oil and gas extraction	3.7	0.9
Utilities	0.7	0.5
Construction	7.0	7.5
Manufacturing	12.0	8.5
Wholesale trade	3.1	4.1
Retail trade	10.4	11.2
Transportation and warehousing	6.3	5.2
Information and cultural industries	1.2	2.6
Finance and insurance	2.1	3.8
Real estate sales, rental, and leasing	1.3	2.3
Professional, scientific, and technical services	3.8	7.3
Management of companies and enterprises	.09	0.1
Administrative support, waste management, and remediation services	3.0	4.4
Educational services	7.2	6.9
Health care and social assistance	8.4	9.6
Arts, entertainment, and recreation	1.5	2.3
Accommodation and food services	7.3	8.1
Other services	4.5	4.9
Public administration	5.6	5.0
Total experienced labour force by occupation	177,955	2,193,600
Labour force by occupation (% of experienced labour force)		
Management occupations	7.5	10.5
Business, finance, and administration occupations	13.7	17.1
Natural and applied sciences and related occupations	5.0	6.3
Health occupations	4.4	5.5
Social science, education, government service and religion	7.6	8.1
Art, culture, recreation and sport	1.6	3.5
Sales and service occupations	22.6	25.3
Trades, transport and equipment operators, and related occupations	21.1	15.5
Occupations unique to primary industry	8.3	3.9
Occupations unique to processing, manufacturing, and utilities	6.6	4.2

Source: Statistics Canada, *Census of Canada*, 2006.

a Following Statistics Canada's use of the North American Industry Classification System.

b Figures may not add due to Statistics Canada's rounding procedures to protect anonymity.

Table 3

Change in structure of labour force, Northern BC and all of BC, 2001-2006

	Northern BC		All of BC	
	2006 (*n*)	Change from 2001 (%)	2006 (*n*)	Change from 2001 (%)
Total experienced labour force by industry[a]	177,945	-1.3	2,226,380	8.1
Labour force by industry (%)[b]				
Agriculture, forestry, fishing, and hunting	16,230	-4.2	76,485	-2.7
Mining and oil and gas extraction	6,580	48.7	20,025	42.6
Utilities	1,170	-14.0	11,250	-3.4
Construction	12,385	8.6	166,095	39.9
Manufacturing	21,310	-13.2	189,120	-2.7
Wholesale trade	5,455	19.0	92,020	11.6
Retail trade	18,475	-5.9	248,955	6.9
Transportation and warehousing	11,135	1.0	114,915	0.6
Information and cultural industries	2,205	-11.8	58,905	-5.3
Finance and insurance	3,670	-3.7	84,215	4.5
Real estate sales, rental, and leasing	2,370	18.2	50,725	22.1
Professional, scientific, and technical services	6,790	10.0	162,435	18.6
Management of companies and enterprises	165	175.0	3,100	126.3
Administrative support, waste management, and remediation services	5,305	10.1	97,310	20.4
Educational services	12,790	1.2	152,565	9.2
Health care and social assistance	15,010	-0.5	213,085	6.5
Arts, entertainment, and recreation	2,745	8.5	51,370	11.3
Accommodation and food services	13,065	-2.6	180,055	7.7
Other services	7,970	-1.7	109,900	11.8
Public administration	10,015	-9.5	110,585	-2.0
Total experienced labour force by occupation	177,955	-1.3	2,193,115	8.9
Labour force by occupation (%)				
Management occupations	13,435	-8.1	229,945	5.3
Business, finance, and administration occupations	24,310	-0.7	375,975	6.3
Natural and applied sciences and related occupations	8,810	-0.6	138,955	12.3

▶

◄ *Table 3*

	Northern BC		All of BC	
	2006 (*n*)	Change from 2001 (%)	2006 (*n*)	Change from 2001 (%)
Health occupations	7,755	11.3	120,360	13.9
Social science, education, government service and religion	13,580	2.3	178,040	10.8
Art, culture, recreation and sport	2,880	13.8	76,460	13.6
Sales and service occupations	40,140	-2.3	555,880	7.9
Trades, transport and equipment operators, and related occupations	37,495	6.7	339,500	17.5
Occupations unique to primary industry	14,755	-4.4	86,460	2.3
Occupations unique to processing, manufacturing, and utilities	11,730	-14.5	91,545	-5.2

Source: Statistics Canada, *Census of Canada*, 2001, 2006.
a Following Statistics Canada's use of the North American Industry Classification System.
b Figures may not add due to Statistics Canada's rounding procedures to protect anonymity.

new towns. The regions outside of Vancouver and Victoria saw the in-migration of hundreds of thousands of people. At the time, most of these in-migrants were young families coming in response to the promise of new jobs and new opportunities.

Resource-producing regions develop according to the logic of exploitation. There is not only exploitation of renewable or nonrenewable natural resources, but also of in-place public infrastructure (e.g., highways) and the communities. The places where raw resource production occurs see only a limited set of benefits including employment (income to workers) and property taxes (revenue to municipalities). Control over production and the profits from that production are concentrated in distant head office locations. BC's rush after the Second World War to develop its industrial resource base firmly established a set of persisting heartland-hinterland relationships in the province. The social contract underscoring the allocation of public resource tenures to large corporations stipulated that they would generate local benefits via high levels of local employment and contributions through property taxes. Use of the term social contract in this case may be a misnomer. As a hardware store owner from Kelowna, Premier WAC Bennett well understood the benefits that increasing basic-sector employment had for indirect employment and local economic investments, growth, and prosperity in small towns. The cycling of local incomes through local stores produced all of the benefits that still underscore our attention to GDP indicators today.

Table 4

Socio-economic characteristics of Northern BC and all of BC, 2006

	Northern BC	All of BC
Average annual family income ($)	77,810	80,511
Population receiving income assistance (%)	5.2	3.8
Population receiving employment insurance benefits (%)	5.0	2.8
Population without high school completion (%)	19.4	11.1
Population without post-secondary credentials (%)	49.8	37.2
Life expectancy at birth (years)	78.6	81.1

Source: Statistics Canada, *Census of Canada*, 2006.

Rather than a social contract, implementing policy supports for growing local employment was a sensible economic approach for extracting more value at all levels from BC's resource sector.

More than forty years later, these interior and northern hinterland regions are undergoing a second round of transformation. Since the 1980s, pressures from social, economic, and political restructuring have changed the way resource industries operate, and these changes have affected the demographic structure of nonmetropolitan BC (Halseth et al. 2004). Hayter (2000) describes how pressures from environmental debates, consumer demands for more specialized products, continuing demands for low-cost products, international trade disputes, increasing relative labour costs, and increasing competition from low-cost global competitors are pushing resource companies to focus on progressively leaner production techniques.

As rural and northern resource industries are concentrating, technology is continuing to expedite the corporate rationality of shedding labour in these sectors. Faced with competitive pressures, resource industries are reducing their costs. This includes enhancing the substitution of capital for labour and enacting a price squeeze on subcontractors and other suppliers. During the early years of the 2000s, the practice of many resource companies in BC was to focus on their core business via an increasing concentration on staples production. This is a strategy clearly favouring short-term investor benefits (through quarterly profit returns) versus long-term investor outcomes. Many firms are undertaking investments in low-cost production regions themselves. For example, two of BC's largest home-grown companies, Canfor and West Fraser Timber, have invested heavily outside of Canada. Canfor (2009) describes itself as "a leading Canadian integrated forest products company based in Vancouver, British Columbia with interests in over 32 facilities in British Columbia, Alberta, Quebec, Washington State and

North and South Carolina." Investments outside of BC and Canada have been recent. In 2003, Canfor acquired two privately owned lumber companies in Quebec. In 2006, and again in 2007, it acquired mills along the US east coast and in South Carolina. In their 2007 annual report to shareholders, West Fraser Timber (2007: 5) reported that they had "completed the acquisition of 13 sawmills in the southern United States [Texas, Alabama, Florida, Georgia, North Carolina, and South Carolina], adding to our two existing mills in Louisiana and Arkansas. West Fraser is now a truly North American wood products company. We are one of North America's largest lumber producers with significant panel board and pulp and paper assets as well. Approximately one-third of our lumber production is now based in the United States. This is an important strategic step for West Fraser as it significantly increases our geographic, product and currency diversification." Investments in the southern United States and outside of North America underscore the late stages of industrial models that would run down existing assets while repositioning to be more competitive in lower-cost commodity-producing regions. The Canadian experience of Schefferville and the relocation of iron ore mining decades ago mirrors what may be occurring in BC.

The significant change involved in shifting from producing products to producing stock market value can be found in the story of the last years of MacMillan Bloedel. Once a symbol of the BC forest economy, by the 1990s, the company was struggling and recording low share values. In September 1997, the company hired a new president and CEO (Tom Stephen). According to *Report on Business Magazine*:

> He arrived in Vancouver with the kind of orchestrated plan for "the first 90 days" that might have been helpful at D-day. By January, 1998, Stephen had fired 2700 staff – nearly a quarter of the 13,000-plus workforce – and had approval to sell off MacBlo's paper manufacturing subsidiary and its two medium-density-fibreboard plants. Plans were well underway to refocus the building materials and distribution businesses, shut down the research and technology centre and, perhaps most important of all, to recast the company's relationship with its unionized workers. (Martin 1998: 60)

The editor of Madison's *Canadian Lumber Reporter* described the plan as the "first step to dismantling the trouble-plagued logging giant, which last year generated $4.5 billion in sales but incurred a net loss of $372 million. 'I'm certain Stephen is maneuvering MacBlo into a position where it can be sold lock, stock and barrel'" (Brunet 1998: 19). In 1999, Weyerhaeuser acquired MacMillan Bloedel. At the time of the acquisition, the MacMillan Bloedel president stated, "The value created for MacMillan Bloedel shareholders is a reflection of the benefits of the restructuring and transformation program underway over the last 18 months" (Canada Newswire 1999: 1).

Economic restructuring focused boardroom attention exclusively on shareholder value rather than on responsibility to communities and workers. Short-term strategies such as selling off corporate assets to boost share values were replacing long-term stewardship of industries and communities.

Against an era marked by the increasing recognition of transformation, northern BC remains predominately reliant on a staples economy, and resource towns continue to exhibit dependence on single-resource enterprises. While regional development lessons from elsewhere spoke about an increasingly critical need to diversify, many of the rural and small-town places in northern BC found themselves becoming more dependent on a single resource as local companies closed non-core product lines, and the provincial government pushed a resource bank agenda. The scope of such continuing dependence is aptly demonstrated by the first decade of the twenty-first century, which includes the provincial economic downturns of the early years, the boom of the middle, and the downturn at the end. Each of these events was linked directly to the global economy's demand for mineral and forest product commodities.

In the following section, we narrow our profile lens to illustrate how nonmetropolitan BC is now transforming itself into at least four or more economic development regions, with each of these regions having different population structures and pressures. As shown in Figure 3, these demographic changes create significant challenges for development policy.

To set a foundation for discussing regional change, it is first important to look at the macro-trends. Figure 3 shows the pattern of population change across BC for the period 1971 to 1981. Data are from the Canadian census and are for regional districts – local government administrative units that correspond to Statistics Canada's census divisions.[1] Through the early years after the Second World War, BC's expanding resource industries supported extensive population growth across the nonmetropolitan regions of the province. New resource developments over this period typically generated large numbers of new jobs. These new employment opportunities attracted young families, which, in turn, supported the development of retail and service support jobs through various multiplier effects. The period 1971 to 1981 represents the full maturity of the expanding northern and hinterland economy based on the industrial resource development policies enacted during the early years of WAC Bennett's Social Credit government.

By the 1980s, however, the impacts of recessions and global economic change began to drive processes of resource industry restructuring. This was felt across all of BC's resource industries and dramatically affected levels of employment and associated rural and small-town population levels. Figure 3 shows the pattern of population change across British Columbia for the period 1981 to 1991. During this period, the continuous growth that had dominated nonmetropolitan BC since the Second World War was broken in a number of regional districts. Fitting with descriptions of how resource industry restructuring is more rapidly affecting older industrial areas, the locations of these population losses are not necessarily a surprise. The southeast corner of BC, the northern parts of Vancouver Island, and the north coast are some of the province's oldest and most remote resource industry areas. Although adjustments and change in any particular area may be linked to different industries (mining and forestry in the southeast; forestry and fishing on Vancouver Island; and fishing, mining, and forestry along the north coast), the cumulative impact is the same: accelerating change, instability, fewer resource sector jobs, and an out-migration of residents (especially young people) looking for work. Just as the creation of new jobs through the 1950s, 1960s, and 1970s supported additional retail and service sector employment, resource sector job losses through the 1980s led to cutbacks and retrenchments in these other sectors as well.

Figure 3 shows the pattern of population change for regional districts across British Columbia for the period 1991 to 2001. As with the preceding ten-year period, some regional districts show population declines. In this case, the northern parts of Vancouver Island and the adjacent central coast, the north coast, and Haida Gwaii all show population losses. Again, these are some of the province's oldest and most remote resource industry areas, and the locations of population loss would not necessarily come as a surprise. Local and regional job losses in particular resource sectors were exacerbated by concomitant losses in retail and service sector employment. One further change of note is that the southeast corner of BC, which had previously recorded population declines and where restructuring of the mining and forestry industries continues, now recorded gains. This suggests, perhaps, that some other dynamic was beginning to exert itself in that region.

Job losses and out-migration were not only driven by the resource sector restructuring processes described above but also affected by changing federal and provincial government policies regarding the provision of services and the maintenance of public sector offices in nonmetropolitan communities. From the late 1980s onward, the federal government led with the closure of rural services such as post offices, human resources offices, and employment insurance offices in many smaller places (Halseth et al. 2003). The provincial government followed suit by closing many local ministry offices for Forests, Transportation, Children and Family Development, and Environment, and downsized other services in many nonmetropolitan communities. The BC government has extended this practice in recent years through an "offloading" process that has meant that many services such as courthouses or highway corridor maintenance are no longer being carried by the provincial tax base. Particularly troubling over this period of government service closures is that the size of the provincial and federal public sector continued to grow. Where cutbacks occurred, they were at the "service delivery" end, where

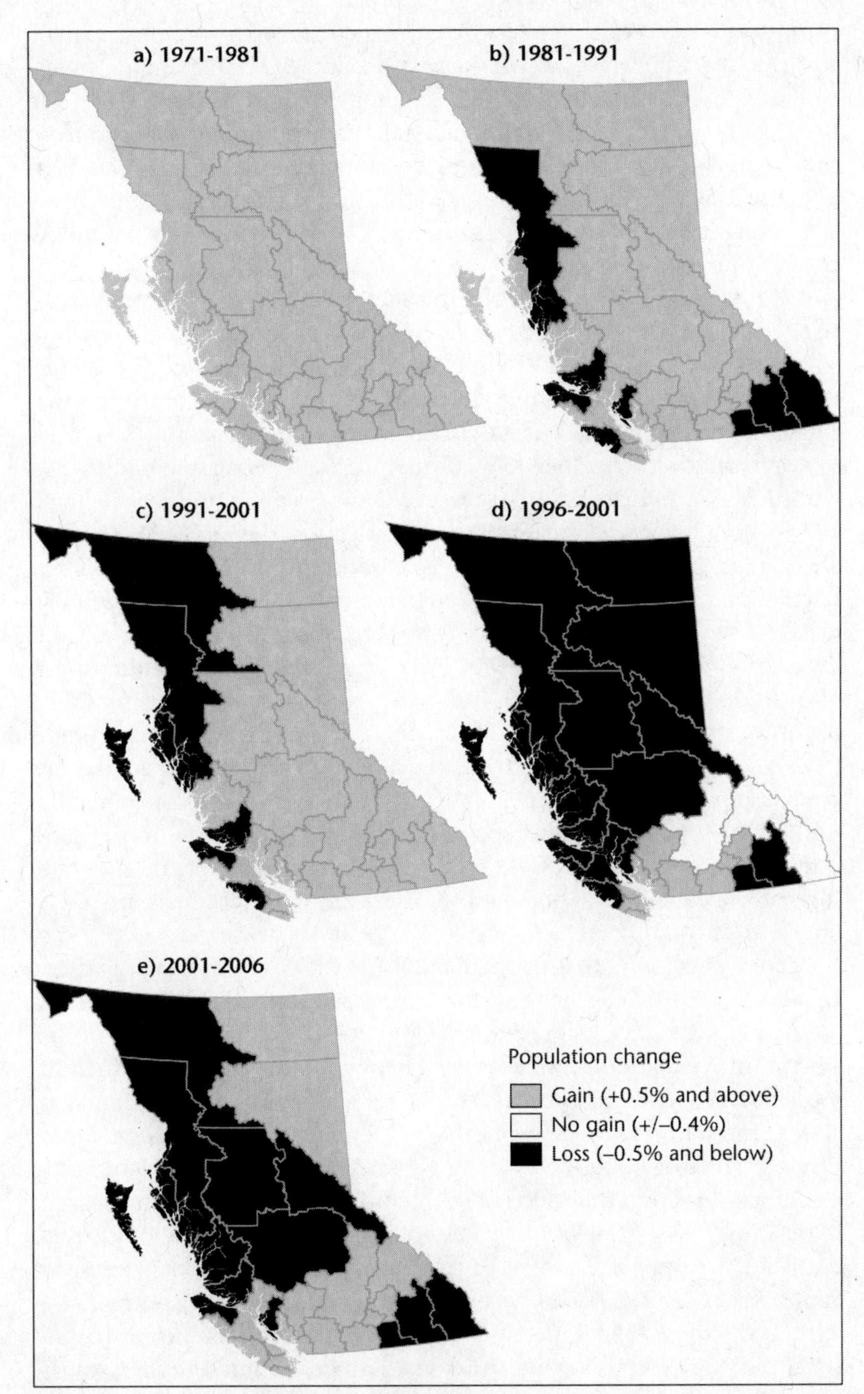

Figure 3 Population change by regional district, 1971-2006. *Data source*: Statistics Canada, *Census of Canada*, various years.

people actually accessed services directly, and they were in rural and small-town places where people would have trouble accessing these services through other means. It is startling to compare the service loss pattern in northern BC with that of northern Alberta, where the provincial government maintains a significant presence and workforce in places with populations as low as 1,500 to 2,000 people. Again, these shifts and service cutbacks are not wrought by "natural or market forces": they are driven by purposeful policy choices.

The 1990s were, however, a chaotic decade for BC's resource industries. In the early years, high prices for both pulp and timber pushed growth in some regions. In the north-central BC town of Mackenzie, for example, market prices and demands pushed production at almost all mills such that they were running 24/7. The additional shifts increased population levels in some communities, albeit temporarily. To illustrate the tremendous flux within BC's resource industries, Figure 3 shows the pattern of regional district population change for the five-year period 1996 to 2001. The data are dramatic and suggest a clear regionalization of BC's nonmetropolitan population change (Halseth et al. 2004). Metropolitan Vancouver and Victoria, along with the metropolitan fringe of Nanaimo, Whistler, and Chilliwack, all show population growth. This is continuing a longer-run pattern of urban expansion along with the spatial extension of the metropolitan region's urban fringe (Halseth 2004). Across the nonmetropolitan hinterland, where most places had experienced more than fifty years of continuous growth, most now recorded population losses. Yet, even with those population losses, some places recorded relatively little population change, and some recorded large increases. Again, these patterns of population change suggest that a different population (and economic) change dynamic is underway in these areas.

Figure 3 also shows that the period 2001 to 2006 reinforces the patterns already described. One change is that the resource boom in the oil and gas industry of the Peace River region has, both literally and figuratively, fuelled a boom in population as well. As we describe in later chapters, if met unprepared, these economic booms cause as many problems as economic busts.

As restructuring processes work themselves out across BC's hinterland, it is important to emphasize two points. First, resources are not uniformly distributed, and thus the effects of restructuring are differently experienced. For example, the fishing industry has not only declined generally along the coast but has also contracted "back" into its original regional centres of Vancouver and Prince Rupert. Second, the regions experiencing restructuring impacts are themselves differentially equipped with assets such as natural resources, transportation infrastructure, climate, picturesque landscapes, and proximity to metropolitan centres that can create opportunities for new economic activities. For example, the south-central Okanagan region has shown population growth at a time when population losses were the norm elsewhere in BC's hinterland. It appears that in the Okanagan, new growth is coming from amenity and retirement in-migration supported by a reorganization of traditional staples production in agriculture to include high-value estate wineries and other innovations. This is affecting population levels and structures and the social dynamic of the communities. The Thompson-Kootenay areas of southeastern BC contain a suite of traditional resource hinterland communities in which resource job losses are being compensated for by an expansion of tourism and second-home amenity industries. The more northern regions of the province continue to be a resource hinterland where population losses during economic downturns mark ongoing vulnerability. Such examples underscore Hutton's (2002) suggestion that BC's resource-producing hinterland is diverging into a suite of different development regions, each with different growth drivers and trajectories. In this case, each of these development regions is "anchored" by a regional centre: namely, Prince George, Kelowna, or Kamloops.

Most problematic of these diverging hinterland regions is the north. It is clear from the pattern of population change that the north is being left behind in terms of community and economic renewal: it remains stuck in the staples economy. Despite periods of booms, and a provision of wealth that still drives the provincial economy, the tools and perspectives are not in place to allow northern BC to mobilize its place-based assets under the new economy in ways similar to those pursued in regions such as the Okanagan and the East Kootenays.

As we explore the question of renewal for nonmetropolitan BC, the region's changing population profile underscores three key points. First, nonmetropolitan BC is diversifying into a complex set of development regions each with different demographic profiles. Second, in northern BC, the population profile is poised to shift dramatically from young to old, and while this follows the Canadian pattern of population aging, it will occur at a more rapid pace and in communities with very limited experience in dealing with the service and care needs of older residents.[2] Third, the First Nations population across nonmetropolitan BC has a very young demographic profile, which further complicates questions around community and economic development, as we cannot simply shift service resources from young to old – we will need to support both.

Shifting Regional Demographics

Patterns of population growth or decline across nonmetropolitan BC reveal changes in the age structure of the populations. Depending on the area, both in- and out-migration have specific implications for certain age groups.

For example, as noted above, growth in the Okanagan region stems, in large part, from amenity and retirement in-migration (de Scally and Turchak 1998). Although the region's population has long included a large share of older people, this retirement-age cohort has grown relative to the rest of the population. Trading on climate and a revitalized agricultural sector, the Okanagan benefitted from the tremendous public sector investment in the Coquihalla highway system that, since the mid-1980s, has made access between Vancouver and Kelowna far more efficient and played a large role in fuelling and directing this population growth. In the Thompson-Kootenay areas of south-central and southeastern BC, while resource industries are sloughing jobs (as they are in BC's other resource communities) an expansion of amenity industries may be compensating for that loss. Proximity to Vancouver (by new highway links), to the Okanagan (where property prices are increasing), and to Alberta (where development restrictions in the national parks have pushed many to invest "next door" in southeastern BC) may be driving a more mixed economy.[3]

A Northern Resource Hinterland

The current round of economic booms and busts reflects the ongoing vulnerability of northern BC to global resource commodity markets, with the result that the story of population change has been mixed. Places such as Prince Rupert and Masset experienced population losses through temporary or permanent closures in public service and resource sectors, while others such as Terrace, Smithers, and Fort St. John have remained steady or have shown growth. In Terrace, this reflects its emergence as a regional service hub for the northwest, while Smithers is growing through economic diversification that includes tourism and amenity migration. In Fort St. John, the oil and gas boom has spurred considerable growth. Even along central and northern Vancouver Island, places such as Gold River and Tahsis lost population due to forest industry restructuring, while historically resource-based communities closer to Victoria experienced considerable growth through the in-migration of retirees.

In 1981, most places across northern BC showed a population structure typical of developing resource hinterland regions. Large numbers of industrial jobs attracted young workers and their families. As a result, the largest share of the population was in the 24-34-year age group, and many of these young adults were starting families. Resource sector jobs have traditionally been "male" jobs (Reed 2003a, 2003b; Halseth and Ryser 2004a), and the population structure of some communities and regional districts reflects this in the larger shares of the populations that are young males. There has always been female labour in the resource sector, but this is becoming even more common – pushed, in part, by the labour and skills shortages experienced during the economic boom of 2006-2007. By 2006, there had been a considerable transformation in the structure of the region's population. The working-age population had "aged-in-place" because of limited new expansion of the industrial base. Figure 4 illustrates the population structure changes using the example of Williams Lake. As has been noted in regard to other mature resource regions, the lack of new job creation has limited the opportunities for high school graduates and young people to enter the workforce (Lucas 1971; Neil et al. 1992; Halseth 1999a, 1999b). The implications of this rapidly shifting demographic extend to the provision of health care and social services. As Hanlon and Halseth (2005) have argued, the process of "resource frontier aging" is creating significant demands in places not used to coping with these types of needs. This is occurring at the same time as the retrenchment of many rural and small-town health care and social services. As a result, coupled with this older workforce has been an out-migration of younger people looking for work.

In this northern resource hinterland, the regional centre of Prince George has reinforced its position as "BC's northern capital." In addition, several secondary regional centres are emerging. These include Fort St. John in the northeast and Prince Rupert and Terrace in the northwest. Terrace and Fort St. John have each grown (or remained stable) relative to their neighbours and are becoming nascent regional centres for their parts of the province. In both cases, public policy over the consolidation of services, followed by market concentration of retail and commercial services, appear to be reinforcing their rise in spatial importance. Recent decisions with respect to health care consolidation follow a pattern set by past government decisions that have seen smaller public service offices closed in neighbouring towns and relocated to centralized offices in Terrace and Fort St. John. These outcomes reinforce the argument that public policy is having an active role in shaping the destinies of rural and small-town places.

A First Nations Demographic

In outlining a First Nations demographic, it is important to remember that population data for First Nations communities are somewhat problematic. First, while the census records and presents population data for geographic communities like those found on Indian reserve lands, Statistics Canada recognizes that there are "undercounting issues" due to a range of valid personal and political statements that are made through lack of participation. A second challenge concerns the more general question of how to count "community members." This can include people who are not living on-reserve, those who are temporarily away from the community, as well as those added to or taken off band and tribal council lists of community members because of changing definitions under the Indian Act or band

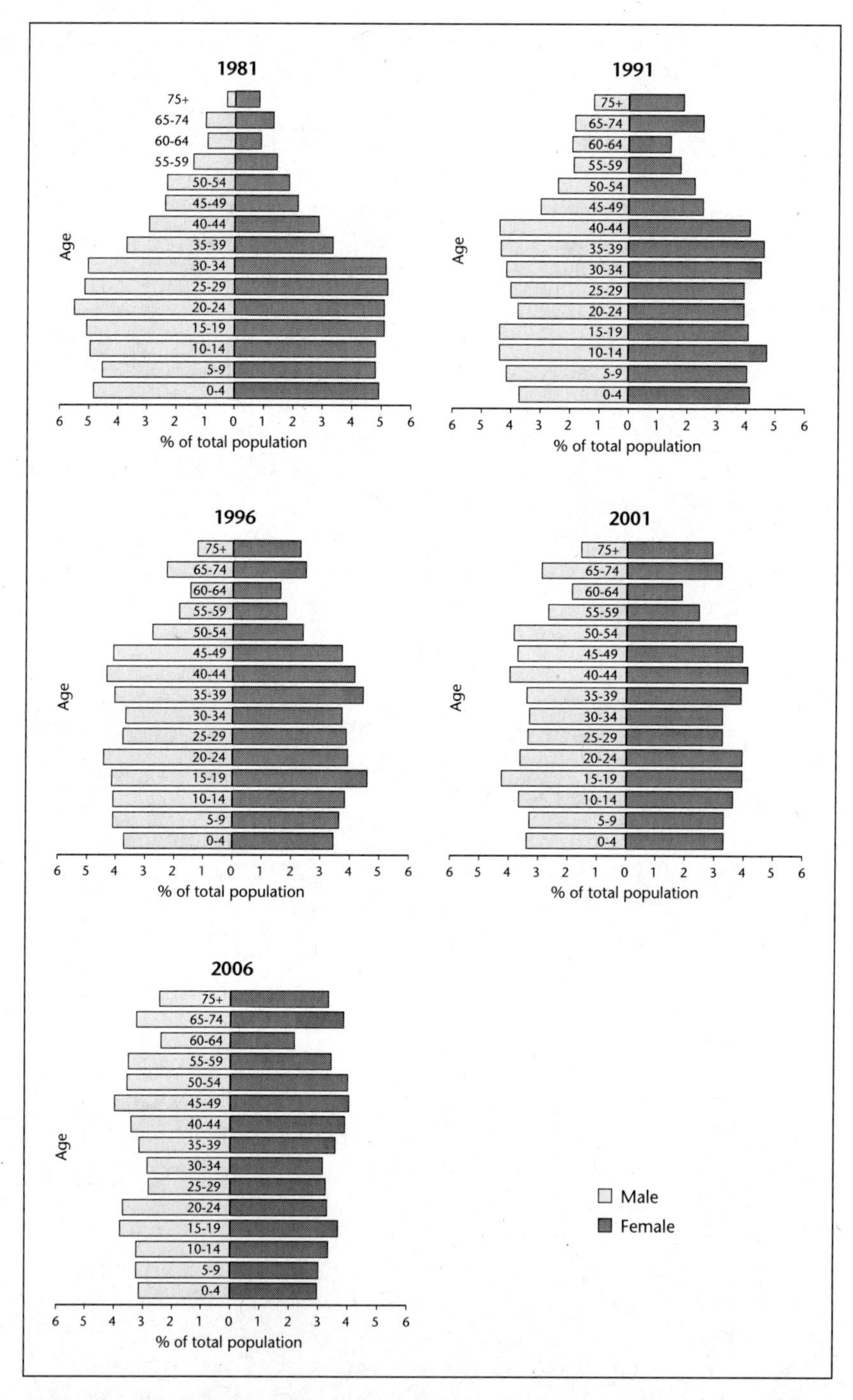

Figure 4 Williams Lake population structure for the years 1981, 1991, 1996, 2001, and 2006. *Source:* Statistics Canada, *Census of Canada.*

Table 5

Northwest First Nations community population data, 2003

Community	Total membership	First Nations residency	Non-First Nations residency	Total community residency
Gingolx	1,874	472	23	495
New Aiyansh	1,674	835	125	960
Laxgalts'ap	1,536	550	15	565
Kitkatla	1,597	466	12	478
Lax Kw'alaams	2,746	627	34	661
Old Massett	2,512	799	20	819
Skidegate	1,277	849	67	916
Kitamaat	1,521	705	3	708
Gitanmaax	1,926	827	30	857
Gitwangak	1,025	522	62	584
Kispiox	1,351	776	30	806
Moricetown	1,693	829	20	849
Telegraph Creek	1,621	325	18	343

Source: Skeena Native Development Society (2003).

and/or tribal council governance documents. A third challenge is in how to enumerate the urban Aboriginal population under the evolving structure of federal, tribal council, and band jurisdictional frameworks. Finally, there is the underlying question of how to define and understand the Aboriginal population in order to be inclusive of métis, nonstatus, and other individuals with Aboriginal identity. These large issues remain unresolved even by those very organizations whose sole interest is with enumerating populations.

Table 5 shows a range of community population data for thirteen First Nations communities in northwestern BC. The data were collected by the Skeena Native Development Society as part of a labour market census completed in 2003. As an Aboriginal organization, the society has adopted a flexible approach to population data collection. The first column in the table represents the total community membership as identified by the community itself. The last column identifies the total number of people who were living in the community in 2003, when the labour market census was undertaken. The intervening columns show the distribution of the people living within the community by "First Nations" identification.

The population age structure within these places shows a relatively "young" population; however, other groups also need attention in the debates on development and services. Gitanmaax Village, in the heart of Gitksan traditional territories, has a large proportion of young families with children, and the community has been able to retain its "post high school" youth. Skidegate Village, at the south end of Graham Island on Haida Gwaii, repeats this pattern. A large proportion of the local population is comprised of youth and children, while the working-age population appears to have aged-in-place, and there is a growing share of the population over the age of 60.

To gain a more complete picture of First Nations development issues in northern BC, we need to be mindful of the economic development and policy challenges associated with other places across nonmetropolitan BC, while recognizing ongoing challenges associated with the legacies of colonialism. These include residential schools, long-term unemployment, paternalism, limited attention to capacity development, a lack of sustainable economic development planning, underinvestment in service and community infrastructure, and efforts to destroy languages and cultures as part of an "assimilation" agenda (Mitchell and Maracle 2005; we will discuss these issues in greater detail in Chapter 4). A significant and growing body of research across many disciplines now ties historically disruptive processes with contemporary issues of poverty and dependency, based on exclusion from northern BC's resource industry economic boom, to explain much of the social malaise and community problems that challenge Aboriginal community and economic development. Histories of colonialism (Harris 1997, 2002), as well as current work on community social, health, and economic well-being (Royal Commission on Aboriginal Peoples 1996a, 1996b; Romanow 2002; Tang and Browne 2008; Loppie Reading and Wien 2009; Wien 2009; National Collaborating Centre for Aboriginal Health 2009/2010a, 2009/2010b), all point to community development as a critical foundational step towards successful economic development. In their "highlights" discussion, the Royal Commission on Aboriginal Peoples (1996b) note, "After some 500 years of a relationship that has swung from partnership to domination, from mutual respect and co-operation to paternalism and attempted assimilation, Canada must now work out fair and lasting terms of coexistence with Aboriginal people."

BC's Provincial Health Officer (2009: xxxvi), in the second annual report on the health and well-being of Aboriginal people, observed the long-lasting effects of this swing:

> A long history of colonization, systemic discrimination, the degrading experience of residential schools, and other experiences have led to adverse, multigenerational health effects on Aboriginal families. These experiences have been the root of inequities in the health and well-being of the Aboriginal population, and these inequities have continued through the generations. Colonization and cultural deprivation have created an environment that

> has negatively impacted the social structures, personal psychology, and coping strategies of many of the Aboriginal population.

Particularly important to these lasting impacts has been the legacy of residential schools; a campaign targeted at the young. The final report of the Aboriginal Healing Foundation's inquiry into residential schools found:

> Aggressive civilization to accomplish colonial goals was thought to be futile in the case of adults. Residential schooling was the policy of choice to reshape the identity and consciousness of First Nations, Inuit, and Metis children. The persistence of colonial notions of superiority is evidenced in the fact that residential schooling that punished the expression of Aboriginal languages, spirituality, and life ways and attempted to instil a Euro-Canadian identity in Aboriginal children, continued from 1831 into the 1970s.
>
> The devastating effects of this program of social engineering were brought into public view in the hearings, research, and Report of the Royal Commission on Aboriginal Peoples. (Castellano et al. 2008: 1-2)[4]

The Mountain Pine Beetle

In addition to social, demographic, and political changes, northern BC is adjusting to environmental changes. One of the most dramatic of these is the largest recorded infestation of mountain pine beetles (MPB) in North America. These beetles are natural inhabitants of lodgepole pine forests. They attack pine trees by laying eggs under the bark. When the eggs hatch, the larvae mine the phloem layer beneath the bark and eventually cut off the tree's supply of nutrients. MPB populations have traditionally been contained in equilibrium with the natural regeneration cycles of the interior forest ecosystem by cold winter temperatures. Warmer winters and the exacerbating effects of climate change have meant, however, that extremely cold weather (e.g., -20 C in the fall or -40 C in late winter) has not occurred in recent years, resulting in the swift spread of the epidemic. Given weather trends, the infestation is only likely to halt once most of the mature pine forests in BC's central and southern interior are dead. Current projections anticipate an end to the infestation by 2013 (British Columbia 2007a).

The economic implications of the MPB infestation are potentially devastating. Outside of the more obvious forest industry impacts, there are a variety of other impacts, including landscape aesthetics, the likelihood and severity of forest fires, water quality, wildlife habitat, property values, and others.

In response to the MPB infestation, the provincial government created an MPB Action Plan in 2001 to help to coordinate MPB-affected interests and actors with a goal of sustaining the long-term economic well-being of impacted communities and the forest industry (British Columbia, 2007a). The Action Plan identifies seven objectives to guide implementation:

1 Encourage immediate and long-term economic sustainability for communities.
2 Maintain and protect worker and public health and safety.
3 Recover the greatest value from dead timber before it burns or decays, while respecting other forest values.
4 Conserve the long-term forest values identified in land use plans.
5 Prevent or reduce damage to forests in areas that are susceptible but not yet experiencing epidemic infestations.
6 Restore the forest resources in areas affected by the epidemic.
7 Maintain a management structure that ensures effective and coordinated planning and implementation of mitigation measures.

The province has helped to facilitate community economic transition through investments in regional development trusts, beetle action coalitions, and other MPB recovery projects. Despite these investments, a 2006 forum on the MPB epidemic stressed that research was overly biased towards the timber supply implications and "offered little information about mitigation and solutions across a broad range of potential economic sectors" (Forrex 2006: 33).

The MPB epidemic is but one example of environmental stress for northern BC's communities and economies. A more general example is climate change. A Canadian Senate report on the risks of climate change notes that already challenged rural systems may be ill-prepared to deal with a changing climate (Canada, Senate Standing Committee on Agriculture and Forestry 2003: 56):

> Because rural Canada relies largely on natural resource-based industries, it will be more vulnerable to climate change ... The livelihoods of rural Canadians are already stressed by low commodity prices and by trade conflicts such as the softwood lumber dispute and climate change will bring additional challenges, which may aggravate the current situation. Climate change will have significant financial and economic repercussions on natural resource-based industries, and physical infrastructure will also be challenged by increased weather-related damage.

British Columbia accounts for only 0.2 percent of global greenhouse gas (GHG) emissions; however, on a per capita basis, the province emits significantly more than many other developed and developing countries (British Columbia 2003c, 2006). The largest source of provincial emissions comes from transportation (40 percent), followed by other industry (18 percent) and oil and gas (14 percent). The extent of hydro-generated power in BC significantly lowers our overall emissions, but it also places limits on our ability to achieve further reductions.

Davidson et al. (2003) submit conditions that negatively affect the ability of rural places to adapt to or mitigate the affects of climate change. First, neoliberal policy changes have significantly reduced the capacity of local governments to mobilize surplus resources to address planning and action for climate change.[5]

Second, rural residents face challenges associated with the transition to employment outside of the resource sector, including the little amount of attention given to rural competitive disadvantages or to local and regional diversification, such that places will be hard-pressed to cope with the multiple shocks of climate change.

An Urban-Rural Divide?

The above sections illustrate that the entire region is set within a clear metropolitan/nonmetropolitan division of provincial space (Davis and Hutton 1989). Historically, core-periphery and heartland-hinterland are concepts applied as part of a Canadian tradition of trying to understand the relationship between metropolitan centres and resource-producing regions (Evenden 1978; Bradbury 1987). Canadian historians such as Careless (1989) and economists such as Innis (1956) developed the notions behind these models to illustrate the physical or geographic relationships that characterize Canada's political economy. At its simplest, such models argue that political and economic control are maintained by a core region, which uses its structural advantage to organize staples or resource production activities in a much larger geographic periphery. Wealth generated by the periphery supports the core and is for the benefit of the core. As long as economic and political decision-making power remains concentrated in the core, opportunities for diversification and advancement in the periphery will remain limited.

The challenge from a development perspective is that many of the assumptions that serve to inform our policy and public understandings of change in rural and small-town northern BC are false – or, more specifically, overly general. For example, not all rural places are losing population. As Bollman and Clemenson (2008: 3) describe for Canada, "the rural population is growing. Most, but not all, of the growth is in areas adjacent to metro areas. [The perceptual challenge is that] growth of the rural population is less than the growth in urban areas." In northern BC, towns like Fort St. John and Dawson Creek have recorded steady growth over the past decades coincident with the growing oil and gas economy. A second generalization emerges from the use of select measures to gauge economic impact, such as GDP, that are useful in showing the circulation of monies – an action that urban areas are quite good at as a result of their dense network of services and administrative functions. The more crucial question, however, and the one brought into sharp focus by the 2008-2009 global economic collapse, is how that money originally got into the system. As made clear in studies of the BC economy, the money comes into our system through exports, exports that overwhelmingly originate in rural and small-town BC (Baxter and Ramlo 2002; Baxter et al. 2005). Rather than a "cities" agenda, it is more useful to understand BC's economy through the notion of interconnectivity – with rural and small-town industry continuing to support metropolitan GDP and quality of life.[6] When policy and infrastructure investments support emerging new global economy trends, we find places, like Smithers, that have moved into the new place-based economy and are growing.

McCann (1987) applied the notion of cores and peripheries to Canadian geography. His descriptive model employs notions of heartlands and hinterlands to illustrate relationships between places and between regions. At its simplest, a metropolitan heartland holds control over a vast resource-producing hinterland.[7] Heartland locations typically begin as places of original settlement within regions, chosen for a range of geographic advantages, including access to wide transportation networks and export opportunities through facilities such as ports. Heartlands provide access to markets, including local markets, because of their metropolitan size and because of their transportation and/or port connections. Because of their command-and-control functions, they develop diverse internal economies with many high-order functions including government, legal, insurance, finance, and management. In other words, heartlands maintain a structural advantage as centres of political and economic power. Because of their size, they contain a great many points of economic transaction so that simple measures of economic activity, such as GDP, capture the density of those transactions. The "cities as drivers of the economy" dialogue incorrectly identifies this density of transactions as indicative of basic economic activity. What such measures hide, however, is that the source of the "original dollar" being recirculated through metropolitan transactions overwhelmingly comes from hinterland resource production.

Hinterlands, on the other hand, are places of primary resource production, defined by an economic relationship with command-and-control heartlands. This relationship rests on the generation of profit from natural resources, which means that growth and investment in the hinterland remains focused on resource extraction and basic processing. With such a focus, hinterland regions remain predominately undiversified and suffer an inherent vulnerability resulting from a dependence on commodity prices and market demands. This dependence creates the structure for economic "booms" and "busts" as BC's resource industries remain "price-takers" – that is, they are reactive to the prices set in the marketplace by commodity purchasers. Such dependencies have meant that few resource-producing regions in Canada have been successful in diversifying into service-based economies and, instead, remain ensnared in a "staples trap" (Barnes 1996).

In the case of staples-producing regions in British Columbia, resource production is limited to "break the bulk" exercises, converting raw material into a basic commodity: such as reducing mineral-bearing rocks into ore concentrates or cutting trees into dimension lumber.

Given BC's highly complex ecological and geological structure, natural resources in specific locations depend on the type of resource and the availability of requisite ecological and geological supports. As a result, in the hinterland there are numerous small settlements located close to where the resources are. These settlements typically have small populations, geared to supplying labour for local resource industries. The hinterland's urban structure is a loosely organized system of small places. There are some interregional ties, but most settlements have more direct and strong ties with the heartland. Individually, they exercise relatively little economic or political power; instead, they are very much dependent on decisions made in metropolitan locations by provincial governments or corporate head offices.

The strength of the heartland-hinterland model lies in its applicability at a variety of scales. McCann (1987) first applied the model at a Canadian scale, identifying the central Canadian heartland's dependence on resource production activities carried out in the nation's far-flung resource hinterlands. Bradbury (1987), as well as Davis and Hutton (1989), showed how British Columbia has functioned as a heartland-hinterland model in microcosm. The critical point is that both heartlands and hinterlands are mutually dependent on one another – they function in a symbiotic relationship. There is no "us" or "them."

The Vancouver-Victoria metropolitan region has dominated BC's settlement structure since the province joined Canada in 1871. In 2006, this metropolitan core contained 59 percent of BC's population.[8] This concentration of population and political power is geographically removed from the resource-producing communities and regions that drive the provincial economy. As widely noted, this geographic separation has the effect of "hiding" BC's economic dependence on natural resources (Baxter and Ramlo 2002; Hutton 2002). It also has the effect of isolating decision makers and major media outlets from the circumstances of hinterland communities, the long-run detrimental impacts of not reinvesting in those communities to maintain their competitiveness, the transitions affecting resource industry workers, and the emerging place-based economic opportunities.

The settlement landscape of BC's hinterland is a set of regional centres and a constellation of small resource-dependent towns. Many of these settlements have limited economic diversity. In concert with expectations derived from staples theory, both public policy and business interests have built and rebuilt a provincial infrastructure designed to extract and export large volumes of minimally processed raw resources and concentrate the benefits from that activity in the metropolitan core (Gunton 1997; Hayter and Barnes 1997a; Hutton 1997). The result is an isolated set of small settlements, dependent on resource extraction controlled from a metropolitan heartland, and with few local economic alternatives. Restructuring of both resource production and public service provision, both of which are purposefully driven by corporate/public policy decision making, has meant that the past twenty years have been marked by accelerating instability, change, and job losses in many of BC's resource communities (Barnes and Hayter 1994; Halseth and Sullivan 2002). Indeed, rural and resource industry restructuring is a common story in developed economies (Marsden et al. 1990; Neil et al. 1992; Mackenzie and Norcliffe 1997). Despite many long-term indicators that economic restructuring is altering northern BC's rural and small-town landscape, the dependence of the provincial economy, and the dependence of many rural communities, has remained on resource extraction (BC Stats 2006; Schrier 2007; Hallin 2008).

The hidden dimension of BC's dependence on natural resource revenues contributes to supporting a resource bank approach to development policy in much of rural, and especially northern, BC. The most recent iteration of this resource bank approach appeared with the initial Gordon Campbell government of 2001-2005. When that government was first elected, the provincial economy was in a difficult position due to a general global downturn in commodity prices and demands – the one bright spot was BC's oil and gas industry. The policy response was to expand every possible opportunity for oil and gas development. Rights leases and exploration permits became a key revenue booster, and the province pushed heavily for the opening of offshore oil and gas exploration. Within a couple of years, the "China boom" began to drive mineral prices up, and BC provincial policy added aggressive expansion of the mining industry. Once again, revenues from rights leases and exploration permits were key as the province started an on-line claims-staking process that resulted in a tremendous increase in the territory covered by mineral claims. Once the provincial economy had recovered (due in large part to the widespread general recovery of a range of commodity prices and demands driven by global markets, not by BC government policies), the provincial government quietly let the controversial offshore oil and gas issue drop.

Increasingly, there is a strong sentiment across northern BC that recent governments and industry are simply drawing down from the assets of the north without making adequate reinvestments (Gunton 2003; Halseth et al. 2007). There is concern that community and infrastructure foundations are crumbling. Aside from local concerns, a range of literatures relating the role and importance of place to the development process informs us that continuous withdrawals from the resource bank will undercut both present and future prospects for development. Given that urban and rural BC are intimately interrelated, better support for rural development will provide net benefits to both.

Our Collective Future

The foundation for rural and small-town renewal should be built upon working together. Calls for increased attention to place in supporting rural and small-town renewal across northern BC do not provide an excuse for senior governments to off-load or abandon their responsibilities for providing coordination, infrastructure, and vital services. Throughout this book, we argue that top-down and bottom-up support for renewal must work in concert.

We refer at times to issues specifically affecting Aboriginal or non-Aboriginal communities. At these points, historical contingency underscores this separate treatment. However, when we talk of renewal in northern BC's rural and small-town places, we are referring inclusively to both Aboriginal and non-Aboriginal communities. The future of all our places and communities lies in developing effective relationships between all our interests. The functional reality today is that our future is a collective future.

This collective future will meaningfully address and move beyond a history of exclusion through a colonial past that separated Aboriginal peoples and communities from the resource economy (Notzke 1994). In British Columbia, successive governments used the idea of "empty lands" to justify the social and economic marginalization of Aboriginal peoples. The empty lands thesis "legitimized the denial of Aboriginal title and sanctified the new white doctrine that all land in the colony was not only under British sovereignty but also directly owned by the Crown" (Tennant 1990: 41). The BC government historically and persistently argued that Aboriginal title did not exist in the province. The *Calder* decision (*Calder v. British Columbia (Attorney General)* [1973] SCR 313, [1973] 4 WWR 1) overturned this argument, and the *Delgamuukw* decision (*Delgamuukw v. British Columbia* [1997] 3 SCR 1010) legally recognized the existence of Aboriginal title in British Columbia. These and other decisions, including the 1990 *Sparrow* decision (*R. v. Sparrow,* [1990] 1 SCR 1075), provide the underpinnings of the modern treaty-making process and the "new relationship" process in British Columbia (Foster 2002).

We do not underestimate the challenges in building these relationships. A range of historical processes supports "separateness." To start, there are the separate governing structures that manage the reporting and support foundations for municipalities and Indian reserves. Municipalities come into existence through provincial legislation, and they undertake tasks as delimited through the Municipal Charter. Indian reserves come into existence through the federal Indian Act, and their activities fall within reporting structures organized by Aboriginal Affairs and Northern Development Canada. By simple illustration, the challenges of these separate reporting lines affect even the most mundane aspects of relationship building. It is common across BC that municipalities and Indian reserves are located adjacent to each other – an historical product of the intersection of two "resettlement" processes.[9] A need to rebuild a joint water supply line, for example, between a municipality and an Indian reserve means that the municipalities move via council resolution and then apply to the provincial government for funding assistance while garnering the remainder of funds from their local tax base. The partner Indian reserve similarly moves via council resolution and then applies to the federal government for both approval of the proposed actions and for funding support. For both jurisdictions, key decisions are out of local hands.

Additional challenges work to create simplistic stereotypes that affect relationship building. BC's long history with treaty negotiation, especially the historical position held by provincial governments that they did not have a role or responsibility in treaty negotiation and the 2002 provincial referendum on treaty negotiation create impressions on both sides. The challenge many First Nations have in getting their grievances and needs heard has meant that public demonstration and blockades are often the only way to bring attention to these pressing matters. While such actions are a completely common practice across all of Canadian society in this age of intense (albeit fleeting) media attention to "protest," they also create and/or reinforce impressions and stereotypes on all sides.

There are, however, many positive signs that suggest that foundations for building more effective relationships are underway. For example, the Northwest Tribal Treaty Nations (NWTT 2004) completed an extensive economic development project and accompanying reports. These reports complement the messages of this book around reorganizing local assets to meet with local aspirations. They highlight the embeddedness of Aboriginal and non-Aboriginal economies in regions and small places. The resolution and then operation of the Nisga'a treaty has demonstrated that interinstitutional working relationships between governments can work "on the ground" with day-to-day issues.

On the provincial side, the "new relationship" is another positive step. Following the 2005 provincial elections, the BC government and BC's First Nations leadership started working to create a more effective framework for interaction. Building on recent court decisions, the provincial government committed in February 2005 "to a process with the First Nations provincial leadership to openly discuss how we can establish a new relationship" (First

Nations Summit 2005). More recently, the BC First Nations Summit, the Union of BC Indian Chiefs, the BC Assembly of First Nations, and the BC provincial government endorsed an agreement titled "A New Relationship." The document, which is the product of senior-level discussions, describes commitments on "how to establish a new government-to-government relationship based on respect, recognition, and accommodation of Aboriginal title and rights" (First Nations Summit 2005). For those long experienced with the intransigence that had marked treaty resolution talks in British Columbia, the use of a term like government-to-government is remarkable language indeed, even if formal processes have stalled (Burke Wood and Rossiter 2011).

The business community is increasingly aligned with a more attentive and collaborative approach. An early bold statement drawing attention to how unresolved treaty issues are harming the provincial economy was made by the management and accounting firm of PricewaterhouseCoopers, which calculated in 1990 "the cost to BC of not settling treaties to be $1 billion in lost investment and 1,500 jobs in the mining and forestry sectors alone" (Price Waterhouse 1990). More recently, the BC Competition Council (2006: 15) argued that the provincial government should "move forward in an expeditious way to renew the Treaty 8 Revenue Sharing Agreement and renew or enter into agreements or Memoranda of Understanding (MOUs) with other First Nations in order to fully implement the New Relationship initiative." (An agreement was signed in 2010.) In the spirit of the "working together" framework that marks the earlier NWTT report, the BC Competition Council argues that this would allow First Nations to establish their own agreements and arrangements with industry.

Robinson (2007) examines another circumstance for relationship building. In this case, the communities of Likely and Xats'ull share a common interest in a large forested landscape. Through an application to the BC Ministry of Forests community forest agreement program, they are working together to develop local community and economic capacity for mutual benefit. Despite the communities' living close to one another, this was another case where there was little formal contact or connection between them. The first steps of the community forest agreement involved getting to know one another and to start building trusting relationships.

Regional economic development literatures are replete with the importance of effective social capital and social cohesion as key building blocks to successful renewal.

Conclusion

The purpose of this chapter has been to sketch elements of a socio-economic profile of northern BC's rural and small-town landscape. Organized within a heartland-hinterland or core-periphery provincial structure, this region has experienced considerable social, economic, and political restructuring since the early 1980s. The diversity of local places and economic transformations reinforces the notion that place-based assets are playing an increasing role in local development trajectories. In the following chapters, we build on this material. In the context of transition from space-based to place-based economies, we detail the need for both top-down and bottom-up supports, the intimate connectivity between economic and social processes, and the importance of reviving the ability of rural and small-town places across northern BC to be resilient and flexible in their responses and reactions to challenges and opportunities.

3
The Whole Community Approach

> The economic development I've seen depends too much on outside investors and depends too much on the global economy and for the most part has failed or has been very short-lived. Development has to be something that's based on the fact there is a solid core of people in this region that aren't going away. If you build economic development around their needs then that economic development tends to hold. (Resident, northern BC)

The development challenge in northern BC's rural and small-town places is about how to support community and economic renewal to meet the opportunities of the twenty-first century economy. Renewal is about having a vision and mobilizing assets to both meet challenges and take advantage of emerging opportunities that fit with the economic, community, environmental, and cultural aspirations of our places. This process requires a transition, in action and policy, from a space-based economy to a place-based economy. It entails a reorientation from development based on comparative advantage to one that seeks to build on and reinforce our competitive advantages.

Moving to a place-based, competitive economy requires a whole community approach to development. We need to move beyond short-term thinking and narrow development strategies by re-equipping our places to be flexible, responsive, and more diversified. In a rapidly changing global economy, we need to ensure that flexibility extends to our rural and small-town economies. To achieve this, we need to change the mindset that views public sector investments as expenses. Rather, we need to reinterpret such expenditures as investments for the future that will continue to pay returns as assets for years and generations. The economic booms of the 1990s and 2000s have been exploiting the human and physical infrastructure investments of the 1960s and 1970s. Those investments have now run their course. We need a new vision of community and economic renewal in the place-based economy, and we need a new approach to investing in development assets to realize that vision. Again, this is not a utopian undertaking. It is an approach to development that is grounded in extensive Canadian and international research and experiences in rural and small-town community and economic development and is rooted in the best lessons from BC's own past.

The purpose of this chapter is to provide an outline of the renewal imperative. It starts with a description of the whole community approach to renewal – which understands that economic development rests on a solid foundation of community development. A robust community development foundation, in other words, can support a host of options for economic renewal. This is especially important as we seek sustainable options within the fast-paced, changing, and flexible global economy. A description of the foundations for renewal follows, including an extended description of what is meant by space-based and place-based economies and the impact of change on mobilizing for community and economic development. We follow these building blocks of our development model with a series of vision and strategy statements that come directly from the residents of northern BC. Together, this material – the building blocks and the strategies – provides direction on the path to renewal.

Understanding Whole Communities: Development Foundations

The complexity of the global economy requires that we adopt a broad approach to equipping our rural and small-town places and economies so that they can respond with flexibility to both challenges and opportunities (Dale et al. 2008; Marsden and Sonnino 2008; Woods 2007). This flexibility requires a foundation that enhances community capacity to plan, act, and react. To start, this includes attention to community development as a critical foundation for economic development.

In approaching renewal, attention to the development of community capacity and infrastructure is a needed prerequisite for creating a platform on which communities can pursue potential economic development opportunities. Figure 5 illustrates how economic development opportunities and flexibility rest on strong community development foundations. The figure illustrates a selection of the components and processes involved in community and economic development that we will expand on in the following sections. When communities have a strong foundation of community development, they are better able to respond in a timely fashion to whatever opportunities (or crises) emerge.

In a general sense, community development concerns improvements to local social and cultural infrastructure. Community development is most often identified with increasing the skills, knowledge, and abilities of residents to access information and resources and to then use these as tools to create

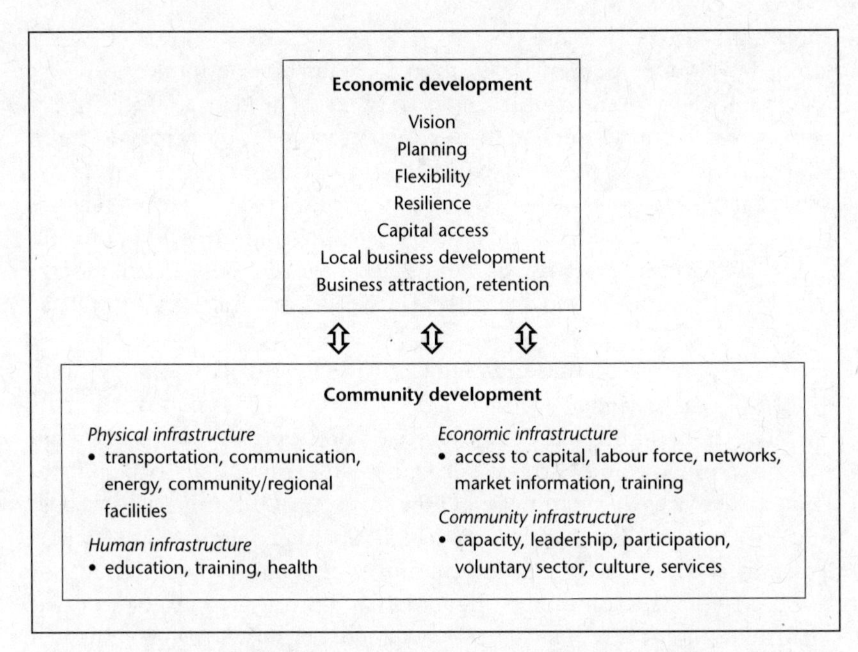

Figure 5 Community development foundations for economic development

strategies and partnerships that can capitalize on changing circumstances (Douglas 2010; Reimer 2006; Halseth and Halseth 2004). Communities need such a foundation, in other words, to realize their full potential and allow them to respond effectively to change. The community development foundation is informative when trying to understand how and why one community is successful in pursuing development strategies and/or responding to crises, when other apparently similar communities are not able to take action (something that will become evident when we describe community stories in the following chapters). Community capacity and the ability of decision makers within a community to work together within an integrated community and economic development process are critical for mobilizing place-based assets and being organized to respond to change.

One significant challenge to facilitating economic renewal is that pressures of social, political, and economic restructuring have withdrawn much from our present community development foundations. As we encounter new development opportunities, we find that we have removed or weakened the very supports that would give us the flexibility and resources to adapt and act. The example of the skills shortages now limiting resource development across northern BC highlights the shortsightedness associated with the withdrawal of support for trades and skills training after the 1980s. We need a new commitment to enhancing the community development infrastructure for northern BC.

Community Infrastructure

Robust development foundations need to focus on community capacity building. To develop community capacity, there is a need for strategic investments in service provision and the voluntary sector. People across northern BC are adamant about the need to provide health care, education, and social support services across the region in a manner that recognizes the realities of rural and small-town life. Such services are important not only for community development but also as a foundation for economic development, in terms of retaining and recruiting business and industry as well as residents.

A critical part of accessing and mobilizing the full capacity of community infrastructure is to ensure broad-based participation of community members and interests. Including a wider cross-section of people and moving beyond the "usual suspects" in creating community plans strengthens local innovation and leverages different networks and sources of information (Canada, Industry Canada 2003). By diversifying and opening opportunities for participation, the full spectrum of community assets – many of which may not be apparent using traditional scoping tools and processes – can be revealed and included in the mix of possible development options. Bringing individual capacities together similarly includes supports to develop the skills of working together and facilitating constructive local debate while resolving perceptual, strategic, or ideological differences. The purpose and goal is to acquire the education and skills required for success in the ever-changing global economy.

Physical Infrastructure

Physical infrastructure is another critical dimension of community development that serves as a bridge to economic development. Community amenities such as swimming pools, recreation centres, and a host of cultural facilities play important roles in enhancing the attractiveness of places for both investment and residents. Similarly, the networks of infrastructure including roads, rail lines, ports and airports, and others, enhance the connectivity of places so that economic opportunities do not face overwhelming competitive barriers (AGRA Earth and Environment 2000; Kjos 2002; Northern Alberta Development Council 2002; Northern Priorities 2002).

Transportation investments in the Kamloops airport and the highway running north to the Sun Peaks ski area illustrate the need to support private sector development initiatives through public service investments. Similarly, the cruise ship expansion and containerization at the port of Prince Rupert is widely supported across northern BC given that potential benefits may be created for a range of innovative businesses and economic sectors. This support is accompanied by recognition that access for small operators to these potential opportunities needs to be enhanced. Viewing the main

▼

THE CRITICAL ROLE OF SERVICES: ATTRACTING INVESTMENT

A lack of investment in new services, and the closure of existing services, negatively affects the attraction of new business and economic opportunities. One clear example of this phenomenon comes in a story relayed to us from a small town in northern BC. The town was working to attract a small software company. It had five or six co-owners. As long as the business location was connected by high-speed Internet, they could do their work, but, as is increasingly common with creative economy workers, they really were more interested in seeking quality-of-life assets. These particular software designers liked the outdoors, especially skiing and snowboarding. They really liked the town because they thought it was a terrific place to grow their company and raise their families. They had only two questions for the economic development officer. The first was "where is the hospital?" Since they were all young, they expected to soon start raising families. Unfortunately, the local health centre had been downgraded, and it was not possible to deliver babies locally. Instead, expectant mothers had to travel to a distant town to await the births of their children. The second question was "where is the school?" There was an elementary school; however, the secondary school was really not able to provide a broad range of courses for students. Given these answers, the software company did not locate in that town or anywhere else in northern BC.

highways as transportation corridors (such as the Northern Gateway Corridor of Highway 16) reinforces the connectedness of northern BC's economy and supports the idea that opportunities abound along the length of these corridors when significant infrastructure investments are made at any point along them (Northern Development Initiative Trust 2009).

One area of lagging infrastructure investment in northern BC has been for new information technologies. Although programs such as the federal government's Community Access Program (CAP) site initiative and the wider Schoolnet project have been important, they reinforce the principle that public sector leadership will continue to be critical in the face of limited private sector participation in low profit-generating localities. If the new economy is an information economy, then the capacity to move information is as crucial to rural and small-town renewal as were the older investments in roads and rail lines (Bandias and Vemuri 2005; Ramírez 2001).[1]

Human Resources Infrastructure

Human capacity improvements concern education and training, both for youth and for an established workforce seeking to compete in new economic sectors. As such, human resource development is a crucial support to regional diversification, and it demands enhanced access to a range of educational facilities at the elementary, secondary, and postsecondary levels. The terms "flexible" and "dynamic," so often used to describe the new economy, must become descriptors of the educational and training mechanisms by which we prepare our residents and workforce. Both bring home the point that BC needs to get ahead of the curve in preparing the "next" northern BC workforce. As will be noted later, increasing the flexibility of and access to education will require a reimagining of the way we manage and deliver high-quality elementary and secondary school education in small places.

In addition to education and training, human resource development requires a broad suite of health care and social services. For individuals, families, and communities, human capacity builds on intellectual, physical, and emotional health. To mobilize flexibility at each of these levels, the availability of health care and social services is critical. We discuss strategies for providing these services in the rural and small-town setting in later chapters.

Economic Development Infrastructure

People across northern BC assert that regional economic development and renewal needs to be concerned with creating stable, income-earning jobs that are the key building block to long-term community viability. In this sense, infrastructure renewal must include our economic and business support and training services, innovation supports, and increasing access to capital and business development advice, especially for small and emerging businesses. A recent report by Statistics Canada shows that rural and small-town places across the country have slightly more business enterprises per capita compared with Canada's larger urban centres, but that many of these firms are very small (one to four employees). This foundation of entrepreneurship creates an ideal potential setting for innovation (Rothwell 2010). Investment in community development to support creativity and competitiveness contributes to this drive for competitive innovation (Greenwood et al. 2011).

The Innovation Resource Centre (IRC) in Prince George reported on how the potential benefits of improving rural innovation performance are significant to the province as a whole. The report they commissioned describes a range of transition challenges and that the "future standard of living in our regional communities will be determined, in large part, by our ability to respond to these and other issues by developing new products and services, improving productivity, reducing costs, adding value, and differentiating our products and services through innovation. The technology industry will play a major role in this process" (Ference Weiker 2003: i).

To take advantage of opportunities to expand economic activity across a range of existing and emerging economic clusters, rural and small-town businesses must overcome a range of challenges, including the fact that such businesses tend to be:

- smaller in size and with less development experience
- geographically dispersed and thus challenged to take advantage of cluster attributes
- less aware of the resources available to assist with business development
- less experienced in developing new products, processes, and technologies
- limited in their access to the Internet and various e-business tools and/or opportunities. (Ference Weiker 2003)

Building on the notion that rural BC companies account for over 50 percent of the province's manufacturing shipments, and that they produce a higher per capita income from exports than do urban companies, both the IRC and the "Promoting Innovation and Commercialization in Rural BC" reports (Ference Weiker 2003) argue for better business development support infrastructure. Such infrastructure and support technology includes the following:

- research facilities in northern, rural, and small-town regions
- enhanced research capacity in nonmetropolitan colleges and universities
- improved access to financing and development funding such as through the National Research Council of Canada's Industrial Research Assistance Program (NRC-IRAP)
- expanded rural representation on the BC Regional Science and Technology Network
- extended services of industrial and trade organizations to regional communities
- enhanced access to professional and technical development supports and opportunities
- greater attention to community development to help with recruiting and retaining university and college graduates.

Existing support agencies should have their roles strengthened and their mandates refined to fit the needs of a region participating in the global economy (Amin and Thrift 1994). This recognition fits well with community-based calls for more cooperative policy development and implementation to support economic and business infrastructure renewal.

Critical to new and expanding business development are marketing, international sales, and the use of new information technologies such as marketing and sales tools. Many entrepreneurs across northern BC have shown themselves to be good at creating a product – the problem often becomes how to get that product into the marketplace and how to manage the sales and shipping side of the business. In our work, we have seen brilliant product ideas, but the entrepreneur has no idea about how the Internet can effectively manage marketing, sales, and shipping. This is an area in which scaling up by collective marketing associations could be of assistance and existing business services agencies could do more.

The central point associated with a flexible and robust community development foundation is that it allows places to respond to any economic development opportunity that fits with local assets and aspirations. For example, an economic development approach geared towards creating opportunity for a new steel mill has limited flexibility should that mill not materialize. However, building a robust suite of community development foundations that address the four critical capacity areas of human, community, economic, and physical infrastructure will allow for the adoption of a smelter, or any other economic development opportunity, should the fortunes of economic change for particular industries or firms align with local conditions. This is not a location decision based solely on site criteria, but it is about maintaining and fostering flexibility to meet opportunities in a rapidly and continually changing global economy. If a hallmark of the global economy is change, then a hallmark of renewal must be to create a flexible foundation for rural and small-town responsiveness. This position, of approaching the social and physical infrastructure needs that underscore effective community development as investments that will pay dividends over the long term by supporting competitive place-based approaches to renewal, finds further support in recent reports from the Canadian Chamber of Commerce (2011), the Conference Board of Canada (2011), and GE Canada's Remote Communities Strategy (2011). Attention to community development creates the foundations for flexible economic development.

The type of development that we outlined in the introduction, place-based development, is the conceptual partner of the whole community approach. In the following section, we contextualize the application of place-based development in the new economy and extend our discussion of the critical building blocks of the whole community approach to community capacity.

Space and Place

The renewal of northern BC's community and economic foundations means shifting from a space-based to a place-based economy. Yet, what is meant by these terms?

Space is very often dealt with in terms of simple Cartesian logic – locations and connections somewhere on an erstwhile "isotropic plain." As described in standard business and economic geography texts, locational and investment decision making is based on balancing three points. The first involves the location of the raw material inputs to the production process. The second involves the location of the target market. The third involves a choice with respect to the location of the production facility, a choice that typically balances the costs of moving raw materials versus finished products (usually based on the bulk transport costs of each) with other key inputs such as the cost/skills of the labour force, regulation or taxation costs, power/energy costs and availability, etc. Over time, the costs of transportation have been declining relative to other costs such that many industrial processes can now be located almost anywhere in the world, to access large target markets around the world, and still be coordinated in real time via communications technologies (Bollman and Prud'homme 2006). Energy price increases have been more than offset by increasing efficiencies in bulk long-distance transport.

Being staples based, the BC economy is fundamentally about moving natural resource products across great distances, through trade, to more advanced industrial economies. In other words, we can understand BC's 1950s-1970s economy as the "old economy" where space, and the challenges of overcoming its costs, was the central policy issue. The investment process was driven by the need to reconcile local assets with distance and topography. The result was the creation of instant towns to support a labour force for local extraction, and roads, rail lines, and port facilities to support the movement of extracted resources. The government established policies for the development of resource frontiers to overcome space in order to access remote resource sites, facilitate harvesting and production, and transport resources to markets for the benefit of the local, regional, and provincial economies. This approach defines the "roads to resources" policy era, and it was via those roads that the vast resource bank of distant rural spaces was accessed for provincial benefit (Mitchell 1983).

Despite the scale associated with mobilizing investments to access the resource bank, the simplicity of constructing a space-based staples economy is that it has a narrow economic focus on exploiting raw resources and facilitating extraction and commodity export (Hayter and Barnes 1990). The landscape of the space economy is narrowly comprised of a set of disjointed settlements linked to the export points and managed from a core that directs the valuing and extraction of those natural resources. However, in the new economy where (1) capital is much more mobile, (2) the resources of governments are more limited in terms of directing development decisions, and (3) there are a myriad of competing values associated with particular places and resources, the simplistic model of the space-based economy begins to fragment. This phenomenon was summarized by the question posed in Chapter 1: if capital can locate/invest anywhere in the world, why would capital locate/invest in your community? The answers led us to the beginnings of an understanding of place-based development (Halseth et al. 2010).

A place-based economy takes quite a different approach to conceptualizing and valuing nonmetropolitan landscapes and resources. It focuses on a broader and more complex view of the economic and intrinsic value of places (Birkeland 2008; Dale et al. 2008; Hirczak et al. 2008). The intrinsic value of localities includes the myriad of resources (natural and otherwise), both in and on the ground, and the ways that such places are understood and valued.

Although more complex, a place-based economy is not a strange or difficult phenomenon to understand. For example, there are differences between places around the world, and these are the things that we look at in creating opportunity – people go to Tuscany not because the landscape looks like the Okanagan, but because it has thousands of years of culturally rich history. People come to the Rockies from around the world not because it looks like the mountainous terrain found on other continents, but because of its special landmarks, histories, sites, and features. At a more mundane level, Canadians have long flocked to "cottage country" to enjoy the special character and lifestyle of summer homes on the lake. Places can be valued in many ways, and those alternative valuations can become community and economic development opportunities.

The unique mix or bundle of place-based characteristics can thus influence capital investment. This bundle of assets includes local variables such as location, natural amenities, technological and communications infrastructure, population and labour force attributes, built landscapes, cultural heritage, and much more. It includes the "story" of the place, its external images, its leading characters, its reputation in the media, and the folklore that attends its history. Place-based characteristics include, or in some cases are overlain by, many factors that localities cannot control like the federal and provincial regulatory and taxation systems. To be effective in mobilizing those place-based characteristics that are under local control, communities need to understand how to work effectively within their localities and in cooperation with other communities to both protect and realize place-based assets and values. Cooperation with adjacent communities is critical because externalities (both positive and negative) from decisions and actions in one place affect other places. Overcoming the disjointedness of the space-based economy was simply about connecting resources, labour, and markets across distance; the place-based economy involves this and much more.

A significant challenge for place-based economies is to recognize that our actions or inactions can affect our choices and flexibility for many years into the future. As places have an enduring quality, when we make a decision in the new economy we have to make sure it does not harm potential opportunities in the future.[2] A dramatic example of this is the ice jam and flooding issues along the Nechako River in Prince George during the winter of 2007-2008. Since 1994, there have been a number of spring and winter flood episodes along the river, and each time millions of dollars are spent to address impacts. If we look back to the 1910-1914 period, however, we will find what is at the root of this problem: the policy of the Grand Trunk Pacific Railway to capitalize on land development opportunities around its new line across northern BC. In the Prince George area, land speculators had already staked out the level high ground in South Fort George and Central Fort George. The only large area left was Indian Reserve no. 1 which, following typical colonial patterns of locating reserves away from lands deemed "desirable" to settlers, was in a swampy area adjacent to the junction of the Nechako and Fraser rivers. Negotiating to relocate Indian Reserve no. 1, the Grand

▼

SPACE- VS. PLACE-BASED DEVELOPMENT: A SMALL AIRPORT STRATEGY

A few years ago, the BC Progress Board (2004) published a report with recommendations for a provincial transportation strategy. One part of the report dealt with the question of small airports around northern BC. The strategy demonstrates a clear space-based orientation such that the recommendations highlighted the key role of Vancouver's International Airport as well as a set of regional airports that could feed into the main hub. The report's recommendations for the smaller airports were to downsize and merge in order to obtain better scale and efficiencies.

In a place-based approach to rural and regional development, connectivity is critical. In the very northwest region of BC, there is a small landing strip at Bob Quinn. This landing strip is absolutely vital to the region as it is the base for the large mines in the area (past and future). As well, it serves as the air shuttle drop-off point for American and European guests coming to the Belle II heli-skiing lodge. Without that landing strip, neither of these economic activities could be as successful as they are. Various groups such as the Canadian Airports Council (2006) and the Northwest Corridor Development Corporation have long supported the creation of a small airport strategy. A study of economic development potential across Canada's four western provinces conducted by the Canada West Foundation (2008) highlighted the important role of a regional airport structure and strategy. To create the flexibility necessary, not just for renewal but for ongoing success in the global economy, we need place-appropriate policy as demonstrated by the critical need for a small airport strategy in northern BC. These facilities contribute to the economy in ways that far exceed the investment we have been putting into them.

Trunk Pacific Railway was able to create the townsite that became downtown Prince George. While the Grand Trunk Pacific Railway made a few thousand dollars on land sales (before the company went bankrupt), that long ago decision committed the city to forever spending money and effort to deal with regular flooding threats. What we do now not only has consequences for the future: it commits and limits us in the future. Understanding the long-term consequences of different development decisions involves a more holistic approach to decision making that place-based development helps to facilitate.

Space and Place in the New Economy

The ascendancy of place within the context of rural development appears in a variety of ongoing rural research themes, including postproductivism, different conceptualizations of the role of competitiveness within the new economy, and the adoption of a territorial as opposed to a sector-based orientation to rural policy development. Each of these themes provides insight into the role and meaning of place within the rural development process.

Postproductivism refers to the transformation, in values and economic activity, associated with a de-emphasis on primary resource production in favour of more diversified economic activities (Reed and Gill 1997). Mather et al. (2006) indicate that in rural debates, the tendency is to present post-productivism in terms of dimensions. These dimensions include the nature and type of production (from commodity to noncommodity outputs), the multidimensionality of objectives associated with landscapes and resources (including environmental, amenity, and ecosystem service values), and the rise in governance concerns (representing a greater diversity of actors and institutions in development decision making).

Despite the proliferation of the concept, writers such as Troughton (2005) and Wilson (2004) remind and caution us that the extent of an actual transformation from productivism to postproductivism within rural economies remains controversial. Even in the absence of consensus around definitions, indicators of postproductivism are informative as they highlight the increasing relevance of place within rural development. Through the varied changes wrought by both productivism and postproductivism, place exerts itself as a more dynamic factor in processes of social and economic development. Niche products that are more dependent on location and local capacity compete for attention with generic and "placeless" commodity products (Filion 1998; Dawe 2004). Place branding has become a vital element of product development and competition for market share. France has aggressively pursued place-branding trademarks for its wines. In British Columbia, the Peace River region is well ahead in developing a Peace Country brand for regional agricultural products. Further, natural resources, in general, are increasingly viewed as local assets that may be used as vehicles for economic diversification. Finally, within new governance arrangements, local actors and institutions are playing more important decision-making roles. This local voice emerges as a response to both senior government withdrawal and to legitimate concerns for bottom-up representation and control (Polèse 1999). Ultimately, postproductivism views rural regions as more than economic spaces from which to extract resources and thus provides a useful construct to challenge the resource bank model that continues to pervade BC's nonmetropolitan development policy (Reed and Gill 1997).

Conceptualizations of competitiveness within the "new" economy represent a significant stream of place-based research. This work includes, but extends beyond, the resource orientation of postproductivism. However, much like the definitional confusion surrounding postproductivism, the concept of competitiveness remains poorly understood (Turok 2004). Despite this, debates around economic restructuring and the transition from Fordism to post-Fordist production have paid considerable attention to the shift away from the importance of comparative advantage in favour of considerations of competitive advantage (Kitson et al. 2004).[3] Comparative advantage is determined more narrowly by the fixed existence and quality of resources (Gunton 2003). Competitive advantage is more complex. Competitive advantage is dependent on the inherent assets and actions (to capitalize on those assets) of a particular place to attract and retain capital and workers that have each become much more mobile over the past several decades (Kitson et al. 2004). As a result, constructing competitive advantage demands that places consider a wider variety of both quantitative (i.e., physical infrastructure, production, location, etc.) and qualitative (i.e., social capital, innovation, institutions) variables in their economic development planning (MacLeod 2001a). In the Canadian context, both Ray Bollman (2007) and Peter Apedaile (2004) argue for greater attention to the competiveness of place-based assets in creating new foundations and opportunities for rural and regional economies. For Bollman, the issue is finding new sectors where place-based assets create competitive strength. For Apedaile, it is about the creative rethinking of assets to take advantage of inherent opportunities.

In response to the dynamics outlined by forces such as postproductivism and the new economy, the rural development literature has increasingly advocated in favour of a territorial rather than sectoral approach to policy and planning (OECD 2006). Territorial planning offers a variety of advantages. First, the model can allow for the integration of economic, environmental, community, and cultural dynamics in planning at a more manageable scale. Second, a territorial approach recognizes the importance of contextual specificity to the process of development (Barnes et al. 2000; Markey et al. 2008a), and how sector-based policy approaches can create inconsistencies and unintended barriers, and even work at cross-purposes to community and regional development. Drawing on the work of Barnes et al. (2000), Florida et al. (2010: 279) reiterate, "Economies need to be understood as local and contingent. It is clear that Canadian geographers have become aware of the historical settings and narrative of place. This has encouraged Canadian geographers to adapt across the board popular theories of economic development for Canada. As Barnes et al. (2000) acknowledge, globalization has made place more important, not less, and this has led to the creation of regional development theories that focus on innovation and creativity as the drivers of growth."

Rural development itself has struggled through and, for the most part, learned from the failures associated with top-down, uniform, nonparticipatory models of development (Booth and Halseth 2011; Halseth and Booth 2003). Attention to territoriality is necessary to attain local buy-in and to benefit from local and regional knowledge, leadership, and development assets. Finally, despite the seeming contradiction of scale inefficiency, territorial planning models can reduce duplication and lead to more effective and lasting policy interventions (Pezzini 2001; Bradford 2005).

The New Regionalism

Although the territorial approach to policy and planning brings certain advantages, it does not necessarily address the problem of realizing development at different spatial scales. For this, the literatures surrounding new regionalism and community economic development (CED) are helpful. Regional and community-based research seeks to understand the complex junction of micro- and macro-development processes within places (Pierce 1992; Massey 1995; Savoie 1997; Porter 2000).

The origins of new regionalism are linked with the broader economic transformation to post-Fordism and the subsequent attention that this brought to the question of regional disparities that were, to some degree, hidden by a combination of the Fordist industrial structure and government support (Scott 2000). With the breakdown of these investment and equalization levers, new regionalism has been tracking the reconfiguration of both economic competitiveness and governance at different scales. Economically, new regionalism understands development as a socially embedded process in which the social capital of a region exerts influence on economic performance (Cooke and Morgan 1998; Barnes and Gertler 1999). The governance theme is equally pronounced as regions experiment with different institutional structures and relationships in an attempt to compensate for government withdrawal and innovate to establish better local participation, competitive advantage, and economies of scale (Storper 1999; MacLeod 2001b).[4]

Key within new regionalism is the potential to improve a region's economic, community, or environmental situation through appropriate intervention (Polèse 1999). From this perspective, the region represents a manageable scale for understanding impacts and designing mitigation strategies.

Community Economic Development

At a more local scale, community economic development has become an umbrella term for understanding the benefits of local bottom-up development. Community economic development is defined as "a process by which communities can initiate and generate their own solutions to their common economic problems and thereby build long-term community capacity and foster the integration of economic, social, and environmental objectives" (Markey et al. 2005: 2). Three themes within the CED literature address the role of place in the development process. (1) CED seeks to rebalance traditional economic development by linking economic and social processes and needs to support a more integrative approach that can realize the full benefits of development and not simply achieve more growth (Shaffer et al. 2006). (2) CED has adapted alternative development theory to promote the benefits associated with local participation as a way to address issues of marginality at the scale of both the individual and the community (Stohr and Taylor 1981; Lo and Halseth 2009).[5] Finally, (3) attention to the topic of participation generally, and to the roles of economic and social sector participants specifically, have focused on the importance of local actors and leadership in directing development processes (Bryant 1995; Halseth and Booth 2003).

From these literatures, a set of broad themes helps to inform and consolidate our understanding of the role of place in development. First, although an economic focus remains, there is now greater consideration of culture, the environment, and the community, as these are now desirable assets in the new economy. The appeal of rural and small-town places must now emphasize access to recreation, culture, amenities, affordable retirement living, a sense of community, and lower land costs that will make these communities attractive to private individuals, business, and industry. The ascendancy of place brings a greater diversity of values (and understandings of value) to economic development. Through place, we gain an appreciation of a more comprehensive or "whole" economy than is often externalized and ignored in the narrow space-based interpretation of resource exploitation in peripheral hinterlands. In addition, within the place economy, an appreciation for diversity means that difference matters. Place can become a factor, for example, in product differentiation as a source of market value. This rethinking of place rather than space challenges homogeneous interpretations of rural, potentially uncovering the latent diversity noted in other rural research (Randall and Ironside 1996).

Second, a place-based economy demands much more of local capacity. From a value-added perspective, local actors and institutions are a source of contextual knowledge that helps to identify community and regional assets. Local capacity must accommodate and forge new relationships and partnerships that represent critical sources of innovation in social and economic development within the context of a more globalized economy (Aarsaether and Suopajärvi 2004). Perhaps the greatest challenge to this increased role for local capacity concerns compensating for state withdrawal from the functions of, and responsibility for, service provision (and the technical capacity that it entails). Importantly, this transition burdens senior governments, as they strive to find the correct policy and program balance between top-down management and support for bottom-up direction and control (Bradford 2005). Both value-added and -subtracted dimensions of local capacity introduce a greater likelihood of social and economic variability across the rural landscape. This, in turn, situates this concept and strategy well within the heterogeneity of the post-Fordist world.

Third, governance regimes are more prominent within a place-based economy (Aarsaether and Baerenholdt 2001). While potentially stressing available local capacity, there are two positive place-oriented by-products associated with enhanced governance. (1) Governance implies a redrawing of the lines of accountability and control, away from centralized state power, to be dispersed among a greater diversity of local and extra-local actors and institutions. In the fast-paced global economy, centralized state governments simply cannot respond quickly to changing conditions. As part of this remapping of decision making, governance mechanisms may initiate regional dialogue and cooperation, altering the direction of traditional heartland-hinterland flows of communication and resources. (2) The participation inherent in governance fosters a sense of local ownership, over decisions and ultimately resources, which did not exist under previous top-down regimes. Thus, a more focused attention to "place" reveals a greater variety of assets and fosters an awareness that those assets are local and may be used for local purposes.

Fourth, a place-based economy demands investment to construct and maintain place competitiveness. The dynamic nature of an economy driven by competitive advantage requires renewal. Platforms of new infrastructure may have enduring value, but the "draw-down" approach inherent within the late stages of a comparative economic structure will not foster the adaptive capacity necessary to thrive within a place-based economy. Rather than viewing outlays for infrastructure within a space-based economy context as expenses against a short-term bottom line, such outlays must be viewed within a place-economy approach as investments that support long-term local and regional adaptive capacity.

Within the context of place-based development, questions of rural decline are set within a much more complex system. Certainly, rural areas will struggle with capacity challenges associated with place-based economic transition – but they are already struggling. These same rural areas contain many of the scarce assets that are highly valued within the contemporary global economy – assets that go well beyond what can be mined or harvested. Development policy that fails to recognize this potential makes a passive but, nevertheless, strong contribution to rural decline.

Community Capacity: Human Capital, Social Capital, and Social Cohesion

Under changing social and economic conditions, communities need to draw from a variety of capacities in order to respond in proactive and timely ways. Community capacity refers to the ability of residents to organize and mobilize their assets and resources to achieve development objectives that they consider important. These objectives may be reactive, where people are faced with a challenge, or innovative, where new visions are established and pursued. Community capacity is built and maintained by the norms, traditions, regulations, and social relationships enabling otherwise disparate individuals to coordinate their actions for collective ends.

To start building community capacity, Alasia and Magnusson (2005) examine how important ongoing investments in human capital – education, skills, health, experiences, etc. – are for rural and small-town regions. This focus is echoed by the BC Competition Council (2006) in its attention to enhancing the province's economic competitiveness by investing in human resources through education, training, and professional development. Similarly, the BC Progress Board (2006) identifies the need for attention to skills, education, and research to build a "culture of productivity" in the new economy as a crucial public policy area. Although neither the BC Competition Council nor the BC Progress Board reports address the specific context of rural and small-town BC, work by the New Rural Economy project of the Canadian Rural Revitalization Foundation (www.nre.concordia.ca) and by the Canada West Foundation (www.cwf.ca) reinforces the need to address human capacity issues as a key building block for enhancing the competitive advantages of rural and small-town places.

The economic development potential of places is dependent, at least in part, on the ability of local social institutions to mobilize effective responses to the pressures generated by a new economic environment (Aarsaether and Baerenholdt 2001). Such institutions will necessarily reflect past patterns and practices of economic and social development; however, they need to be adaptive and innovative. Failure to create these conditions is what Florida (2002) refers to as "institutional sclerosis," which can become a major constraint on the capacity of places to adapt to ongoing socio-economic change.

Historically, rural regions have faced barriers to community capacity investments. An instrumentalist view would report low return on education investments, as the skills needs of resource industries have traditionally been low, while union pay rates were relatively high. Those views (and those days) are long past. Within resource extractive industries, the ongoing application of flexible production and new technologies means that the workforce must now be well educated and possess a range of skills. Trades tickets, computer literacy, and a host of other specialty training courses are now requirements for employment.[6] Once on the job, a "learning environment" is the norm. Innovative places and businesses put a premium on education and the application of new ideas in creative ways. Rural and small-town regions will not attract capital to develop innovative ideas if they continue to be perceived as concentrations of low-skilled employment.

Another challenge for rural and small-town educational investment has been the mobility of skilled workers. Such mobility reduces the incentives for firms, or even regions, to invest in education for fear that the investment will be recouped elsewhere – this is the "if we train them they might leave to work for someone else" mentality among some businesses. Two points are important for placing this concern within a broader perspective. For one, the locations of advanced educational training facilities will remain relatively limited. In Canada, institutes of technology and universities with research training capacity exist in select locations. To access these, people will need to move. The question for rural and small-town businesses is how to create a competitive and attractive working environment so that those workers will want to return. For example, the province of Quebec is taking a sophisticated approach to the question of youth out-migration from rural and small-town regions. Understanding that it is natural for youth to leave their home towns (e.g., to learn about the world, to gain job skills, or to go to school), the public policy emphasis is on creating welcoming rural and small-town places to draw these people back when they are starting their careers, their businesses, and are seeking a familiar place to raise their family. Interestingly, much the same approach to rural out-migration is found in Japan (where some rural places even have scholarship opportunities to let residents go out and explore the world), where the emphasis is on attracting young families and businesses back with place-based investments. Investment in training and education must confront and overcome the "chicken and egg" situation: should we invest in education to attract investment and new firms or attract new firms and then invest in needed education? The answer, of course, is that we need both, at the same time. A well-educated workforce is a crucial recruitment tool, and the need to support ongoing training in the workplace and beyond is now the norm for most businesses and industries.

The second main point concerning mobility is that places themselves need to focus on the recruitment and retention of the mobile labour force. Just as businesses need to create supportive work environments to attract and hold workers, so too do regions and communities. In the 1950s and 1960s, the emphasis was on creating attractive towns, separate from the noxious outputs of industry, with quality amenities for their target labour market of young families. Today, much of this remains important. Quality-of-life (including increasing attention to a healthy environment) services for the now wider array of young through to older age groups and access via new information technology can bring many of the benefits of urban life to the more affordable and human scale of the rural and small-town community. As communities and regions undertake these investments, decision makers should not be under any illusion that people who feel more at home in the crowded cores of Canada's large metropolitan centres will suddenly rush to live a rural life – instead, they should target those for whom a "connected" small-town life is desirable.

A major driver of a holistic community capacity approach to regional development is the concept of clusters, as developed by researchers such as Porter (2000, 2004), whose work focuses on "industrial clusters." Components of industries that share proximity, networks, supplier chains, relationships, and a host of additional supporting institutions are much more effective in responding to market challenges and opportunities. Through processes of competitive cooperation, such clusters are able to share not only facilities and infrastructure, but also information and networks. In other words, there is a blending of hard infrastructure with the soft, intangible factors associated with community capacity. The inclusion of both economic and social contributors to competitive success function through networks set within unique places.

One of the challenges in adapting Porter's cluster approach to resource economies has been the depth of vision applied to the question of what constitutes a cluster. A vivid example is the identification of Prince George as home to a cluster of companies producing forest products. The presence of three large pulp mills, together with a wide range of other forest products mills, bears witness to the validity of this cluster argument for the city. Opportunities in the new economy for growing within and across this cluster certainly exist. However, if we adjust our vision of local economic activities, it is clear that Prince George serves as an incubator for a robust high tech sector. This sector emerged as the transportation and forest products sectors become increasingly automated and computer based. More than a hundred high tech firms now operate in the city, undertaking a range of technology, hardware, software, and management activities. Application of a cluster approach to economic development requires attention to the argument in this book that we must rebundle and reimagine our assets in order to appreciate the scope of opportunities available in the new economy.

A recent project by the 16-97 Economic Alliance examined economic possibilities for the growth of a mining cluster in northern BC. This project was creative in exploring a host of opportunities that might typically be hidden from a more simplistic conceptualization of the mining industry as a market for heavy equipment sales. The resulting Northern Interior Mining Group is working "cooperatively to access new markets, boost profiles and awareness of regional services, and advocate for business related issues [to become] a 'go to' industry organization ready to provide information and support to the mining development community" (16-97 Economic Alliance 2010).

Social Cohesion and Social Capital

By drawing attention to both economic and social contributions to competiveness, clusters and new regionalism in general focus considerable attention on the strength and resilience of communities. Within these approaches to fostering a foundation for development, there is a significant emphasis on social dynamics and the associational nature of creating economic opportunity in place. Exploring new economic opportunities and exploiting competitive niches within communities and regions requires a high level of collaboration between different community, government, and business actors and institutions. Clusters, for example, feed on the delicate balance between businesses competing with each other and finding ways to work together for mutual benefit (e.g., lobbying policy makers, investing in training facilities, etc.). Two concepts useful for exploring how communities organize and respond to change are social cohesion and social capital. Both terms are complex and have a considerable literature and debate behind them (see, e.g., Wall et al. 1998; Wallis 1998; Putnam 2000; Korsching et al. 2001; Schuller 2001; Keast et al. 2004); for our purposes, however, we understand social cohesion as involving interaction and social capital as involving trust.

The concept of social cohesion can be used for examining how a community develops networks and processes of exchange. It is associated with processes of interaction and the resulting partnerships, networks, and relationships that emerge from, and are sustained by, that interaction. Social cohesion involves, therefore, the central ways by which a sense of community is created and recreated over time. It can be founded on shared values, shared experiences, and cooperation. It is normalized through routine relationships and social interaction; and in a reflexive manner, it can reinforce local values and patterns of interaction (Beckley 1995).

A good example of social cohesion in action is the community response to the withdrawal of private and public sector services. The responses of local voluntary sector groups – in addressing the resulting gaps – can provide a foundation to build networks and interactions that help to develop social cohesion. Service providers and voluntary organizations, such as post offices, seniors' centres, recreation or cultural organizations, schools, and a host of others provide locations for people to engage in routine social interaction (Potapchuk et al. 1997; Bruce and Halseth 2001). Such social interaction and any resulting networks then become a social asset that may help the community to respond collectively to economic, social, political, or environmental change. Over time, the confidence people feel in the networks, and the forms of trust they generate, become a form of social capital that may be mobilized to help communities cope with sudden or stressful events (Lowndes 2004).

Social capital refers to the social assets available to a person, group, organization, or community (Reimer 2002). In general, social capital encompasses key features of trust and cooperation. It involves other features of social organization, "such as networks, norms, and trust that facilitate coordination and cooperation for mutual benefits" (Korsching et al. 2001: 81). As such, social capital is an important concept for examining the development of successful communities. As communities work together, they build social capital, and as they cope with challenges or change, they employ that social capital.[7] In other words, the foundation of trust and prior relationships are local resources that can be drawn on to accomplish things for individuals, groups, or communities.

A word of caution is needed at this point. Over the past number of years, government programs or policies have targeted the development or enhancement of social capital and social cohesion. Such programs and policies are often based on an interpretation of social capital and social cohesion as "good" for community development. While we argue that these are important elements within community development, we caution against labels such as "good" or "bad." Rather, what matters is the use or purpose to which social capital and social cohesion are put. If employed to support participation, community functioning, access to information and resources, etc., then the value is clear. In some cases, however, social capital and social cohesion can be so strongly developed that the groups tend to be closed to new people and new ideas – thus creating a form of exclusion that is counterproductive to the goals of community development. It is with this caution in mind that community developers should make use of concepts such as social capital and social cohesion.

To be useful in rural and small-town renewal, we need to recognize that social capital has a spatial dimension. Trusting relationships formed locally or within groups are often called bonding social capital since they intensify local ties and strengthen the ability within groups or organizations to work together to solve problems and address needs (Larsen et al. 2004).

Examples of bonding social capital include community events or social clubs (Potapchuk et al. 1997). Trusting relationships between groups inside or outside of the community are often called bridging social capital since they link specific groups to a wider pool of ideas, experiences, advice, and support outside of their regular circle of interaction (Putnam 2000; Wallis 1998). Such networks may provide information about how other groups or places are arranging or providing needed services. In many rural and small-town places, organizations such as Lions or Rotary clubs, the Legion, and a host of others have been especially important since they work locally to develop social cohesion and bonding social capital – and they link to much wider national and international networks of support, programs, and advice. Bridging social capital will become more important within the communities of northern BC as we progress towards the resolution of treaties. Renegotiating the landscape of ownership and economic opportunity will require that Aboriginal and non-Aboriginal communities work together to identify those opportunities and to resolve the inevitable tensions that will accompany the transition.

Vision and Strategic Foundations

As noted earlier, the collective body of our research has explored the components of a foundation for community and economic renewal in northern British Columbia. In this section, we review the key components of economic renewal as told to us by the citizens, organizations, and communities in the north. If we are seeking to adopt a whole community, place-based approach to development, it is important to begin with local knowledge, perceptions, and strategic priorities as identified by northern residents.

When asked about transition to a future economy, people in northern BC talk about moving from northern strength to northern strength. This renewed northern strength includes a resource economy foundation, diversified community and economic development opportunities within existing sectors, and work to add new economic opportunities.[8] Diversification within traditional resource sectors to include additional value-added manufacturing finds support in recent reports from Statistics Canada. For example, Beshiri (2010) finds that resource sector manufacturing is not only a very important component of rural and small-town employment, but that its share of total manufacturing in Canada had increased during the period 2001-2008 preceding the global recession. This existing strength provides an ideal platform for further value-added expansion and growth.

Renewal includes a greater retention of the benefits generated by the northern economy for use by northern communities. To achieve this, we have synthesized feedback from northern voices to identify components of a vision for renewal and a variety of strategic directions for attaining the vision. It is through these frameworks that northern BC must explore creative ways to rebundle its assets to create new strategic opportunities and development advantages.

Vision

People spoke passionately to us about how a northern economic vision is clearly rooted in the interactions between people, the environment, and a high quality of life (see how these same issues are reflected in work by Ostry 1999; Frame et al. 2004; Goebel et al. 2004). In describing the key elements of a northern vision, our research has recorded the following eleven core areas of interest:

1. diversity
2. inclusivity
3. cooperation
4. lifestyle
5. sustainability
6. northern perspectives
7. connections
8. human resources
9. foundation for community development
10. attitudes
11. regulatory framework.

These vision components provide a framework with which to approach economic development.

People argued that *diversity* across northern BC is a multifaceted characteristic. Not all communities will desire to have the same level of economic development or the same path to an economic future. Across the rich diversity that is northern BC, different peoples, cultures, and communities may choose different approaches to economic development. This diversity extends to the multilayered ways in which different genders, and different community and cultural groups, may seek to participate (Reed 2003b). To this we can add that the needs of different age groups, including access to training and jobs for youth, and access to health care and other services for an aging population, help to bind this diversity with our need to build robust community development foundations. Finally, people spoke about the rich and diverse physical geography of the region and about how opportunities for co-constructing a robust economic base must extend across industry types, firm sizes, and economic sectors.

When talking about community and economic development visions and strategies, people spoke about how these should be *inclusive*. They argued that First Nations participation must feature in all discussions and actions. Such processes must be "bottom-up," to include participation by the entire spectrum of economic sectors active in the region, and involve all levels of government, as well as industry and business interests in the private sector (Counsel on BC Aboriginal Economic Development 2002; Indian and Northern Affairs Canada 2004; NWTT 2004). This approach to participation reaches beyond the legislated, stepwise consultation so common in today's resource development approval processes. Rather, authentic and inclusive participation builds on the idea of respectful and ongoing dialogue that helps to build relationships, understanding, trust, awareness, and most of all, readiness to respond to challenges and opportunities in a collaborative fashion.

People spoke about how the region needs to move away from bitterly competitive, intercommunity relations towards *cooperation*. Competition can be healthy and boost creativity; however, rural and small-town places across northern BC should build a more collaborative environment where government and community players interact with trust. Such cooperation extends to, and focuses on, the need to settle treaties and develop effective working relationships between Aboriginal and non-Aboriginal communities. For example, the figurative distance that Aboriginal and non-Aboriginal communities need to travel in order to achieve an effective working relationship was clearly demonstrated during our Northern BC Economic Development Vision and Strategy Project. Across northern BC, there are many circumstances where non-Aboriginal communities are located close to, and sometimes even immediately adjacent to, federally demarcated Indian reserves. During three of our workshop meetings, it became clear that representatives of adjacent Aboriginal and non-Aboriginal communities were getting together to engage in a collective dialogue about the future of their communities and economies for the first time. One speaker was so moved by the experience that she wept. The challenges facing each community aligned quite closely, and participants identified a possible mechanism for collaboration to resolve one such mutual challenge. Clearly, much more attention needs to be devoted to an ongoing and inclusive multicommunity dialogue across northern BC.

As noted above, *lifestyle* issues are becoming key economic development assets in the new economy, and these can be used to help build on the already significant contributions that rural communities make to regional and provincial economies. Northern characteristics, such as friendliness, resourcefulness, self-sufficiency, safe and healthy communities, a lack of urban congestion, affordable housing, and the sense of community that comes from knowing each other are identified by people as being increasingly important. Linking economic development with workforce needs, these lifestyle issues are important in the decision making of the next generation of young workers and need to be vital components of any development vision in the future.

Those who spoke through our community interviews, workshops, and meetings are adamant that economic development must support the people, environment, and quality-of-life assets so valued in northern BC. *Sustainability,* for northerners, is not an abstract concept but is grounded in the connections between generations and with the land (Ostry 1999; Pierce and Dale 1999; see also Sasaki et al. 1996). People argued that a northern vision should be robust and flexible enough to ensure continuity between government changes and the booms and busts of economic cycles. They also felt that a northern vision should ensure that more of the wealth generated in the north stays in the north for community and economic development – a notion that highlights how residents of BC's resource bank are increasingly tired of having resource withdrawals made without adequate reinvestment in their social and economic foundations.

It is clear from the contributions of individuals and groups that northern BC has developed a strong sense of its place within the province and a strong sense that it must have the tools necessary to shape its own destiny. People argued that a *northern perspective* recognizes that the north needs to speak with a stronger and more united voice, that there needs to be more local control of resource revenues, and that the revitalized vision for industrial development must support northern communities first and foremost. This northern perspective will evolve from the growing number of *connections* that define the region. These include connections between individuals and between communities, through infrastructure that facilitates communications and development, through the environment, and through the quality of life supported by that environment.

A vision for renewal must recognize the growing significance of *human resources* (Saunders 2004; Scott 2004). Individuals, businesses, employers, and other stakeholders spoke about how the realities of a new economy are demanding a more flexible and responsive human resource base in order to take advantage of opportunities as they arise (see similar arguments in Kunin 2003; LeBlanc et al. 2003; Nicol 2003; Petroleum Human Resources Council of Canada 2003). They said that education, training, and capacity building are critical parts of a northern vision and should be core values in northern BC. To this end, they offered strong support to the network of postsecondary institutions in place across the north and to other key institutions of our human resource development infrastructure.

Community development, including adequate health care facilities, access to quality education, cultural opportunities, recreational facilities, connecting infrastructure such as road, rail, air transportation, and the various forms of communications technologies are all felt to be important for a robust rural and small-town foundation to recruit new people and economic activities and to retain existing people and businesses. People were very clear about how community development and economic development processes

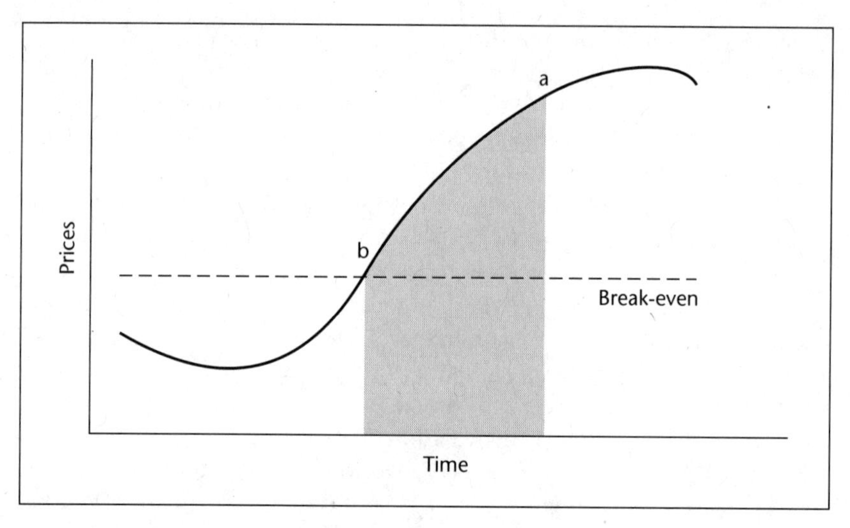

Figure 6 Product or commodity price curve

are interlinked and how both are crucial to the future of the region. These processes include tools to focus on our strengths, to balance northern aspirations with economic realities, to "brand" northern communities and assets for investment purposes, and to tap into the existing array of community and economic development support structures and services (Bruce and Lister 2001). A wide array of economic development organizations and resources already exist, but further coordination between these resources and community users is necessary to ensure that we get "the most bang for the buck," that gaps are addressed, and services extended.

People argued that a new northern vision must take a positive and proactive *attitude* towards economic change. The pattern of simply being reactive to opportunity or to crisis has to be changed. Figure 6 captures this sense of relocating from a reactive to a proactive approach. The curve uses the example of a price curve for a product or commodity over time. The x-axis represents time, and the y-axis represents the changing value or market price for the product or commodity. As prices go up and down over time, they cross a break-even point, above which the business can make a profit and below which the business will lose money. As prices go up, economic actors and investors move into the new opportunity in hopes of securing market share and making money. As shown by point a, a reactive approach to price increases encounters the curve long after it has moved above the break-even point. In an economic upswing, we have lost valuable time in the competitive race to win both market share and profit. In a report for UNBC's Community Development Institute, Graham Kedgley (2009) uses the example of BC's mining industry to illustrate this phenomenon. As the provincial government's former coal commissioner, Kedgley writes that we cannot wait until mineral or coal prices are high to start planning for a new mine. We need to be ready to ship product immediately when prices reach the profitability level. We need to be proactive and must move our approach to development so that we encounter improving opportunities at point b. The shaded area under the curve represents lost revenue – while the shaded area above the curve and above the break-even point represents lost potential profit.

Finally, many of the individuals and organizations that spoke with us about the issue of a renewed northern vision mentioned the important elements of *policy and regulation*. They raised three key issues. First, there is a general need for greater policy coordination so that the actions of different governments and agencies can build together rather than work at cross-purposes (Pezzini 2000; Isaksen 2001; Drabenstott and Sheaff 2002a, 2002b). At present, policies and regulations are too piecemeal and limited to bureaucratic "silos." Second, there is a general feeling, reinforced by observation, that the region is a "have" area of the province – if only more of the wealth it generates stayed in the north. Thus, a northern vision should include a renewed public policy framework that creates more employment and an enabling context for increased northern investment. Third, as part of a move to more place-based policies and regulations, there is a need to apply a "rural" and a "northern" lens to ensure a better fit and guard against unanticipated negative consequences.

Strategic Directions

Together, the eleven elements identified for a northern vision point to areas of organization, capacity building, and investment. To support these, the following twelve strategic directions serve to guide the development of opportunities for renewal:

1. education and training
2. community capacity building
3. youth opportunities
4. economic strength and diversification
5. financing, investment, and funding
6. infrastructure
7. marketing and branding
8. a collective voice
9. partnerships in decision making
10. a framework
11. a northern context
12. support mechanisms.

People spoke to us about how the new economy is an information economy where *education and training* are key to capitalizing on changing opportunities. They suggested that the region's education strategy should ensure that people are trained in the north and are able to take advantage of new forms of technologies and delivery options; offer basic education as well as advanced skills training; meet the needs of lifelong learning; meet the needs of present and emerging industrial sectors; and support ongoing human capacity upgrading in northern BC (Rosenfeld and Sheaff 2002).

Moving to the level of *community capacity building,* people pointed out that the needs of the new economy are creating new demands across the region. In both Aboriginal and non-Aboriginal communities, they talked about the need for new administrative and management training and how community capacity development would equip places to deal with change and opportunity. All of these recommendations reinforce the need for lifelong education and training, and they extend to all segments of the community and economy.

There is a strong feeling that one of northern BC's strategic advantages is its large cohort of *young people.* In many ways, this youth component in the population sets northern BC apart from many of its OECD competitors. To energize this economic advantage, we were told that northern BC's youth strategy should include education and skills training opportunities, a youth perspective and participation in creating a northern vision and strategy, links to a global culture to create socially progressive communities, and jobs (Dupuy et al. 2000; Jentsch and Shucksmith 2004). For Aboriginal youth, the strategy needs to include a strong grounding in traditional cultures and languages to provide the base from which youth can make their own decisions about how to participate in changing traditional and market economies.

Jobs come from *economic strength and diversification.* The region's diversification strategy should recognize the value and quality of our resource base, ensure that more resource industry benefits are left in the north, and then build on this base to create a diversified economy that includes value-added and processing sectors as well as other economic sectors. Opportunities within and between sectors were the focus time and again (see also Statistics Canada 2003). Our participants emphasized that new economic development must create employment opportunities for northerners. They pointed out that development based around fly-in/fly-out workers, or temporary workforces, drained the region of development benefits and left only the costs to be borne by the region's future generations.

One of the lessons individuals and businesses shared was that a flexible global economy requires flexible options for *financing* economic diversification. Among the potential mechanisms suggested were community trusts, resource revenue sharing, expansion of existing programs such as Western

Economic Diversification and Aboriginal Affairs and Northern Development, and the creation of new institutions such as a "Northern Bank" or a union of northern BC credit unions to "scale up" the level of support available for community economic development. Into this mix, the Northern Development Initiative (NDI) Trust has been a valuable addition. A second issue concerns insurance coverage – an already considerable challenge as places deal with changes in basic services and the more conservative approach to risk that insurance companies are taking. New financing mechanisms will also help with much-needed improvements in community *infrastructure*.

We heard how part of northern BC's marketing strategy should include place-based *branding*. The global economy values the region's characteristics of dramatic physical landscapes, clean natural environments, and rich cultural heritages. Historical examples such as the North Pacific label to market sockeye salmon in Britain, and new initiatives such as Branding the Peace illustrate how valuable place-based brands can be in the global marketplace. Dawe (2004), for example, has shown how effective the Orkney Islands region of the United Kingdom has been in using place branding to market local products at a considerable premium into the global marketplace.

To increase the visibility and *voice* of the region in policy debates and the marketplace, people suggested that one of the guiding principles for the region's strategic directions is to "scale up" from the community to the regional level. Past approaches to development across nonmetropolitan BC have been characterized by intercommunity competition. These put the organization of places in a heartland-hinterland regional development schema where small towns sought to "outbid" their neighbours for new industry or government investments. As noted by Turok (2004) and others, such rivalry generally results in a wasteful allocation of resources, duplication, and a temptation to make showy investments rather than foster more authentic ingredients of competitiveness. Achieving economies of scale through collaboration can support places as they search for their own competitive advantages as regions in the global economy, and as they debate how to access and mobilize distinctive local characteristics or assets that will ground an economic future that fits with their aspirations.

Building on this, people noted the intimate connection between the region's communities and economies. Recent changes in both the global economy and provincial legislation around resource development were mentioned as developments that reinforced this connectivity. As a result, people suggested that decision-making *partnerships* for northern BC should connect within communities and sectors, between communities and sectors, between Aboriginal and non-Aboriginal communities, and across northern BC's subregions.

To move forward, people argued, any *framework* within which northern BC might interact and discuss regional strategic directions has to be based in the north and developed from the bottom up. This was said at the same time as recognizing that individual places will have their own assets and aspirations and that these can be set within and positively affected by what happens across the region. Participants asserted that a *northern context* for developing such a framework would allow it to recognize the "quadruple bottom line" of economy, community, environment, and culture so important across northern BC. These are the four elements that underscore northern lifestyles and development visions.

Finally, to move forward on any form of northern BC development strategy will require *support mechanisms*. People were very practical in their suggestions and recommendations, arguing that we must make efficient use of existing educational and economic development tools and institutions (MacKinnon 2002; Markey 2003). Similarly, they spoke to us about how the development of strategic directions for the region needs to involve tools that create economic and community knowledge. They see these as important building blocks that could facilitate development exercises.

Recommendations and Postscript

Building from the vision statements and strategic directions noted above, our research has garnered the following five core recommendations for renewal.

1. Settle treaties in a fair and timely fashion.
2. Complete the electrical power grid across the region to facilitate new economic development opportunities in northern BC.
3. Move forward with the next steps in discussions about creating some form of a robust and inclusive northern BC regional development council.
4. Move on the various suggestions for a resource revenue-sharing arrangement with the region's Aboriginal and non-Aboriginal communities.
5. Develop greater cooperative and coordinated policy within and between all levels of Aboriginal and non-Aboriginal government to support economic and community development across the region.

In various presentations of our work, we have received both support and criticism for these recommendations. We insist that these issues reflect directions that northerners themselves feel are crucial to both supporting long-term goals and initiating steps in the short term to renew northern BC's communities and economic strengths. We include them here so that they may resonate throughout the remaining chapters to facilitate a better understanding of opportunities and barriers to seeking economic renewal in northern BC.

Recent events support the validity of these core recommendations. At the 2008 Northern Economic Summit in Prince George, the NDI Trust submitted that the coming decade needed to be a "northern decade," and argued "making the next decade 'the northern decade' is the best investment to ensure long-term provincial prosperity. Make no mistake about it – the North drives our economy" (NDI Trust 2009). Investments in power, infrastructure, research, and education and training – all through a coordinated and supportive public policy environment – will create the foundations for this northern decade.

Although there has been limited progress concerning the resolution of treaties, there was wide support for the position that participating governments should work towards settling treaties in a fair and timely fashion. While working to complete such treaties, participants in our research noted that it will be important in the interim to move forward with building effective working relationships between Aboriginal and non-Aboriginal communities (BC Treaty Commission 2002; Skeena Native Development Society 2003a, 2003b; Usher 2003). The future of northern BC involves all our people and all our communities. As noted, since the 2005 provincial elections, the BC government and BC's First Nations leadership have been at work to create a more effective framework for interaction (First Nations Summit 2005).

Since the Northern Economic Vision and Strategy Project (NEV), we have argued that it is critical to complete the electrical power grid across the northern parts of BC. Both communities and industries identify access to power as one of the biggest factors in realizing economic development opportunities and as an area of potential opportunity both within traditional energy sectors and in alternative sources of energy production and use. When this recommendation first came out, the response by government was profound silence. There was a pervasive but faulty sense that BC had all the energy it needed and had had for a long time. Since then, fluctuating oil prices, the inability of industry to commit to regional development where there was no access to the power grid, and even BC Hydro advertisements that now recognize how BC is in an energy deficit have all worked to change that mindset and emphasize the importance of this recommendation.

Progress on energy, however, has been slow. The communities of Masset, Old Massett, and Port Clements on Haida Gwaii, for example, consume almost 20,000 litres of diesel fuel per day to provide power through the Masset diesel-generating station (16,000 L/day average through August and 23,500 L/day average through February), and they have no electrical power to spare for new economic actors. Any renewed interest in mining puts the spotlight on the incomplete power grid across northern BC. A number of mining proposals along highways 16 and 37 north are debating power supply options with the provincial government, but without a comprehensive plan for power, the expensive process of extending the grid is still years away (Terrace Standard 2005; G.E. Bridges and Robinson Consulting 2005).[9]

Through all components of our research, and related to each of the recommendations, there was a strong desire to move forward with further discussions concerning the creation of some form of northern BC regional development council. We have identified a set of principles to guide such organization(s) and some next steps for debating potential options. It is now worth noting that regional coordination processes have become the preferred development and funding mechanism of the BC provincial government. First among these was the creation of the Northern Development Initiative Trust from funds generated by the BC Rail-CN Rail Agreement, which we will profile in more detail in Chapter 6. The NDI Trust created a regional forum that covered much of the area included in the NEV. As originally set out, the province envisioned the creation of a set of smaller, subregional committees. One of these separate committees involves a special allocation of funds to First Nations. Building on the successful Columbia Basin Trust, the NDI Trust involves a trust fund for supporting economic development investments. Evaluated against the set of principles identified above, the NDI Trust is challenged by its economic focus (rather than overtly recognizing the intimate linkages between economic development and community development), the lack of First Nations participation (rather than creating a forum for bringing together all of northern BC's peoples and communities), and its limited governance structure, drawing largely on mayors and provincial government appointees (something that does not build in other interests).

Building on the NDI Trust model, one of the provincial responses to the mountain pine beetle crisis, as noted above, has been to fund regional beetle action coalitions. By September 2005, two such coalitions were active in northern BC, using a funding and governance structure similar to the NDI Trust. The challenges identified above remain for these coalitions as well. Finally, two subregions in northern BC (the northwest and the central interior) have initiated regional economic alliances to take advantage of working synergies among local economic development offices.

There is wide support for the principle that local resources should generate benefits for local communities. Wide reference is made to the Fair Share Agreement in the Peace River region (profiled in greater detail in Chapter 8) and the need for the province to move on the various suggestions for a resource revenue-sharing arrangement with northern BC's Aboriginal and non-Aboriginal communities (Union of BC Municipalities 2004). In recent years, the provincial government has moved in these directions through an expansion of some existing resource-sharing arrangements, such as community forest and forest and range agreements. Furthermore, the NDI Trust and beetle action coalition funds have directed monies into regional bodies that are governed in northern BC, and their original funds have been periodically supplemented by additional resource revenues. These funds are on top of processes like the 1988 South Moresby Forest Replacement Account to assist with changes following creation of the Gwaii Haanas National Park Reserve and Haida Heritage Site.

Finally, our research consistently supports a need for dialogue to help build greater cooperative and coordinated policy development within and between all levels of Aboriginal and non-Aboriginal government to support economic and community development across the region. Included among the action items was the call for a multilevel government meeting on cooperative policy development and implementation strategies. The various regional economic forums and bodies that have been created to date appear to have initiated (albeit in a much more limited way than imagined) some of this dialogue.

The concepts, principles, and recommendations provided in this chapter – all grounded in the voices and experiences of northern BC – serve to inform the place-based development approaches and responsibilities that follow in later chapters. Before progressing to our framework for renewal, it is important to obtain a deeper understanding of the historical development patterns and processes of economic and political restructuring that have shaped the current landscape of northern BC. Place-based development is, above all else, a highly contextualized form of development. The following historical overview will inform a deeper understanding of development in northern BC. This will allow us to see beyond any particular snapshot in time and base our recommendations on a more nuanced appreciation of the internal and external forces that compete and overlap to create the multiplicity of northern BC experiences.

Part 2
Creating a Space-Based Economy

4
Province Building

> WAC Bennett's vision for BC was to a considerable degree a "northern vision," where the "modern north is a land of minerals, huge forest stands, uranium, coal, oil, natural gas, hydro-electric power. This is a land of the future ... The Government and the people of British Columbia have started a revolution." (Mitchell 1983: 260)

The roots of the present economic and settlement landscape in northern BC are found in two development eras. Through the 1950s and 1960s, the BC provincial government followed a coordinated public policy approach based on a model of industrial resource development (Williston and Keller 1997). This led to twenty-five to thirty years of rapid economic and community growth across the region (Halseth et al. 2004). New communities and high-quality local infrastructure were the backbone of industrial centres drawing from the province's rich resource base (Horne and Penner 1992). This resource industry growth was instrumental in creating a wealthy province and in transforming BC's urban and rural economies alike.

Prior to this period of civic and industrial investment, BC was a "have-not" province within the Canadian federation, meaning that the province relied on the federal government for transfer payments to meet basic public service requirements. The boom created by the demand for resources during the Second World War was an exception; prior to the war, the economic status of the province suffered because of its small and relatively inefficient resource sector. While being quite entrepreneurial, the resource sector (mainly forestry) lacked scale, generated few secondary and support industries, and contributed relatively little wealth (that was subject to wide fluctuations) to provincial coffers (Marchak 1983; Hayter 2000). In its hinterland regions, BC had but poorly developed community and industrial infrastructure and, as a result, was not experiencing either economic or population growth.

Against this disjointed backdrop of economic and social life, the election in 1952 of WAC Bennett's conservative Social Credit party marked a turning point in resource exploitation. This period after the Second World War became a directed enterprise with clear policy goals aimed at "province building" (Williston and Keller 1997). As was happening elsewhere in Canada (Himelfarb 1976), BC's resource endowment was imagined as a foundation for provincial prosperity.

To set up later discussions about future opportunities and challenges, this chapter provides an historical context for understanding how BC arrived at the current state of resource development. As McArthur (2010: 14) argues, the "BC economy is, as with all economies, a product of its history, its people, and its natural endowments." It is important to remember that this "destination" was not the product of historical inevitability but, rather, it involved the creative reimagining of public assets and an active and bold development vision mobilizing those assets to take advantage of opportunities growing within the global economy of the times.

First Nations: A Legacy of Marginalization

What is now British Columbia has long been a trading region. Prior to European contact, this territory was a fully occupied, interlinked, and functional region that demonstrated high levels of economic and political organization (Harris 1997; Peters 2000). The First Nations living here traded local goods and commodities as part of complex arrangements for meeting practical, economic, and social needs. In such an ecologically diverse landscape, trading was necessary to make different foods, construction and ceremonial materials, and other products available in places where they did not naturally occur or at times of the year when they might not otherwise be available. The region's strength lay in its vast and diverse resources, and trading to capitalize collectively on these local assets accounts for the resiliency of the First Nations economies.

European contact, and the organization of the fur trade economy soon after, began a long process of transformation for the First Nations peoples. The ease with which the fur trade economy settled into BC's colonial landscape is explainable, in part, by its fit with the generations-old expertise of First Nations with trade and barter systems (Fisher 1992). Markey et al. (2005: 57) note the importance of Aboriginal participation, arguing that through the fur trade, "Aboriginal peoples played a crucial role in facilitating the economic development of the nation." However, the breadth of relations and commodities that the older trading networks had long supported were eroded by the more focused and lucrative economic exchange associated with the fur trading companies.

Some First Nations across northern BC actively reorganized their political and economic strength to take advantage of the new fur trading economy. As noted by Fisher (1992: 26), when the Hudson's Bay Company began to establish operations on the north coast, First Nations there "had lost none of their trading acumen. They were still discriminating about types and quality of goods and could still drive a hard bargain." Under the guidance of their creative and visionary Chief Legaic (various spellings, including Ligeex), the Lax Kw'alaams Band, for example, moved their main village to the Port Simpson area (part of their traditional territory) in order to build stronger relations with the Hudson Bay's factor and trading post – a bond further cemented when Chief Legaic married his daughter to a senior HBC trader. Thereafter, the Lax Kw'alaams Band became the key trading partner between interior First Nations and the post.

The impact of early fur trade and colonial contact remains a controversial subject. Fisher (1992: xi), for example, made a distinction between the fur trade and the settlement frontier, asserting:

> The early period of European contact and the fur trade may have been a mixed blessing for the Native people of British Columbia, but it was not an unmitigated disaster. The trade itself was a reciprocal relationship in which Native demands had to be met. While the indigenous cultures changed and evolved, change was not new, nor did it run out of control. By contrast, during the period of settlement beginning in the mid-nineteenth century, Native cultures came under assault ... Cultural disruption was most clearly exemplified in the extent to which the first inhabitants of the province were deprived of their land, but losing land and resources was not the only form of dispossession.

Harris (1997: xvii), on the other hand, asserts that the prosperity of the economic and settlement enterprise that became BC "has been built on others' misfortune, and we should appreciate the havoc European contact has wrought. Colonialism is not pretty."

Over time, however, the devastating effects of European contact have become increasingly clear. Two key impacts are associated with the ravages of disease and an increasing marginalization within the European organized political structure and resource economy. Disease went through First Nations communities at different times and in different waves, but it nonetheless took a massive toll. We know, for example, that even before contact, the trade routes that linked First Nations within BC to wider continental trade routes played a role in bringing European diseases to the various regions of the province (Harris and Galois 1994; McGillivray 2005). In terms of marginalization, Markey et al. (2005: 57) argue, "As economic activity advanced to staples which either required a settled population or facilitated settlement and fixed patterns of land use (i.e., lumber), Aboriginal peoples became increasingly economically isolated. Even when Aboriginal peoples did participate in the staples economy, primarily as a labour force, they were unable to control the benefits derived from resource exploitation" (see also Peters 2000).

Traditional First Nations economies were destroyed, first, through a reorientation towards the fur trade and, later, by their removal from land-based activities as use rights were increasingly allocated through colonial, and then provincial, administrations to non-Aboriginal economic interests. Most significantly, as part of a strategy to make lands available for colonial settlement, an entire process of deterritorialization was purposefully realized (Harris 1997, 2002). As has been well documented, the identification of Indian reserve lands was part of a strategy to remove First Nations from desirable property that could then be made available to settlers (see also Leonard 1996). First Nations reserve lands not only were too small to maintain a land-based economy, but also they were often removed from locations of spiritual and cultural importance. These actions had lasting impacts on the social, cultural, economic, health, and community conditions of Aboriginal peoples.[1]

Additional policies exacerbated cultural loss through deterritorialization and destruction of land-based traditional economies. Specific among these were policies that prohibited the potlatch system and then supported the development of an extensive series of residential schools. The impact of the residential school process cannot be underestimated. The biography of Justa Monk (Moran 1994) describes in detail the forced removal of children from families who were attempting to maintain a semblance of traditional lives and lifestyles. Moran further describes the experiences of Justa and many other children in the abusive setting experienced within residential schools. Accompanying this were processes of cultural loss. Residential schools were about inculcation into white culture, complete with linguistic and religious cleansing:

> You could say that Lejac was like a correction centre, a jail, and like those places you get good guards and you get bad ones. One day you would be treated like a king and the next day you were being slapped around. They didn't discipline us by explaining things, teaching us to work together as we were taught in our culture, nothing like that. Instead they ordered us around, and they didn't care whether we liked it or not. It was as if we were not human beings. Our feelings were not considered. They were not important. If a nun or a priest told us to go swimming in December, we went swimming in December. It was like that about our language. It didn't matter that Carrier was the only language we knew – we were told not to use it and if we did, wham! right now. I think now that it was the worst thing that happened to

> us in Lejac – being punished for using our language. I never thought about it at the time but now it really bothers me. I love my Carrier language. The teachers insisted we not speak our language, just as they insisted about everything else they wanted to change in us. (Moran 1994: 55-56)

Recent court cases and decisions in favour of residential school survivors have made plain for the Canadian public the injurious costs of the residential school program. Less clear is that these costs remain significant and will continue to affect First Nations into the future. The paternalism of the Indian Act, and the separation of children from their parents that limited the experiences of how one raises a family, have created social consequences that will take generations to resolve. Renewal within the First Nations will require significant attention to healing.

In addition to processes of healing, a critical barrier to renewal is the lack of resolution to the historic grievance of treaty settlement. As occurred almost everywhere else in Canada, the advent of European settlement came after the signing of treaties with resident First Nations. The foundation for this process is the Royal Proclamation of October 1763. The proclamation "recognizes Indians as 'Nations or Tribes'; it extends British sovereignty and protection over Indians to the west of the existing colonies; it asserts that the Indians are not to be interfered with; and it acknowledges the Indians as continuing to own the lands which they have used and occupied" (Tennant 1990: 10). Acquisition of Indian lands could only be made by the Crown and then only through purchase treaty. Across western Canada (with the exception of most of BC), the principles of the proclamation were followed as European settlement arrived in concert with treaty signing.

The British established the Colony of Vancouver Island in 1849 and extended this to the mainland in 1858 with the creation of the Colony of British Columbia. James Douglas was the appointed "governor of Vancouver Island from 1851 and of both colonies from 1858 until his retirement in 1864. The two colonies were united into the one colony of British Columbia in 1866" (Tennant 1990: 17).

As the colonial government under HBC Factor Douglas initially got underway, he sought to follow precedent from the Proclamation of 1763 and from the rest of western Canada. Right from the start, however, the foundations of BC's long and considerably complicated treaty odyssey were set when the HBC instructions to Douglas differed considerably from the proclamation:

> With respect to the rights of the natives, you will have to confer with the chiefs of the tribes on that subject, and in your negotiations with them you are to consider the natives as the rightful possessors of such lands only

> as they are occupied by cultivation, or had houses built on, at the time when the Island came under the undivided sovereignty of Great Britain in 1846. All other land is to be regarded as waste, and applicable to the purposes of colonization. (HBC Secretary Archibald Barclay, as cited in Tennant 1990: 18)

Treaty 8, in northeastern BC, was part of western colonial expansion in the prairies. Another suite of initial treaties, the "Douglas treaties," involves the region around Victoria. At this point, however, the treaty process essentially ground to a halt. The explosion of non-Aboriginal settlement accompanying the gold rushes to the Cariboo and Omineca put such intense pressure on the colonial government that there was no negotiation of treaties, although a system of reserves was set up.

Tennant (1990) provides a comprehensive discussion of the evolution of Aboriginal rights and treaty negotiation in BC. Two key points we can take from his summary are the length of time the process has taken and the many ways by which the colonial and then provincial governments have sought to avoid responsibility for, and participation in, treaty negotiations. It was only through successive "victories" by Aboriginal claimants at the Supreme Court level, such as Calder (in 1973), Sparrow (in 1990), and Delgamuukw (in 1997), that the federal and provincial governments came to acknowledge their treaty obligations (McGillivray 2005; BC Treaty Commission 2007, 2008). The BC Treaty Commission was established in 1992, under an agreement between the government of Canada, the BC provincial government, and the BC First Nations Summit. The commission is to be the steward of a "made-in-BC treaty process." BC's first modern treaty – the Nisga'a Final Agreement – came into effect on 11 May 2000 (although the Nisga'a had negotiated this treaty outside of the BC Treaty Commission process). Figure 7 shows First Nations territories in British Columbia today.

There continues to be considerable angst regarding the process and approach of treaty resolution. The failure to address this crucial issue has continuing social and economic costs (PricewaterhouseCoopers 2009; KPMG 1996; Price Waterhouse 1990). Yet, as we look forward, the renewal of non-metropolitan BC involves a First Nations future. The demographic profile of northern BC is clear in that First Nations are already a significant part of the northern BC population, and their youthful population profile will increase this significance (McArthur 2010).

In the following section, we discuss in more detail the pattern and legacy of resource development in the province. The fur trade, which so intimately involved First Nations, initiated a trajectory of subsequent exploitation of resources that facilitated political, economic, and spatial expansion across BC.

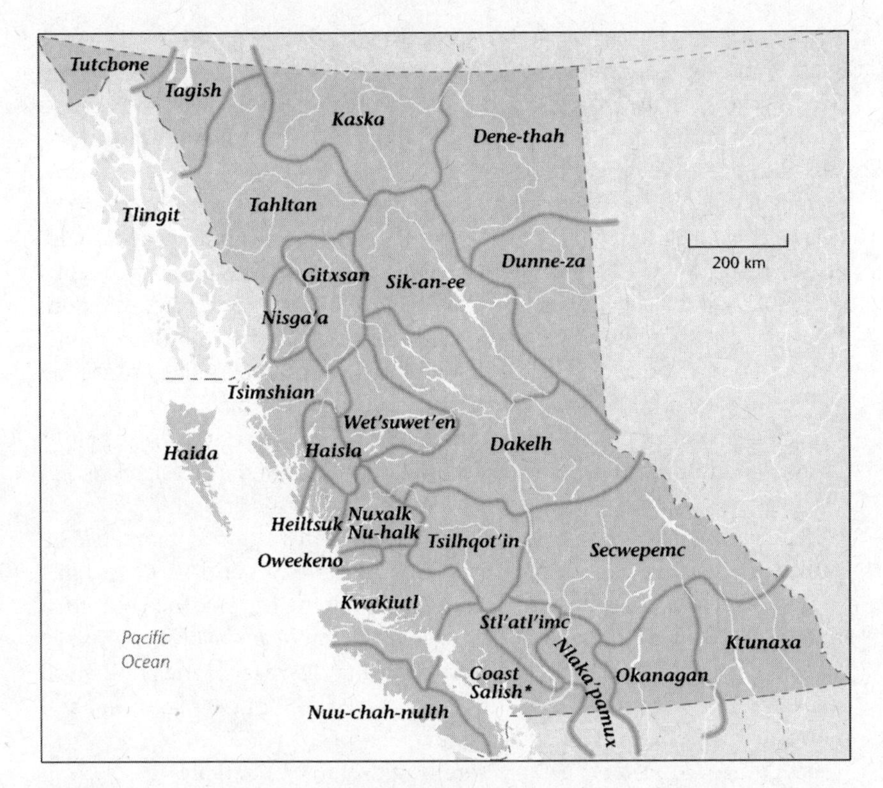

Figure 7 First Nations in British Columbia. *Source*: British Columbia, Ministry of Aboriginal Relations and Reconciliation (2010). *Note:* Although Coast Salish is not the traditional First Nations name for the people occupying this region, this term is used to encompass a number of First Nations peoples, including Klahoose, Homalco, Sliammon, Sechelth, Squamish, Halq'emeylem, Ostlq'emeylem, Hul'qumi'num, Pentlatch, Straits.

Staples and Innis: Resource Foundations

Harold Innis, with the publication of his seminal book in 1933, sketched a description of the Canadian economy over time as being dependent on the export of raw resource commodities to more developed economies. Innis argued that the economic development of Canada was dependent on the successive exploitation of resources, supported (even driven) by external sources of capital and technology (Innis 1933; Watkins 1981, 1982). The theory provides a useful foundation for understanding the characteristics of economic development in Canada; a uniquely Canadian foundation different from linear, more universally oriented, market-based theories of development (Drache 1976; Mackintosh 1991). Over time, Innis traced a shifting pattern of reliance on different commodities: fur, forests, minerals, power, etc. These raw resource commodities are "staples." As a staples-based economy, Canada was very dependent on its export relationships with manufacturing economies in the United States, Europe, and elsewhere. Innis (1950) argued that through a series of resource development eras, Canada served as a staples-producing hinterland for these more economically and technologically advanced countries.

Dependence on the demands of external markets for unprocessed raw staples commodities not only supported levels of economic development, but also left Canadian regions dependent on the demands and prices set by those external markets. As Barnes (1996: 216) notes, "most staples regions tend to be vulnerable to demand shifts in markets that are both highly competitive and price-elastic." Such vulnerability and dependency continues within an increasingly fast-paced global economy in which world demand for various staples commodities can fluctuate significantly and rapidly. During economic booms, where staples demand (and prices) increases, resource-producing regions experience rapid economic growth.

The development of BC's hinterland demonstrates a clear dependence on staples production. Provincial policy through the 1950s and 1960s specifically used expanded staples production as an engine for province building. In the pre-1980 period, the staples macro-environment and a localized Fordist compromise facilitated the rapid expansion and dispersal of the population and economic activity of northern BC. Forestry, oil and gas, mining, and hydroelectric activities fuelled the expansion of the region.

As described by Innis (1950), there is an outcome to staples production that is much more dangerous than the vulnerability inherent in being a price taker in the international marketplace. Dependence on the export of staples commodities creates a challenge known as "truncated development." Large-scale resource developments require significant capital investment. BC has long used various policy levers to provide incentives to attract large industrial capital into the province (Williston and Keller 1997). As Hayter (1982: 277) argues, "foreign investment replaces and pre-empts economically viable indigenous development." Without a driving need for diversification, foreign-controlled firms are often content to continue exporting basic resource commodities needed in their home economies or for other components of their multinational production chain. The resource hinterland remains just that, a hinterland with little additional economic diversification or investment (Davis and Hutton 1989). This has been referred to as the "staples trap."

The truncated development argument extends to include the implication that external and/or foreign ownership "relates to a loss of autonomy over strategic investments and technology decisions" (Hayter 1982: 281). When demand for staples commodities wanes (or prices fall below production costs), multinational firms may idle their resource production facilities. For example, this process of idling production facilities has taken on a modern nuance within the mining industry. The operations of modern mines are highly automated and technologically advanced; however, they operate as "turnkey" industries. An established mine can be closed down relatively quickly should prices fall below those needed to ensure profitability. Once the mine is closed, a small staff is kept on to monitor vital equipment and environmental protection. If prices rise, the mine's operations can be quickly started up to take advantage of the upswing (no matter how brief). One additional result, however, is that there is little investment in new infrastructure that is regarded as superfluous to the company's operations.

In Tumbler Ridge, the first coal mines built in the early 1980s included massive roadworks, parking, and office areas. The new mines that opened in the mid-2000s have made few such investments. Road access to one site near the former Quintette mine looks like a couple of dump trucks lost their gravel loads along the shoulder. While such moves may support firm profitability, they do little to assist with the types of long-term infrastructure and employment investments that renewal in the new economy requires. When research develops new technologies for the industrial process, these may be reinvested in low-cost production regions rather than in traditional staples production regions. In those traditional supply regions, the older industrial infrastructure is allowed to run down as capital extracts the last value from its investment.[2]

For our purposes, staples theory offers a contextually grounded approach to understanding the impacts and patterns of development in northern BC. As such, it provides a suitable link to regional inquiry. The focus of staples theory is on the effects of transporting raw materials over long distances (causing weaknesses in other lines of development); dependence on external industrialized areas for value-added processing, markets, and supplies of manufactured goods; and dependence on external sources of capital to cover the high costs of resource development (Hayter and Barnes 1990). For these reasons, staples theory has powerful explanatory power with regard to the challenges and resistance associated with adopting a place-based approach to rural and small-town development in northern BC.

Resource Hinterland Development in Ontario

We can trace the seeds of BC's future provincial approach to managing resource development in hinterland areas to similar actions undertaken in Ontario between 1850 and 1920. The comparison is informative for understanding development patterns in British Columbia. Nelles (2005) has provided a well-regarded and exceptionally detailed description of Ontario's "politics of development" during this period. His study details the early creation of forestry, mining, and hydroelectric industries in northern Ontario. Key principles set in place during this period include the following: the maintenance of public ownership of resource lands; the security of industrial investment via long-term lease rights; attention to critical infrastructure investments by the public purse to support private resource development; and finally, an emphasis on steady flows of resource revenues to the provincial coffers as well as the creation of local employment to stimulate regional economies. Nelles (2005: xviii) argues, "The state in the form of the provincial government had played a major role alongside private initiative in the development of Ontario's natural resource economy." Underscoring this provincial government approach was a measure of pragmatism that spanned the ideologies of successive governing parties.

The attention to maintaining public ownership of resource lands was driven, in large part, by earlier experiences. Nelles (2005: 39) submits that in forestry and mining, provincial policy and public opinion were moulded to favour the promotion and control of industrial growth while maintaining public land ownership "in order to stimulate rapid utilization (of the resource), prevent monopoly and speculation, and extract from this new resource a regular income for the consolidated revenue fund." The goal was to find effective ways to stimulate and "maximize local industrialization based on natural resources as the continental market opened up" (xviii). The undertaking in Ontario – of situating resource development within burgeoning new opportunities created by new industrial organization – would later be repeated in British Columbia via the reports of the Post-War Rehabilitation Council. In Ontario, "the principle that a portion of the 'bounty of nature' properly belonged to the public had become one of the basic political values" (31).

As the continental market began to open via trade liberalization, the Ontario provincial government sought to build on Canada's historic position as an exporter of staple commodities. To do this, ways had to be found to stimulate some degree of local manufacturing. For example, the development of extensive sawmilling was promoted by industry and public policy as a counter to the export of raw logs and the capture of more economical and employment value within Canada. In turn, the expansion of sawmilling created massive amounts of wood waste. Technological changes were soon married with the resource and power advantages of northern Ontario to set the foundations for an emerging pulp and paper industry. Going into the mid-1800s, much of northern Ontario was still considered to be "wastelands" in the minds of colonial agriculturalists, but with the opening of new trade opportunities, the resource wealth of these wastelands increasingly became the focal point of provincial policy and action.

This position was not a natural outcome of experiences in resource development in North America. As Nelles (2005: 39) notes, "the principles of reservation, crown ownership and lease-hold tenure which characterized Ontario resource policy stood in bold contrast to their 19th-century American counterparts." In the development of the forest industry, many factors, including the challenges imposed by the landscape of the Canadian Shield, resulted in the lumber industry choosing to protect and foster their interests, "by defending rather than reducing the power of the state."

In the forest industry, experimentation led to a system of Crown land leases that maintained the balance of public ownership while providing industry with relatively secure and long-term access to timber. This access then allowed industry to secure the capital investments needed to develop large processing facilities. Industry saw the advantage of regulation requiring investment as a safeguard against the participation of new producers/competitors who could threaten the viability of these earlier investments. The requirement to create processing facilities would reduce threats from the exports of unprocessed logs to US markets.

The organization of the mining industry necessitated a somewhat different approach. Fundamental to this have been the separation of surface and subsurface rights, and the retention of subsurface rights by the Crown. Industrial investors resisted the imposition of royalties, but the cost to the provincial tax base of providing the support infrastructure for new mining activities justified the application of royalties. Added to the experiences from the forest industry, where sawmilling created both jobs and economic spin-offs locally, additional pressure was brought through policy to encourage not only the development of mines, but also smelters.[3] One of the most extensive of these developments emerged in the Algoma-Sault Ste. Marie area, where Francis Hector Clergue organized a complex industrial empire: "From deep in the forests and mountains of the interior, armies of men extracted nickel, iron ore, pulpwood and construction timbers which were hauled to the shore on Clergue's railway, then transferred to Clergue's ships for the journey to Clergue's smelter, pulp mills, reduction works, and in the latest in the evolutionary chain, a steel rail mill" (Nelles 2005: 59-60).

Clergue's motivation for moving up and down the production chain was that Canadians ought to resist the temptation of exporting raw materials to the United States and, instead, earn the profits that would otherwise be exported. This pattern of resource development, involving the maintenance of public ownership, a close alliance with business and industry to stimulate resource sector investment, and the extensive participation of labour across hinterland regions set in place an alliance that presaged the "Fordist" resource development alliance of government, industry, and labour that emerged later in British Columbia. Public ownership, and regulation based on principles of wise use, allowed for considerable flexibility in provincial policy responses over time. This proved valuable in Ontario as recognition through the early 1900s arose around the need to conserve forest resources and replant for future benefits.

To support hinterland resource development, Ontario recognized the need to set in place the infrastructure to connect resource production locations with markets. Overcoming access and the cost of distance constraints were companions to the use of public lands and policy to stimulate economic development of not just hinterland regions but of the province as a whole. Prospects around the growth of stable revenue flows to provincial coffers, and Bay Street investors, supported a new round of province building. Attention to the basic infrastructure needs of resource industry development focused on roads, rail lines, and power.

In addition to extensive support for the development and maintenance of roads, the Ontario government participated in railway construction. Both roads and railways were critical infrastructure for opening up resource development regions in northern Ontario. As described by Nelles (2005: 11), by these actions of infrastructure investment, "the provincial government strove to bring land, labour and capital into productive combination in the north by improving transportation to the region." The creation of "development roads" brought the hinterland resource regions "both physically and psychologically" (118) to the attention of investment communities.

The early development of hydroelectric power potential across Ontario presented the provincial governments of the day with the question of maintaining public ownership and control versus releasing the development rights to allow private investment and businesses to capture the profits from power generation. In the end, access to power was a critical support for new industrial activities, and thus public ownership became a critical tool for development.

Beyond roads, rail lines, and power, a fourth type of infrastructure supported the development of new resource industry. As part of stimulating innovative growth, and in partial recognition of the inherent conservative nature of business, "the province maintained what today would be called an industrial research program and provided at public expense, a variety of industrial services" (Nelles 2005: 122). To stimulate industrial transition, for example, the provincial government purchased diamond drills for use in exploration and undertook extensive resource-mapping exercises. It provided support for the development of mining schools (such as at Queen's University), field training camps, and the training of professionals in "scientific forestry." A forestry school within the University of Toronto, reforestation research at the Ontario Agricultural College, and other such investments supplied the trained personnel and research capacity to keep industry at the leading edge of change. This approach presages by about a hundred years the now common recognition for the key roles of information and ongoing training opportunities in the knowledge economy. In this description, our purpose is not to provide an historical critique of Ontario's resource development process. Rather, it is to identify that the core elements of what would become BC's resource-dependent policy framework were, in fact, grounded in tested strategies from other jurisdictions.

The Post-War Rehabilitation Council

The WAC Bennett government is widely credited with transforming BC's small and inefficient resource industry into an industrial force that propelled the province into decades of prosperity. But what were the blueprints that the Bennett government used? Where did the ideas come from? As noted above, there were key examples of similar initiatives in other provinces. In BC, during the last years of the Second World War, the provincial legislature established a Post-War Rehabilitation Council to develop a framework for action once the people and industry of the nation returned to peacetime.

The work of the Post-War Rehabilitation Council illustrates the value of vision and the importance of public attention to long-term development planning. The attention to building robust community and economic development foundations gave British Columbia a level of flexibility that allowed it to respond to new opportunities and industries as they emerged. In addition to collating expert advice and available information, the Council travelled extensively around the province to learn about opportunities and barriers and to hear what the people living in various places had to say based on their own experiences and intimate regional knowledge.

The Post-War Rehabilitation Council was to be very influential to the investment-oriented approach of the Bennett vision for BC. Part of this influence is attributable to the fact that WAC Bennett was himself a member of the Council and participated in its regional visits. The Council advocated for expanding the comparative advantage of BC resources in all sectors and linking economic growth with social development in order to absorb and resettle the postwar labour supply.

Importantly, the Council's report presented a balanced view of the role of government, relative to private industry, in the development process. It rejected a policy of "laissez-faire for one of intelligent, positive action" (British Columbia 1943: 5). Such intelligent and positive action required actions that are planned, coordinated, and conducted in cooperation with the other sectors of society and other government authorities. This pragmatic approach clearly influenced Bennett's understanding of the levers of development and facilitated the acceptance of an interventionist approach within a person and political party more ideologically associated with free enterprise. As Mitchell (1983: 259) states:

> Bennett's perception of the relationship between private enterprise and provincial development was highly pragmatic. When private interests failed to co-operate with his vision, he never hesitated to fill an economic void through public-sector participation. Apparently he did not push public enterprise for its own sake, for he steadfastly acknowledged and approved private enterprise as the foundation of the BC economy. But neither did he shrink from taking direct government action if he felt that private industry

> would not act ... A fitting working motto for his government and his era would be intervention if necessary, but not necessarily intervention.

The Post-War Rehabilitation Council recognized that the postwar problems in BC, as elsewhere, would be so complex that government alone could not solve them. The complexity of the time (emerging from a world war, going into a cold war, the rise of communism in Eastern Europe, the clear ascension of the United States as a superpower, the rise of an industrial economy on a scale unknown in history and organized on a global scale) must not be underestimated. This complexity belies comments that those "times were simpler and solutions easier." To move forward, the Council recognized roles for government at all levels, workers, and industrialists and entrepreneurs.

Linking the emerging global industrial economy with the older Canadian role as a staples-trading nation led to a recognition that BC's prosperity would be

> inextricably bound up with the well-being of the thickly populated regions elsewhere on this continent ... Europe and the Far East. The forest, mining, fishing, and certain branches of agricultural industries have been built up by the demands of consumers many miles distant ... Thus has foreign trade in the past provided a foundation for the provincial economy. Until the day arrives when the population of Canada is sufficiently numerous to provide adequate domestic markets for the bulk of our produce, the prosperity of this Province will probably continue to reflect the ups-and-downs of world trade." (British Columbia 1943: 4)

The Post-War Rehabilitation Council developed the framework for a planned and coordinated approach to economic development. In doing so, its task was to "co-ordinate the information that is already available and to secure the essential technical advice and intelligently to plan for the progressive development of our resources and the welfare of our people for a long period ahead ... [to do this] it is necessary for the Government of British Columbia to undertake 'regional planning' of the whole Province" (156).

Recognizing the geographic complexity of the province, and that the resources, infrastructure, and other assets necessary for the type of resource industry development they envisioned are not uniformly available, the Council argued for the creation of eight regional plans to support economic and social development. The regions were:

- Vancouver Island
- Peace River and Northern Interior of BC
- Central BC and Cariboo
- Northern BC's Pacific Slope

- Lower Mainland Coastal Area and Fraser Valley
- Railway Belt
- Okanagan
- Kootenay and Southern Interior.

The broad scope of thinking that supported the Council's work is clear in the range of factors they identified as necessary to include in such regional development planning. These include attention to land ownership and management, assessing resource inventories and classification schemes, and general planning and marketing of uses and opportunities. When resource industry development was ready to get underway, proactive policy surrounding soil conservation, transportation, crops, markets (existing and possible), water use, and reclamation all had to be in place. Delineating and organizing not only access to but also management of resources was something akin to today's economic language of rebundling our assets to stimulate innovation and new investments. Local industries could generate employment and extract value from staples production. To be successful, not only were local industrial plants needed but also the support industries so important to the maintenance and development of an industrial resource economy (akin to current debates about clusters).

All of this new investment had to occur in places that would support settlements, and therefore a robust framework supporting city, town, and village communities was essential. The war experience brought out the problems of labour shortages and the costs of labour turnover. Social policy investments had to support recreation and cultural facilities, community planning, housing, schools and opportunities for higher education, highway connections and local road systems, as well as medical and health care services. Such investments would attract and retain the workers who were essential to "growing the province by growing employment opportunities." Alluring to Bennett's practical side was that, besides industrial revenues, one of the key funding streams for the provincial government was a greatly expanded personal income tax base.

The Council's mandated messages of coordination and planning were heeded. We are able to trace the development of policies linking the following: land (especially the principle of continuing public ownership), resources (as "attractive" for bringing in investment capital), local industries (as in the earlier Ontario case to extract more value from staples production), communities (to bring stability to industry and to recirculate monies to grow local and provincial revenues), and employment as the foundation for growth. As seen above, these policy areas build on ideas already tested in the resource frontier expansion of the late nineteenth and early twentieth centuries in Ontario. They also build on, and extract, additional local, regional, and provincial value from the traditional staples production role that the Canadian economy had come to play in the continental and global marketplaces.

The reports of the Post-War Rehabilitation Council outline strategies for action by ministries responsible for forests and parks, mining, agriculture, transportation, and land management. These include coordinating settlement and industrial development; growing manufacturing and new industries; securing and increasing markets for BC products; new transportation infrastructure to link the province's resource-producing regions and its export ports and rail lines; and managing water resources (especially in support of future power generation). The report notes that transport investments included terminal facilities, air transport, the interprovincial highway systems, express highways, and port facilities.

Broad in scope, we can take five key lessons from the Council's work. (1) Policy actions and public investments need a forward-looking perspective built around a long-term time horizon. (2) BC's future development opportunities lie within the dominant economic system of the times. (3) Reject emphatically a laissez-faire approach in favour of positive and coordinated action to support all of British Columbia. (4) The geographic complexity of the province has to be recognized and opportunities tailored to assets. (5) Province building includes both economic and social aspects.

Our approach to economic renewal is not solely based on an industrial resource model; nevertheless, the lessons from this earlier period still resonate.

WAC Bennett's Era of "Province Building"

In 1952, the Social Credit government of WAC Bennett came to power in BC's provincial legislature. The province was ripe for development; it was a rich frontier ready for experimentation and innovation. The Second World War had demonstrated that BC's natural resource endowments were in growing demand by the burgeoning industrial regions of the world. As both premier and finance minister, Bennett would balance the spirit of innovation needed for regional development with a fiscally conservative approach that emphasized partnerships and long-term cost-benefit analysis. As pointed out by Mitchell (1983: 257):

> Public policy was crucial to the path that BC followed during this era and to an amazing degree that policy was centralized in the person of WAC Bennett. The premier promoted a particular type of economy which emphasized the province's traditional and natural strengths: resource development. Critics of Social Credit have suggested that he would have done better to encourage the growth of secondary industries, but federal tariff walls and the lack of a sizable population for a local market or labour force worked

> against that approach. Bennett strongly felt that the province should concentrate on its obvious comparative advantage over lesser-endowed regions. He subscribed wholeheartedly to the economic ethos of the era, that resources and markets were inexhaustible. The idea that there could ever be an end to the boom and expansion was unthinkable.

Bennett was a firm believer in free enterprise and despised mindless government intervention in the marketplace. However, as premier, he defined the role of government as a dynamic agent of development. His government's primary mandate was that "the task of government is to manage the economy in a way that will achieve larger social goals" (Mitchell 1983: 258). By this vision, large-scale industrial developments would have the effect of making the province an integrated economic engine. In support of this vision, the Post-War Rehabilitation Council's rejection of a laissez-faire approach to regional development echo in Bennett's belief that government involvement in large projects was from time to time necessary for the well-being and development of BC, especially when private sector interests had either no interest or no business in them. Bennett "was not hesitant to involve the hand of government, but did so only after giving the private sector a reasonable chance to act" (271).

In accordance with the recommendations of the Post-War Rehabilitation Council, the Bennett government made strategic investments in a variety of areas. Wood waste became an input to support a new pulp mill industry in the province's interior. Hydroelectric power was expanded as a key support to new industry; and a full highway network, an integrated rail network, and regional airports were developed (Tomblin 1990). A supportive and coordinated policy framework was put in place including changes to the forest tenure system to facilitate greater certainty (and thus capital access) for emerging large-scale forest companies (Hayter 2000). As Mitchell (1983: 257) states, "no frontier has ever experienced a more concerted push towards economic expansion; this was British Columbia's Great Leap Forward."

Part of this "Great Leap Forward" aimed investments at transforming the BC hinterland into a more integrated economic and political landscape. Social Credit policies during this period intentionally sought to address regional disparities across the province (Barman 1996; Munro 2004; Tomblin 1990). The Bennett government enhanced the industrial, energy, and communications infrastructure of the province and undertook an aggressive program to improve the transportation network to open up the north to resource and community development (Larson 2004).[4] The "Bennett era" established the foundation for the northern economy, and these remote regions of BC remain largely reliant on the (now-dated) infrastructure provided during this period.

The province facilitated new employment opportunities, with a foundation of town economies and a sense of broader support for the regions that were generating BC's resource wealth. The hinterland was a resource bank, but one that required active and sizeable investment from which to expect social and economic returns long into the future. Ultimately, the longevity of the Bennett government, matched with a vision for postwar (re)construction and a willingness to invest, radically transformed the economic and social landscape of the province.

It is not our intention here to idealize the Bennett era. We do seek to learn from the vision, consistency, and investment orientation of this period. Nevertheless, several negative consequences for the future development of the province stem from that era. The narrow focus on specialized resource commodity industries seeking to export minimally processed raw materials left the province vulnerable to market demands and prices. It severely hindered local adaptive capacity, and it exacerbated tendencies towards environmental degradation (e.g., compensating for lumber price downturns by putting more wood through the sawmills). All of these are consequences that currently hinder efforts at economic diversification (Barnes and Hayter 1997; Marchak et al. 1999). The "Fordist compromise" brought the interests of the state, capital, and labour into close alignment with the result that, over time, they grew resistant to needed policy changes within BC's resource industries no matter which political party was in power (Hessing and Howlett 1997; Hayter 2003). Furthermore, the complete marginalization of First Nations from title and treaty rights during this period (continuing a trend reaching back to first colonial contact) exacerbated social problems and planted the seeds of investment uncertainty that have stifled economic development and adaptation across nonmetropolitan BC (KPMG 1996). As such, we must view the next phase of development in the province in an historically interdependent manner.

Postwar Economic Model: Capital and Communities

The processes and consequences of the province-building resource development boom of the 1960s and 1970s have been well described for BC. A key first point is that this boom built on a staples economy tradition and the Post-War Rehabilitation Council's edicts of delivering more value from resource opportunities. BC's economy has experienced a succession of resource development waves over the years and remains closely tied to its natural resource base.

The period after the Second World War became a directed province-building enterprise (Williston and Keller 1997). As was happening elsewhere in Canada (Himelfarb 1976), BC's resource endowment was imagined as a foundation for provincial prosperity and settlement expansion. In terms of hydroelectric power development, the Bennett government launched a two rivers policy: extensive damming in the Columbia River basin to mitigate flooding and supply a steady flow of water to US power generators earned immediate development cash; and, two hydroelectric dams in the Peace River basin created the power source to expand industrial activity in BC.

The vision in the years after the Second World War of expanded industrial resource development demanded that every facet of the resource industry needed to "scale up." An economically competitive industry that could ship large volumes at a guaranteed level to emerging markets needed large processing facilities. The cost of such facilities would be considerable, and the province actively sought policy and incentive mechanisms to attract large multinational capital. Hayter (2000) examines the rise of MacMillan Bloedel from a small timber-trading house into an industrial giant through acquisition and merger; his study illustrates how Bennett-era policies in support of large-scale capital were, in many ways, an extension (with a public policy push) of long-running private sector imperatives within the forest industry.

To feed the envisioned new large processing facilities, the province reorganized access to resources. In the forest industry, for example, the many small tenures that had fit with the needs of family-run or portable sawmills were replaced with large tree farm and pulpwood-harvesting tenure areas. These tenures came with significant regulation such that they would demand the participation of large industrial capital. As with the Ontario example from much earlier, these large tenures provided secure long-term access to resources that capital could then take to the investment community as security for loans to construct new processing facilities.

Using the example of the forest industry, regulations associated with the new form of large resource tenures required the construction of processing facilities to create employment where those resources were accessed (Hak 2007). WAC Bennett was keenly aware of how important local employment was to creating spin-off economic activity and growing higher levels of local wealth from the publicly owned resource base. As a populist, he knew that BC's erstwhile underdeveloped rural and small-town regions would not take kindly to shipping raw materials out for processing when they could have been creating local employment.

The province encouraged the transition to large industrial forestry firms to provide a stable flow of resource royalty revenue to the provincial government, to generate local employment and thus additional provincial income tax revenue, as well as to cultivate opportunities for industrial support services (Hayter 2000). Various additional policies, such as the requirement to cut a minimum percentage of their timber allowance each year regardless of market conditions, ensured that these large firms would supply a reliable base income for the province. In fitting with these times, policy makers imagined rural BC as a vacant resource bank ready for "productive use."

The transformation of rural BC during this period did not just accommodate capital; it made provisions for people and communities. In addition to implementing the sweeping policy changes needed to carry out large resource developments, the provincial government recognized that it needed a mechanism to recruit and retain a stable workforce while at the same time bringing fiscal discipline to the previous pattern of ad hoc company town development. The Instant Towns Act of 1965 mandated that where "it is in the public interest to establish a municipality in conjunction with the development of a natural resource ... [the provincial government] may, by Letters Patent, incorporate ... any area of land ... into a municipality on the receipt of a petition from at least five owners of land within the area" (British Columbia 1998). Thus, resource companies could purchase small blocks of land and petition for incorporation. Once it granted incorporation, the province shared with the companies the costs of town development. Once residents moved in, however, the benefit for both the companies and province was that the workers (as local property tax payers) would now assume much more responsibility for the town and its infrastructure.

Historically, new resource towns typically came about in the chaotic fashion of boom-town growth (Louden 1973; Bowles 1992). This was an expensive and often wasteful process. In Cobalt, Ontario (circa 1905), that chaos included a townscape that

> was a battlefield of mud, tree stumps, and rock dumps. Land was at a premium and fresh water hard to secure. The camp spilled out from the train station like tossed baggage. There were no streets to speak of, just a profusion of squatters' shacks and boarding houses limited to the narrow band along the railway or forced to seek space deeper in the surrounding bush." (Angus and Griffin 1996: 22)

As with rejecting the uncertainty inherent in a laissez-faire approach to economic development, leaving the new resource towns to chance was not an option. They needed to support a stable labour supply and create robust local economies. Canada and BC both have long experience with resource-dependent and single-industry towns. "Company towns," "planned communities," "resource towns," and "instant towns" are in all provinces (Bowles 1982; Randall and Ironside 1996). These towns share an economic dependence on a single industry, their economies are overwhelmingly natural resource dependent, and they suffer under fluctuating global demands and prices for their resource commodity. The province put considerable effort into the planning and construction of BC's postwar instant towns to create attractive and diverse communities (Gill 2002).[5] These towns offered a suite of social and community services in an effort to stabilize the workforce, secure additional local economic investment, and foster an atmosphere of permanence (Porteous 1970, 1987). Government service providers generally thought this to be a good idea, hoping to minimize the social costs of isolated living, and so did resource companies, who anticipated the benefits of a stable workforce (Hayter 1979; Bradbury and St. Martin 1983; Gill 1991; Halseth 1999a, 1999b). The resource companies also supported the establishment of stable independent communities, as they no longer wished to be involved in the running or maintenance of these towns (Stein 1952; Bowles 1992).

The earliest and most prominent example of BC's new resource town model is the manufacturing centre of Kitimat, built to support Alcan's new aluminum smelter and designed in the early 1950s by eminent US land use planner Clarence Stein. Founding president of the American Planning Association, and world famous for his urban and residential design ideas, Stein had a vision for the new town that blended the economic needs of Alcan to have a stable labour force with the social needs of the families and workers to feel part of a stable, permanent, and welcoming community. As Stein (1952: 3) stated in introducing his master plan for the Kitimat townsite:

> The purpose of Kitimat is the industrial success of the plant. That success will depend on the degree that workers are content, that they like living in Kitimat. Unless the town can attract and hold industrial workers, there will be continuous turnover and difficulty ... The workers must find Kitimat more than temporarily acceptable. They must be enthusiastic about it as a particularly fine place in which to live and bring up their families. It must become the place they want as homeland, the town they are going to make their own.

The elements behind the design of Kitimat were threefold. First, site planning separated land uses. This meant grouping uses such as residential and commercial, and separating uses such as industrial from residential. Second, Stein used neighbourhood design ideas to create functional housing areas. This meant designing for the target population of young families with small children and included elementary schools, ample parks and playgrounds, and neighbourhood walkways and green spaces separated from roads and traffic. Finally, wary of the boom and bust nature of single-industry towns, Stein supported industrial infrastructure principles to ensure some level of built-in economic diversity for Kitimat. This meant preplanning the town's design to accommodate other industries or economic sectors.

Although not always implemented, these lessons – of attention to broad economic foundations and high quality of life – endure. Historically, we have done a good job in providing quality-of-life services in our northern communities, but we have paid little attention to diversification. Sadly, as we now pay more attention to diversification, there are threats to local quality-of-life services from public sector cutbacks and closures.

Interpreting the WAC Bennett Legacy

The WAC Bennett government confronted a resource frontier that required significant investment to overcome the constraints of space and "open up" the province to development. Policies and investments sought to reconcile regional assets with the formidable distance and topography of BC's hinterland. By virtue of the dual forces of province-building and resource-extraction practices that needed comprehensive settlement patterns, the postwar period featured a commitment to building the economic and social infrastructure of the province. Against this vision are the challenges inherent in a staples economy. Staples theory, with its insights into the dynamics of the space economy, provides a useful tool with which to interpret the legacy of the WAC Bennett government as we prepare foundations for renewal.

During the 1950s-1970s, public policies and business interests built and rebuilt a provincial infrastructure designed to extract and export large volumes of minimally processed raw resources (Gunton 1997; Hayter and Barnes 1997a, 1997b; Hutton 1997). This approach views the hinterland narrowly, as an economic space from which to extract wealth. The implications of this development pattern are in the many excellent treatments of the "rise" of BC's forest industry as the exemplar of the industrial resource model. Drushka's (1998) review of the interior forest industry from the early 1850s through to the early 1990s is an "on the ground" discussion of how companies and technologies affected work and communities in the woods. Big dreams, larger than life people, and heavy labour founded the industry, but government policies and stock market pressures later came to guide its future. Similarly, Bernsohn's (1981) history of forestry in BC's central interior is firmly rooted on the ground, with the workers and in the communities. His introduction notes that the story has moved from being about pioneers and heroes in the woods to one "of people trying to make money, for a firm or for the provincial government, all too often ignoring the effect on the forest. It tells why the goose that lays the golden eggs – the forest that provides the majority of the money in and from the north – is suffering from anemia and a variety of other illnesses" (7).

Marchak's *Green Gold* (1983) added tremendous depth to our collective understanding of the staples economy and its vulnerability. Focusing on the men and women who live and work in forest industry towns, and drawing from case studies in northern BC, she warns of the transition noted by Drushka and Bernsohn to making decisions based on corporate or stock market terms rather than community or ecosystem needs. Importantly, for our work on renewal, she highlights the need for strong provincial government intervention if we are to redirect how the public resource is to be used to benefit the people and the province. In fact, she details a range of specific policy areas for attention. Her insights about the need for significant change echo our own comments about how British Columbia has known about the need for renewal since the recession of the early 1980s, but has not acted on that knowledge.

Building on Marchak's interest in the position of men and women in resource towns, Reed (2003b) draws from the forestry towns of northern Vancouver Island to update our understanding of the social marginalization of women within communities affected by a geographic marginalization in the resource economy. Drawing together a portrait of the complex ways in which gender and place contribute to women's work and activism, this introspective study is in women's own voices.

Thus, while successful in creating growth during the long postwar boom of the industrialized economies, staples production carried both social and economic costs. The two underlying weaknesses of a staples-based economy are the following: first, BC remained dependent on demands and prices set within more economically and technologically advanced countries. In staples theory terms, BC was a resource hinterland for those industrial heartlands – a dependency that created commensurate levels of market vulnerability (Barnes 1996). Second, in terms of truncated development, levels of diversification and product innovation have been relatively low, and BC remains mired in the "staples trap" as a resource hinterland.

Discussion of where we have been must lead into discussion of where we are going. As described in Chapter 3, the vision for nonmetropolitan BC is about moving from a resource production strength to a diversified economic strength that builds on continued strong resource sectors but adds diversification within those sectors and across to other sectors. This move to broaden rural and small-town economies away from continued reliance on staples commodities is not new, and several literatures have dealt with the need. As we have already briefly introduced, one theoretical debate concerned with this shift from resource economy dependence to more diversified rural and regional economies is that of "postproductivism."

Towards a Post-Staples Economy

Neil Argent (2002) describes the productivist approach to development in rural economies dominated by basic commodity production for nonlocal markets. It involves intensive, industrially organized activities driven by the imperative to grow and expand operations in order to continue generating profits against the backcloth of long-term declines in prices. The role of the state in a productivist approach is to support primary outputs and facilitate increased productivity. Most post-1980 policy moves by a succession of provincial governments have focused squarely on reducing costs for resource companies to allow them to remain profitable.

Reed and Gill (1997) argue that the transformation from primary resource production to more diversified economic activities is part of a move away from this productivist framework. Looking specifically at potential opportunities within the tourism, recreation, and amenity industries, they argue that the new form of "product creation and marketing" varies tremendously from old-style resource commodity production. BC has been questioning the primacy of the commercial exploitation of resources, and economic proposals now centre on a new understanding of both economic assets and economic development opportunities. In turn, they generate a need for new institutional arrangements that break down the power structure of traditional land use agencies. To mobilize opportunities in a postproductivist economy, there needs to be more of a partnership between decision-making levels. Senior government planning has to include bottom-up development and local participation in decision-making processes that affect local lives. In BC, some experiments with building such relations, such as land and resources management plans (LRMPs), have been only partially successful. This partial success is explainable by a continued narrow concentration on resource production.

Mather et al. (2006) identify a range of shifts in the nature and type of production experienced in the countryside. They especially note shifts from commodity to noncommodity outputs. These shifts are multidimensional and seek to address broader objectives through enhancing the environmental, amenity, and ecosystem services of the countryside. Like Reed and Gill, Mather et al. note that effective decision making to achieve these broader objectives requires a governance structure that includes a greater diversity of actors and institutions.

Wilson (2004) cautions that while there is continuing debate about the nature, pace, and even existence of a transition to postproductivist rural and small-town economies, it does provide a useful framework for understanding the mutual coexistence of productivist and postproductivist actors. Drawing on examples from Australia's "landcare" movement, he suggests there are postproductivist indicators within senior government policy change, resource production practices more linked to environmental values, and reorganized governance structures that comprise a diversity of interests including local actors.

Banks and Marsden (2000) argue that these changes, whether they be labelled postproductivist or not, serve to underscore a new approach to rural development. This new approach includes the adoption of environmental and conservation policies to facilitate a more multifunctional rural landscape.

Needed are appropriately designed and regionally embedded new developments to support more flexible and sustainable rural and small-town economies. For those rural and small-town economies, this transition is taking place during a time of expanding market opportunity through which consumers with increased disposable money and time are making new demands on the countryside for high-quality amenity products, healthier foods from small and large producers alike, and expanded opportunities for pursuing leisure and retirement and/or recreation housing.

Looking into a future that will include greater attention to postproductivist economies, work by Bollman (2007) is instructive in characterizing key areas of concern and attention within a retooling of rural Canada. Bollman argues that there are three drivers for rural Canada: technology, prices, and demography. In terms of technology, the ongoing substitution of capital for labour means primary sector industries will employ fewer people. If rural development means the growth of jobs and/or local population, then resource production will not be the future driver of rural development. As a result, successful communities will necessarily have to find new goods or services to "export."

In terms of prices, the falling relative cost of transporting goods helps rural Canada to be competitive in manufacturing where lower land prices and costs of living for labour further enhance this attractiveness (Baldwin et al. 2001). Rural Canada has always had manufacturing jobs (basic resource commodity processing), but new manufacturing opportunities need to be set within just-in-time delivery systems. Low production costs and access to efficient transportation are key ingredients. Beshiri (2001) identifies how rural Canada has been increasing its share of total manufacturing employment. As a result, rural Canada appears to be competitive in manufacturing. Rural and small-town places without a significant natural amenity attraction may find a successful future in manufacturing.

One of the historic challenges to rural manufacturing has been the lack of central institutions like research universities, corporate research centres, sophisticated financial intermediaries, and the ability to access/move information as and when needed (Freshwater 2003). Bollman (2007) notes that the falling costs of information access can assist with this challenge. It means, however, that rural and small-town communications infrastructure needs to meet the standards of the twenty-first century economy.

In terms of changing demographics, three issues are important. First, growth within Canada's Aboriginal population will create a host of new economic opportunities and labour force possibilities. Second, for rural and small-town places within commuting distance (daily for work; and on a weekend basis for recreation and/or recreation property development) of urban centres, there are opportunities to build on future urban growth. Third, evidence shows rural areas are competitive in attracting both young families and early retirees. Young families are drawn to jobs, lower costs of living, and the attractiveness of these places to raise children.

An additional point to consider about demographics concerns the question of immigration. As noted earlier in this chapter, the in-migration of settlers had supported the historical "resettlement" of traditional Aboriginal territory. Most rural and small-town places across Canada have links to many of the source origins for Canadian immigration. Most new immigrants to Canada locate in one of three large metropolitan centres; however, some rural regions are competitive in attracting immigrants (Beshiri 2004). The challenge will be turning what we know about immigrant attraction and retention into community-based solutions that will both attract and retain immigrants by creating a more welcoming approach (Nolin et al. 2009).

Summary and Transition

British Columbia has a long history of resource exploitation and trading. First Nations employed the rich natural and biological resources of their territories to support healthy communities and economies. Early settlers and settlements came to the region for the rich resource base. After the Second World War, BC embarked on ambitious industry-based resource development: the WAC Bennett regime scaled up BC's resource production to accommodate the emergence of massive industrial-processing capacity.

The new scale of economic development seen in BC was not unprecedented in Canada. Principles such as maintaining public ownership, providing long-term tenure access to industry, and supporting the economic foundations of infrastructure and community development had been well tested in places such as Ontario. Building on the work of the Post-War Rehabilitation Council, the WAC Bennett government adopted a specific vision for industrial resource development and approached this vision very pragmatically. To start, they looked for opportunity in the emerging global economy and rebundled BC's natural resource assets to attract industry that could mobilize those opportunities. Most significantly, they set in place policy and public investments designed to pay dividends back to the province over a long period.

This approach centred on a space-based economy. Crucial to mobilizing opportunity in such an economy is overcoming the costs and obstacles of distance. In other words, there was a need to connect resource-producing regions with points of export. BC's postwar approach was extremely successful in that it supported thirty years of unbroken rural and small-town community and economic growth. It was well suited to, and situated within, a space-based economy. However, the characteristics and organization of the global economy have been changing. We need to know more about the forces that have led to the breakdown of a space-based economic development approach. This knowledge will help to identify new opportunities and directions for renewal and reveal the importance of strategies and approaches that we have forgotten or minimized in importance.

5
Restructuring and Response

> The BC forest economy is a troubled landscape. Environmental protests, Aboriginal claims, reduced forest yields, lower allowable annual cut, labour saving technological change, fierce outside competition, trade restrictions, consumer boycotts, and lower wood-product prices reflect on this trouble, providing sharp contrast to the thirty golden years of Fordism. (Hayter 2000: 391)

Throughout the earlier chapters, we argued that British Columbia has evolved very much as a resource periphery. The current industrial base, communications and transportation infrastructure, and nonmetropolitan settlement structure were set in place during the economic boom that followed the Second World War (Williston and Keller 1997), when revenues from the export of resources built the province. Today, the economy remains dependent on limited-manufacture resource commodity exports. Following arguments by Hayter (2000: 35), the province's "geographic marginality" has been the defining context for the evolution of both its resource economy and settlement system.

In a province where our rich natural resource endowment has been the base for a particular type of development, we have witnessed the unfolding of staples theory arguments that dependence on external markets and multinational capital acts to limit industrial diversification beyond raw commodity processing. The recent business mantra of "focusing on our core business" has only acted to narrow the product range and focus of large forest products companies (in particular) at a time when the marketplace for dimension lumber has become choked with international competition from low-cost producing areas. The result is less stable and more vulnerable companies. When confronted with challenges in the market, successive governments have adjusted policy to allow industrial capital (and to a degree organized labour) to remain competitive and export oriented in order to maintain provincial tax revenue. This has occurred despite the fact that, since 1980, massive change has affected all of BC's resource industries.

There is now a wide literature that identifies how the recession in the early 1980s marked a fundamental shift in the Fordist compromise that linked industry and government with labour and, indirectly, with rural and small-town communities (Young 2008; Hak 2007). Nonmetropolitan BC has experienced considerable job losses, firm consolidation, and plant closures. Layoffs and closures have meant that the region began to lose population for the first time since the Second World War (Hutton 2002). Hanlon and Halseth (2005) describe how the impacts of this restructuring continue to place downward pressure on the region's population base. The problem has been that while the global economy has undergone a shift from space-based economies towards place-based economies, BC regional development policy has not made the shift and remains focused on propping up a staples economy with short-term investments and benefits.

This chapter outlines some of the issues embodied in the breakdown of rural and small-town BC's space-based economy. Under a succession of crises to the Fordist regime of production, industry began to adopt flexible production systems closely linked into the global economy and increasingly used technology to reduce costs and the size of the labour force. Such changes have since become associated with deep restructuring and change across BC's resource industries. The provincial government followed suit by undertaking a series of refocusing and retrenchment actions commensurate with trends predominant during an era of neoliberalism. Key in this has been the closure of public services in small places and limited reinvestment in the human and transportation infrastructure of resource-producing regions. Against this tide of industrial and state "pull-back," local governments and communities responded to economic change and challenge with an ever-decreasing set of tools. The chapter describes the erosion of some of these fundamental tools and identifies areas in which rural and small-town BC has carried the burden of governance and development.

Post-1980s and Restructuring

It is widely recognized that the early 1980s marked a sea change in BC's resource industries within an increasingly globalized economy. During the early 1980s, the economy was in a deep recession initiated by all of the circumstances of a staples-dependent economy (reduced demand and reduced prices for a range of resource commodities), and exacerbated by larger forces that were reorganizing both the engagement of the state and industrial capital in the development enterprise. Hayter (2000) and Markey et al. (2005) describe the impacts of restructuring within the forest industry and its implications for businesses, governments, and communities.

Much of the postwar industrial era saw a pattern of production associated with Fordism, or mass production (Cater and Jones 1989). Fordism involves single and repetitive tasks, an assembly line style of production, little or no worker input into production practices or product design, stable production chains, large production runs, and little product differentiation. Such a production pattern was a good fit for staples industries that relied on one type of commodity, and produced it in large volumes, with little change in that product from year to year (coal, dimension lumber, crude oil).[1] Throughout this Fordist era, BC was growing but was not moving beyond basic processing to create advanced manufacturing and related "downstream" industries.

As noted in preceding chapters, a staples production system within a space-based economy suffers internal contradictions that generate crisis and pressure. While the leadership and vision coming out of an earlier province-building era had taken us to this point, external corporate control and truncated development (not to mention provincial government dependence on continuing resource sector revenue flows) meant that we have become very much "stuck" in that old economy. A variety of product life cycle models all show that firms will experience decline if they do not adapt and invest in the future. Rooted within product life cycle models are notions adapted from economic and social diffusion curves. More directly, typical models of product life cycles in the industrial and economic literatures emphasize the growth and decline of products as substitutes become available or as markets shift (Coles 2006). Another example is the tourist area life cycle model developed by Butler (1980). This model, which describes the hypothetical evolution of a tourist or resort area, posits that development will move through a series of stages: exploration, involvement, development, consolidation, stagnation, and rejuvenation, and/or decline. After the emergence and development of the tourist area, there comes a crisis in that it is not able to grow its visitor numbers further. Options include stagnation that will lead to slow decline or reinvention of the tourist amenity to facilitate a period of rejuvenation.

Since the 1980s, the Fordist "regime" of production has been under increasing pressure to change. Hayter (2000) described this pressure as creating a crisis for BC's forest industry spurred by increasing consumer demands for more specialized products, increasing relative labour costs, increasing competition over the use of resource lands, and increasing competition from low-cost production locations (Barnes and Hayter 1997). In BC, this change has accelerated as a result of ongoing trade disputes with the United States over softwood lumber, environmental debates, the uncertainty around Aboriginal land claims negotiations, and ideological shifts in resource policies by successive provincial governments (Hayter 2003).

Whenever BC's space-based staples economy had confronted declining commodity prices or competition from low-cost producers, the response was to cut costs. Over short-term periods, this included idling plants or reducing shifts. Over the longer term, BC's resource companies have been aggressively restructuring towards a more flexible style of production (Hayter 1997). This most often includes larger plants with increased levels of technology and fewer employees to keep per unit production costs low and production flexibility high (Hoekstra 2002).[2] For towns and communities that had thrived under the high employment regimes of resource industry production from the 1950s through to the 1980s, there have been considerable social and economic impacts associated with this transition.

To organize the discussion of restructuring impacts on rural and small-town BC, the following subsections deal with a definition of flexible production, industrial restructuring, political restructuring, local government responses, the restructuring of rural and small-town provision of services, and the changing role of civil society in renewal debates. Throughout these subsections, however, it is important to remember that these are interacting processes and each affects the others. In some respects, the consequences of the whole are much greater than just the sum of the parts.

Flexible Production

The pressures on BC's resource economy since the 1980s have meant lay-offs from the introduction of technology, strikes and lockouts due to the struggle by labour against corporate demands for more flexible contracts, and a sense of increased vulnerability within resource-dependent towns. The pressures of international competition and the need to keep profit levels consistent and high have forced firms to revise production processes. Vulnerability includes not only traditional concerns about global market prices and demands, but also an accelerating level of expectation among stock market investors for good quarterly profit results. Because of these types of pressures, forestry firms are restructuring towards a more flexible style of production.

A flexible regime of production centres on retraining workers so that they can undertake multiple production tasks and reorganize work so that the industry can produce a greater variety of products tuned to the needs of individual purchasers. Workers now undertake multiple tasks in a production process that involves the wide application of computer-based automation. The flexible regime model of industrial organization allows firms to profitability execute smaller-scale production runs, based on market and customer demand, and achieve wider product variation to reach niche markets.

The flexible regime model appeals to companies for a variety of reasons (Walter 1997). Important among these is global competition and rising production costs. Global competition in resource industries has created a need to capture niche and specialty markets. In a rapidly changing marketplace, and in competition with low-wage countries, companies find it important to adapt quickly to changing customer needs. In the timber industry, there are questions of rapidly changing the dimension lumber outputs of mills to fit the demands of market prices. There are innovations such as "adding" features like predrilled studs and finger-jointed remanufactured wood to product lines. In the pulp industry, there are the changing demands of a vast range of publishing and packaging buyers. Even the coal industry must be able to blend grades of coal to meet specific customer demands for costs and qualities. Niche marketing and product differentiation are characteristics of the flexible regime model. Other examples include market-driven pressures for companies and products to be "green" through various forms of environmental certification.[3]

A flexible regime takes increasing advantage of technology throughout the production process to permit greater efficiencies in making small batch and specialized products. Advanced technologies market products directly to consumers and move the production process towards just-in-time production among various suppliers. The role of technology in shifting the relationship between commodity suppliers and their customers has been wide ranging. For example, the ability to track individual products – from production in a sawmill to ultimate sale to a household consumer – has meant that forest companies now often do not get paid by some of the larger or "big-box" retailers until their product actually goes out the store's door in the arms of a customer.[4]

Additional motives for companies associated with flexibility are the advantages of increased productivity and reduced labour costs (Binkley 1997). Automation and computers enable a smaller, more highly skilled workforce to replace a large contingent of manual labourers (Leach and Winson 1999). A Canadian study of restructuring in a set of pulp and paper towns through the 1990s clearly showed significant job losses (Mackenzie and Norcliffe 1997). For the remaining workforce, issues such as retraining, skills upgrading, and the process of "lifelong learning" are now more important than ever (Bonnell et al. 1997; Rennie and Halseth 1998).

In addition, some of the more specialized functions are contracted out to consultants or contractors on a "needs" basis. Contracting out not only reduces the ongoing wage bill, but it also means reducing the firm's commitment to long-term benefits packages for employees. A dramatic example in the forestry sector has been the way log hauling has been spun off by sawmills. In the boom after the Second World War, company employees driving company trucks typically did the log and lumber trucking. Today, these truckers are independent entrepreneurs who very often work as "owner-operators." Benefits to the companies are similar to those noted above, and now include that these owner-operators can be encouraged to bid against one another for jobs. A significant downside for the owner-operators is that if a company declares bankruptcy (such as in the case of Skeena Cellulose in BC's northwest region, in 2001), the owner-operators can be left with enormous bills for equipment, fuel, repairs, and labour already committed, and yet they are so low on the creditor priority list that they, too, will likely go bankrupt.

There has been increasing interest in the notion of corporate social responsibility, but the impacts of economic restructuring within the BC forest sector have resulted in an increased focus only on corporate bottom lines. Historically, forestry companies provided a number of ways to support the small-town communities in which they operated. One of the most community-oriented and socially responsible of those companies was BC forestry giant Slocan Forest Products under the direction of founder Irving K. (Ike) Barber. Canfor adopted the slogan "our roots are in this community" as a reflection of this relationship and its importance for corporate success. Increasingly, however, industry has focused only on their core business and is doing everything possible (in the areas of regulation, taxation, labour, and technology) to drive production costs down. This focus on the short term negates attention to long-term value development:

> There is only one world and we are open to the forces that affect it, environmentally, economically, culturally, politically, scientifically. If we "stick to our knitting," as a recent corporate buzzword advocated, we put our forest sector at a competitive disadvantage. If all we know is our own forest, then we are managing it without a full understanding of how unique it is. It's hard to see a picture when you're standing in the frame. (Apsey 2006: 183)

In reference to sawmill closure announcements, former Canfor president and chief executive officer David Emerson said, "Difficult times call for difficult decisions. We have had to rethink everything we are doing to find ways to get our costs down and improve profitability. Decisions about mill closures are never easy but [are] the best thing we can do for shareholders" (Canfor News Release 2003). Closures, as well as a sell-off of company holdings, are part of a more general trend "to re-deploy capital from non-core assets into our core businesses" (Canada NewsWire 2003). Such moves relegate the local community to being just one of many stakeholders – and one with minimum leverage.

Retooling to a flexible production regime requires increased capital investment. This has, in some cases, become a challenge where resource industries have transformed into income trusts, where the goal is now to transfer income to shareholders – with less attention to the long-run needs for capital reinvestments. This demand for retooling and investment, coupled with a search for additional economies of scale, has resulted in an increasing participation by large firms. For those who argue that BC should remain within a space-based commodity economy, these business trends around large production facilities and increasingly large firms are evidence that BC is still on track for industrial investments. However, this trend is only exacerbating the problems Innis identified long ago: only now the effects may be accelerated by the fast pace of global market dynamics.

A potential positive outcome associated with the transition towards flexible production regimes for resource towns may be to embrace the ethos of flexibility within the more appropriate framework of place-based economies. In this case, a traditional emphasis on extractive industries broadens to include possibilities rooted in the unique character and location of each place. The search for a flexible, place-based community response to restructuring demands a re-evaluation of local assets so that they can be rebundled and then mobilized to meet local aspirations.

One example of such flexibility and a place-based focus to community development is Terrace. In this case, the emergence of Terrace as a diversified regional service centre economy has included attention to the potential mining opportunities in northwestern BC. The significant mining potential along Highway 37 north has been known for a long time. To play a larger role in that mining economy, and to provide a platform for area residents to see more benefit from jobs in the mining sector, a number of groups and organizations in Terrace have come together to support a regional mining initiative. At the heart of this mining initiative is an exercise by Northwest Community College to offer a training program in mining trades and technology. Again, foresight and preparation have the potential to support a more rapid response to opportunities in the area.

Restructuring and the State

State withdrawal in both social and economic terms best characterizes policy responses after the 1980s. First, the social policy response is characteristic of a shift in government policy across Canada, and in other industrialized countries, from an equity-based orientation to less-defined attempts at enabling regional and community development (Polèse 1999). This means that successive governments have been gradually withdrawing from a commitment to providing equitable access to standardized services across the province, while making modest (and incomplete) efforts to assume a secondary role of facilitating transition through various community and regional development programs (Markey et al. 2007). This change in approach is partly a response to demands for greater bottom-up representation and control. However, a negative interpretation of enabling strategies is that they serve as cover for government abandonment (Lee 2003). In this vein, some local governments in northern BC have noted how they have been nearly "enabled" to death. More seriously, there is recognition in the literature that enabling strategies often underestimate the continued necessity of senior government investments in supporting, through material and policy means, any emergent forms of bottom-up development (Lovering 1999).

Across northern BC, examples of state withdrawal are commonplace. Starting in the 1980s, the federal government began closing rural post offices, employment insurance offices, and human resources offices (Valley Sentinel 1992a, 1995, 1996a). Federal government cutbacks in transfer payments to the provinces have meant a reduction in health care and education services in smaller communities (Valley Sentinel 1992b, 1994). The provincial government has closed and/or reduced health care services and various line-ministry offices (Valley Sentinel 1996b, 1996c; Lawlor 2002; CBC News 2002a). A trend towards off-loading has meant that the provincial tax base is no longer covering some basic public infrastructure (CBC News 2002b; Armstrong 2002). If rural places wish to have these services, they must take on an additional financial burden.

In light of the critical role that services play in supporting local and regional development, many recent service cuts just do not make sense. For example, a decision to cut back vehicle ferry service across Francois Lake was panned by both residents and forest industry representatives. It was reported that "the scheduled cutbacks are saving the Highways Ministry $250,000 a year ... but calculations show the Forests Ministry is losing $60,000 a week in timber revenues" (Hoekstra 2002). A policy approach holding ministers of the Crown accountable for delivering their service plans at or under budget too often defeats the more important cumulative benefits, efficiencies, and cost savings that can be had by working across ministries and across government program "silos."

The policy transition commensurate with our space-based to place-based economic shift will involve a move from sectoral to place-based policies. The basis of this transition to place-based policies is the notion that the positive and negative externalities of policies are experienced in localities on a day-to-day basis. It is in these localities that the unintended negative consequences of disjointed and uncoordinated policy processes can have their biggest impacts. The European Union is ahead in adopting place-based policy frameworks in support of rural community and economic renewal, and this approach is becoming more common across the United States as it, too, seeks to respond to a changing global economy. Canada lags in this regard, but possibilities do exist (Reimer and Markey 2008).

Continued application of urban-based models of efficiency and market parameters against which to evaluate public services is simply unsuited to the needs and realities of rural places and rural geographies (Hanlon and Rosenberg 1998). Service closure through the application of inappropriate models directly affects rural and small-town sustainability. Troughton (1999:

28) argues, "As the reductionist process goes on, the loss or retention of key institutions, including local hospitals or health centres, can represent the difference between community survival and collapse." The shift from co-ordinated community development support in the 1950s and 1960s to the piecemeal and fragmented withdrawals of the post-1980s period is a purposive policy shift that undercuts opportunities for hinterland regions to move beyond the staples trap of resource commodity production (Polèse 1999; Gunton 2003).

As described by Hayter (2003), debates about resource development policy in BC have been part of and affected by a "contested remapping" of the province's physical and policy landscapes. On the physical landscape, the northeast coal project, the extension of the northeast oil and gas development, and renewed pressure to develop offshore oil and gas represent contemporary versions of metropolitan command and control over an erstwhile empty resource hinterland. Similarly, BC's parks and protected areas strategy clearly targets the northern hinterland as the location to "make up" the province's share of protected eco-systems. Some of the largest parks in the BC provincial parks system, and the bulk of BC's protected landscapes, are in remote hinterland regions well removed from the metropolitan core. Such policy decisions may create or may limit future rural development opportunities, but all have been enacted with little direct influence by the northern BC communities that are most affected.

On the policy landscape, there has been an opening up of the decision-making process to consider other interests including environmental, Aboriginal, and community issues. Processes such as land and resources management plans (LRMPs) were meant to provide a forum for sorting through competing values and claims (Duffy et al. 1998). Despite these changes, however, provincial governments remained committed to the notion that BC's hinterland is a resource bank. Despite changes in most social, economic, and policy contexts within which it functions, the province's policy imperative has remained the same – generate resource rents from nonmetropolitan BC to support the provincial economy.

A number of other researchers have contributed to our understanding of the impacts of restructuring in BC's staples economy. Markey et al. (2005) outline a variety of negative externalities associated with staples development including a net reduction of the capacity of communities and regions to cope with economic transition. Munro (2004) follows a similar tack in describing the inability of provincial government policies to provide significant assistance to such communities and regions with economic transition. In part, one can link this inability to the complexity of the transition from a historic comparative advantage structure that drove resource sector economic dependence to the more flexible competitive advantage context required in a diversified global economy. Gunton (2003) provides a case study illustrating the regional implications of BC's comparative advantage in coal production. Importantly, Gunton shows that a lack of local reinvestment, potentially drawn from resource rents, exacerbates community instability and retards economic diversification. This is not productive or sustainable because the transition from a space-based to a place-based economy demands much more of both policy and places.

Provincial Government Responses

In community development and revitalization debates, it is clear that some institutional players simply carry more weight. The BC provincial government manages and controls a number of transition activities, and its resource policies can create or limit local development opportunities. A second key player is the local government, which acts for local interests and can drive local activities through its council and economic development office. Local governments often become the official conduits through which senior government aid and programs flow. In addition to municipal and/or regional district governments across northern BC, many First Nations and Aboriginal government and governance organizations play similarly important roles. A third key player, increasingly important since the 1990s, is local civil society organizations. In this section, we focus on the provincial government.

Successive BC governments, regardless of political orientation, continue to endorse and reinforce a large-scale industrial resource development policy. As discussed, the hinterland resource bank has endured "withdrawals" from the store of resource wealth without a consistent commitment to reinvestment (Halseth 2005). There are three important dimensions to the resource bank approach with respect to prospects for renewing northern BC's community and economic foundations. First, viewing the north as little more than a space for resource extraction perpetuates a one-dimensional view of the northern economy. The diversity and variability of northern communities (economically, culturally) is lost from this perspective, hindering innovative approaches to rural development. This narrow viewpoint is a by-product of both an economically restrictive ideology and considerable lack of understanding of the realities of northern BC. Northern people associated with our research consistently cite the barrier to development posed by a lack of understanding or awareness about life in the north from metropolitan-based bureaucrats and politicians, many of whom have never visited the region.[5] This poses serious consequences for investment prospects in northern BC, in addition to providing the occasional episode of comic relief when visiting representatives fail to notice that a community they originally thought was landlocked is, in fact, home to the province's largest privately operated port (i.e., Kitimat).

Second, within the resource bank mindset, the allocation of service and infrastructure investments to northern BC is primarily an expense, rather than a potential investment. This follows a longer and more general pattern in Canadian public sector spending. The expense mindset certainly drives the trend towards the rural service withdrawal referred to above; however, a secondary impact occurs as individual government departments lose sight of the interdependency of their functions (e.g., the story of interministerial disconnect surrounding a decision by the Highways Ministry to cut back vehicle ferry service across Francois Lake recounted earlier). Government miscommunication is certainly not exclusive to the rural experience; however, the Francois Lake story is telling in terms of revealing the underlying perception of rural "costs" within government decision making. An expense mindset limits a more holistic and long-term approach to viewing rural economies and can cause a variety of unintended negative consequences or missed opportunities.

Finally, as a by-product of the first two factors, the resource bank model of development has impeded a significant and coordinated commitment to infrastructure renewal and expansion in northern BC. Community and development infrastructure from the WAC Bennett era across northern BC is crumbling under the weight of overuse, as well as changing technology and demand, and it is wholly inadequate to service the requirements of the new economy. As the following sections illustrate, successive provincial governments have repeated this pattern of neglect and path dependency associated with the resource bank.

In 1972, the people of British Columbia elected the social democrats of Dave Barrett, who had proposed a radical agenda to change BC's resource policies. This agenda included diversifying access to resource tenures for small-scale operators, increasing competition, forcing out inefficient operations, and increasing net provincial royalties. This proposed radical agenda was thwarted, however, by the demands of the provincial treasury for industrial resource revenue flows and resistance from both the corporate sector and unions (Wilson 1997). Preservation of the status quo satisfied all three players. Industry inefficiencies (i.e., small firms, outdated machinery, and techniques) identified in the early 1970s, particularly with respect to coastal forestry, continue to plague the BC industry forty years later. In the view of a long-time forest policy expert, "it became more and more apparent that either they [the Barrett administration] did not know what to do with the forest sector or that they could not agree amongst themselves what their policy ought to be" (Apsey 2006: 93).

The election in 1975 of Bill Bennett's conservative Social Credit government brought little change to the province's resource policies. In fact, the government response to a provincial recession in the early 1980s was to look back to the early 1950s and the use of resource development mega-projects to "jump start" provincial prosperity. The updated version involved the northeast coal project. Costing nearly $3 billion, it involved the creation of two huge mines in northeastern BC, the creation of Tumbler Ridge as the town to house the coal miners and their families, significant upgrades to the BC Rail and CN Rail transportation networks across northern BC, and the construction of a bulk-loading terminal at Prince Rupert (Gill 1984). Again, both social democratic and conservative governments looked to rural BC for revenues to bolster the provincial economy and provide financial support for services increasingly concentrated in metropolitan areas.

The return of a social democratic government in 1991 meant another set of governments following a well-worn pathway based on a geographic imagination of a rural resource hinterland that would support provincial prosperity. Two significant policy directions did not divert this dependence. Introduction of the new Forest Practices Code and the development of extensive resource-planning processes sought to bring "'peace in the woods,' and a soft landing transition to a more sustainable forest economy" (Wilson 1997: 83). The Forest Practices Code brought in stringent harvesting and management guidelines while the resource-planning processes sought to identify lands for protection as well as lands for resource development and/or extraction. In many respects, these were clearly aimed at ensuring continuing market access vis-à-vis international environmental boycotts, real or threatened (Hayter 2003; Gunton 1997).

A second policy adjustment was in response to the recognition that many regions of the province had been harvesting more timber than was sustainable. To deal with increasing uncertainty around timber supply and annual harvests (and the provincial revenues based on those harvests), the province reviewed the calculation of stumpage rates (Wilson 1997). This is the levy charged to forest harvesters for the right to cut on Crown land. The forest industry argued that both the terrain and the cost of retooling industrial plants varied across the province and they appealed for relief. The policy response was "waterbedding"; that is, lowering stumpage rates in one forest region while compensating by raising stumpage rates in another forest region. Again, the provincial dependence on steady resource revenue flows meant that there was no fundamental change to the large resource tenure systems and the industries based on them.

The provincial Liberal government, led through three election victories by Gordon Campbell, perpetuated the provincial focus on "resource revenues at all costs." This includes policy directions to loosen government regulations and allow larger firms enhanced freedom and the potential for greater profitability. It includes the expansion of raw log exports in order to maintain provincial revenues during the long and extended softwood lumber dispute with the United States. Finally, the government's initial push to open up coal-bed methane exploration and to have the oil and gas development moratorium on the northwest coast lifted were clearly driven by the provincial treasury's need to replace proportionally dwindling fishing and forestry revenues as the provincial population continues to grow. A recent iteration of this approach is the 2009 action plan, Generating More Value from Our Forests (British Columbia, Ministry of Forests and Range 2009), which focuses almost entirely on dimension lumber production and pressing to grow new markets for that lumber.

Young and Matthews (2007) note three dimensions to neoliberal reform in BC under the Campbell government: rights, market, and spatial liberalization. Provincial rights liberalization has occurred primarily in two resource areas: forestry and mining (noting that fisheries are under federal control). In forestry, changes in tenure agreements allow forestry firms to subdivide, lease, and trade their tenure rights. In mining, the provincial government made more land available to mining firms, while easing regulations and expediting rights acquisitions. Some may see increased exploration expenses as a sign of a revival in the mining sector; rapid increases and decreases in mining expenditures reflect, however, the booming global demand (now largely driven by industrialization in China). Market forces perhaps more than policy changes explain resource sector investments.

Provincial market liberalization has largely occurred in the forest industry. For example, the creation of BC Timber Sales (BCTS), an agency at arm's length from the Ministry of Forests, creates a "market between harvesting and processing operations" (Young and Matthews 2007: 181). BCTS is responsible for the development of Crown timber for auction. Subsequently, stumpage rates are determined through BCTS auctions. Following the neoliberal relationship between local and global regulatory regimes, the province's creation of BCTS is a result of free trade and softwood lumber agreements with the United States that create a framework for competition to challenge perceived government subsidies of resource industries.

Finally, provincial spatial liberalization relates to economic and environmental regulations that connect corporations to place or govern the environmental management practices of different activities. In terms of managing the environment, the province has opted for a "results-based management" approach that places greater responsibility on corporate actors to manage environmental assets. Young and Matthews (2007) note that corporate actors are no longer held to the same regulations of environmental reinvestment. Again, the government implemented these changes with a view to enhancing the competitiveness of the resource sector. The changes, however, reinforce the resource bank approach to development tied to bulk commodity exports that contribute declining levels of return to rural regions. Table 6 summarizes the consistency of the resource bank interpretation of development by various governments after WAC Bennett.

A notable point of departure, in the post-1980s period, from the resource bank approach adopted in the immediate postwar period is a lack of attention

Table 6

Resource bank policy summary, BC governments after WAC Bennett

BC government	Policy summary
1972, NDP	• proposed a radical agenda to change BC's resource policies • intended to address industry inefficiencies • thwarted by demands of the provincial treasury and resistance from both corporate and union sectors
1975, Social Credit	• made little change to resource policies • used resources to "jump start" the economy during a recession • made significant upgrades to the rail network and northern port construction
1991, NDP	• did not divert large resource industry dependence with two significant policy directions: Forest Practices Code and extensive provincial resource-planning process • intended to ensure continued market access vis-à-vis international environmental boycotts
2000, Liberal	• perpetuating the provincial focus on "resource revenues" • directing policy towards loosening government regulations and allowing greater corporate freedom and access • expanding raw log exports to maintain provincial revenues • pushing to open up coal-bed methane in the northeast and lift the moratorium on northwest coast oil and gas development

Source: Adapted from Halseth (2005).

to (re)investment in rural and small-town infrastructure in the north. Simply put, since the 1980s, a proactive or consistent policy response to mitigate negative social impacts and adapt the community and economic infrastructure of hinterland regions has not matched the pace of economic restructuring. Both social democratic and conservative BC governments have looked to rural BC as a resource bank to bolster the provincial economy and provide financial support for metropolitan growth and services. As such, political and economic restructuring in British Columbia since the 1980s illustrates an overt public and private position of rural community withdrawal.

Backfilling needed infrastructure investments once a development boom gets underway is a costly approach that ultimately works against both fiscal and development responsibility. The example of Fort McMurray/Wood Buffalo Regional Municipality is instructive. The pace at which the oil sands development has occurred has far outstripped the available community and industrial infrastructure. The result of this "infrastructure deficit" is needed infrastructure hastily built and at a premium. Fort McMurray has argued that infrastructure and services delivery must, instead, be coordinated with new economic growth.

In BC, there has been a similar infrastructure deficit associated with the oil and gas development booms around Fort St. John, Dawson Creek, and Fort Nelson. Again, investment by the province lagged, and it relied on older inadequate forms of support (property taxes) for too long. In 2005, a fifteen-year provincial infrastructure agreement was signed to provide approximately $250 million to Fort St. John and $170 million to Dawson Creek to help "catch up" with infrastructure. The higher materials and labour costs of this boom period meant, however, that the monies were insufficient. As argued by Fort Nelson Mayor Chris Morey (2008: 1), "what we can learn from this is that massive developments have massive impacts. They require housing, transportation, social, health, and education services that are expanded in synchronization with growth of the resource activity."[6] This lesson, of course, has been with BC since the 1950s, but is one that recent provincial governments seem to have forgotten.

Perhaps the most symbolic change associated with the current Liberal government's neoliberalization of the rural periphery is the removal of appurtenancy. Appurtenancy refers to a policy, established in the 1940s and 1950s (via the 1947 and 1957 Sloan commissions), that established a "social contract" between government, the forest industry, and resource communities that tied the allocation of timber harvesting rights to location-specific processing. The rationale for this approach was to provide stability to local economies and to spread the economic impact of the forest sector across the province. The spread effect was complemented by two additional dispersion policies, the annual allowable cut, which dictated harvesting rates within a specified range for each year (thereby providing stability to regional employment and provincial rent), and utilization requirements to harvest a mix of species to encourage the pulp and paper industry (Young 2008).

The rationale for removing appurtenancy is part of an overall strategy designed to enhance the competitiveness of the forest industry through improved access to timber (e.g., reduced regulatory environment, results-based management) and increased flexibility for timber use. According to the Forestry Revitalization Plan (British Columbia 2003b):

- Timber processing rules were an attempt to create local or regional economic benefits from logged timber. However, these regulations led to a series of unintended consequences that hinder the forest sector's ability to make sound, business-based decisions.

- Overall, mandatory links between logging and processing impair the ability of licensees to make decisions based on economics or market demand, forcing them to be both loggers and processors, regardless of their interest or ability to be in both distinct businesses.
- Forcing licensees to process wood at mills with outdated equipment, or at mills that make products not in demand, prevents valuable public timber from flowing to other, better uses. It can also restrict employment created from the resource.

The repercussions to date, however, run contrary to intended objectives. Although an increase in global competition is a stated reason for dismantling the previous tenure regime, the result has been a decrease in local competition. Mergers and acquisitions have increased ownership concentration in the province and increased levels of specialization. Overall, rationalization in the industry has led to community impacts through employment losses and a loss in property taxes from closed mills. At a broader level, Nelson et al. (2006: 39) state:

> The tenure changes do not appear to have changed firms' focus on cost competitiveness as their key strategy. While there was some small increase in investment it reflects the need to address short-term increases in harvest. The changes to date do not appear to have encouraged either new entrants or investment in the development of new products or offer any kind of offsetting investment that would help expand employment. While a very important contributor to regional economies, this means that even in the short run forestry cannot be expected to serve anymore as a major instrument of regional development.

A further consequence is that the removal of appurtenancy seems to have signalled a symbolic abandonment of rural places by both industry and government (see also Bowles et al. 2002). Recently, over several years, there has been a closure of mills in the Mackenzie Timber Supply Area (TSA), the result of the firms shifting their harvest to the areas affected by the mountain pine beetle further south – they, in effect, put the rich forest resources of the Mackenzie TSA into their "back pockets" for use once access to cheaper MPB wood falls off. The companies are shifting activity, the province is still receiving revenues, yet the town of Mackenzie bears the impacts in its economy, small business sector, local government, and households.

To date, much of BC policy and action has been stuck in a "race to the bottom" to try and level the playing field for older resource industries as they compete with lower-cost and lower-regulation production locations. However, we are now preparing for the new economy, not the old economy;

and in the new economy, the economic, environmental, cultural, and community assets of places all support development. In drawing attention to the economic, environmental, cultural, and community assets of rural and small-town places, we are not interested in a nostalgic return to a bucolic past. Similarly, it is not about privileging rural over urban. As noted above, British Columbia is part of the global economy, and our urban and rural systems are intimately linked through a host of supportive and reciprocal relationships.[7] In moving from a space-based to a place-based economy, however, we need to recognize that rural and small-town BC has many of the key assets now desired in the global economy.

The provincial government is continuing with a policy that is five decades old to support large-scale resource industries through granting use rights to large industrial capital. Despite changes in government, the dependence of the provincial treasury on resource revenues has resulted in successive governments simply reinforcing the existing structure. The recession of the early 1980s, as has been noted, was a turning point from resource industry expansion to resource industry crisis. Despite this, provincial government policy continues to try to repair a system that has repeatedly been identified as needing fundamental change. This pattern emulates shifts experienced in other industrialized nations, whereby governments have withdrawn from an interventionist approach to development planning and have off-loaded responsibility for key community and infrastructure services under the influence of neoliberalism without commensurate fiscal and policy powers (Polèse 1999; MacKinnon 2002; Halseth et al. 2003). Political restructuring has thus maintained an economic position of resource dependence, while fundamentally altering and lessening senior government and industry commitments to hinterland places where few diversification incentives or tools exist.

All of this forcefully reminds us that development is fundamentally political; not in any pejorative sense, but in a practical sense, acknowledging that it is about power, competing priorities, and access to decision making.

Local Government Responses

In the expansionary period of the 1950s and 1960s, major new economic and transportation infrastructure opened BC's hinterland regions to industrial, export-oriented resource extraction. Before this, export-oriented extraction was restricted to forestry and fishing activities along the coast, mining in the southeast, and agriculture in the southwest and northeast. There was one additional significant forest industry concentration: along the CN Rail line east of Prince George. Much of the remainder of the central and northern interior was simply too isolated from major markets to be commercially viable, and what activity there was in forestry, mining, and agriculture was primarily small scale and often intended for intraregional consumption.

Given the size of the region and the abundance of resources, resource extraction policies focused population, investment, and settlement into regional centres. The pragmatic approach of the WAC Bennett government sought to control the expenses associated with the uncoordinated development of settlement. Regional centres made it more convenient to consolidate and deliver community, care, and welfare services. As local governments with property taxation powers, these centres could assume some of the costs in providing these services.

To support economic development, a range of public services had to be available to attract and retain both industry and people. Expansion and welfare investment continued into the 1970s and early 1980s, buffering these remote and rural communities from the more general trends of retrenchment that beset rural agricultural regions in Canada (Joseph and Bantock 1984; Stabler and Olfert 1992; James 1999). An ethos of public investment in social infrastructure and welfare development thus characterized the development of BC's northern communities for much of the second half of the twentieth century.

As a result, resource towns became the backbone of BC's twentieth-century staples economy. They typically have small populations, are dispersed across the regions in which specific types of resources are found, have intense connections to the heartlands for command-and-control directives, and have limited interactions with other resource towns. They are highly dependent on world market demands, on fluctuating market prices, on foreign investment and control, and on decision making by provincial governments and large multinational corporations (Bradbury 1978; Marchak 1983; Marchak et al. 1999).

As has been noted above, the period since the 1980s has seen considerable economic restructuring. Layoffs and closures associated with resource industry restructuring have meant that rural and small-town BC began to lose population for the first time since the Second World War (Hutton 2002). In addition to population losses, restructuring has had a significant effect on the population age structure of BC's hinterland places.

In northern BC, industrial resource growth during the 1960s and 1970s attracted large numbers of young workers and their families. By 2006, there had been a considerable transformation in the region's population structure. The working population has aged-in-place because of the limited expansion within the regional industrial base. This lack of new job creation has limited the opportunities for high school graduates and young people to enter the workforce. Together, the age structure now shows an older workforce and relatively fewer young people. This "resource frontier population aging" suggests a future potential challenge to health care and community support services.

In moving through renewal, government bodies (e.g., Canada, Industry Canada 2003) have identified how local governments will be the key players for improving community innovation. Local governments lead because of their extensive networks of local and regional contacts. Part of this role is to support business development by overcoming resistance to change in ways of doing business and by working to secure community development assets that assist with attracting businesses and immigrants to places outside of major urban areas.

Strengthening the adaptive and innovative capacities of places and regions in supporting community and economic renewal is a theme found in other reports. Ference Weiker (2003: 1) notes that "innovation is particularly important for regional communities as they seek to evolve from resource-based economies to more knowledge-based economies." As such, transition via innovation is about supporting the creation of broad community development foundations so that places can be competitive in the global economy.

The tasks associated with transition from a space-based to place-based economy are challenging for local government. Small offices have limited internal expertise and capacity, funding from the local property tax often does not even meet municipal operating costs let alone additional activities like transition planning, senior government funding programs are often ineffectual in assisting with transition, and pressures from local businesses and workers for "old economy" fixes can stifle both innovation and transition. Past approaches to economic development planning have been difficult. There is criticism of industrial recruitment (euphemistically called "smokestack chasing") on the ground that it cannot ensure that, once a firm is attracted to the community, using local incentives, it will remain beyond the expiration of those incentives. There is the problem of delineating the full net benefits and costs associated with luring firms (Freshwater 2003). One result is that many local governments remain committed to continued resource extraction models. In some respects, this meets the geographic imagination of a local constituency raised under a mill or mining regime. As well, replacement of one major company with another is an easy and familiar pathway.

Eroding Place-Based Foundations

The withdrawal of government from the reproduction of rural and small-town BC's social and economic infrastructure contrasts sharply with a dynamic period of province-building investments in the period immediately following the Second World War. The WAC Bennett government of 1952 to 1972 invested heavily in rural and northern BC. That government understood the need for, and value of, a coordinated policy approach linking social and economic development in a mutually supportive fashion. However, we are now at the point where these original infrastructure investments are crumbling and inadequate. Despite these foreseen limitations, there has been no coherent or consistent policy response to address this development support deficit (Little 2002).

Economic busts result in plant closures and displaced workers, while economic booms result in labour shortages and overextended community physical and social infrastructure. Both booms and busts strain family and social relationships (Gill and Smith 1985). And, in both cases, there are increased demands for a wide range of social, health care, economic, education, and other services (Bluestone and Harrison 1982; Swanson 1990). However, service restructuring trends since the 1980s have resulted in the downsizing or closure of services in rural and small-town places across Canada (Borgen 2000; Halseth and Ryser 2006; Halseth et al. 2003; Meinhard and Foster 2003). In recent years, these changes have been more pronounced with regard to public sector services as provincial and federal governments in Canada have "regionalized" and concentrated their nonmetropolitan services.

Such a withdrawal of government supports runs contrary to the needs of the business community. In Enhancing the Competitiveness of British Columbia, the BC Competition Council argues that government and business have two quite separate, but interlinked, roles in the development enterprise: Business and industry has a responsibility to "operate efficiently and effectively in the pursuit of existing and new business opportunities and, in particular, have competitive management practices, invest in plant, equipment, training and innovation, and ensure that corporate and industry strategies are in line with marketplace opportunities and that they have the proper scale and scope of activities" (2006: 5). In support, the state plays a role "in providing a nurturing environment for investment and business opportunities. It is government's responsibility to establish the fiscal, taxation, regulatory and economic foundations and provide the necessary infrastructure to support a competitive business environment" (ibid.). Erosion of the service sector and long-term inattention to rural infrastructure are limiting the economic foundations necessary for renewal.

In addition to supports for business, the state plays a role in supporting local action. Given that public policy increasingly calls for bottom-up community development, services provide the foundations for local actions to cope with renewal (Furuseth 1998). Services provide jobs, create training opportunities, nurture leadership skills, and support other forms of economic development (Bruce 2001; Leroy 1997). Services provide opportunities for building relationships and trust – all of which can lead to new partnerships and innovative ways for delivering services where they might not otherwise exist. Finally, services play an important role in recruiting and retaining residents as well as attracting and holding economic activity (Fitchen 1991; Johnson and Rasker 1995).

Halseth et al. (2003) describe three eras of service provision in Canada. Historically, rural and small-town places were isolated and looked after their own service provision. This resulted in tremendous service variability from place to place. Wealthy places were able to afford better schools and better protection services, for example. In the economic boom years after the Second World War, such principles as universality – referring to the ability of any resident to access services, regardless of financial or other barriers (Canada, Department of Justice 2007) – resulted in government funding for services such as education and health care, and these became more evenly available across rural and small-town Canada. Since the 1980s, however, there has been a retrenchment of support for government services (Meinhard and Foster 2003). This trend in rural and small-town service reductions has continued and is marked by an increased concentration of services in higher-order centres that are able to offer goods and services needed less frequently (de Souza 1990; Konkin et al. 2004; Halseth and Ryser 2004b, 2006). Such service closures and regionalization affect the most vulnerable residents, such as senior citizens and people living in poverty (Liu et al. 2001). It places pressure on residents who must now travel for needed services, and this can be difficult for those who lack access to reliable or affordable transportation. As a counter to the discourse around economic and patient efficiencies found in regional concentrations, the Northern Health Authority has found it necessary to set up and operate its own bus line, which now runs regular service across northern BC, moving patients to services.

The withdrawal of local services limits the contributions that service providers can make to the local economy, to networks both inside and outside of the community, and to community capacity. There are many examples of the impacts of service closure on community capacity. One involves the town of McBride. The Ministry of Forests awarded the town a community forest tenure, and that same ministry at the same time closed the regional Forest Service office in McBride. The result was that a good deal of professional expertise was lost as there was a relocation of staff, and the lack of a local contact office hampered liaison between the community forest and the ministry. The good side to the story is that the McBride Community Forest persevered through these challenges, and it has gone on to become one of the most successful community forests in the province and a model for others. Unfortunately, applying inappropriate urban-based models means withdrawing rural and small-town services at times when they are most needed (Konkin et al. 2004; Northern and Rural Health Task Force 1995; Windley 1983). The application of a "one size fits all" type of service limits responsiveness to local circumstances and stifles innovation to resolve challenges of scale and distance, so typical of northern BC's community landscape.

Reliance on the Voluntary Sector

Increasingly important players in local renewal debates are local civil society organizations. Many of these are voluntary, and most work to address some local need. For renewal, voluntary sector or civil society groups play three critical roles. First, they meet local needs for services and activities that support local quality of life. Second, they develop local leadership. Third, they participate actively in renewal debates and processes.

An important component of a community's capacity to respond to social and economic change lies in the strength of its community-based voluntary groups (Halseth and Sullivan 1999). Voluntary groups often respond to crises or stresses related to unemployment, government cutbacks, limited services, or the increased use of emergency shelters (Berman and West 1995; Keast et al. 2004). Voluntary organizations can provide the local foundation to support government-financed programs and services. Examples include the Comox Valley Nursing Centre (Attridge et al. 1997) and Ontario's Guthrie House (Halseth and Williams 1999), where services are organized and delivered in an alternative way to the formal health care system. Guthrie House, in Elgin, Ontario, is a community-based health and wellness centre managed by volunteers that supports services formerly provided by mobile units. Without voluntary organizations, many of the services they house would not be available in the local area.

In this context, voluntary groups have been filling many of the emerging service gaps in rural and small-town places. Often, however, these services are involved with complex problems such as unemployment, community revitalization, or community health. Such complexity demands information, support, or assistance from a range of sources and institutions. At the same time, there has been a movement in government policy to encourage voluntary organizations to develop partnerships with government departments, the private sector, service providers, and other voluntary organizations in order to qualify for funding programs (Borgen 2000; Bradford 2003; Osborne and Flynn 1997; O'Toole and Burdess 2004; Zahner 2005). Partnerships can build collective capacity; but they can also sap the strength of small organizations, as they may become more and more distracted from the problems they originally set out to address. Funding and support for voluntary groups, although it is often "soft" (i.e., temporary, limited), is critical to successfully responding to emerging needs.

Within this context, rural and small-town voluntary groups face challenges in their daily operations. They have fewer staff and specialized skills compared with their urban counterparts (Barr et al. 2004). Bruce et al. (1999) found that almost two-thirds of the seventy-one voluntary organizations in their study had member-related challenges, including a lack of members and members who offer little participation. Members lacked adequate training to carry out activities (Marshall 1999). With a smaller population pool to draw from, voluntary groups may face a loss of staff and volunteers due to physical and psychological burnout, and they may have difficulty in recruiting or motivating volunteers (Bruce and Halseth 2001; Huxham and Vangen 1996). People may not be able to participate because of their work schedules, lack of resources, costs, distance, and a lack of education. Another challenge faced by voluntary groups surrounds limited financial resources. Throughout the 1980s and 1990s, the Canadian government reduced core funding to voluntary organizations, which were encouraged to seek private funding or develop partnerships if they wanted government support (Burnley et al. 2005; Lesky et al. 2001). Such activities require stable human resources to coordinate and sustain partnerships and deliver services (McDonald and Warburton 2003; Milbourne et al. 2003).

Through these types of actions and activities, voluntary sector and civil society groups play an important role in the development of local leadership. These groups provide one relatively easy avenue by which people can become involved in their communities, thereby building overall levels of community capacity. People are able to help as they can, and they are often able to move into leadership roles by taking charge of some activities. These groups are especially useful vehicles for new residents or young people to get more actively involved in their communities.

Some civil society groups play important roles in debates about economic renewal. Their roles are often critical to bringing local ideas and options forward for consideration. Where there are debates, these civil society groups provide venues for hearing them and bring forward information to assist with making decisions. However, the array of civil society groups within even small communities can be quite diverse, to the point where they can create an often-conflicting landscape that precludes local consensus. In debates over the closure of resource industries, for example, some local civil society organizations may look for a replacement of resource jobs, with their high wages and union contracts. Other local civil society groups may argue that such a closure provides an ideal opportunity for diversification. This lack of consensus can be a barrier to local capacity building at a time when the community needs to be at its most effective.

One example of a civil society group playing a significant role in community and economic renewal across northern BC is the Immigrant and Multicultural Services Society (IMSS) in Prince George. This volunteer-based group works to provide immigration support and welcome services to newcomers to northern BC. Its challenge, however, is that IMSS is the only group offering long-term service delivery in the north, and it has a service area extending fully across all of northern BC (other organizations, like SUCCESS offer contract services in the Fort St. John area). Additional funding has appeared from time to time to support local offices and outreach services in other locations; nevertheless, IMSS regularly finds itself stretched to provide services and maintain supports. This struggle persists even though (1) immigration as critical to the success and renewal of communities and economies has long been identified and (2) both the federal and provincial governments have made clear their strong desire to broaden the destinations for immigrant streams to include more people choosing to locate in rural and small-town places.[8]

Closing

BC's space-based resource economy boomed following the Second World War, with the economic and community landscape ably supported by public policy for and investment in infrastructure and services. Following the deep recession of the early 1980s, however, a host of pressures have eroded these economic and community foundations.

BC's resource industries have contracted operations, both physically and in terms of a concentration on their core business product, and have been pressed to produce profit against increasing completion and general downward pressures on commodity processing. Moves from a Fordist to a flexible style of production have resulted in plant closures and job losses. In concert, senior governments have reduced services and supports in these same hinterland communities. This pincer movement has led to further job and population losses and to a loss of skills and expertise – both very much needed to meet the challenges of transition. Economic and political restructuring has exacerbated the vulnerability set in place by industrial resource development policies and has highlighted the need for a new approach to local and regional development in northern British Columbia.

6 Struggles in Transition

> You have to make sure that the development ideas you are talking about are within your own control. Managing expectations should be made around the strategy. If you don't want people to get depressed about these things, we need government commitment because anything else isn't going to work. The whole purpose is to attract new businesses into our community and we have to ensure this is doable. Otherwise, it is a great vision, with a great plan, with no way of doing it. (Resident, northern BC)

As our review of northern BC's development history illustrates, the period since the early 1980s represents a time of intense economic, social, and political transformation. The purpose of this chapter is to outline various dimensions of the provincial and community-level response to these changes in the post-WAC Bennett era. Questions to guide this inquiry are, simply: How has the province responded to the economic restructuring instigated from the early 1980s? What strategies have communities employed to adjust to the new economic and political landscape during that same period?

In the following sections, we reveal a region struggling with transition and renewal. We begin the chapter with a look at the confusion and tension within senior governments between abandoning and enabling community and regional development. The second section reviews the legacy of community-based approaches to development. We conclude with some observations on why both top-down and bottom-up approaches to fostering renewal have struggled in transition.

Provincial Response: Abandonment or Enabling?

The policy response during the period since the 1980s was state withdrawal in both social and economic terms.[1] This policy response is characteristic of a shift in government policy across Canada and in other industrialized countries from an equity-based orientation to less defined attempts at enabling regional and community development (Polèse 1999). The roots of this political restructuring are grounded in neoliberal theory and incorporate ideas from new public management (NPM) concerning the role of the state (Aucoin 1990; Hood 1991; Hanlon and Rosenberg 1998). The equity-enabling shift has occurred as a response to both fiscal and ideological pressures to lessen the tax burden and increase the role of the market in what were traditionally areas of state control. As a result, governments have been increasingly abandoning a commitment to equity (i.e., the delivery of comparable services and infrastructure in different places). In its place, state intervention via enabling responses means that governments either assume a secondary role, seeking to facilitate or manage development and service delivery through various community and regional programs, or they simply rely on (de)regulation and market forces to determine the level, format, and location of services and programs (Markey et al. 2007).

Within the general thrust of neoliberalism, and its faith in market mechanisms, the much debated and contested topic of NPM has extensively changed public institutions and state approaches to public policy, policy making, and policy implementation (Lane 2000). Although very broad in its conceptualization, most general summaries of NPM emphasize the adoption and implementation of private sector models of management and control, that is, management by unfettered "price signals." There is a strong emphasis on contracting out, the application of entrepreneurial management styles, the disaggregation of public service provision, the use of incentives to increase productivity, competitive cost-efficiency measurement, and increased discipline of the workforce (Aucoin 1990, 1995; Osborne and McLaughlin 2002). As noted by Hanlon and Rosenberg (1998: 559), "the negative impacts of these reforms are most intensely felt among less well-off individuals and communities."

The application of NPM tools within a political construct of neoliberal policy change undermines notions of equity and investment that were so critical to the development of northern BC's comparative advantage economy. Under the guise of enabling grassroots, community, or regional action, the resulting policy and action for the past thirty years has most often limited or actively undercut the supports, tools, and capacity needed to nurture local initiatives into action. Closure of basic local services and the failure to adjust funding mechanisms to better match rural realities are two examples of the ongoing undercutting of basic community development supports. Under the guise of "freedom to act," the policy and action of political restructuring sets in place strong mechanisms that, instead, steer local governments and actions in very specific directions. For example, regulations about how to spend the new gas tax monies, policies that require public-private partnerships (3P), and incentives that hastily push hot provincial government topics are examples of the strong steering that occurs through neoliberal governance and its NPM tools. These forms of political restructuring have especially affected the rural and small-town places of northern BC. They have also had an impact on the ability of rural and small-town places to follow through with transition to a more place-based and competitive advantage approach to development.

Wilson and Poelzer (2005: 12) argue that territories such as northern BC have been

> disadvantaged and marginalized within the political hierarchy, both at the provincial and federal levels of government. This marginalization is reinforced by the fact that the provincial Norths occupy an ambiguous position in the Canadian psyche. Despite the fact that they exhibit all the characteristics of "northern" regions, the provincial Norths are often not regarded as the "true" North – a privileged status reserved for the territories. These realities present significant challenges for the empowerment of these geographic regions. Without regional representative institutions of their own, Northern residents feel alienated from the provincial body politic of which they are a part.

Importantly, state withdrawal is partly a response to demands for greater local representation and control. Although some of this demand comes from local-level frustration with the constantly shifting and reduced commitments from government, there are clear benefits associated with bottom-up, or more balanced, forms of development. Three common arguments present the advantages of local control (Gibson et al. 2000; Bradshaw 2003; Herbert-Cheshire and Higgins 2004). First, local planners and administrators are more directly subject to the repercussions (economic, social, and environmental) of their management decisions. This factor addresses a common complaint, particularly acute in rural areas, that distant managers do not make decisions in the best interests of a particular place. Such external decision makers are not familiar with the complexities and intricacies of particular places, which leads to decisions based on a limited set of criteria (often associated with a narrow interpretation of efficiency). In addition, the social pressures associated with being part of a community influence local decision makers. Their decisions surrounding continuing service delivery, or the implications associated with employment issues over the longer term, are set within a completely different context of understanding.

Second, local managers are able to react more swiftly to change. This adaptive capacity is particularly important within a faster-paced global economy and competitive environment. Macro-economic forces and the overall speed of change affect communities and regions in far less predictable ways than they did in the past. The resilience of place is now determined as much by flexibility and responsiveness as it is by endowed assets.

Finally, familiarity of place is associated with contextually grounded, or tacit, knowledge, which is increasingly critical to innovation and adaptation processes (Bradford 2005; Filion 1998). Competitiveness in the new economy requires an awareness and exploitation of niches – in places and products. Local decision makers are more likely to select development strategies that are appropriate to their particular place, rather than relying on standardized processes or the latest development fad. We introduced this last point earlier in our discussion of research into successful cluster development, where the local exchange of ideas and knowledge about products and market opportunities helps to make place-based industrial clusters more flexible, responsive, and competitive (Porter 2004).

One cannot discount the benefits of local participation and stewardship, and indeed, they form the foundation of our recommendations in the following chapters. Nevertheless, there is clear recognition in the literature that enabling strategies often underestimate the continued necessity of government investment in localist or bottom-up development (Lovering 1999; Markey et al. 2005). Governments will continue to play important roles in capacity building, providing both catalytic and baseline funding, monitoring and evaluation, and assistance with scaling up various initiatives. In an environment of ongoing restructuring, governments may provide temporary or transitional roles while communities and regions reorient themselves to new economic and competitive realities. Instead of abandonment via enabling policy, local places within a neoliberal governance regime need continued top-down partnerships and support as they develop and enact bottom-up economic solutions that take into account local assets and aspirations.

It is difficult to assess the intentionality of government action with respect to enabling or abandoning particular programs and places. Cumulative impacts are hard to trace over time and across different governments. The often-cited "silo effect" within and between different levels of government complicates an understanding of cumulative net effects. However, there is ample "on the ground" proof of state withdrawal across northern BC, and this hinders the ability of rural places to adapt to a new competitive environment.

Our intention here is not to imply that rural communities have the right to access a full range of services on par with urban areas, regardless of cost and considerations of community economic viability. Rather, in keeping with the overall theme of this book, the following factors speak more to the role that government investment may play in leveraging social and economic development in rural areas. In addition, a thoughtless or ideologically driven approach to government withdrawal stifles the potential for developing innovative and collaborative alternatives to the traditional practices of rural service and program provision.

Regional Development: Enabling the Local Response

Despite the dominance of the resource bank approach to northern development, the period since the early 1980s has witnessed a variety of enabling efforts. Enabling here refers to government relinquishing of direct lines of responsibility for development in favour of facilitative approaches whereby responsibility then becomes either shared or entirely downloaded to local or regional levels of governance. Aside from the benefits attributed to bottom-up development (discussed above), the social and economic impacts associated with restructuring since the early 1980s clearly motivated the need for some type of a government response.

As outlined in the previous chapter, the recession of the early 1980s marked a pivotal moment in the industrial restructuring of the province and a period of considerable employment loss and dislocation throughout hinterland BC (Hayter and Barnes 1997b; Hayter 2004). Munro (2004: 453) suggests that such a shift, or period of change, was to some extent inevitable given that "further expansion in resource extraction became impossible, world markets began to be served by competing suppliers, and questioning of the environmental and the social consequences of continued rapid economic growth became more intense." As described by Halseth et al. (2004), the impacts of the shifts and changes in northern BC have included economic volatility, population declines (with locales of "boom economies"), out-migration of working-age families, and accelerated population aging. Table 7 provides a brief summary of key regional policy and program initiatives applied to northern BC, dating from the 1980s.

Our review of the various regional initiatives reveals three broad limitations. First, Table 7 illustrates the contrast between the sporadic three- to five-year policy horizons of most government initiatives with what we know is a much longer-term process of community and regional development (Douglas 2003). This inconsistency represents a critical challenge for regional development across northern BC. The relatively sustained regional expansion and infrastructure policies of the WAC Bennett government from the 1950s to the early 1970s are the exception and source of considerable nostalgia for hinterland regions in BC (de Wolf 2002). Second, northerners often criticize the initiatives for their lack of meaningful bottom-up involvement, direction, and control (Edgington 2004). The establishment of organizations or initiatives is often very much a top-down process. There is undoubtedly a high degree of regional variability in the degree of integration between the organizations and their constituent regions; however, many programs

Table 7

BC regional development programs

Date	Model	Description
1987-1992	• ministers of state and regional development officers (RDOs) • minister of regional economic development (1989)	• regional districts assigned a minister of state • regional offices opened in eight regions, consisting of RDO, a regional development liaison officer (RDLO), and clerical staff • mandate to establish regional priorities, implement government programs, and conduct evaluations and reporting
1993-1996	• regional economic development offices and regional development officers (REDOs)	• five regional offices established with REDOs • REDOs responsible for a more community-based approach towards economic development and implementation of government programs
1998-2001	• Northern Develop ment Commission (NDC)	• NDC established by the Northern Development Act and headed by a commissioner supported by a staff of five servicing three northern regions • mandate for advocacy and consultation • management of a small fund to assist development projects
1999-2001	• Ministry of Community Development, Co-operatives, and Volunteers	• variety of community economic development programs and transition funds
2000-2010	• northern caucus • Community Charter • heartlands strategy • development trusts • Rural Secretariat	• macro-environment: tax reductions, deregulation, labour flexibility • tourism promotion (esp. the 2010 Olympics) • transportation projects • First Nations support • sector marketing and support • regional trusts created • infrastructure programs • stimulus spending

Source: Adapted from Lax et al. (2001).

resemble more traditional economic development models that did not pay much attention to local variability or participation. Third, at a strategic level, although the expectation was that the regional development organizations would generate economic activity, they had no control over local and regional resources or the macro-government policy levers necessary to do so. Their functions are generally limited to strategic planning, networking, and place marketing. As a result, regional and community development groups faced the most challenging aspects of short-term time horizons and an uncompetitive development environment with but limited tools.

All of these initiatives lack proper evaluations; it is, however, clear from speaking with northerners that some of the organizations managed to contribute to successful development initiatives. This was often in spite of the narrow parameters or unfocused objectives of the senior government that brought the initiatives into being. For example, select initiatives have cultivated capacity and an initial willingness for communities to work together. Other programs provide useful services, such as the Rural Secretariat (part of the Ministry of Community and Rural Development) and its RuralBC website, which provides one-window access to rural communities for information about funding programs and various government resources. Programs such as Towns for Tomorrow[2] (small-town infrastructure) and Local Motion[3] (sustainable transportation) are to be commended for their focus on core infrastructure. There is a clear orientation towards enhancing the livability of rural and small towns by investing in key amenities. Finally, the recent focus on establishing regional trust agencies, as an institutional mechanism to finance regional development and foster a territorial approach to planning, is perhaps the best indicator that government has learned some important lessons about how to foster community and economic development through regional control and how to create mechanisms for long-term institutionalized funding.

Trusts

Building from the success of the Columbia Basin Trust (curiously, a 1990s product of the WAC Bennett government's decades earlier power sales agreement with the United States), the province has created a series of development trusts in different regions of the province. The government diverts funds into the trusts from resource revenues – and, in the case of the Northern Development Initiative (NDI) Trust, the lease of BC Rail assets – managed by a regional body, for example, a committee of mayors and others. The following is a list of current major trusts:

- Columbia Basin Trust, which supports efforts by the people of the Columbia Basin to create greater self-sufficiency for present and future generations (created in 1995, $276 million to finance power projects, a $45 million endowment, and $2 million per year from 1996 to 2010 for operations).

- Nechako-Kitamaat Development Fund Society, which supports sustainable economic activity in northern communities affected by the Kitimat-Kemano project and by the creation of the Nechako Reservoir (created in 1999, $15 million).
- Northern Development Initiative Trust is an independent regional economic development corporation focused on stimulating economic diversification and job creation in northern and central British Columbia. The trust is independently governed by a board of thirteen regionally based directors (created in 2005, two instalments of $135 million with a supplemental investment of $50 million).
- Southern Interior Trust, which helps grow and diversify the economy of the southern interior of British Columbia through economic development initiatives in 10 key sectors (created in 2006, $50 million).
- Island Coastal Economic Trust, managed by an independent board of directors, which makes strategic investments in regional economic priorities such as forestry, transportation, tourism, mining, economic development, small business, agriculture, and energy to help diversify the economy of central and northern Vancouver Island and the Sunshine Coast region (created in 2006, $50 million).

Additional trusts of note across northern BC include the North Island-Coast Development Initiative Trust (established 2006), the Coast Sustainability Trust (established 2007), the South Moresby Forest Replacement Account (established 1988), and the Muskwa-Kechika Trust Fund (established 1998). The Gwaii Trust was established in 1991 following the creation of the Gwaii Haanas National Park Reserve. The Gwaii Trust started as a $38.2 million locally controlled fund designated to support economic diversification and sustainable development on the islands. Its mission is to enhance and support environmentally sustainable social and economic benefits for the people and communities of Haida Gwaii. The trust is managed by the Gwaii Trust Society (an eight-member volunteer board of directors), and it distributes funds through a range of programs bridging social, cultural, physical, and community infrastructure investments.

Critiques of the NDI Trust gathered in northern communities through our research involve two main areas. First, the NDI Trust has been slow to respond to economic opportunities. The mandate and identified areas of funding limit or close off opportunities in other areas. Second, the trust's focus on economic development has been very narrow. We know that social and economic development issues are intimately interwoven in northern BC;

yet, the NDI Trust has not supported the social development side of community development initiatives. This narrow focus constrains the effectiveness of its own investments. For example, the dimensions of northern BC competitiveness listed by the trust are limited to issues of business costs and tax rates. These are obviously important dimensions, but they lack the whole economy perspective demanded by northerners.

Recognizing these shortcomings, the NDI Trust has created some innovative mechanisms to support community development initiatives. For example, there is annual funding ($1.5 million in 2008) to support economic development positions in municipal government offices that could not otherwise support such a position. The trust now has a program to support the hiring of a grants writer to add capacity to local government offices working to diversify the local economy but challenged with the day-to-day tasks of running local government.

Regional trusts represent perhaps the culmination of lessons learned following a thirty-year period of trial and error. They also reflect the tension between an enabling and abandonment approach to fostering a competitive, place-based platform for development in BC. Trusts and other infrastructure programs enable regional capacity with the promise of institutionalized funding and local governance and determination. However, in the absence of an overall strategic vision for rural and small-town BC, the government may very well rely on the trusts to excuse themselves from tackling broader, structural forces in the reshaping of northern BC. Moreover, the trusts may be adequately capitalized for the long-term sustainability of their organizations; it is argued throughout the north, however, that their funds represent a pittance when compared with the wealth extracted from these regions. Ultimately, the resource bank approach persists.

The Federal Role

The federal government is generally praised for providing a much more consistent and coherent approach to rural policy and regional development than the province. This consistency has been at issue in recent years, under the Conservative regime. Nevertheless, the federal government does provide direct community development and community economic development assistance through programs such as Western Economic Diversification, Community Futures, Aboriginal Affairs and Northern Development Canada, Industry Canada, the Canadian Rural Partnership, and Human Resources and Skills Development Canada – and historically through a variety of regional development programs dating back to the 1950s.

Two particular elements account for the strength in the federal approach to fostering development. First, since the mid-1990s, the federal government has sought to design and integrate various rural programs through a common framework. The framework is the responsibility of the Canadian Rural

Secretariat. Although this has not been a particularly well-funded program – concentrating more on administration than program delivery – it does create opportunities for policy dialogue and coordination at both the national and provincial levels. Second, a federal commitment to the regionalization of development programs through agencies such as Western Economic Diversification (WED) and the Atlantic Canada Opportunities Agency (ACOA) is widely regarded as a successful approach to program delivery to meet the challenges of a culturally and geographically diverse nation.

The program to support Community Futures Development Corporations is an excellent example of consistency in the federal development presence in BC (Ference Weiker 2002). WED Canada came about in 1987 under the Western Economic Diversification Act. The Community Futures initiative began in 1985 out of a legacy of federal government programming around job creation and initiatives like the Local Employment Assistance and Development corporations. Community Futures is a "unique economic development program that, over the past 25 years, has created and maintained thousands of jobs and leveraged more than $620 million of investment money to strengthen and diversify the economies of hundreds of communities across British Columbia" (Community Futures British Columbia 2011: 1). Despite being subject to the changing policy goals of the federal government (something that has routinely modified their mandate over time), the Community Futures initiative was reviewed in 2008 by the OECD and found to be "one of the most innovative and successful rural oriented policies anywhere in the world" (ibid.). The flexibility and success of Community Futures is in its general mandate, supported by a local board of directors, which allows activities to be adapted to local conditions and to better balance business development and community economic development. This movement "towards the adoption of a 'bottom up' approach to economic development [where] local communities knew how to respond to local problems more quickly and effectively than outside agencies" (ibid.) prefaced our argument for a more robust partnership between bottom-up initiatives and top-down supports.

The program of Community Futures Development Corporations (CFDCs) promotes, coordinates, and facilitates community economic development initiatives and serves as a catalyst in promoting strong partnerships between key stakeholders involved in the community economic development process in rural areas. The program supports thirty-five offices throughout the province (twelve in northern BC). These offices provide critical development capacity in rural areas and represent an important source of developmental training and financing for businesses (and communities) that may have difficulty accessing traditional loans. For example, in 2006-2007 alone, the BC CFDCs program provided $31 million in business loans that were able to then leverage an addition $53 million.[4]

NORTHERN DEVELOPMENT INITIATIVE TRUST

The Northern Development Initiative Trust was established in October 2004 through an act of legislation of the provincial government. The territory of the NDI Trust covers approximately 70 percent of the province, which includes communities from Lytton in the south to Fort Nelson in the north, and from the east at Valemount to the west on Haida Gwaii. The NDI Trust is a not-for-profit economic development funding corporation for northern BC that operates independently from government.

The NDI Trust's mandate is to be a catalyst for strategic economic development at local and regional levels in northern BC. Its mission is to help communities create and sustain world-class industries and diversified economies by providing funding and other forms of capacity to identify and pursue new opportunities for stimulating economic growth and job creation.

The trust was established using funds from the lease of BC Rail assets. Additional "deposits" were made to support action on topics such as the mountain pine beetle epidemic. To support sustainability, the NDI Trust sets an objective to achieve an annual rate of return of at least 7 percent on market investments while minimizing investment risk.

The NDI Trust currently offers funding through a range of program areas. These programs are available to local governments, First Nations, and not-for-profit agencies that reside within the trust area. Each project must demonstrate measurable economic benefits such as job creation or increased export sales. Funding mechanisms include grants, loans, venture capital investment, and

A second program that holds considerable potential for community-based planning is the federal government's support for Integrated Community Sustainability Plans (ICSPs; Federation of Canadian Municipalities [FCM] 2007). Federal governments have made commitments of $13 billion over a ten-year period (2005-2014) for municipal investments in public transit, water and wastewater treatment, community energy systems, solid waste management, and road and bridge infrastructure from funding collected through gas taxes (Canada, Infrastructure Canada 2009). These gas tax agreements specifically link infrastructure investments and sustainability through the requirement for all recipient municipalities to complete or enhance existing ICSPs by the end of the funding agreement (i.e., 2015). However, given that municipalities are not required to develop sustainability plans prior to accessing funding, the inclusion of conventional road and bridge repair as "sustainable" infrastructure, and the much larger ($12 billion over two years) economic stimulus package for "shovel-ready" infrastructure interest-free loans. Examples of projects include support for a Visitor Information Centre for the Village of Valemount, the Mount Timothy Ski Hill in Lac La Hache, a Tourism Discovery Centre in Williams Lake, airport expansion in Prince George, and a broadband initiative and network infrastructure for Bella Coola. Most of the projects funded by the trust are in small communities with populations of fewer than 5,000.

The NDI Trust is managed by a volunteer board of directors. Of the thirteen directors, eight are elected local government representatives; two from each of the four regions (Cariboo-Chilcotin Lillooet, Prince George, Northeast, and Northwest). Five directors are appointed by the government of BC based on their previous business leadership abilities. The board is advised by four regional advisory committees to ensure that local knowledge is incorporated into the strategic plan for the trust and for its funding-approval processes.

The NDI Trust is supported by an executive staff and is centrally located in Prince George.

For further information, see

- British Columbia (2004), *Northern Development Initiative Trust Act* (Victoria, BC: Queen's Printer) http://www.bclaws.ca/EPLibraries/bclaws_new/document/ID/freeside/00_04069_01
- Northern Development Initiative Trust, homepage, http://northerndevelopment.bc.ca/. Northern Development Initiative Trust, (n.d.), *Strategic Plan 2006-2008* (Prince George, BC: Northern Trust).

projects, the effect of these programs on transforming Canadian communities towards new platforms of development is questionable. However, they do represent much needed capital resources to rebuild strategic community infrastructure for the twenty-first century if incorporated into well-articulated rural development strategies. The gas tax funding on which the agreements are based also represents a source of institutionalized funding that addresses, in part, municipal concerns regarding the fiscal imbalance associated with Canadian tax structures.

Unresolved Treaty Negotiations as Barrier to Reinvestment

In contrast to the variety of laudable provincial and federal funding programs, in terms of establishing patterns and structures of place-based competitive development, the performance of both levels of government has been poor when it comes to resolving perhaps the greatest impediment to renewal in rural and northern BC: the resolution of treaties with First Nations.

No factor better illustrates the continuity of the resource bank model of economic growth in the province than the delays associated with the modern treaty process.

The lengthy court processes associated with the federal and provincial acceptance of the rights of First Nations to traditional territories has fostered a climate of uncertainty that has impeded economic investment and development. Resolution of treaties now rests with the BC Treaty Commission process. In the words of the commission, "Treaty making is unfinished business in British Columbia. A just relationship has to be established for historic and legal reasons, but also for practical purposes – to restore the social and economic well-being of First Nation communities and to reach agreement on land, water and resource use and protection throughout the province" (BC Treaty Commission 2009: 8).

The BC Treaty Commission process is comprised of the following six stages (BC Treaty Commission 2009):

Stage 1 Statement of intent to negotiate
Stage 2 Readiness to negotiate
Stage 3 Negotiation of a framework agreement
Stage 4 Negotiation of an agreement in principle
Stage 5 Negotiation to finalize a treaty
Stage 6 Implementation of the treaty.

There are now sixty First Nations participating in the BC treaty process. Because some First Nations negotiate at a common table, there are forty-nine sets of negotiations. There are forty-four First Nations in Stage 4 agreement-in-principle negotiations and six First Nations in Stage 5 negotiations to finalize a treaty. The Maa-nulth First Nations and the Tsawwassen First Nation are in Stage 6 (BC Treaty Commission, 2012). While primarily a federal responsibility, the province of BC shares in the costs and benefits of the treaty process and is an active player at the negotiation table. For a variety of reasons, the pace of the treaty process exemplifies the lack of understanding associated with the shift to competitiveness within the resource bank model. First, the estimated cost of the cumulative impact of land use uncertainty is over $1 billion in lost investment (forestry and mining sectors alone) and 1,500 jobs (KPMG 1996). Second, outside of lost opportunities, the government is losing the direct investment associated with treaty settlement. The estimated total financial benefit of all treaty settlements to BC's First Nations is between $6.3 and $6.8 billion. After BC's share of the costs, including cash, pretreaty and negotiation costs, as well as BC taxpayers' share of federal costs, the net estimated financial benefit to the province as a whole is between $3.8 billion and $4.7 billion over the next forty years (Thornton 1999). Third, delays and uncertainty associated with the treaty process help to perpetuate and foster new divisions between First Nations, and between Aboriginal and non-Aboriginal communities. Furthermore, some First Nations feel they did not get adequate resources (time, fiscal, information) to support their full participation in the treaty process.

There are examples of adjacent communities working together to facilitate a positive post-treaty future; however, the potential for friction impedes efforts to foster necessary regional cooperation and to make collaborative investments in needed infrastructure. Interim measures agreements, which provide a temporary process to reconcile competing interests until there is final reconciliation through a treaty, have helped to alleviate this pressure and allow progress on economic activities and joint ventures despite the lengthy formal treaty process. Beyond the macro-impacts on stifling economic development in the province, the length of treaty processes places increasing debt burdens on First Nations communities. Finally, the resistance to treaty resolution signifies a resistance to place-based development. Thornton (1999) indicates that there will be investment displacement concerning the transfer of rights to land and resources. However, the rights and new investment opportunities will be going to communities that are firmly rooted and entrenched in the northern landscape. These dollars are much more likely to stay in the province.

As outlined earlier, the provincial government's New Relationship, and its more recent advocacy for Aboriginal rights in BC, signal positive directions for the future and a recognition of the benefits associated with the treaty process. The New Relationship outlines an action plan and states simply in its opening paragraph: "We are all here to stay. We agree to a new government-to-government relationship based on respect, recognition and accommodation of aboriginal title and rights. Our shared vision includes respect for our respective laws and responsibilities. Through this new relationship, we commit to reconciliation of Aboriginal and Crown titles and jurisdictions" (British Columbia 2007b: 1). Similarly, a recent federal decision to establish an arm's length treaty negotiation body (in effect, preventing the process through which the federal government is caught, between ministries, in a conflict of interest within the treaty process) is a step in the right direction.

Local Response: Stuck in the Middle

Various senior governments have made periodic investments in the hinterland and have established some promising structures. However, they have been piecemeal, not attuned to the complexity and flexibility of rural development, and they lack a comprehensive and integrated vision for development. In this section, we narrow our lens to investigate local development efforts in the transition from a space-based to a place-based economy.

A common refrain within rural and small-town economic development networks is that local development policies are either not working or not having the impact communities and governments might like. Part of this shortcoming is attributable to the transformative scale of economic restructuring and the abilities of places and local governments to cope with the increasing pace of transition. Yet, another explanation rests with development policies themselves and the capacity of communities or regions to organize, plan, and most importantly, implement economic strategies effectively.

Responses to this "implementation gap" are varied. Some argue that the failure to implement comprehensive local or regional development strategies is proof that local initiatives lack efficacy (Filion 1998; Nutter and McKnight 1994): local development processes are too variable and vulnerable to internal weaknesses and external forces. At the extreme, these arguments suggest that local development efforts are counterproductive to the "natural" evolution of rural and small-town space (Soloman 2003; Stabler and Olfert 1992). In other words, the market should determine development, and the places in which it occurs. As we have seen, however, there is nothing "natural" to such market processes given the significant roles of policy, and policy change, at all levels.

From a more positive perspective, while rural and small-town change is complex, a body of localist research is demonstrating that we can both understand development processes and intervene in productive ways. Local and regional economies, from a competitive perspective, are composed of both inherited endowments, such as location and available resources, and human intervention in terms of choices, policies, capacities, and leadership. Furthermore, within a context of senior government withdrawal, the health of local economies is increasingly a community responsibility. As Douglas (2003: v) argues:

> As local government, particularly municipalities, undergo extensive and intensive restructuring, and as the information and technology-driven economy transforms so much of rural society, the health of the local and regional economy is becoming more and more important for the sustainability of rural communities. The survival of communities and their quality of life (e.g. cultural amenities, social services, public health infrastructure) are increasingly dependent on a vibrant and sustainable local economy. While always important, and so acknowledged, the local economy is becoming increasingly central to the viability of the rural community.

Despite the currency of local development approaches, the actual skills and policies associated with adopting local development take time to build

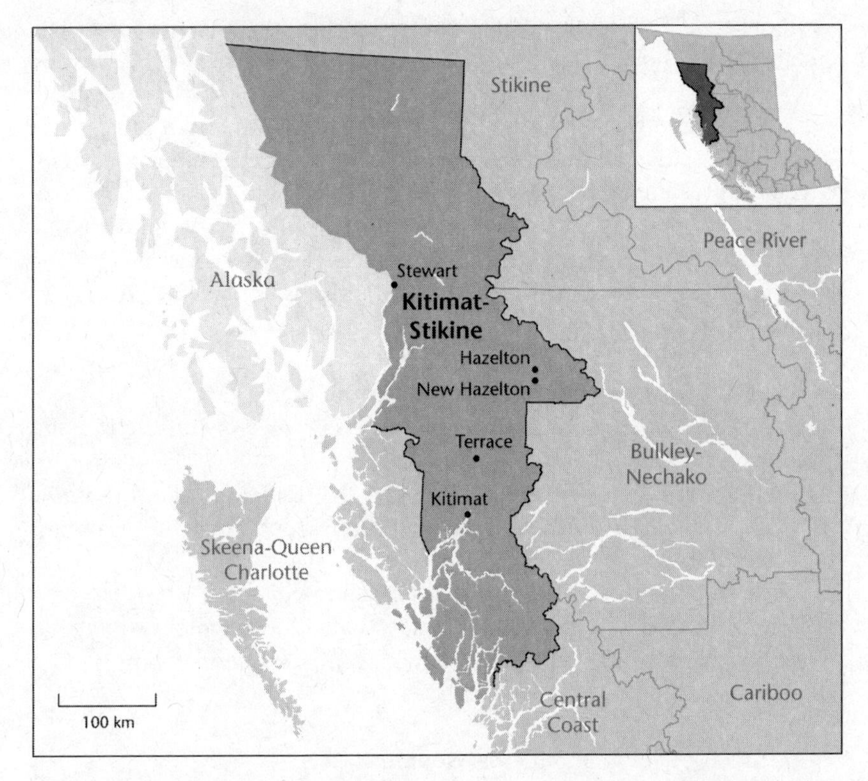

Figure 8 Northwest region of British Columbia. *Source*: BC Stats (2009).

and must counter powerful external forces as well as internal legacies of past development. In BC, the period since the early 1980s, during which communities have been pursuing localist development strategies in more formal and organized ways, represents a period of experimentation and learning for such approaches. We undertook an investigation that compared and contrasted local development studies and processes in one region with their outcomes to better understand the dynamics associated with the local development process. Generalizing about the local development experience is challenging given the variability associated with local and place-based development processes, which are dependent on local resources and capacity. Nevertheless, our findings resonate with observations in the literature and speak to the challenges associated with overcoming past development legacies and building local capacity.

The targeted case research took place in the Terrace-Kitimat-Hazleton area of northwest BC (see Figure 8). This region contains a population of approximately 42,000 people in four municipalities and includes more than ten First Nations reserve communities, providing a useful illustrative sample for northern BC as a whole. In brief, the findings indicate that not adequately incorporating the regional context into local development processes too often leads to "process without product." There is an inability or an unwillingness to engage with what is ultimately the messiness and complexity of adapting best practices and general processes to reflect the human resource, infrastructure, and locational realities within a specific place.

The research findings are in five key themes showing the specific dynamics responsible for the implementation gap. These themes isolate the local experience, rather than simply revisiting the impacts associated with the external dynamics of restructuring covered in previous chapters:

1 Economic development processes lack depth of analysis.
2 Recommendations often fail to account for issues of jurisdiction and meaningful levels of local control.
3 Contracting out responsibility for local development planning limits opportunities to build community buy-in and may limit process accountability.
4 Social and economic planning are not well integrated.
5 Doing things is important, but a coordinated development strategy to facilitate commitment to implementation over the longer term is often lacking.

First, a review of economic development research and strategy reports finds them lacking the depth of analysis that would make them ultimately useful as implementation or action documents. We temper our criticisms here, noting that the intention of many of these plans is not to serve as fine-grained analyses to guide social and economic investment decisions; rather, they are often broad-brush efforts intended to stimulate discussion and further research. However, for a variety of reasons (funding, program changes, political and administrative turnover, etc.) such follow-up discussion and feasibility research is rare. When finer-grained or business plan-level analysis does occur, the linkage to the now dust-gathering reports is limited. Local economic development participants argued that:

> [The study] is an example of what's been done provincewide maybe in the rural areas but not really identifying the specifics of each region and then the results don't identify the problems that exist in each region to overcome those economic obstacles or barriers. They didn't take the time to get to know the communities, which results in a superficial view of the region where you can't really identify what the obstacles are.
>
> These reports consistently talk about what we want to become but not clearly how we get there, what the obstacles are, and what the priorities are. It is the absence of practical economics that make these "wish lists." People

become more pessimistic when they don't see the reports getting beyond the planning stage.

A by-product of shallow analysis is that many of the recommendations flowing from local studies and planning processes lack sensitivity to critical issues of context. People in the region spoke about how there are a multitude of generic recommendations associated with how to promote competitiveness, or build social capital, or generate economic diversification. However, without a true appreciation for local context, human capacity, location, access to resources, transportation and communication infrastructure, etc., these recommendations are conversation starters only (see, e.g., Table 13 in Chapter 7 for a sample of these economic development recommendations for Tumbler Ridge in northwestern BC).

The danger with this implementation barrier is that dialogue may remain trapped in the abstract, create false expectations, and lead to ill-suited program interventions based on passing policy or development fads that are without substance. At a more basic level, the reports themselves can be expensive, consuming limited resources and the even more limited time and energy, usually volunteered, of the people and organizations earnestly working towards a new economy.

Second, local development plans do not adequately consider realms of jurisdiction and realistic levels of community reach and control. Many areas fall outside of municipal control or jurisdiction. The following is a list of sample topic areas to consider in making recommendations for economic development (Markey et al. 2006a):

- Resolve treaties.
- Enhance tourism.
- Foster an entrepreneurial-positive investment climate.
- Work closely with First Nations.
- Attract retirees.
- Develop an enhanced service sector.
- Provide tax relief.
- Eliminate red tape.
- Pursue new markets.
- Improve transportation networks.
- Cut unnecessary regulation.
- Promote value-added wood processing and manufacturing.
- Increase opportunities for education.
- Increase access to financing.

People told us about how local development processes must more carefully and realistically forward recommendations that fall within the areas over

SAMPLES OF ECONOMIC DEVELOPMENT RECOMMENDATIONS (MARKEY ET AL. 2006B)

Land Base Certainty

- Establish a new government-to-government relationship with First Nations.
- Expand use of memoranda of understanding and interim measures.
- Resolve the treaty process.

Regulatory Reform (Liberalization)

- Establish log market (BC Timber Sales).
- Increase flexibility of tenure allowances.
- End appurtenancy and other spatial commitments (utilization requirements and minimum annual harvests).
- Increase land base access.
- Establish results-based environmental management.
- Expand community-based tenures.
- Reduce taxes.
- Simplify the legal and regulatory environment.
- Work with other jurisdictions to harmonize regulations and processes.
- Improve the business cost climate through actions such as reducing personal and corporate taxes.
- Position and actively market the area as a key place to do business.

Capacity Building (Education and Training)

- Expand access to kindergarten to Grade 12.
- Increase trades training.
- Review immigrant access to trades.
- Focus on First Nations youth education and training.

Entrepreneurial Development

- Financing:
  - Provide direct government contributions or use tax credits to encourage the creation of early stage capital.

which communities have jurisdiction. When development decisions depend on other levels of government, or involve the private sector, processes must focus on these as areas of promotion. A detailed analysis of jurisdictional and interest boundaries for municipalities, regional governments, the prov-

  - Develop community venture capital funds.
  - Use government pension funds for venture capital investments.
  - Facilitate the matching of angel investors with regional high technology companies.
  - Provide financial incentives to encourage banks to loan to businesses in designated sectors.
  - Provide education programs, showcases, and investing seminars, targeted at both investors and companies.
- Establish more regional trusts.
- Provide resource dividends.
- Use government purchasing power.
- Support Economic Development Officer positions.

Innovation

- Explore the clustering potential of different sectors.
- Expand research capacity.
- Make strategic use of government purchasing power.
- Promote the early adoption of new technologies.
- Collect and disseminate market information.
- Foster the development of strategic alliances as a means of helping local companies gain market knowledge and access to distribution channels.
- Promote the harmonization of common regulatory standards.
- Assist companies in export market planning, proposal preparation, and export marketing.
- Promote awareness of industry capabilities within the regions of British Columbia.
- Promote the strategic use of e-commerce.
- Increase access to broadband Internet.

Infrastructure

- Expand communications access (and close the digital divide).
- Update and expand transportation networks.
- Expand access to power grid.

ince, the federal government, and First Nations is complex, messy, subject to change, and perhaps difficult to disentangle. People spoke about the need to understand jurisdictional issues and how they may influence the ability of communities and the region to implement local strategies.

The problem with this implementation barrier is that a failure to incorporate jurisdiction creates false expectations. Reports that list opportunities, but do nothing to analyze their viability within a given context create a false impression that nothing is being done – or that local development processes have failed to capitalize on the many seemingly ripe economic opportunities. In this sense, local and regional development is unfairly criticized for being ineffectual.

Third, perhaps the most complex part of community and economic development planning concerns community involvement. Involving local people in the development processes that will affect their lives yields a variety of positive changes that enhance implementation. This is well known. As stated above, these include greater buy-in, appreciation for and integration of local knowledge, and conflict resolution prior to making major investment decisions. That said, numerous people in the study identified frustrations with either the level or the format of community participation in various strategy or research processes. Local economic development participants stated that they felt left out of the research and strategy processes, were unaware of strategy processes, were unaware of various earlier development or strategy reports, and/or were unaware of where to find current or past reports.

There is a wide array of models for including community participation in economic development processes. Ultimately, such processes face limited resources of time and money. As a result, decisions concerning levels of community involvement must be strategic. However, the statements drawn from interviewees help us to identify a variety of additional implementation barriers associated with this issue. Failure to embed economic development and strategy processes, and their outcomes, in the community or region can lead to wasteful circularity, as there is no collective memory either to preclude duplication of effort or to make incremental progress through each effort.[5] In addition, other positive outcomes, such as enhanced trust and knowledge of networks and organizations, produced through either direct involvement or well-communicated process transparency, are lost opportunities.

> The document that we have was done a while ago. It is an excellent report that was done on the area and includes both development and infrastructure ideas about what is required for us to move forward in the tourism sector. It's been sitting on the shelf for quite a while. Just recently I had time to read it and was surprised the study was done but just sitting on the shelf. Intentions were there, yet it sat on the shelf – it's kind of like "OK ... why wasn't this actually implemented, why didn't somebody take it to the next step?" This is where the question comes from our local government when they look at it as "oh yeah, this study is done," but yet they don't act on it,

> and the problem with that is that the community in the end will suffer in the long run. There is no accountability for implementation. This report has been done, recommendations were made, how are we going to implement them? – there is no accountability back to the community, saying this is what we're doing to make us move forward.
>
> The strategy is just fine. But if it truly wants to be carried on, then it has to be owned by the community.

Fourth, a number of economic development participants expressed concerns related to the perceived dominance of economic planning relative to the resources allocated to social planning. The main problem with this trend is that strategies and processes are considering the economic and the social factors in isolation from one another (see the next chapter for a more detailed analysis of this practice). It is clear from the people who spoke to us that the economic and the social are interwoven in the region. People spoke to us about how communities and regions will not be able to diversify or renew their local economies, let alone consider long-term prospects for growth, if there are not equal mechanisms to support healthy communities and healthy community development across all age and cultural groups. Within the uncertain context of boom and bust resource-based economies, local development processes can become overly concerned with questions of economic activity, leaving matters of social development as residuals or outcomes of economic processes. Instead, it was clear from the interviews that the economic and the social reinforce and support one another and that they must move forward together.

Our increasing knowledge of economic development within a more globally competitive context now tells us that we separate economic from social (and environmental) issues at our peril. We can no longer disassociate social well-being from issues of productivity and economic growth – whether linked with individual and family well-being or, increasingly, with important factors such as regional economic attraction and retention of people as well as businesses. Economic development participants noted:

> Our challenge with the reports is that they are not functional for the planning of our social services and that's our biggest barrier – we're not linking the economic development reports with the social planning reports.
>
> There is not enough attention paid to sustaining or developing healthy communities at the same time as we explore economic opportunities.

Our final observation concerns the tension between reactive and proactive planning. There is a need within communities to see local development planning as an ongoing process. Despite the increasing need to work proactively on local development, many communities still do not have active strategic plans. Planning processes may emerge as a response to economic crisis (or opportunity), but the dedication to continually adapting a coherent vision and plan for development is often lacking. Recognizing the tremendous energy and resources required for planning processes, the lack of adequate plans leaves communities in more reactive positions and removes any potential for continuity (and memory) with previous planning processes.

When resources are perpetually consumed by "the immediate," a community or region will be challenged to realize its strategic vision; thus, plans will forever appear incomplete. This is a barrier associated with reactive planning. "Doing things" is important to build momentum and to sustain community energies (no one likes to participate in endless process). However, there is a lost opportunity when communities fail to link isolated projects with strategic coordination at a higher level. Communities do not want to be overly structured and miss emerging opportunities, but adherence to a broader vision serves as an important check and balance through long-term economic development processes and potentially shifting local and senior government priorities.

Summarizing the significance of the above five planning process implementation barriers, it is clear that the northwest region during our review period was "stuck in the middle" with economic strategy and planning. The many planning processes and reports we reviewed and discussed with the people of the region have no true beginning and they have no definitive end. The majority of the reports are missing a thoughtful and participatory grounding in the community (the beginning), and they fail to provide the deeper level of analysis necessary for making and implementing real decisions (the end; see Figure 9). As a result, local development processes are meeting with limited success, and they continue to be more reactive than proactive.

Communities across northern BC are struggling with issues similar to those witnessed in the northwest. Increasingly, however, our research has uncovered a strategic shift in thinking and approach that is seeking to build capacity and address many of the local planning limitations outlined above. Community actors are realizing that they receive a poor net return on "booster" strategies, and there are many latent community and regional assets of competitive significance. There are numerous examples of communities organizing and networking with each other in order to share information and construct a collective voice for change and advocacy. In the following chapters, we outline these competitive approaches, and how they may create community and regional economies that are more resilient, while we probe more deeply the development tensions that must be addressed before substantive local change can be achieved.

Beginning	Middle	End
Phase 1: Strategy	*Phase 2: Blue Sky options and possibilities*	*Phase 3: Implementation*
• community process (participation, vision, values, etc.) • goal identification	• opportunity identification • possibilities list ↓ • context of place (assets and infrastructure; regional setting; global setting) • business case	• partnership development • long-term commitment • long-term funding • flexibility • transparency and accountability • technical capacity

Figure 9 Three elements of economic strategy

Struggle for a New Approach

Given the levels of social and economic change witnessed throughout northern BC since 1980, it is fair to consider why senior governments were either unwilling or unable to deviate from the resource bank model of hinterland development. As mentioned earlier, a common perception regarding the inevitability of rural decline explains, in part, trends towards government withdrawal and the passive approach to facilitating development. Rural decline is not, however, inevitable but, in fact, facilitated by purposeful public and private sector policies.

A number of additional factors contribute to the inertia. First, deviating from the established path of industrial resource development towards a more integrated, diversified, and knowledge-based economy is a complex process, and one that most of rural Canada has not successfully grappled with. The complexity manifests itself not only in terms of the challenge associated with designing appropriate responses, but also (and perhaps more importantly) in political expediency: tackling complex problems supported by an entrenched power structure leaves decision makers vulnerable to both political opposition and bureaucratic opposition (House 1999). Second, as Clapp (1998) outlines through the concept of "resourcism," an ideological and often personal closeness between the political and corporate elite stifles change.[6] Transition from resource dependence is difficult. Marchak (1995: 12-13) argues that once land rights are allocated and a resource industry has developed:

> corporations have subsequently held enormous power to influence government action because their bargaining position is too strong. If they exited a region or curtailed production, whole areas dependent on sales of the resource and its products would be harmed, unemployment would rise, and government revenues would plummet. Once captured in this way, governments are rarely able to extricate themselves from the long-term obligations they have incurred to the granting of land or harvesting rights. They provide further subsidies, reduce tax obligations, and create new incentives to keep the industry operating in their territories. The system becomes self-perpetuating. We see this process in British Columbia and the Pacific northwestern United States over the past century; it is just beginning in many tropical countries.

Third, in the absence of articulating a robust and coherent vision, Wilson (1997) examines the policy barriers associated with a lack of public support for change and a "stunted public imagination" about viewing our economy from a more progressive perspective. From this perspective, politicians are not being led by an electorate to facilitate change. In Wilson's review of the attempts at policy change within the 1972 and 1991 NDP governments, he states that challenging the established power structure led to threats of a capital "strike" that are compounded by the overall vulnerability and volatility of the resource-based economy. Contemplating change during a time of bounty is not appealing, for obvious reasons, and cries for assistance quickly displace attempts at change during downturns. Finally, at a broader level, the character of Canadian economic leadership is, perhaps, more managerial than entrepreneurial (Laxer 1989). This trait suppresses innovation and risk taking, while maintaining the status quo of commodity resource production and dependency – facilitating declining employment and economic prospects in hinterland areas.[7]

A recent study by the Conference Board of Canada (2007) reinforces the perspective that Canadian industry lacks entrepreneurial initiative, assigning a "D" grade to Canada's performance on innovation. The Board defines innovation as, "a process through which economic or social value is extracted from knowledge – through the creation, diffusion and transformation of knowledge to produce new or significantly improved products or processes that are put to use by society" (53). Innovation is critical to enhancing productivity and competitiveness in the global economy; it applies to all sectors and industries and extends to the provision of social and environmental services. The Conference Board continues:

> In the Innovation domain, Canada places a lowly 14th – fourth to last among the 17 countries in our comparator group. Not only does Canada lag on the basic input indicators – such as investments in R and D, training and development, and machinery and equipment – but we produce relatively fewer graduates in science, engineering and trades. Without increased private and public investments in these most basic areas, Canada will find it difficult to make significant improvements in innovation performance. (63)

The provincial approach to hinterland and northern development in the post-WAC Bennett era, and particularly following the intense period of restructuring in the early 1980s, has struggled to define a new direction. Efforts to align the province with an emerging competitive global economy have been largely piecemeal and reactive. The resource bank has continued to fill provincial coffers, owing to the richness of the BC resource base and increasing global demands for primary resources. At the same time, however, northerners have experienced increased uncertainty, regional variability, and an overall trend of decline. The perception in the north, reinforced by infrastructure decay and government withdrawal, is that the benefits associated with resource production are increasingly accruing to the metropolitan areas of the province. Northerners argue that there is a burgeoning internal trade imbalance between the flow of resources from hinterland areas for returns in government transfer payments and investment.

The impact of this imbalance on the north has been severe, and it has motivated local responses to foster development. However, as we have seen, these local development efforts have struggled with issues of capacity, jurisdiction, and an ability to foster a consistent development strategy over the long term.

Internal barriers associated with community capacity and the complexity of development planning complicate the transition to a diversified and resilient rural economy. The capacity of rural communities to engage in complex community planning processes is variable and often limited. Devuyst and Hens (2000: 90) remind us that capacity is a common concern, "Canadian municipalities generally did not possess the capacity to do an effective job of integrating or harmonizing assessment and planning. Moreover, there is little prospect that impact assessment and municipal planning procedures will be blended or harmonized in the future."

There are a variety of dimensions to considering community planning capacity, including expertise, access to information, and the ability to mobilize a critical mass of individuals willing to engage with and sustain ongoing planning processes. The literature identifies rural communities as facing challenges in each of these areas. Related to issues of capacity, the scale and complexity of the community planning process presents a challenge to rural communities. The issue of complexity represents a common theme in the literature (Bulkeley 2006; Guy and Marvin 1999; Morrison 2006; Wells 2002). Complexity manifests itself in a variety of formats within the planning process, including the following:

- a broader context of restructuring and long-term planning capacity
- management capacity related to community planning
- technical expertise associated with different components of the planning process and infrastructure components
- the relationship between the local and the extra-local
- knowledge of and uncertainties associated with sustainable options and alternatives
- monitoring and benchmarking sustainable thresholds
- measuring infrastructure performance
- the integration of various community plans (official community plan, financial plan, etc.).

The scope and scale of community development planning represent added dimensions of traditional community planning (e.g., official community plan). Rural communities, in particular, will likely not have surplus capacity, let alone easy access to expertise, to address these new areas of responsibility. The managerial approach to governance that prevails in North America (which treats local governments much like a corporate entity) makes local bureaucracies very lean institutions (Osborne and Gaebler 1993). Inevitably, limited capacity and expertise make it difficult to sustain long-term community-based processes (as evidenced above with the lack of "memory" associated with the multitude of planning efforts in northwestern BC).

Structural Change in Comparative Perspective

Viewed from a cumulative perspective, both the senior government and local development policy response after the WAC Bennett era have experienced limited success in facilitating positive structural change within BC's northern economy and society. The period has failed to achieve any kind of significant renovation of the industrial resource economy framework. While rapid changes are taking place within a globally competitive environment, we remain, at both the provincial and local levels, very much stuck in the middle. Successive governments in BC continue to coast on the vision and the infrastructure constructed during the WAC Bennett policy era, and they have failed to fully articulate and galvanize support for a new direction. Similarly, local responses struggle with their ability to implement plans and commit to long-term strategies for renewal because of limited local capacity not adequately and consistently supported by senior governments.

The WAC Bennett government confronted a resource frontier that required significant investment to overcome space and "open up" the province to development. Policies and investments sought to reconcile local assets with the formidable distance and topography of BC's hinterland. By virtue of the dual forces of province-building and resource extraction practices that needed comprehensive settlement patterns, the period after the Second World War contained an equal commitment to building the economic and the social infrastructure of the province. Within the context of resource and infrastructure growth, there was an appreciation for the multiple spin-offs associated with community and regional economic benefits and development.

In contrast, the post-1980s period has continued the economic dimensions of the staples tradition (in terms of continued resource dependence), but has fundamentally altered its commitments to hinterland settlements and social infrastructure. Recent governments in BC have stubbornly maintained a narrowly defined space-based approach to development of the resource bank. During resource "boom" times, this approach is capable of generating tremendous wealth for the province. However, outside of the variability of boom and bust commodity patterns, this approach may be reinforcing deeper structural weakness in the economy vis-à-vis the broader global context of an emerging place-based competitive economy.

Our assessment is that despite global change, the dominance of the comparative advantage mindset and economic structure has not substantively changed. Although we are seeing early traces of recognition and programmatic language that signal an awareness of competitive approaches to development, and the need to support such initiatives, British Columbia lags behind our competitors both nationally and internationally. In order to more thoroughly investigate the origins, significance, and strategies of place-based competitive development approaches, the following chapter outlines the place-based literature and offers an assessment of the competitive landscape of northern BC from a place-based perspective.

Part 3
Moving to a Place-Based Economy

7
An Economy of Place

> People form attachments to place – attachments that are strong enough to create intense reactions when they are challenged. Globalization and mass culture have not eliminated the importance of family, ethnic, cultural, and local ties for people's understanding of the world and their place in it ... Policies that fail to recognize how places and people-in-places form an important basis for our sense of self, view of the world, and our capacity to act in it, are liable to undermine the social and human capital on which those policies rely. (Reimer 2009: 5)

The previous chapter outlined many of the challenges and repercussions associated with top-down, space-based, and comparative approaches to development by both senior and local governments. The switch from comparative to competitive advantage is a complex process that requires fundamental shifts in both vision and method. The purpose of this chapter is to look more closely at the dynamics of competitiveness and its application and relevance to rural and small-town northern BC. Our analysis explores various interpretations of place and competitiveness found in the literature, and we further ground the investigation in an examination of the competitive characteristics of northern BC. Given that economic renewal in the north will demand more of place, what are the place-based assets that can form the foundation of a new northern economy? How do communities begin the process of adopting a place-based approach?

Variables of Regional Competitiveness

Part of the challenge of adapting to a more competitive economy is that the concept itself is poorly understood (Turok 2004). The looseness with which the term regional competitiveness is applied is a problem, further complicated by the fact that the idea of competitiveness has assumed "fadlike" qualities at both macro- and micro-economic scales (Kitson et al. 2004). The adherence to the idea of competition fits well within the traditional bravado of economic boosterism and the contemporary rhetoric surrounding neoliberal economic and policy adjustments. As a result, "competitiveness" has become a favourite and casual term for economic development consultants and policy makers.

The complexity of the notion of competitiveness is not just a challenge because of its loose application. The complexity of new regional competitiveness separates it, in a constructive way, from traditional forms of boosterism and territorial marketing. Malecki (2004) differentiates between old and new forms of place promotion through the useful metaphors of "low-road" and "high-road" competitiveness.

Low-road competitiveness is associated with traditional booster techniques such as tax incentives, tax holidays, grants, and similar incentives to entice firms to a particular locale. The main problem with this approach is that it can provide minimal net benefit to communities or cause debt dependence on the scale of the incentive offered versus the scale of the return benefits (Freshwater 2003). An additional challenge of low-road approaches is that the mobile firms they seek to attract may retain their sense of mobility and simply leave when offered a better deal by competing jurisdictions. Despite these limitations, this approach has certainly not disappeared from the repertoire of regional planners and economic developers. In fact, the trend of communities continually undercutting one another may have increased as the impacts of restructuring make all places more vulnerable to the mobility of capital and workers.

High-road competition rests on nonprice quality measures designed to instil a more enduring competitiveness over time and across a region. It involves collaborative efforts between competing jurisdictions, the private sector, and government to foster learning, innovation, and positive place attraction (Malecki 2004). The regionalization of high-road competition seeks to avoid the wasteful allocation of resources and the duplication associated with negative intercommunity rivalry. The approach allows regions to compete at a more effective scale and establish economies of scale on regional infrastructure and related investments.

Researchers have identified a number of variables associated with high-road competitiveness. Kresl (1995) and MacLeod (2001a), for example, refer to a useful organizing framework by distinguishing between quantitative and qualitative competitiveness variables. Quantitative variables include traditional economic development features such as infrastructure, production processes, location, economic structure, and amenities. These are critical in terms of establishing the platform on which community and economic development can take place.

Table 8

Quantitative and qualitative competitive variables

Quantitative	Qualitative
• infrastructure • transportation, communication, industry, power	• social capital • trust, collaboration (firm, industry, communities, public bodies), social networks
• production factors • productivity, technology	• innovation • networking, learning, human capital development (capacity), tacit knowledge
• location • proximity to market, resources, growth corridors	
• economic structure • diversity, firm size, support services	• institutions • coordinating bodies, regional strategy, flexibility, governance stability and consistency
• amenities • cultural facilities, recreation, climate, natural environment	

The quantitative variables listed in Table 8 provide an interesting mix of challenges for fostering a more competitive environment. First, many of the ideas listed are fixed, meaning that policy or program intervention cannot affect them much. Factors like location, the status of the surrounding environment, and climate may represent assets or barriers to specific types of economic activity and are beyond our immediate control or intervention abilities. Second, other variables are sensitive to investment decisions. Infrastructure investments provide the framework for economic activities. Transportation networks, communications infrastructure, power, and built amenities are critical ingredients for determining the type, scope, and scale of economic development. Third, we see from the list that the legacy of development matters, that is, the economic structure and make-up of a particular locale is cumulatively shaped over time. This speaks to the importance of fostering competitive advantage over time. Constructing a competitive place – inclusive of the built environment and human capacity – takes time and is beyond the scope of single programmatic interventions. Finally, the list highlights the importance of production factors or productivity.

Productivity, often featured as the holy grail of competitive performance, refers to the value of products and how efficiently they are produced and put into the marketplace. Thus, if your jurisdiction is able to produce a higher-quality product at a lower price, you will be more competitive. Ingredients in the productivity mix include labour and workable hours, capital resources such as land and natural resources, and the quality of machinery and equipment. Significantly, for our overall message of the importance of investment, productivity is dependent on continual upgrades in the quality of physical capital and people, as ongoing innovation within the economic system makes the productivity threshold a moving target.

Quantitative variables represent the more traditional terrain for economic development policy and practitioners. Within the new regionalist literature, however, recent attention is associated with the rising significance of qualitative competitive variables. These previously ignored elements represent the intangibles within the development process. To some extent, quantitative variables may be the same within any jurisdiction. Conversely, qualitative variables are much more place sensitive, and this helps to explain, in part, why all other things being equal, certain places are more competitive than others.

Qualitative elements are generally associated with three interconnected themes: social capital, innovation, and institutions (see Table 8). First, research has identified social capital as a prominent force in fostering a suitable balance between competition and cooperation within regions. Concepts such as the "associational economy" and "untraded interdependencies" are descriptive of social relations between economic agents within a region, are not tradable, and are not easily substitutable (Apedaile 2004; Scott 1998; Cooke and Morgan 1998; Storper 1997). Social capital facilitates productive economic relationships that can spur innovation, create coordination between policy actors, and speed the sharing of information that can make a region more responsive and adaptable to shifting economic conditions. Research into social capital relations provides insights into the positive externalities (at the micro-level) associated with "social" or "relational" embeddedness (Iyer et al. 2005). This embeddedness refers to the linkages and levels of trust among community and economic actors that play a role in, among other things, facilitating commitment to a particular place. This is especially important for rural areas.

Second, innovation refers to strategic processes of area networking and investments that can stimulate intersector and interfirm advancement. The OECD (2005: 46) defines an innovation as "the implementation of a new or significantly improved product (good or service), or process, a new marketing method, or a new organizational method in business practices, workplace organisation or external relations." The OECD describes four different types of innovation (47-50):

- Product Innovation involves a new or significantly improved good or service. This may include significant improvements in technical specifications, components and materials, incorporated software, user friendliness, or other functional characteristics. For example, in the education sector, a product innovation can be a new or significantly improved curriculum or new educational software.

- Process innovation involves a new or significantly improved production or delivery method. This may include significant changes in techniques, equipment, and/or software. In education, this can be a new or significantly improved pedagogy.
- Marketing innovation involves a new marketing method involving significant changes in product design or packaging, product placement, product promotion, or pricing. In education, this can be a new way of pricing the education service or a new admission strategy.
- Organizational innovation involves introducing a new organizational method in the firm's business practices, workplace organization, or external relations. In education, this can be a new way of organizing work between teachers or organizational changes in the administrative area.

These improvements come about through the creative application of ideas and are facilitated or advanced through inter- and intrasector cooperation. Innovation grows from the density of these local and regional linkages, supported further by a recursive commitment to learning and ongoing human capacity development (Greenwood et al. 2011; MacKinnon et al. 2002; Florida 1995).

To capture the complexity of factors and interrelationships affiliated with the concept of innovation, it is common within the literature to refer to an "innovation system" (Torjman and Leviten-Reid 2003). Components of the system include research institutes and organizations, sources of funding for research and development, technology transfer organizations and facilitators, education and training, sources of business capital, and institutional support for commercialization. The idea of an innovation system reveals the reflexive relationship between macro- and micro-roles and responsibilities associated with fostering competitiveness through continuous advancements in innovation. Communities have a role to play in terms of capitalizing on their local knowledge and facilitating the local processes that lead to innovation (Canada, Industry Canada 2003). Researchers cite the importance of "tacit knowledge," which refers to the experience, motivation, and behaviour of individuals and organizations (Alasia 2005). At the macro-level, senior governments must work to construct and adapt the political, legal, and macro-economic conditions that support (or do not excessively impede) the innovative potential of regions (see Table 9).

The most prominent recent strategy for fostering innovation is to facilitate the development of sectoral clusters. Clusters are "geographic concentrations of interconnected companies, specialized suppliers, service providers, firms in related industries, and associated institutions (e.g., universities, standards agencies, trade associations) in a particular field that compete but also cooperate" (Porter 2000: 15). As noted earlier, the key to clusters is that businesses within the cluster are able to capture the positive side effects of

Table 9

The innovation system

Political, legal, and macro-economic

- stability and predictability of the political system
- legal and regulatory environment
- macroeconomic conditions

Community/regional environment	*Company operations and strategy*
• demand conditions	• company strategy
• competitive environment	• culture and climate
• inputs:	• internal structure and processes
– R&D/technology infrastructure	• human resource capabilities
– human resources	• linkages with other organizations
– capital	
– production inputs	
– physical infrastructure	
– commercial information	
• related/supporting industries	

Source: Adapted from Ference Weiker (2003).

cooperation, while maintaining an overall competitive environment that continues to stimulate innovation. Clusters can form within specific places given the proximity effects associated with building trust, encouraging collaboration, developing a critical mass of human skills and capacity, and constructing a jurisdictionally appropriate policy environment.

Building and sustaining clusters may occur spontaneously; however, researchers are increasingly identifying how economic development intermediaries may support the development of clusters (Isaksen 2001; Christensen et al. 2002). Strategic interventions can include the following:

- workforce development: university and college training, linking educational institutions with the business sector
- shared resources: incubator facilities, financing mechanisms, and business development services
- market information: industry and market research
- networking: seminars, trade shows, social events, information exchange
- public policy: encourage public sector investment, support for research and development activity, tax regime, and others.

Third, a supportive institutional environment is critical for coordinating strategic intervention and advocating beyond jurisdictional boundaries

(Markey 2005; Aarsaether and Suopajärvi 2004; Amin 1999). Within the literature, the concept of *institution* is used in various ways, often without clarification. Institution can mean a single actor (e.g., government) or a diverse set of social practices and norms such as money or language (Hodgson 1998; Jones 2001). Institution can comprise decision-making mechanisms and frameworks of responsibility and accountability. Within the context of competitiveness, the institutional environment refers to the collective identity and functionality of economic and social actors within a particular place. These organizations include firms, financial enterprises, local chambers of commerce, training agencies, trade associations, unions, government agencies, and business service groups. In terms of mobilizing this collective for the purposes of fostering a more competitive environment, Amin and Thrift (1994) refer to the concept of "institutional thickness." This describes the relative level of regional interaction between actors with a commitment to being involved in a common project, thereby avoiding the consequences of negative competition and unleashing the development potential associated with collaborative governance. The "thickness" develops based on experiences of successful collaborative ventures. The institutional environment represents an interesting qualitative dimension within the context of competitiveness because of the linkages between individual agency and collective action, both of which are variable and place-dependent.

The qualitative variables in Table 8 collectively identify a larger issue of significant importance to successful place-based competitive economy transition: that of a shift in the local and regional culture of politics. This needed shift in the culture of politics has several facets. First, at the local level, there is a needed shift from short-term thinking to long-term strategic decision making. Too often, local councils and elected or unelected elites push agendas of tax and service cuts in order to satisfy small but noisy local interests. Uncompetitive property tax regimes will harm transition efforts; however, it is important to remember that infrastructure renewal, support for existing and new quality-of-life services, community economic development, and community development foundations all require investments, and by not starting today, decision makers simply push costs on to future councils and future generations. This is practically, fiscally, ethically, and morally wrong. Moreover, attention to long-term strategic investments in community development supports for a competitive place-based rural and small-town economy extends to the provincial government's activities and actions as well.

Second, a shift in the culture of politics is hampered by the fact that local governments are bound by the structure of their municipal boundaries. The local electorate and the legislation governing local governments create an implicit and explicit demand to focus on the community first (if not solely).

If they do not bring new investment or new money into the town, elected local governments are likely to be rejected by voters. The proliferation of stories across northern BC of mayors undercutting each other to attract an investment has created a climate of mistrust and negative competition. There will need to be a profound political culture shift among local elected leaders and the local electorate alike to allow for the local, regional, and provincial partnership approaches so needed in the future.

Third, building from the second point, northern BC needs new tools for working cooperatively as regions, while still allowing for the flexibility of local initiatives and actions. The long-standing possibilities embodied by organizations such as regional districts, and the newer dialogue tables associated with beetle action coalitions and the NDI Trust are practising a new culture of politics across northern BC. The success of the Northern Transportation Corridor, for example, is providing concrete evidence to support a culture of speaking with one political voice on key issues in order to effect positive change in places and across the region.

Together, the qualitative competitive variables create the foundation for a new culture of local and regional politics. Working cooperatively at a local and regional level contributes to the development of trust and social capital. The opportunities for exchange that such a cooperative undertaking create support opportunities for innovation, information exchange, and mutual approaches to investments that are beyond the capacity of individual small places. New models of collaboration will help to guide northern BC towards more effective and flexible mechanisms for regional governance that have the stability to act over the long periods required by transition and development.

The regional literature is helpful for identifying the complexity of place-based competitiveness. However, the majority of the research comes from metropolitan areas. This leads to assumptions of scale and capacity to supply the ingredients of competitiveness that may challenge rural and small-town jurisdictions. The lessons drawn from urban-centric research are informative; however, many of the observations and strategic recommendations do not translate well to the nonmetropolitan setting.

A Rural Lens on Regional Competitiveness

Before turning to aspects of rural competitiveness, it is important to note Amin's (1999) warning that it is not possible to simply take one model of regional development from one place and graft it onto another place. Each region develops, and importantly, inherits, its own competitive circumstances. This reflects the earlier warning by Massey (1984: 9), who argued in the "new regional geography" debate that "'general processes' never work themselves out in pure form. There are always specific circumstances, a

Table 10

Variables of rural competitiveness

	Quantitative	Qualitative
Asset	• cheap land • access to resources • natural amenities • increasing access to education	• strong social networks • strong commitment to place • high quality of life
Barrier	• weak economic base • low population • declining population • aging population • distance from markets • capital • expertise • weak communication infrastructure • declining employment in primary industries • limited access to financing • business structure	• low levels of education • "thin" organizational and institutional infrastructure

particular history, a particular place or location." As such, the application of any model or concept requires a finer grain of application in practice. This finer grain is one that must recognize, and build around, the individual circumstances and geographic context of places and regions.

Using an adaptation of the quantitative and qualitative framework presented above (in Table 8), Table 10 includes a number of competitive variables isolated by rural researchers (Terluin 2003; Malecki 2004; Caffyn and Dahlström 2005; Hanlon and Halseth 2005). These competitive variables are representative of generalized conditions and characteristics commonly associated with "ruralness." First, the economic dependency of many rural areas on primary industries creates a variety of potential competitive barriers, including population decline, relatively lower general levels of education, and a lower skill base across the labour force – all characteristics necessary to compete within the new global economy that is so dependent on knowledge-based activities. Such dependence may inhibit transition as the local political culture and institutions are both practised in, and comfortable with, protecting the status quo interests of "their" local resource industries. As Bollman (2007: 4) states, "Primary industries (specifically, the traditional primary sectors producing commodities) would not be considered as drivers. Primary industries are shedding labour. If rural development is the growth of jobs and/or the growth of population, then commodity production is not a driver of rural development." From a more positive perspective, access to resources represents opportunities for local economic diversification through such mechanisms as community resource management. Similarly, viewing natural resources as amenity assets underscores a significant component of a rural quality of life that may encompass opportunities for tourism, a second house, and amenity migration.

Second, distance (and isolation) represents perhaps the greatest competitive barrier for rural economies. Dependent on the quality of connecting infrastructure (communications and transportation), distance may present a cost-prohibitive barrier for rural enterprise. Through technological and procedural efficiencies, relative prices associated with truck and rail transportation and the communication of information (e.g., telecommunications) have fallen steadily since the 1970s. The falling price of distance is an important factor in the overall ability of rural communities to be competitive in sectors such as complex manufacturing. As a result, rural Canada has increased its share of total manufacturing employment over the past three decades.

Third, the comparatively weak institutional capacity of rural areas represents a competitive barrier to the extent that intermediary organizations play important roles in facilitating and coordinating the soft externalities associated with place-based economic development. Locally constructed political cultures can affect the development of local and regional institutional capacity to support transition, and constructing competitiveness is increasingly a responsibility shared between the public and private sectors. Rural areas that lack supportive organizations (such as economic development agencies) and lack government and/or governance capacity (owing to cutbacks and downloading) will face challenges when seeking to plan or adapt to the competitive challenges of the new economy.

Compensating somewhat for the lack of institutional capacity is the commitment to place commonly attributed to rurally based individuals and businesses. Thus, while the number of individuals and organizations may be limited (thereby potentially limiting the diversity of skills), the participatory commitment of existing actors may be strong. Given the long timelines associated with development processes, and the continual need to update plans and respond to change, commitment to place represents a competitive asset for rural areas.

Fourth, the comparatively lower levels of education within rural places are a significant barrier to both facilitating endogenous development and attracting new economy actors. Barriers to enhancing education levels exist at both regional and personal scales. At the regional level, the mobility of labour is a disincentive for industry to invest in human capacity development.[1] At a personal level, reliance on primary industries and limited local opportunities for diverse employment provide a disincentive for individuals to invest in advancing their own education prospects (Alasia 2005).

Aiding in the development of human capital within the rural context, however, is the increasing variety of rural educational opportunities. For example, advances in distance education and the enhanced flexibility of programs to accommodate part-time studies create new opportunities for prospective rural students. Flexibility has been key to the delivery of coursework at UNBC. One recent example is the creation of an Executive MBA program; designed for in-service professionals and business people, this intense two-year program brings students together on a regular basis for weekend coursework. Another is the application of "cohort-based" educational models. If, in a particular region, the number of interested students reaches the critical mass necessary to deliver a specialized program, then that program is delivered locally. These cohort-based programs have been especially popular in the education and social work fields. Again, the range of opportunities for investing in human capacity across northern BC is a vital aspect of creating the broad community development platform so necessary for community and economic renewal.

There also exists the opportunity to take advantage of rural economic and knowledge clusters. The long-standing economic organization of rural economies provides not only the surface areas of focus (forestry, agriculture, etc.) where there are skills, expertise, and a density of firms, but also the tacit or hidden clusters of skills and knowledge that can be grown into full economic sectors needed in, and competitive in, the twenty-first century economy.

Finally, the business structure in rural communities (particularly in BC and Canada, more generally) is comparatively less robust and diversified than in metropolitan areas. This speaks to the legacy of development and difficulties associated with creating a critical mass of diverse industries in rural settings. Studies completed in BC reveal that rural companies are:

- smaller in size and younger in development
- geographically dispersed
- less aware of supportive resources
- less technologically advanced
- more limited in their access to information and information technologies.

These general trends may, however, be compensated for by the necessity of innovativeness required by rural companies to survive within a globally competitive economy (North and Smallbone 2000). From this perspective, innovation is a nonuniform concept with multiple dimensions. The key for rural enterprise success depends on finding niches and being adaptable.

Overall, the variables in Table 10 provide useful benchmarks for considering the relative competitiveness of rural communities and regions. The problem here is that we get a false sense that rural competitiveness, in its simplest form, derives from being "not urban" (Marsden et al. 2004). In the following section, we step from the generalities of rural competitiveness to explore the prospects for regional competitiveness within northern BC.

Competitiveness in Northern BC

People in northern BC are very familiar with the variety of competitive disadvantages that affect their region. The challenge in terms of shifting from an economy of comparative advantage to a competitive position – from space to place – is how to identify, rebundle, and mobilize the assets of the region. We begin by listing five prominent barriers and follow this with a discussion of competitive assets (see Table 11).

First, a lack of capacity exists in two distinct forms in northern BC. On one hand, a dependency on staples-led development has meant that there is a lack of entrepreneurial capacity to translate into reality many of the competitive recommendations common in economic diversification and business innovation reports. On the other hand, although the north contains strong individual leaders, many people expressed concerns about a lack of depth in institutional leadership and a declining pool of qualified people who traditionally assume such roles. Organizational restructuring that has witnessed losses of personnel (and experience) through office closures and staff relocations in government and industry reinforces this lack of depth.

Second, related to the issue of human capacity, northerners spoke about the overall fragility of local institutions concerned with northern governance. This relates specifically to nongovernmental agencies, such as economic development corporations, that play important roles in facilitating economic development through information sharing, advocacy, advice, financing, training, and support. The indirect benefits associated with these

Table 11

Competitive barriers and assets in Northern BC

Barriers	Assets
• limited capacity	• social networks and lifestyle fostering commitment to place
• leadership	• resource wealth
• fragile governance institutions	• untapped local economies
• limited reinvestment	• embedded regional connectivity
• no tradition of cooperation	• proximity issues
• cumulative uncertainty	• youthful labour force relative to OECD
• proximity issues	
• research and development	
• business and marketing skills	

organizations are difficult to sustain in the face of the narrow and sporadic funding mechanisms from which most of them draw their support. Given the importance of institutions in fostering regional competitiveness, this lack of attention to institution building and maintenance represents a serious shortcoming. For example, institutional realities throughout the north make blanket recommendations for the creation of sectoral clusters (common in all reports concerning the northern economy) somewhat hollow. Even where cluster recommendations briefly consider "ruralness," for example, by advocating for virtual rather than close proximity networking, a strong institutional base is still required to facilitate such relationships. With institutional staff and fiscal resources already thin on the ground, such suggestions for economic and regional development are bound to fail without an infusion of additional human and financial capacity.

Third, the north struggles with a poor record of reinvestment from its bountiful resource wealth. We refer below to resource wealth as an asset. One clear on-the-ground ramification of this issue, however, concerns the north's crumbling or nonexistent infrastructure. For example, people identified the lack of access to electrical power as one of the biggest impediments to economic development in the region. Recommendations in economic development reports call blindly for the development of value-added resource activities (always a catch-all recommendation in any case). Such recommendations are of little help where aged transformers are being blown from telephone poles as businesses pursue manufacturing opportunities, where existing sawmills run the saws in the day and the planers at night because of power shortages, and where guiding and lodge operators cannot even plug in a commercial freezer.

Fourth, BC's north does not have an ingrained history of cooperation. Intercommunity, intracommunity, and business cooperation are necessary to create the innovation necessary to exploit new or latent competitive advantages. Communities within the region have no legacy of cooperation because, up until quite recently, there was simply no need to cooperate. The strength of the industrial economy, and the belief that resource booms would follow natural bust cycles, exacerbated a cultural remoteness across the region, already instilled by geographic distance. Transition to a place-based competitive advantage economy will need local and regional transition in political cultures.

As described some time ago by Bradbury (1987), the structure of the resource economy reinforces direct linkages between individual hinterland communities and the provincial metropolitan core (for public policy and management functions) and with the headquarters of the resource industry (for employment, investment, and other economic functions). Such a structure truncates the development of, and need for, intercommunity dialogue and cooperation across northern BC. At an industrial level, Patchell (1996:

498) adds the observation that the BC forest industry (the dominant industry) "exemplifies how a short horizon and domineering control limit the evolution of cooperation." Interviewees and workshop participants in a number of projects from different communities were very direct about recognizing the social distance between them. This was particularly obvious in some cases by the fact that our project workshops provided the first opportunity for representatives from different communities to gather to discuss their regional economy.

Finally, the cumulative impact of the direct and indirect competitive challenges facing the north creates an underlying tone of uncertainty and lack of capacity that inhibits both economic and social investment. The ongoing dialogue surrounding First Nations treaty claims and treaty negotiations exacerbates the impacts of uncertainty and continues to affect all communities in northern BC. In combination with trade disputes and price fluctuations for resource commodities, such uncertainty means that the region finds it difficult to sustain the critical mass of people and investment necessary to underwrite a competitive community development environment.

Returning to the competitive assets of northern BC listed in Table 11, northerners speak of how strong social networks and an appreciation for the northern lifestyle create a resilient commitment to place. Our participants spoke about how quality of life and many of the other characteristics that have long described rural and small-town places can now become a focus for the region's economic development. For example, an outdoor lifestyle and wilderness setting create opportunities for tourism, amenity, and resource development. The small-town characteristics of safe and familiar communities provide an ideal setting for recruiting both young families and retirees. In fact, many of the characteristics that have long described rural and small-town communities are valued assets in the new economy. This finding corroborates the regional advantages associated with social embeddedness referred to earlier. Here, social capital plays both recursive and reinforcing roles in supporting local investments and interpersonal as well as interfirm linkages, and a commitment to place.

Commitment to place is important beyond any direct economic development benefit. The dedication expressed to us by northerners creates enthusiasm for the necessary development processes and allows for the transition time necessary to construct new economic relationships and patterns. Fostering a more competitive economy in the north will take considerable time, first, to come to terms with new economic realities and, second, to tolerate the inevitable failures and missteps associated with change. This issue of requiring time to make adjustments should not come as a surprise. The regional and community development literatures have long recognized that transition requires a significant time commitment. In northern BC, it took about twenty years (1950 to 1970) to establish most of the social and physical infrastructure needed to support the comparative advantage-driven resource industrial model.

Resource wealth is obviously an asset to northern BC. If there was one issue that all of the individuals and groups in our interviews and workshops spoke forcefully about, it was the clear need to reverse trends that have seen a net outflow of economic wealth from the region. They spoke not only about the need to create more local opportunity but also about how a greater share of economic wealth should stay in the north rather than being recirculated to the north through government channels. Thus, there were calls for increased community and regional control or management of resources.

Third, the focus of most strategies for economic and community development throughout northern BC includes a combination of continued reinforcement of the existing industrial resource economy and attraction of external business opportunities. In many ways, this focus reflects an outdated "smokestack-chasing" approach to economic development. A significant gap, and potential competitive advantage, exists within the local economies of the region, but it is often overlooked or undervalued. People frequently pointed out that a pervading booster mentality among economic planners essentially takes the local economy for granted. In no way does this diminish the cornerstone significance of the industrial economy to the north. Undoubtedly, however, within the existing localized business community there are hidden economic opportunities that are not adequately identified, supported, and exploited.

One regional example rests with the "clusters" of large forest-processing mills in northern BC towns. These clusters today suffer from such competitive pressures that they employ every technology and computer application possible to reduce their costs of production – hence, our earlier suggestion to think of these as incubators for a regional high tech industry (of which many small software and design firms already exist). "Industry-ready" high tech solutions may become a significant export from northern BC. A similar nascent cluster within a forest sector cluster can include the set of skills and businesses involved in environmental management and restoration – a cluster that will grow (in scale and technical sophistication and readiness) as northern BC grapples with the aftermath of the mountain pine beetle epidemic. Moreover, the local economy plays a particularly critical role for a significant portion of the regional population that is not benefiting from the high wages associated with the industrial resource economy. In this sense, the north must consider the meaning of competitiveness across a broader spectrum of the population.

Finally, there are a variety of existing forces of connectivity that serve to unite an otherwise geographically, economically, and culturally diverse region. Given that strategies for regional and rural development must increasingly rely on a critical mass of people, businesses, and governments working together, the following sites of connectivity serve as important potential sources of competitive advantage:

- effective political relationships within provincial government and organizations such as the North Central Local Government Association
- economic flows between resource production sites and processing centres, as well as between production centres and shipping points that, among other examples, bind the region together
- infrastructure that connects the diverse places across the region
- services that have been consolidated into larger communities creating more connections
- new factors such as attention to lifestyle and the environment that connect the north via watersheds and valleys.

These barriers and assets represent only a portion of the observations expressed by the people who live with the competitive realities of northern BC. They provide important insight into the rural dimensions of regional competitiveness that are not detailed in either the academic literature or the circulating policy documents about the conditions of rural and small-town regions such as northern BC.

Recognizing the assets of place throughout northern BC is one thing, devising a strategy to realize their potential for economic and social development is another. We have seen in previous chapters the tremendous uncertainty and pressures that communities are dealing with in terms of adapting to external forces and the dynamics of political restructuring. Within this flurry of activity, where the limited capacity of municipalities struggles to cope with day-to-day activities, how do communities plan for change?

Developing Place

In the following stories, we present two different planning approaches. Smithers and Valemount are places that have made consistent efforts through planning to adapt their communities to shifting economic and political realities by using a place-based approach. Tumbler Ridge tells of a different route to action – one for communities that do not have the luxury of long-term planning and face a particular crisis in a moment in time. For Tumbler Ridge, the commitment to place founded on a high quality of life and quality natural and built amenities provided a foundation that enabled the community to confront crisis and build for the future.

Place through Planning: Smithers and Valemount

The Town of Smithers, which is located in northwestern BC (see Figure 10), is a good example of a community capitalizing on its regional assets and

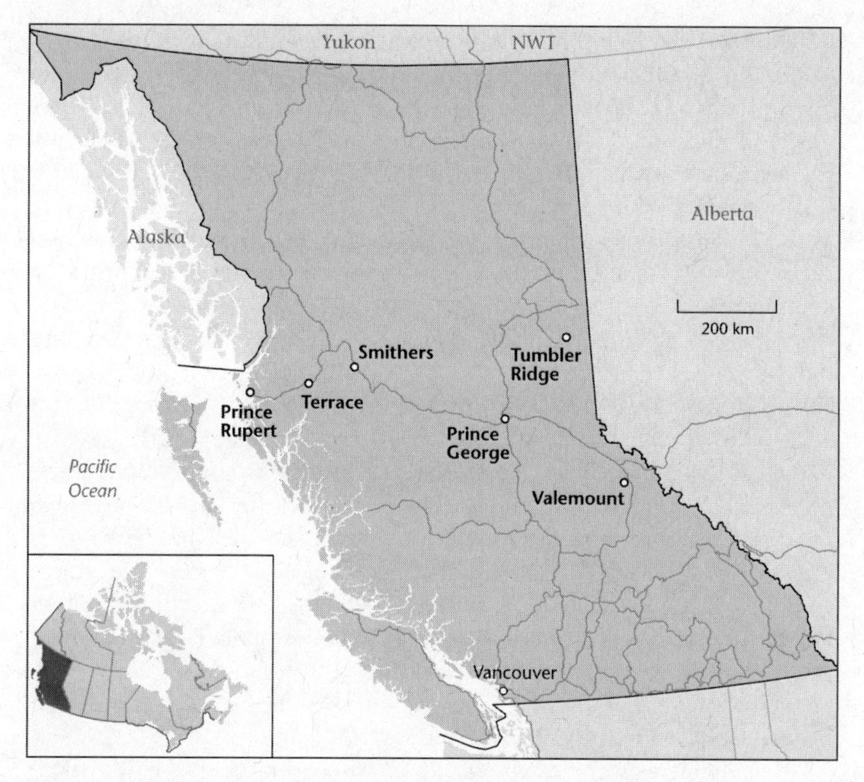

Figure 10 British Columbia, including Smithers, Valemount, and Tumbler Ridge.

amenities through a place-based approach to community economic development. Smithers promotes the high quality of life in its community as a means of retaining and attracting residents and has incorporated this focus into its economic development plan.

Smithers identified its core strategic objective: to move the community from "Boomtown to Sustainable Town." In 2007, an Economic Development Committee was created to identify future economic development objectives. While Smithers has traditionally been dependent on resource extraction, their new focus is to accentuate community amenities to attract both people and investment.

Smithers is located midway between the two larger regional hubs of Prince George and Terrace. With a population of approximately 6,000 people, the community has a surrounding rural population of over 12,000 people. The town has land-based constraints, a struggling forestry sector, and growing regional competition for attracting investment, employment, and services. To meet these challenges, the Smithers Economic Development Committee developed a strategy to concentrate on existing amenities, encourage growth in existing sectors, and attract people and investment to the community. The new economic development strategy identified the continuing opportunity for the community to promote itself as a central service hub for the resource sector, appealing to the mining industry through the development of mining support and service businesses. Infrastructure improvements such as the expansion of the Smithers Regional Airport are crucial to attracting the mineral exploration and mining sector to establish offices within the community.

The Bulkley Valley Economic Development Office (BVEDO), a joint inititative of the Town of Smithers, the Office of the Wet'suwet'en, Village of Telkwa, and the Regional District of Bulkley-Nechako, recognizes the importance of the aiport for "visitors, commercial operators and industrial activities in the Northwest. The crossroad of these three freight transportations modes and the quality of life in community gives the Valley a potential competitive advantage for transportation equipment servicing and intermodal transfers, e.g. heavy equipment, particularly if major mining and hydroelectric projects go ahead along Highway 37" (BVEDO 2010: 20). Four scheduled airlines, two charter airlines, and three helicopter companies service this small regional airport. An airport of this nature in a community of this size is an example of how the town has focused on upgrading the infrastructure and services needed to attract both people and business.

Other strategies include capitalizing on the natural assets of Smithers to attract nature-based tourism, retirees, amenity migrants, and new businesses through branding Smithers as a community with a high "quality of life, community engagement, and attractive natural and built environment" (City Spaces 2008: 13). The Town of Smithers, in cooperation with the BVEDO, is working towards creating stability for the community and region as it negotiates the cyclical investments of the resource sectors. This is to include the establishment of a new sustainable economic development agency, a new branding campaign emphasizing the community's facilities and services, a business care program to assist new business start-ups, and continued dedication to maintaining high-quality infrastructure and community amenities. Through innovation and forward thinking, Smithers is using its place-based assets to position itself as an important service centre in northern BC. A developed network of support for existing businesses complements the community's emphasis on quality-of-life assets. Their competitive advantage is in their ability to organize and implement the development of amenities needed by both residents and businesses.

The second planning example is the community of Valemount (see Figure 10). Smaller than Smithers, Valemount has a local population of approximately 1,018 (in 2006). Located at the entrance to the Yellowhead Pass, Valemount sits at a crossroads of highway and rail corridors. For much of its history, Valemount has been a centre for forestry and sawmilling; in 2001, it was home to three sawmills, and most of the local working population was employed in the forest sector.

Beginning about 1995, the local council and administration in Valemount recognized that increasing fluctuation and uncertainty in the forest industry demanded that they look to a more diversified economic future for the community. Separate from the current health of the local forest economy, local decision makers stayed focused on the need to build a flexible community development foundation to support other economic actors and to support the current forest sector.

As part of its creative reimagining of assets, Valemount recognized that it is located at the entrance to both Mount Robson Provincial Park and Jasper National Park. Given restrictions in the national parks regarding additional resort, hotel, and tourist development, Valemount was ideally situated to capture tourism investments. It already had a burgeoning tourism sector because of the high-quality snowmobiling trails throughout the region, and proximity to transportation corridors meant additional opportunities in highway commercial and transportation services.

The approach in Valemount was to build flexible community development foundations. For example, the town needed to improve the water system and so investments were infused to improve it not just for current needs but also to design those improvements in such a way that capacity could be expanded if additional large water users (such as a destination tourist hotel) came to the community. Once the water system was in place, the town was, in fact, able to attract significant hotel investments because it was able to highlight that local services were ready to receive this commercial private sector investment. Another example of the creativity employed by Valemount concerned the need to replace the local municipal government offices and the need to upgrade the local visitor information centre. Using a wide range of funding sources, the town created a single new large building adjacent to the highway. Highway improvements and exit ramps made the property more accessible than ever before. The main floor and front parking area of the building were geared towards the visitor information centre (VIC). This VIC is much more than just a small closet with a rack of promotional brochures; rather, it contains community facilities for presenting art and cultural assets from the region to entice visitors to stay locally. The basement of the new VIC building was transformed into a state-of-the-art small-town municipal office complete with requisite technologies for land use and management planning.

By 2009, all of the forest products facilities in Valemount had been closed; yet, the community continues to have local economic activity and a robust housing market because of the long-term planning given to creating a flexible and diversified economic future. In the resource sector, there is quarrying activity underway, and the community was recently successful in acquiring and then operationalizing a community forest. In the tourism sector, the nascent winter tourism of snowmobile activity has greatly expanded and is one of the key areas for this activity in northern BC, which attracts large numbers of users from northern Alberta. The summer tourism industry has similarly grown with bus and drive tourism traffic making use of local hotels and amenities such as horse trail riding. Many international tour groups now make Valemount a key stop in their tour of Western Canada and the Rocky Mountains. Transportation services and various truck stops, gas stations, and restaurants upgraded as exit and entrance ramps to the Yellowhead Highway were improved. Finally, the stunning mountain and valley setting within which Valemount is nestled has meant that recreational property development and amenity migration have helped to bolster and stabilize local real estate markets.

The Valemount 2020 Vision – Implementation Strategy, produced as part of a comprehensive "Socio-Economic and Land Use Impact Analysis Study and Report" for the Valemount area, describes the following vision (Valemount 2004: 1):

> By 2020 Valemount is a dynamic and successful place with a multifaceted, blended economy, based primarily on tourism, resort and real estate development as well as continued forestry. It is centred on a well-balanced and attractive Village core that authentically reflects its past. Further, the residents of Valemount have recognized the importance of protecting both the area's natural setting and its access to mountain-based backcountry recreation. Likewise, they have embraced the opportunity to offer tourists access to unique and special attributes – attributes, which in some cases are found nowhere else in the world. It is a socially strong and engaged community that celebrates its history while at the same time championing cutting edge technologies and innovative approaches to new challenges.

Realizing this vision will not be easy. As fits with a community that has already undertaken more than twenty years of planning and action for economic and community renewal, the Valemount 2020 plan recognizes that "there is not a quick fix for the long-term social and economic sustainability of the Valemount area" (ibid.: 10). Instead, "Valemount will need to embrace a strategic vision that has strong leadership from decision makers as well as substantial community buy-in" (10).

Although Smithers and Valemount are different in size, they both have a long and successful history as resource industry towns. Both communities recognized that increasing uncertainty and fluctuation within that economic base demanded attention to diversification. The key to their success has been that despite economic up- or downturns in the local dominant industry, decision makers remained focused on the need to build a flexible community development foundation to take advantage of local opportunities and to feature a reimagined set of local assets.

Place through Crisis: Tumbler Ridge

We use the example of the mine closures in the early 2000s in Tumbler Ridge (see Figure 10) to show how places can be successful in meeting the challenges of a specific crisis to renew their local economy and community.

Located in northeastern BC, on the eastern slope of the Rocky Mountains, Tumbler Ridge began as a coal-mining town during the 1980s (Gill 2002; Halseth and Sullivan 2002). Its economic heart was two open-pit coal mines, Quintette (operated by Denison Mines) and Bullmoose (operated by Teck Corporation). As part of the Northeast Coal Project, Tumbler Ridge was BC's last great experiment in instant town development. Planning began in 1976, and the provincial government issued letters patent to incorporate the town on 9 April 1981. Town construction started in earnest in 1982 following the signing of a fourteen-year deal to ship coal to a consortium of steel mills in Japan. The extensive project development costs formed part of a provincial strategy to kick-start a recession-mired economy and expand industrial development in the region.

The letters patent issued by the province to found Tumbler Ridge describe how this was to be a provincially important resource development project. They go on to identify that the townsite was to be "completed by the time the permanent residents arrive so that there will be a socially cohesive and well-planned community conducive to attracting and retaining a stable work force" (British Columbia 1981).

Unfortunately, coal prices fell almost as soon as Tumbler Ridge opened (Tumbler Ridge Tattler 1984a, 1984b), creating concern about the viability of both the mines and the town. A 1990 contract dispute with the Japanese buyers led Quintette, the larger of the two mines, to file for bankruptcy protection. The bankruptcy plan transferred management of Quintette from Denison Mines to Teck Corporation. Through the 1990s, falling coal prices meant successive rounds of layoffs. In March 2000, Teck announced that the Quintette mine would close two years ahead of schedule. Local leaders did not heed years of warning signs about the likely demise of the local resource industry, and announcement of the mine closure triggered a crisis.

The reaction of the provincial minister for energy and mines to the announcement was that he had been "blindsided." In fact, his ministry had been in active negotiations with Teck on a new rail and shipping deal in order to lower company costs and keep the mine viable. When confronted with the closure announcement, the minister responded that "the town was

Table 12

Tumbler Ridge Revitalization Task Force

	Position
Victoria	Minister of Energy and Mines
Victoria	Ministry of Energy and Mines
Victoria	Assistant Deputy Minister
Peace River	MLA
Peace River Reg. District	Administrator
Peace River Reg. District	Chairperson
Tumbler Ridge	Mayor
Tumbler Ridge	Administrator
Tumbler Ridge	Councillor
Tumbler Ridge	Councillor
Tumbler Ridge	Councillor
Tumbler Ridge	Councillor
Tumbler Ridge	Councillor
Dawson Creek	Mayor
Dawson Creek	Administrator
Fort St. John	Mayor
Fort St. John	Administrator
Chetwynd	Mayor
Chetwynd	Administrator
School District #59	Chair
School District #59	Administrator
South Peace Health Unit	Chair
Peace Health Unit	Chief Administrative Office

Source: Tumbler Ridge Revitalization Task Force (2000).

built for one purpose, as a place to house the workers for the two mines, and without the mines, I don't know that you could convert the town to some other use" (Hunter and McInnes 2000: D2).

Local residents and elected officials were also blindsided. Quintette had recently signed a five-year export agreement with its Japanese buyers, and people felt the mine would operate until at least 2003. Despite the provincial minister's gloomy response, town leaders were committed to renewal. The tone in the local newspaper was defiant (Tumbler Ridge Community Connections 2000: 1), arguing that "despite the media messages, and the abandonment of Tumbler Ridge as a disposable [town] by provincial politicians, there is a strong current of confidence about our future running through town. Many residents are survivors from other mining towns ... [they] call Tumbler Ridge home and are not willing to move." Six days after the closure announcement, the local council created an emergency action plan. As a first stage, they convinced regional, provincial, and federal government offices to support Tumbler Ridge through a transition period. With that support in place, the next step involved the creation of a Revitalization Task Force. The task force included a broad range of interests (see Table 12). According to its terms of reference (Tumbler Ridge Revitalization Task Force 2000: 1): "The Tumbler Ridge Revitalization Task Force Committee is to focus on the [town] and its ability to deliver municipal, educational, community health, and social services to a viable and stable community infrastructure. Special emphasis will be put into creating an economic environment that creates economic diversity."

Stabilization Strategy

Workers were offered immediate assistance with respect to unemployment insurance, retraining, and relocation. The task force identified three time horizons for action. In the short term, the stock of rental, vacant, and company-owned houses was to be sold to create a municipal property tax base. Local services (especially education, health care, and social services) were to be stabilized through Emergency Services agreements to last for a period of five years (Sullivan 2002). Over the intermediate term, population change and municipal operations were to be founded on an orderly transition plan. In the long term, a strategic marketing and diversification plan was to be developed because only a diversified economy would help create a more stable population. The high-quality residential, commercial, and industrial service infrastructure of Tumbler Ridge featured prominently in economic development promotional materials.

One of the first areas of concern was returning the town's housing stock to private households in order to secure a residential property tax base. About 80 percent of local housing was rental housing owned by either the mines (Quintette or Bullmoose) or Canada Mortgage and Housing Corporation (CMHC). With the announcement of the Quintette closure, the town negotiated with CMHC and Quintette to acquire 985 units and then marketed them through the Tumbler Ridge Housing Corporation (Hope 2001). Houses initially sold for $25,000 and apartments for $12,000. The housing sale went far better than expected, and within two years, 97 percent of the properties were sold. These homeowners now began to pay property taxes, something that helped pay for municipal services such as sewers and water, road maintenance, and the local recreation and aquatic centre.

A second early area of concern was key education, health care, and social services (Halseth et al. 2003). Each of these priority areas was the focus of a services agreement to guarantee funding through the transition period. With respect to education services, the provincial Ministry of Education was to provide 75 percent of the pre-Quintette closure funding. The agreement was to last for five years, with the goal of providing certainty of access to education for people wishing to remain in, or move to, Tumbler Ridge. In fact, the population transition in Tumbler Ridge was so successful that the number of students remained relatively stable over the entire period.

In terms of health care services, a similar emergency funding package was set up. Health care funding was especially important for both seniors moving to town and families with young children wishing to stay in town. The package was sufficient to secure the services of two physicians and nursing staff. Tumbler Ridge, like most of rural Canada, still faces difficulty in recruiting nursing staff, but the arrival of a large number of older residents seeking a retirement community has bolstered physician caseloads to the point at which three physicians work in the town.

For social services, the challenge was to continue providing a full range of services on a reduced budget. The Ministry of Health had previously funded assessment and referral services, counselling, and self-improvement programs as separate services. These were consolidated into one office, and a social worker was added specifically to assist youth going through the transition process. This umbrella office then received support from the Tumbler Ridge Family Support Society – a local volunteer group with a long history of local service, and by community groups like the informally organized "Women in Transition" gathering.[2]

A third area of concern was the town's debt. Tumbler Ridge still owed $10.8 million in infrastructure debt left over from the original town construction. Town debt can be a significant encumbrance on local diversification. To eliminate the debt, expected future payments were "front-loaded," and this allowed the provincial Municipal Finance Authority to provide $5.3 million, the provincial government to provide $3.7 million, and the town to provide $1.8 million. Tumbler Ridge cleared its debt on 22 December 2000.

Even though Tumbler Ridge was built using a space-economy approach, the community had become a place: a place with intrinsic values, commitments by families, and affinities forged within a community and the surrounding landscape. In other words, the community was rooted in place, and the community mobilized its place-based assets to create a transition plan when the provincial government did not have one. Their approach capitalized on the very high quality local infrastructure, attractive setting in the eastern foothills of the Rocky Mountains, proximity to nature, and town design that emphasized accessibility. Tumbler Ridge rebranded and marketed itself as a place where young families could raise children, seniors could grow old in a supportive community, new tourism and outdoor recreation adventure companies could flourish (as evidenced by the photo cover of this book), and the natural history of the area could support new amenities to draw visitors and tourists. Coincident with this exercise was the discovery

Table 13

Recommendations to improve the economy of Tumbler Ridge

	Respondents (*n*)
Better shopping / stores	75
Big resource industry	68
Cell phone – high speed Internet	11
Diversified resource industry	142
Expand post-secondary education	11
Expand small businesses	112
Fix roads / bus service	47
New vision at Town Hall	29
Reopen mine / new mine	100
Ski hill	26
Tourism	147
Other	17

Source: Halseth and Ryser (2001).

of fossil beds and dinosaur tracks in the river valleys immediately adjacent to the town that provided further assets for attracting tourism activity.

In support of its long-term priorities, the Task Force developed an economic diversification strategy. Consultants hired to research local economic potential focused on a diverse range of opportunities from traditional resource development to the growing sectors of recreation and tourism for remaking Tumbler Ridge into a retirement or education centre. These opportunities included the following (Sullivan 2002):

- resource development (forestry, mining, oil and gas)
- recreation (backcountry, ecotourism)
- tourism (wilderness, park-based)
- home businesses
- retirement centre
- educational centre.

Although the town's services and infrastructure are ready to accommodate most of the suggestions for diversification, many residents and decision makers still look towards big resource sector projects.

We conducted a survey in Tumbler Ridge a year after the Quintette mine closed. One of the questions was about resident opinions for diversifying the town's economy. In many respects, Table 13 mirrors the consultant-driven Economic Diversification Strategy suggestions. A look at the top five suggestions reveals the potentially conflicting visions for this small community. Resource development and tourism set the foundation for two very different rural imaginations positing two very different economic development futures.

At the close of its first two years of community transition, the plans of the Tumbler Ridge Revitalization Task Force had met with considerable success. Following the Quintette closure, many households moved out of town, but people attracted to the community and the town's available housing almost entirely replaced this departing population.

Not all steps in the Tumbler Ridge transition process worked well even given the close participation of provincial ministries. One particular disjuncture occurred within the tourism sector. Tourism was identified as one of the key viable economic options for the community. This option was based on the beautiful and dramatic natural surroundings of the area, and it became more significant with the discovery of dinosaur tracks. These finds have been the foundation for the creation of a local paleontology museum and a summer program of "dino camps" that brings many children and young people into the community. In addition to local hotels, Tumbler Ridge was fortunate to be relatively close to three small provincial parks, each of which contained camping and picnic sites. The disjuncture occurred when, during the early summer following the mine closure announcement, and local tourism strategies were just starting to move into action, the provincial ministry announced that two of the three provincial parks in the area were to be closed as a budget-saving measure. It was only through the actions of the local member of the Legislative Assembly (MLA) and the area local governments, that this ministerial decision was reversed. As with the McBride Community Forest example mentioned earlier, it is very easy for distant bureaucracies to make cost-cutting decisions with little regard for their collective impact on area plans for renewal.

The local government is working with broad support for diversification, but it has also been clearly searching for a replacement large resource industry. The town's website stated in 2003 that Tumbler Ridge "has a strategy to encourage growth and development in every sector of the community. The main areas of focus are natural gas exploration, forestry including silviculture, tourism and recreation" (Tumbler Ridge, District of, 2003). With an eye to diversification, the town council has supported initiatives in each of these areas, and it has supported the re-establishment of a local service sector. In addition, the seniors who have moved into the community represent a form of basic sector economic activity and have spurred the local economy through spending in stores and on services.

As early as 2000, Western Canadian Coal Corporation was exploring properties between the Quintette and Bullmoose sites (Vancouver Sun 2001). By 2004, reserves were proven, and the development process for a new mine was well underway (Prince George Citizen 2004; Tumbler Ridge News 2004). In 2003-2004, Duke Energy undertook a series of oil and gas pipeline and processing plant expansions and upgrades in the Tumbler Ridge area (National Post 2003). Both projects build on the provincial government's resource expansion policies, much as had been the case with each successive provincial government for the previous fifty years. Today, several coal, gas, and other resource initiatives are active in the Tumbler Ridge area.

The lessons of recent history are not lost on the Tumbler Ridge leadership. With the opening of new mines around the community, the approach of the town council has been to welcome these industries while at the same time recognizing that the community does not want to go back to single-industry dependence. In addition to coal mining, local economic development work has attracted forestry and forest-product processing, oil and gas support industries, and some significant investment in new hotels.

The work of the town council is aided by an array of civil society groups. Just as these community groups supported the development of Tumbler Ridge's Transition Plan, so too, are they playing a role in supporting a diversified economy. Included among these groups are the local Bed and Breakfast Association, Tourism Co-operative, and the Dinosaur Museum Society, together with existing naturalist, outdoor recreationalist, and environmental groups. All of these groups are working on small-scale diversification away from resource dependence.

From Development of Supply to Development of Demand

The concept of competitive advantage resonates with the people and planners in northern BC, who clearly understand the nature of the fast-paced and shifting global economy. The attractiveness of the concept appears to be part "fad" and part realization that the three decades of decline of the region (despite the continued wealth of resource extraction and more recent boom facilitated by the demand for oil and gas) calls for new approaches to building the northern economy and its communities. A closer examination of the concept, and its application and significance to the north, is needed. Moreover, the initial enthusiasm fostered by a greater awareness of competitiveness requires long-term, and structurally significant, responses and investments at all levels. The following thoughts related to these issues are organized into two areas: conceptualizations of competitiveness and the approach to planning for the transition from comparative to competitive advantage.

First, perhaps the most damaging aspect of the fadlike interpretation of competitiveness is that it borrows recommendations drawn mainly from urban areas. This often results in a misapplication of programs and skews both political and public expectations. We witnessed this most dramatically with the cut-and-paste recommendations advocating for a supply-side approach to fostering regional competitiveness in an attempt to attract both people and investment to the north. This entails providing general infrastructure and services that would be appealing to businesses and residents. There are very real attraction assets in the north. Yet, a deeper analysis of how to implement a supply-side approach, and who benefits from such investments, never properly accompanies such blanket statements. These recommendations play on the nostalgia for the aggressive investment of the 1950s and 1960s, without acknowledging how restructuring has fundamentally changed both the economic and social environments in the north.

The application, or misapplication, of development notions from urban settings is especially problematic for rural and small-town places. There is no universal definition of "rural" or "small-town" in the research literature; however, there is consensus that definitional frameworks must be appropriate to the national and research context in question (du Plessis et al. 2004). In the resource periphery of northern BC, for thirty years, the advancement of resource development based on comparative advantage has been confronting in a very uncomfortable way the restructuring imposed by a transition to a competitive global economy framework. Small towns with populations between 5,000 and 20,000 people, and rural areas whose populations often number less than 1,000, have limited human and economic resources on which to draw when working to understand and react to this transition. Coupled with the legacy of a staples economy in which nonlocal firms control access to most of the land base and economic infrastructure, coping with the transition is even more problematic. The development and deployment of social capital may support embeddedness and a commitment to place by residents as well as community and business leaders. Strong social capital has long been a defining element of rural and small-town communities and, as noted above, it does seem to have supported both local responses and a wider sense that the region must take greater charge of its destiny within the global economy. The local linkages and levels of trust effective in supporting quality of life at the community level are now increasingly recognized as important at the regional level as northerners realize that similar pressures affect all of their rural and small-town places, and through collective mutual support they can more successfully address such pressures.

Rural and small-town areas like northern BC can benefit from an adaptation of the supply-side model (e.g., thinking about new infrastructure), but nonmetropolitan areas must act much more intentionally to mesh supply-side investments with a realistic assessment of capacity. This is not to say that advocates of the supply-side approach in urban areas are calling for random investment; but the elasticity to absorb investments is much greater in metropolitan regions. If planners adopt similar approaches in nonmetropolitan environments, communities and regions risk prospects of an ever-declining net return or, at worst, bankruptcy (think of a multiplex recreation complex that is too large for the community and not attracting external demand). With limited financial resources, and with increasing investment needs across the range of human, community, economic, and communications infrastructure, a careful and realistic regional assessment of current and future capacities and needs must be built from a cooperative base that recognizes mutual interests and interdependencies.

Competitive investments geared towards regional growth in northern BC will require even greater analytical capacity. Rural communities and regions must place more emphasis on the demand side of development (i.e., thinking about their specific assets of place and culture that will draw residents and businesses and about targeting local production to meet a specific market demand). This will ensure a greater likelihood of project success, and importantly, draw attention to whether and how the benefits of new investments accrue to the people and the region. Ultimately, the demand-side approach cautions northern developers through a rural adaptation of the common expression that might read something like this: "if you build it, they still might not come." Enthusiasm is present in terms of embracing a new competitive mindset. There needs to be a corresponding shift in not confusing or grafting the development benefits associated with traditional comparative patterns of development to a new competitive environment.

A second observation drawn from our research concerns the planning models we witnessed throughout northern BC. If a region is to switch the emphasis of its approach to community and economic development, the planning process must respond accordingly. Regional development in northern BC would benefit from two process-oriented considerations. First, attention to northern capacity requires more than simply mention of the problem. There are deeper levels of the complicated problem of community and regional capacity analysis that would greatly benefit processes of regional planning. There is a need for exploring different models of capacity assessment in specific settings across the north. This finer-grain analytical complement to the "big picture" perspective requires governments to extend beyond the usual parameters associated with funds allocated for economic renewal. Long-run capacity assessment and analysis cannot be separated from long-run support for capacity building and development. As one economic development participant suggested, there is usually only enough funding to get to the next report; this needs to change.

Next, planning must start with the aspirations of the people of the north. It is no longer enough to simply include weak accommodations for consulting northerners as a small part of an externally developed and managed process. This shift in favour of a different underlying philosophy (that reprioritizes the role of northerners) will ultimately embrace what all recognize as the greatest competitive advantage in the north: its people. A secondary advantage associated with this philosophical shift is that the gap between regional aspirations and the region's ability to control the levers of development will become more apparent. As noted above, with respect to governance and government, it makes little sense and has little long-term value to download regional development planning and responsibility without similarly downloading the appropriate tools, resources, and authority to follow though on plans. Economic development priorities and strategies developed for rural and remote regions that continue to hinge on the decisions of distant and urban political and bureaucratic elites are likely to fail (House 1999).

Closing: Context and Competitive Advantage

The shift from comparative interpretations of development to competitive advantage in the north is a complex problem for a complex region. This chapter has applied a rural lens to explore the regional development literature and its renewed interest in competitive advantage as a tool for regional rejuvenation. It has also explored the relevance and meaning of competitive advantage in the nonmetropolitan setting of northern BC. The findings suggest that the application and execution of a regional development approach based on competitive advantage is hampered by a poorly formed understanding of the core terms and consequences that come from policy decisions focused on promoting regional "bottom-up" strategies. To execute competitive advantage-based development, rural and small-town regions must first have the conviction, tools, resources, and authority to create and execute appropriate strategies. This means knowing not only the context of the global economy and the opportunities it creates, but knowing the context of the assets and aspirations of the place, of the region, itself. Contextually demanding analysis and planning certainly does not seem as sexy as pumped-up exhortations of competitiveness. Ultimately, however, this is where a more sincere and practical strategy for northern development lies. In the next chapter, we present conceptual and practical tools that can assist the process of designing and supporting place-based development from both bottom-up and top-down perspectives.

8
Mobilizing for Change

> It started as the dream of a growing northern mill town determined to be more than a place known for long, cold winters and world-class bar-room brawls. Sixteen thousand people paid $5 each to sign a petition in 1988 and 1989 demanding a university. The campaign was energized in 1989 by a story in *The Globe and Mail* quoting Stan Hagen, then B.C. Minister of Advanced Education, who waved a red flag in front of the northern bull. "In the Interior," he said, "people don't think of education beyond Grade 12. The questions they ask at the end of the day are, 'How many trees did you cut today?' or 'How were things down in the mine?'" ... Within two months, the government in Victoria announced that plans were under way for a new university for the Interior with its campus at Prince George, the geographical centre of the province. (McInnes 1995: D3)

Establishing a place-based competitive economy requires the progressive action and coordination of both top-down and bottom-up actors and institutions (see Woods 2007; Masuda and Garvin 2008). In previous chapters, we presented two obstacles to development associated with each of these approaches that are inhibiting the capacity of northern BC to make an effective transition to a place-based economy. From the top-down perspective, the relative abandonment of rural communities by senior levels of government has removed essential capacity from the north and neglected the necessity of ongoing investment in community infrastructure. Communities and regions, meanwhile, are often "stuck in the middle" in their attempts to apply quick-fix solutions and outdated economic development methods to the increasing demands of a new and quickly evolving global economy. Reconciling these deficits requires coordinated and appropriate responses from both the top down and the bottom up.

This chapter presents select conceptual and practical tools that help to address development challenges in the north. We begin with a discussion of governance, a concept that helps to mediate top-down and bottom-up relations and responsibilities within a new economy. We then present specific observations and findings related to top-down and bottom-up action within the context of regional development. Although they are not without criticism, new approaches to regional research are seeking to recover from the poorly conceived and poorly coordinated top-down, uniform, regional development programs in Canada in the period after the Second World War. Regional dynamics of governance and competitiveness represent major themes in a resurgence of the regional approach to community and economic development. We include in these discussions examples from other jurisdictions and select cases from northern BC where places appear to be "getting it right." In this chapter, we begin to address questions about whether it is possible to construct a place-based economy in northern locales, setting the stage for our own recommendations for how best to facilitate place-based development in northern BC.

Governance: Reconciling the Top-Down and Bottom-Up Relationship

Governance refers to a shift in state function from control and direction of economic and social programs to the facilitation of these programs through coordinated partnerships with nonstate actors – inclusive of, for example, nongovernmental organizations and the business sector (Murdoch and Abram 1998). Governing through collaborative mechanisms, which represent a plurality of interests, involves new lines of authority and a redistribution of responsibility for traditional state roles (Douglas 2005). This creates new opportunities for place-based development, as local actors and institutions may exert more influence over the decisions that affect their communities and regions, and support the implementation of more effective place-sensitive actions. Equally, the specific dynamics of a more collaborative governance structure may create challenges, given the variable capacity of different places to participate or fill gaps.

The ideological and structural origins of the governance approach are in a variety of themes. First, Marsden and Murdoch (1998) point to the trend of fiscal restraint by senior governments that have inhibited their capacity to govern national spaces in an all-inclusive manner. Central governments require new mechanisms to facilitate strategic priorities and, from a less cynical perspective, ensure the maintenance of certain standards of program delivery. Second, processes of industrial restructuring that have replaced Fordist models of production with flexible and entrepreneurial alternatives have dramatically influenced regulatory structures (Woods 1998). This puts pressure on government functions to be "run like a business," which can constrain the democratic roles and processes established through a traditional state structure. Third, experiences with top-down (only) regional development efforts in the 1970s were ineffective due to their divorce from the local context. Finally, and within a rural context, the increasing demands on rural space (resource extraction, amenity values, claims to traditional territories, etc.) necessitate the inclusion of new voices and interests within decision-making processes (Hudson 2005).

Not surprisingly, the specific impacts associated with the transition to governance in rural areas are varied. Positive dimensions of a more collaborative approach to governing include the sharing of resources and perspectives, the development of new and innovative partnerships, and the inclusion of a greater variety of interests, opinions, and sources of information (Douglas 2005). The shift to rural/regional governance includes a repositioning of the importance of local government. Local government is the main institutional player within a place-based approach to governing, and it must adapt from being primarily a provider of local services to taking on much more dynamic roles as the coordinator of local representation and advocacy (Woods 1998). Two of Canada's leading local government experts have made this point. Tindal and Nobes-Tindal (2004: 371) argue that local government "must be recognized as a political mechanism for expressing and responding to the collective concerns of members of the community." Positing local governments as an "extension of the community," with a primary "concern for the problems and issues faced" by the community, they emphasized how local governments must now be more "strategic and selective" in their work, strive to "develop community responsibility" for their problems and solutions, and "use their limited resources wisely" (372).

From a progressive perspective, such a transition may enhance access to the democratic process in rural areas. All of these advantages speak to a contextualization of governance and decision-making processes that fit well with the transition to a place-based approach to community development.

Enthusiasm for governance must be tempered, however, with the observation that while enhanced collaborative capacity may be the desired outcome, a variety of negative outcomes identified in the literature may occur given the capacity limitations of rural and small-town places. The transaction costs associated with the collaborative process may simply create an environment of uncertainty that undermines the social and economic investment foundation of rural places (Markey 2005). For example, Kearney et al. (1994: 21) argue that there must "be a shared desire to work towards common objectives, a high level of mutual trust, a willingness to cooperate, share responsibility, accept accountability, and where necessary to alter the prevailing administrative structures." This clearly sets a high standard for collaborative processes. Local conflicts, and the transition to new and more fluid forms of leadership, in fact, might inhibit the ability of communities to make decisions and adapt to the shifting dynamics of the economy. That no one actor has the necessary resources and capacity to respond to multidimensional challenges and opportunities in the new economy may become a source of strength by creating a flexible network of agencies (Scott 2004). However, in a rural environment where the combined resources of local actors may not be enough to achieve the critical mass necessary to maintain services and adapt on a continuous basis, governance may become more symbolic of government abandonment than local empowerment.

Despite the messiness and variability associated with governance in rural areas, state and economic restructuring have essentially forced the adoption of such structures. The challenge for both top-down and bottom-up actors is how to design, implement, and manage the mechanisms of governance that will maximize the positive externalities of collaboration without burning out the players or processes. Here, researchers and policy makers have been seeking to translate the principles of governance into appropriate scales of implementation. For rural and small-town places with limited capacities, working together as regions can be a viable governance option.

Northerners take to the general idea that economic development in the north is very much a socially embedded process. Northerners recognize that their strong social bonds – historically embedded in northern culture by virtue of a more rugged and remote existence that demands greater levels of cooperation – play an important role in the northern economy. In northern BC, the social and the economic are intimately linked. These local characterizations of the northern economy easily relate to concepts within the new regionalist literature; concepts such as the "associational economy," the role of social capital in development, and regional "relational assets" referred to earlier (Storper 1997, 1999; Cooke and Morgan 1998; Scott 1998; MacLeod 2001b). All of these concepts speak to a transformed understanding of governance and competitive advantage that is shifting traditional concepts of government and comparative advantage that established northern BC's social and economic foundations. Northerners know that they need to work together, and regionalism provides a vehicle for organizing such action and mediating bottom-up and top-down relations with governments and economic forces.

Bottom Up: Mobilizing the Community Foundation

Effective regional development demands the active participation, if not leadership, of bottom-up community development participants. Considering the extent of the frustration directed by northerners towards past regional development approaches, we were surprised that our findings have revealed strong sentiments and a willingness to pursue renewed regional efforts.[1] Our northern BC research illustrates that communities increasingly feel that they are "on their own." This was not only reiterated through a profound sense of abandonment expressed in various interviews and roundtables, but was also reflected when northerners spoke of a need for better policy coordination between the various levels of government – a sentiment clearly supported by the literature (Pezzini 2000; Drabenstott and Sheaff 2002a, 2002b; Douglas 2003). Despite open awareness of the need for better government support and coordination, the feeling of abandonment by, and frustration with, shifting and uncoordinated policy serves as a catalyst for sentiments in support of "made in the north" solutions. Communities generally feel misunderstood and ill-served by senior governments, which, in turn, lends currency to bottom-up approaches to development. People argued:

> A northern vision and strategy must be built from the bottom up by northerners.
>
> We must determine our own destiny which will involve taking power from other places.
>
> To move a northern vision forward, public policy development needs a northern voice so that it is workable in the north.

This demand for more bottom-up control, however, presents new challenges for northern capacity. In previous chapters, we reviewed specific problems associated with local development such as being "stuck in the middle" and of broader competitive barriers that pose challenges to local control and reinvestment. In the following section, we examine how a regionalist approach may help to address some of these development shortcomings so that the north can play a more proactive role in creating a place-based economy. Adopting a regionalist perspective may assist development in the north by (1) contextualizing the development process; (2) addressing issues associated with the capacity deficit in the north, for both governance and development; and (3) fostering and mobilizing intercommunity and interregional cooperation.

First, adopting a regionalist approach helps to contextualize the development process. This is by no means an automatic outcome. However, a regional focus may provide an inward perspective as actors consider regional assets and the compatibility of different strategies with local conditions. Our research reveals that this local focus manifests itself in two fundamental ways in the north: awareness of regional resources and attention to the local economy. As demonstrated, northern BC is a significant player in the provincial economy. The global demand for resources that are primarily situated in the north is driving provincial economic fortunes. Given the importance of resources, issues of resource management, and the control and flow of resource wealth are always popular topics in interviews and regional roundtables throughout the north. Participants spoke forcefully about the need to reverse trends that have seen a net outflow of economic wealth from the north and said, for example:

> Northern revenues should flow back to the north.
>
> Government needs to recognize the role resources play in driving the economy of BC and should return some of the revenues to local communities.
>
> We need to keep our revenues in the north – not just flow them back through government programs.

People spoke about the need not only to create more local economic opportunity, but also to keep more of the wealth generated by those opportunities in northern BC. They want a greater share of economic wealth to stay in the north rather than being recirculated back to rural and small-town communities through government channels (Lee 2003; Synergy Management Group 2003). The example of the Town of Mackenzie illustrates community sentiments in the north regarding the ownership of resources and a reorientation of both corporate and government attention concerning the use of resources.

Greater contextual awareness in the development process provides additional benefits to the development process by bringing attention to the subtleties of opportunity within the local economy. Traditional local economic development approaches of place marketing and attracting and enticing industry are the favoured, if not only, approaches to building community economies. Our research reveals that people in the north recognize the importance of making the region attractive to industry in order to bring both business and people to the region. However, they also told us that the existing local economy of the region, and the people supported by it, represent significant latent community and economic development opportunities. Besides looking to attract new business and industry, people reminded us that communities in the north must look to support and grow local businesses and local opportunities.

Local entrepreneurs, and the businesses and industries they run, often have a proven record of commitment to their communities and region. As such, the local economies of the region represent a relatively untapped resource of economic development skills, capacity, and knowledge that directly sustain the economy and society of the region – people and businesses committed to the region and committed to staying in the region.

The participatory aspects of regionalist structures may assist with building rural capacity for governance. A regional approach provides a space for inclusion that helps to identify collective interests that may then contribute to development processes. If the off-loading and budget cuts of central governments have strained the capacity of local institutions (both governmental

▼

TOWN OF MACKENZIE: SAVE OUR COMMUNITY RESOLUTIONS

In 2008, with its forest industry idled as firms drew their timber from areas in BC's Cariboo affected by the mountain pine beetle, the Town of Mackenzie held a civic "Save Our Community Rally" on 23 May. The resolutions coming from that rally speak to many of the issues raised in the transition from a space-based to a place-based economy that would build northern BC's communities. These resolutions included the following:

- Establish forest policies that will tie logs to the community. Logs must be processed in the communities where they are harvested.
- Ban raw log exports. Get more value and more jobs out of the forest resource.
- Northern and rural communities, such as Mackenzie and Fort St. James, have made huge economic contributions to government coffers, paying for their infrastructure many times over. Provincial and federal governments should recognize this contribution by ensuring that infrastructure (e.g., health, education, social services, road maintenance, and other services) is maintained at pre-mill closure levels while communities work to overcome current economic and social challenges.
- Ensure that forest companies reinvest substantially in their operations. Incentives must be in place to reward those companies, whether primary or secondary producers, that invest in more diversified and value-added production.
- Increase funding for training and retraining workers, employees, contractors, and others who have been displaced by the severe downturn in the forest industry.
- Make comprehensive reforestation and silviculture a top priority. Develop a reforestation strategy and increase funding substantially.
- Ensure secure access to timber for value-added production, as well as small and medium companies, cooperatives, and nonprofits. Encourage more community forests.
- Ensure sustainable and scientific harvesting practices that maintain mid- and long-term supply of trees, and a healthy environment, as well as minimize waste.
- Too many important decisions about forest policy, diversification, tenure, and management are made far away in Victoria or in corporate boardrooms in Vancouver, Toronto, and New York City. Workers, employees, contractors, service providers, municipalities, and northern and rural communities as a whole, need more input into and control over how the forest resource is utilized and developed. (Hoekstra 2008)

and nongovernmental) to act independently, regionalism provides a framework through which collective capacity may mobilize for common objectives. Within a specific place or region, this collective effort may transform itself into an institutional actor (implying both scale and resiliency) that can replace the stability previously associated with more traditional government control and responsibility. The importance of a collaborative approach to rural and small-town renewal resonates in the structure and contents of a

BEETLE ACTION COALITIONS: REGIONAL INITIATIVE

Cariboo-Chilcotin communities facing the devastation of the mountain pine beetle (MPB), have created an opportunity to exercise resiliency through a regional approach to cooperation. As a result of the Cariboo-Chilcotin effort, regional beetle action coalitions have emerged in partnership with the provincial government to create community-based plans for renewal.

In June 2005, communities of the Cariboo-Chilcotin Beetle Action Coalition (CCBAC) leveraged the benefit of regionalism, learned in earlier land use planning processes, and designed a model of intergovernmental cooperation to adapt to the challenges and opportunities facing their forestry-dependent communities. The CCBAC is governed by a regional board of volunteer directors composed of elected officials and citizens from participating communities. This includes the mayors of Quesnel, Williams Lake, Wells, and 100 Mile House; a member from each of the three First Nations language groups (Shuswap, Chilcotin, and South Carrier); a director from the Cariboo Regional District; and the chairpersons from the Cariboo-Chilcotin Conservation Society and the Cariboo Licenses Land Use Strategy Committee (CCBAC 2005).

The CCBAC model of regional collaboration, and their proposal for the development of a Pine Beetle Trust Fund to assist with long-term transition, showed how communities can lead senior levels of governments to find solutions for common challenges. The "regional coalition plus government" was designed to be potentially transferable to other regions. In September 2005, a second coalition emerged in what would eventually cover the region between Smithers and Valemount: the Omineca Beetle Action Coalition (OBAC 2007). And in April 2007, a third coalition called the Southern Interior Beetle Action Coalition was established (SIBAC 2011). All three coalitions have received funding from senior levels of government to create regional partnerships to address the impacts that the MPB will have in their regions.

The CCBAC business plan outlined a series of commitments to the communities in the region to assist government to measure the impact of the MPB on their recent Canadian textbook on rural planning. *Rural Planning and Development in Canada* (Douglas 2010) has four sections: livelihoods, policy and governance, life spaces and places, and community development. Individual contributors all speak to the complexity of rural and small-town places and the embeddedness of change in both local and global processes. Community and regional approaches repeatedly appear as the most suitable options for transition planning, action, and investments.

local economies, commitments to regional inclusion and participation; transparent and fair governance; and working with other levels of government to identify solutions to community economic challenges.

The board of directors is supported by a number of advisers, including economic development officers from the participating communities, economic and social sector representatives, and industry and provincial government representatives. Projects were undertaken at a committee level, and advisory and working committees were struck to plan for specific strategic directions and specific activities.

Common issues have united communities, enabling the CCBAC to build on the social capital created through developing a regional partnership. CCBAC is about the people, the communities, and the future of the Cariboo-Chilcotin. The CCBAC mission is to create a community-based coalition that will work with government regarding the MPB epidemic and ensure that the communities are economically stable, that there are jobs in all sectors, and that support is there for the entrepreneurial spirit within the Cariboo-Chilcotin (OBAC 2007: 3).

The coalition identified the following four main themes for economic investment:

1 land base for nontimber uses
2 telecommunications, transportation, sewer and water systems, recreation
3 education and training for displaced workers
4 business attraction and development.

A series of strategies were developed to guide these investments. The CCBAC experience has been influential in developing a model that has moved the conversation out of the boardrooms of provincial and industry leaders, into the community centres of the people directly affected by the changes in their local economies.

The participatory process implied by a governance framework, when merged with the scale and place of regionalism, helps to facilitate a sense of "institutional thickness" within local actors and agencies that will enhance the capacity and resiliency of a community or region to adapt to change (Parkins 2008; Markey 2005). Institutional thickness supports a high level of interaction between regional agencies, fostering a mutual awareness of being involved in a common project. Once this common project focus is

COMMUNITY AND REGIONAL COLLABORATION

The Rural Development Institute (RDI) at Brandon University has conducted a number of projects related to regional and community collaboration. Drawing on earlier work with community-based processes in Manitoba and Nunavut, the RDI created a "vision and model for the community collaboration project: *Empowering Communities and Building Capacity 2005 to 2008*" (Beattie and Annis 2008: 5). That larger project included eighty-five communities organized into six regional roundtables. A recent major report described their key findings.

The purpose of the collaboration projects was to explore the portability of lessons learned through community and regional dialogue and partnerships. Key findings from the project focused on the following five topics.

Organization
The projects recognized that "regional roundtables need to develop organizational infrastructures to be sustainable over the long term. They need visions, goals, and objectives, which should be revisited from time to time and revised as needed ... There should be clearly defined roles and expectations for the executive and for those who carry out the coordination and administrative functions" (Beattie and Annis 2008: 6).

Communication
The projects recognized that communication plays a critical role in supporting the work of roundtables and helps to avoid potential problems and tensions during the process of negotiating relationships. Communication needs to be ongoing and multifaceted.

Policy Support
A third critical lesson was about the importance of government "buy-in." This was especially important given the crucial policy levers that senior levels of government possess.

established, a variety of positive externalities flow to the governance regime, including the dissemination of community knowledge, increased flexibility, increased innovative capacity, and the rise of new leaders and different leadership styles (Amin and Thrift 1994).

A second capacity benefit attributed to regionalism includes the potential to pool resources to address the limitations of individual communities. This benefit is associated with all regional contexts; however, service delivery and

Financial Support

The projects recognized that "governments need to see that investing in community development processes is an appropriate use of public funds. Governments need to move from funding deliverables to supporting capacity development" (Beattie and Annis 2008: 7).

As well, collaborative processes must be adequately resourced for the long term in order to support not only the foundational work of creating effective working relationships and structures, but also for action and the ongoing dialogue that can benefit from these types of collaborations.

Time

The projects recognized that "developing trust and valued relationships and partnerships within and between communities, governments, and academic institutions took persistence, deliberate effort, time, resources, and committed skilled and sustained leadership" (Beattie and Annis 2008: 8).

We have argued in this book that regional collaborative processes take time, support, and resources in order to build suitable relationships and partnerships. In supporting our argument that community development is a crucial foundation for economic development, these cases highlight the critical role that community development plays in supporting place-based renewal.

Beattie and Annis (2008: 103-4) complete their review by identifying a series of considerations for further policy development in support of community and regional collaborative processes. Critical recommendations include the following:

- Communities need to work with their neighbours in a collaborative strategy for the region.
- Governments need to support capacity development.
- Governments need to invest in community development processes.
- Governments need to work better across government departments, and across governments.

infrastructure development in more remote and sparsely populated rural areas can be a particular challenge. Within the rural setting, regionalization may allow for the continuity of basic services such as education, health care, and emergency services – albeit with the potential that distance to services may affect some communities more than others. Similarly, various infrastructure projects are inherently regional in nature, such as landfills, transportation, and recreation facilities. Here a regional approach offers a number of advantages, including economies of scale for construction and cost efficiencies in operation and maintenance.

One of the best examples in northern BC of communities coming together to achieve an improvement in services is the new hospital at the north end of Graham Island on Haida Gwaii. For years, the communities of Masset, Old Massett, Port Clements, and the area's rural residents endured declining

16/97 ECONOMIC ALLIANCE: BOTTOM-UP REGIONAL COOPERATION

The 16/97 Economic Alliance is a regional economic development partnership between local and regional economic development agencies with mandates to improve the economy of north central BC. This region includes the Fraser-George Regional District, the Stuart-Nechako portion of the Bulkley-Nechako Regional District, and the northern portion of the Cariboo Regional District. This region, drawing its name from the transportation corridors of highways 16 and 97, was identified by the group as "a natural economic region" providing resources, energy, water, transportation, labour force, education and health services, supporting businesses, and the services and public infrastructure needed for economic growth (16/97 Economic Alliance 2007). The 16/97 Economic Alliance is composed of government, nongovernmental economic development organizations, and postsecondary educational institutions with similar or complementary mandates to enhance regional economic development.

Participant organizations pay an annual fee, and each organization designates staff members to participate in the Economic Alliance's committees, task forces, and teams. The development of the Economic Alliance was also funded through in-kind contributions from the partner organizations and support from the Ministry of Economic Development.

The 16/97 Economic Alliance is governed by a management committee composed of representatives from the member organizations. The *Working Together – Expanding Our Economies* business plan outlines that the management committee will be composed of the following (16/97 Economic Alliance 2007: 45): two representatives from the private sector, two representatives from First Nations or Aboriginal organizations, one representative from a regional district, health care facilities – including the hospital on the former Canadian Forces Base Masset site. Competition, rather than cooperation between communities, led to the impasses. The federal role in governing the Old Massett Indian reserve lands further exacerbated the challenge of collaboration. When the communities came together, and argued for a collective solution to their communities' needs, their new common purpose proved so powerful that a new state-of-the-art health centre opened in 2009.

The ability of communities to work together – to achieve the institutional thickness required to realize regional advantage – is entirely dependent on the third variable: cooperation (Terluin 2003). Regionalism, as an extension of governance, requires the active collaboration of both governmental and nongovernmental actors. In a context such as northern BC, where there is no particularly ingrained history of cooperation between neighbouring

three representatives from municipalities or regional districts, three representatives from regional or business associations, and at least one representative from training and educational institutions.

The regional economic alliance concept focuses on assisting economic development practitioners and improving the effectiveness of economic and business development activities in the region. As the Alliance has grown, the partner agencies have identified synergies in their efforts and have brought individual projects in line with the interests of other organizations. The alliance is to be "a pragmatic organization managed by 'on the ground' economic development officials seeking to identify and implement high priority, broad regional action through collaboration with local, regional and other groups" (16/97 Economic Alliance 2007: 2). This includes working closely with other regional organizations such as the Omineca Beetle Action Coalition, the Cariboo-Chilcotin Beetle Action Coalition, the First Nations Mountain Pine Beetle Working Group, the Northern Development Initiative Trust, the Nechako-Kitamaat Development Fund, and other municipal, regional, and community economic development agencies.

The 16/97 Economic Alliance (2007) published an *Industry Cluster Report*. The report identifies industry clusters that will be the focus of the development and implementation of regional economic cluster plans, directed at increasing jobs and investment through sustainable growth and diversification of the economy. From this report, a mining cluster study was completed and this led to the creation of a Northern Interior Mining Group. In addition, the Alliance has implemented benchmarking, "green" energy, and networking studies. See http://1697alliance.com (16/97 Economic Alliance 2007b).

communities, this can be a significant hurdle. Equally challenging is the weak structure of regional government in BC, which lacks the structural mechanisms to facilitate regional cooperation. The 16-97 Economic Alliance and the Beetle Action Coalition are examples of regionalist initiatives in northern BC that are seeking to overcome these structural barriers and facilitate regional collaboration.

The emerging regional research, and the policy it has inspired, has been criticized in the literature for being overly optimistic and lacking in empirical evidence to support claims of benefits (Lovering 1999). While we have illustrated specific aspects of the regionalist approach, using examples from the north, it is not a cure-all response to what are often entrenched structural barriers. In northern BC, two of the major barriers to achieving a progressive regional agenda are the continued pressure to preserve industrial resource jobs and the growth-oriented approach that too often drives local economic development processes. Each of these barriers reflects the "momentum" of the past, the resiliency of the status quo, and the inability of some institutions to adapt to new models.

First, the desire for long-term sustainable development is often challenged by the competing time frame associated with immediate employment needs versus long-term management needs. The consequences of local job losses, for example, through a sudden plant or industry closure, are immediate and often accompanied by loud and impassioned local calls for assistance and intervention from senior levels of government. In our interviews and roundtables, such urgency was underscored by the participation of civic and economic development organizations.

As an illustration of such immediate employment needs, the economic downturn of the 1990s across northern BC was accompanied by a significant outflow of population. This out-migration comprised largely young families in search of alternative work opportunities (Halseth et al. 2004). More generally, Clapp (1998) notes how resource industry communities facing the prospect of job losses will take an optimistic view of the resource base and push for continued (even expanded) exploitation despite impending collapse. In Canada, the collapse of the east coast cod fishery and the significant closures experienced by the west coast salmon fishery reinforce the negative consequences of placing immediate pressures for jobs and income and/or local taxes over long-term resource management.

Our research examines various dimensions of the tension between environment and employment. In some cases, calls for local control of benefits were framed around notions that corporate profits and government royalties too often took precedence over local jobs and that pushes for greater competitiveness are achieved through job rationalization. People argued that local control of benefits could then be directed to enhancing local employment. However, in many such cases, these calls were explicitly tied to creating more resource industry jobs rather than building towards a diversified economic strength by supporting new economic sectors and/or options. People told us:

> Resource job losses in small towns often mean that people must move in order to support their households. This means that there is no latent labour pool available to take up new options in a diversifying economy of small industries.
>
> We have to recognize that nonindustry jobs are not part of smaller communities; smaller communities don't devalue lower paying jobs, it's just that you need a larger industrial base to support these types of jobs, and there are always only a handful of them available.

Halseth (2005) argues that while small towns across northern BC generally remain open to alternative revitalization ideas, their actions more often reflect a commitment to continued or renewed resource extraction and export. This may fit with the geographic imagination of a community as a mill or mine town; nevertheless, it continues to leave places highly vulnerable under a restructured global resource economy. The concerns pressed by sudden resource job losses will continue to interfere in a vicious cycle with efforts for more long-term, stable, and even sustainable, economic development.

Second, in Canada certainly, an emphasis on the economic side of local development planning has resulted in the creation of a substantial suite of government, private sector, and voluntary supports for new firms and entrepreneurs (Bruce and Lister 2001). Many of these economic development supports function at local and regional levels and cover many of the pressure areas experienced by small and large businesses alike. This can include economic and business support and training services, as well as assistance in accessing capital and business advice. The approach is generally to support economic growth with the expectation that increases in jobs and the circulation of capital will spur increases in community quality of life.

There are, however, a number of challenges with a "growth approach" in the north. One challenge involves the delivery and coordination of appropriate economic development support. People reported that while many supports exist, they suffer from inefficiency and a lack of coordination (MacKinnon 2002). They pointed out how some programs seemed to repeat what other programs were doing, how programs that are supposed to be working in concert are often more disjointed than coordinated, and how programs lack stability or longevity. They said:

> It will be important not to duplicate efforts. There is a need for overall coordination between different levels of government and different levels of economic development organizations.

> There needs to be coordination of economic development programs and policies. These processes need to be tied together to allow for more effective outcomes.

Second, Mulkey and Murphy (2002) describe the importance of combining community capacity with appropriate economic resources. Too often, however, the growth approach to regional economic development does not adequately address the question of social development. Evidence from recent booms shows significant social costs, service and infrastructure deficits, and a failure to extract all of the available economic benefit.

Rural and small-town lifestyles are central to both social and economic development, and both suffer without investment in the community and services base. Unfortunately, access to a range of community services, including health care and education, has been decreasing due to closures, regionalization, underinvestment, and other cost reduction strategies (UNBC 2003; Halseth and Halseth 2004). Businesses, industries, and northern residents argued passionately that we must not ignore the need to provide community infrastructure to support community economic development. Adequate health care facilities, access to quality education, cultural opportunities, and recreation facilities (in addition to "connecting" infrastructure such as road, rail, air transportation, and other communications technologies) were all felt necessary to support a robust community foundation to recruit and retain people and economic activity. Northerners recognize, however, that control over these supports is often external to the region bearing the pressures of change. They noted how

> it will be important that an independent institution be identified to implement a northern strategy. One of the failures with past efforts was that such institutions either became too political or were dismissed following a change in public policy direction.

People spoke very clearly about how community and economic development are linked and how both are crucial to the future welfare of the region. Too often in the north, however, a growth-oriented approach undervalues the need for regional investment, thereby transferring costs and challenges to the future in an unplanned way.

Top Down: Facilitating Effective Intervention

Since the recession in the early 1980s, government policy towards community intervention has shifted from a direct role in sectoral and infrastructure investment towards person-based policies. This is entirely consistent with the restructuring effects of a neoliberal policy orientation as described earlier. The approach reallocates and downgrades intervention towards supporting individual responsibility and entrepreneurialism. This individual focus emphasizes programs such as job training (and retraining), entrepreneurial development, and relocation assistance, among others.

There are three main factors associated with this policy shift. First, individually oriented policies are significantly less expensive to implement. Minimal investments in training programs maintain a government presence in the development process but represent a fraction of the budgetary commitments associated with larger infrastructure and industrial projects. Given the timing of the policy shift during a recession, cost was a likely motivating force. Second, economists have typically associated policies that aim to create development in particular locations with protectionism (Kraybill and Kilkenny 2003). From a narrow economic perspective, older approaches to regional development policies distort human and business migration decisions, foster dependency, and postpone necessary adjustments in the economy (Partridge 2006):

> Two approaches fuel rural development schemes: restrictions on technology and subsidies to draw people into what would otherwise be low-paying work with no takers. A compassionate society should help those confronted by economic change later in life, but these rural preservation programs typically become a bribe to divert rural young people from the opportunities of youth and trap them in low-skill work, sustained only by other people's money. That creates political vulnerability and dependence. When money runs out or policy changes, folks now in their 40s, 50s, and 60s are trapped, with few skills. Instead of a gradual adjustment to change, communities are devastated overnight. (McMahon 2003)

Third, the migration associated with economic downturns in particular locales may enhance the quality of life of residents, whereas rural intervention programs may be costly and produce uncertain results. Much of the criticism of regional development programs in the period soon after the Second World War, which precipitated the shift to the individual and the market, are entirely justified (Savoie 1992). Regional programs during this period lacked any kind of structural influence, were poorly coordinated between different levels of government, and relied on weak theories of development that were not adequately contextualized to different parts of the country (Markey et al. 2005). Furthermore, the programs were thin on evaluation and tended to measure only narrow economic indicators. Thus, when positive social and economic outcomes did occur, they were not adequately captured and attributed to specific programs.

In the past decade, place-based policies have witnessed a renaissance. From a place-oriented policy perspective, there are clear governance benefits associated with policy and programmatic intervention at the regional level.

First, regions offer a more appropriate scale for action in order to maximize investments in services and infrastructure. Governments can avoid the problems associated with the uniform, or one-size-fits-all, policy approaches of the past by focusing on regions as the scale for implementation. Regions provide sensitivity to local context, while offering economies-of-scale advantages that may realistically accommodate budgetary limitations. Second, unlike past regional programs, new regionalism fosters a sense of shared responsibility between the top-down and bottom-up actors. Regional programs may allow senior governments to set broad policy goals and maintain standards of delivery, while off-loading a share of the responsibility for implementation – and blame, if a particular policy fails to achieve its intended objectives. Regions provide a median between the equity objectives of traditional territorial policies and complete acquiescence to the vagaries of the market.

In support of this position, Douglas (1999: 39) argues "that a 'new' rural region is emerging, and that this reconstituted socio-political framework offers a variety of opportunities as well as significant challenges for the health of rural communities." While his notion of regions is flexible in scope, extending from small rural areas to supranational organizations like the European Union, it does address territories like northern BC where "regional producer groups, cultural interests, various non-governmental organizations, and occasionally local governments [can] form strategic alliances, cooperative structures and other types of associations" (41). Such regional development collaborations are at the intersection of top-down and bottom-up dimensions of action. They involve a wider range of players, especially including civil society groups, and work in horizontal relationships that reach across the jurisdictions and mandates of partners. The motivations behind such regional collaborations are tied not just to global trends of state off-loading and/or downloading, but also to the strong identification of regional ties, histories, and economies that support collaborative dialogue. The actions of collaboration draw on Fuller's (1994) notion of the "arena" society in which rural people now live and interact widely to meet their social, economic, recreational, and environmental goals. The opportunities associated with collaboration and a collective agenda include the additional capacity and potential of combining different people, places, and networks. The challenges include the differential levels of a sense of place and commitment among participants, the additional demands on time and other resources for organizing and managing regional relationships, and the level of community and capacity development among participants that can support their individual contributions and the collective benefit of the collaboration.

A successful regionalist initiative that exemplifies the potential of a co-constructionist approach to facilitating development, in which there are appropriate roles for both senior governments and local and regional actors is the Fair Share Agreement in the Peace River Region.

Regionalism depends on the collaborative interplay between the bottom-up and the top-down actors. In the previous section, we outlined specific bottom-up responsibilities for facilitating development and effective governance. Similarly, we must ask whether there are specific responsibilities that senior governments must assume to make governance work. The answer to this question involves three specific roles: (1) articulating a vision for development across broad jurisdictional space, (2) maintaining a commitment to investment, and (3) ensuring effective policy coordination to mobilize both the vision and investment. We discuss each in the following sections.

Vision

We argued earlier that the WAC Bennett regime was largely responsible for establishing the institutional and policy context that facilitated the emergence of an industrial resource economy in northern BC. Inspired by the comprehensiveness of the Post-War Rehabilitation Council and his own sense of opportunism, WAC Bennett capitalized on postwar growth and provided BC with a "northern vision." The vision was simple and straightforward – create access for large-scale industrial development aimed at the global marketplace in order to transform the province into an integrated social and economic region. The political continuity achieved by the Social Credit party during this period and WAC Bennett's willingness to actively invest in the north played central roles in realizing this vision.

From a research perspective, the central importance of a vision within a regional context speaks to the adoption of a clearly defined strategic approach to community and economic development planning. There are two fundamental contributions provided through the active construction of a vision. The first derives from an understanding of the importance of establishing a shared mindset about future directions (Torjman and Leviten-Reid 2003). Development is a long-term process, and a vision helps to mediate internal tensions and facilitate continuity. Each of these factors helps to avoid policy and programmatic shifts by virtue of changes in government, short-term reactions to market fluctuations, or other events. The role of a vision is to provide a broad guide within which to accommodate change without losing sight of core goals and values, not to "lock-in" communities and regions.

A second contribution is that the importance of place demands a vision constructed with an acute awareness of context. Generic shopping lists of potential development strategies do little to reveal the assets of a particular place and, in fact, may hinder development efforts by creating false expectations and diverting precious resources (Markey et al. 2008b). Including local actors and institutions, in order to appropriately represent context, does not

THE FAIR SHARE AGREEMENT

The Fair Share Agreement (FSA) is a multiyear agreement that reallocates provincial royalties garnered from the oil and gas sector back to the Peace region from which the resources flow. The funds top up municipal budgets to support infrastructure developments and to help mitigate the social and infrastructure impacts associated with the activities of the oil and gas sector. Given the nature of the industry, the region is prone to particularly severe boom and bust patterns of development activity – where both the rapidity of economic cycles and the influx and outflow of the industrial presence present considerable challenges for local and regional planning bodies. The FSA establishes a unique precedent in BC and offers interesting insights into the dynamics and potential of regionalist collaboration and negotiation.

The Peace River Regional District (PRRD) is located in the northeast corner of BC (see Figure 11). The region is 117,761 km^2 in size and is home to 60,743

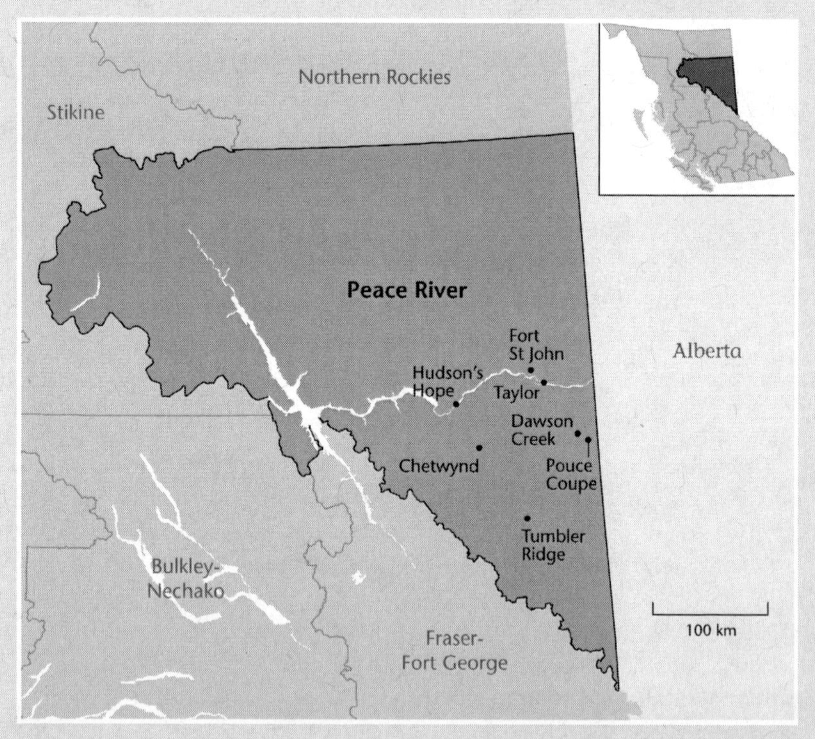

Figure 11 Peace River Regional District, British Columbia. *Source*: BC Stats (2008).

people (in 2008). The main population centres of the region are Fort St. John (18,792) and Dawson Creek (11,420), which are surrounded by a series of smaller rural settlements, including Chetwynd, Hudson's Hope, Pouce Coupe, Taylor, and Tumbler Ridge. Aboriginal peoples represent 12 percent of the regional population (compared with a provincial average of 4 percent) in the following five Aboriginal communities: Blueberry River First Nation, Doig River First Nation, Halfway River First Nation, Moberly Lake West First Nation, Saulteau First Nation. These Nations are part of the Treaty 8 Tribal Association with a mandate to act as a coordinator or facilitator, and to provide technical support on various issues as mandated by the Council of Treaty 8 Tribal Association Chiefs.

Northeastern BC is part of the geologic hydrocarbon-bearing area known as the Western Canada Sedimentary Basin (WCSB). The basin contains the vast majority of oil, gas, and crude bitumen in Canada and is the only current area of BC producing commercial quantities of oil and gas. The sector provided the province with its single largest source of revenue in 2008 ($4.09 billion), creating 34,000 direct and indirect jobs.

Petroleum exploration and development have been active here since the early 1950s; however, the impacts of oil and gas activity began reaching critical levels with the rapid growth in the sector in the early 1990s. This growth has provided considerable economic activity – both direct and indirect – for the region, but it has also exposed significant municipal challenges in terms of service provision, infrastructure stress, and a growing pattern of social ills associated with a highly transient and seasonal workforce.

Impacts

There is a palpable tension in the Peace River region concerning the pros and cons of the oil and gas industry. The economic benefits are obvious in terms of employment opportunities, high wages, strong local spending, and industry contributions to community events and facilities. However, the negative impacts associated with the sector and its operations are highly visible, too, including the following:

- large transient workforce and demands on social services
- demands on regional physical infrastructure, particularly water, energy, and roads
- challenges for local and regional governments to plan for highly variable development fluctuations with uncertain long-term timelines
- general quality-of-life issues for residents, issues associated with industrial activity such as noise, dust, flaring and gas releases from wells, and overall impacts on the cost of living and the affordability of housing.

►

A Regional Response: The Fair Share Agreement

Following the lead of the region's largest municipality, Fort St. John, the region commissioned research to gather information on the oil and gas sector and its impacts on the area. The research reports reviewed case comparisons with other jurisdictions to understand different financial mechanisms and local benefits standards. The reports also outlined the various dimensions of how the industry was affecting the region and the deficiencies of the fiscal imbalance as represented by the existing tax structure (Adams 1992).

During negotiations with the province, it became clear that the government was unwilling to provide the region with any additional taxing authority on the industry. In addition to fears about precedent for other jurisdictions, the province was attempting to position the oil and gas sector to be highly competitive with other producing regions. In 1993, the province recognized the fiscal imbalance facing the region and began negotiations for what would become the Fair Share Agreement. The memorandum of understanding acknowledges that local governments should be compensated for the service and infrastructure costs associated with resource development activities that take place within the region. The original FSA1 provided $4 million to the region ($2 million from a tax on industry and a $2 million provincial grant). The agreement received a positive response from the region, but it became obvious very quickly following the dispersal of funds throughout the region that the agreement was inadequate.

The region pressed for a revised agreement and was met with resistance from the province. It was at this point that the region escalated its position, appearing before the National Energy Board approval process to inform the Board that the region would reject any further developments. The province responded with a $12 million agreement in 1998. This agreement ended early, and FSA3 is currently in place for the period between 2005 and 2020. The current agreement began with a starting contribution of $20 million, with indexing in place to deliver up to $28 million per year (British Columbia, Ministry of Community, Aboriginal and Women's Services 2005).

Specifically, the objective of the agreement is presented as follows: "The objective of this MOU is to address issues respecting parity, responsiveness, local autonomy, accountability, certainty, industrial competitiveness, economic development and regional infrastructure needs while having limited precedent effect with other local governments in British Columbia. In addition the Parties have a mutual interest in ensuring that each local government within the Region has the resources to upgrade, maintain and expand the services and infrastructure necessary to facilitate the economic expansion of the oil, gas, forest and other industries within the Region" (3).

The annual grant is equal to the base year grant of $20 million, multiplied by the rate of change in the rural industrial assessment base between the previous completed taxation year and 2004. The calculation is as follows:

$$\text{Payment} = \$20 \text{ million} \times \frac{\textit{Rural industrial assessment base (previous taxation year)}}{\text{Rural industrial assessment base (2004)}}$$

For communities in the region, the annual grant for 2008 represented a significant contribution to the municipal funding base, roughly doubling taxation receivables. The total $24,954,182 contribution was divided among regional municipalities as follows (there is a separate agreement for regional First Nations):

Examples of transfers made under Fair Share Agreement, 2008

Chetwynd	$1,633,645
Dawson Creek	$8,479,706
Fort St. John	$12,152,470
Hudson's Hope	$582,493
Pouce Coupe	$666,906
Taylor	$535,304
Tumbler Ridge	$903,658
Total	$24,954,182
First Nations	$1,592,821
Total	$26,547,003

The creation of the Fair Share Agreement represents an example of regional collaboration and planning that led to accommodation by senior government – but which maintains ultimate provincial authority. Although the initiative is clearly a boon to the region, interviewees have expressed a number of concerns regarding its long-term sustainability – particularly as it is clear that the impacts associated with the industrial activity are not going away.

necessarily decrease the importance of senior governments. Given that many bottom-up initiatives require the assistance of various state policy levers to come to fruition, it would be unwise to exclude or marginalize the involvement of senior government. As such, visioning must include the dynamic interplay between top-down and bottom-up resources, perspectives, and aspirations. Swyngedouw (2000: 549) argues:

> Of course, the rescaling of the State by no means implies a diminished role for the nation state; on the contrary, global-local forms of governance that are instrumental in reshaping regional and social economies do so in close association with the State apparatus. They rely heavily on the State's legal, regulatory, and financial power to push through their development vision.

Northern BC has not experienced a substantive development vision since the 1980s. As discussed earlier, successive governments following the WAC Bennett era have continued modified versions of the resource bank model, but without a continued commitment to broader community development objectives. Forging a new vision must be primarily grounded in the voices and aspirations of the people in the north. We will explore the components of a renewed vision for the north in the following chapters. Examples of a vision for rural and small-town renewal being realized come from both Europe and Canada.

Norway has been an influential example with respect to the development and deployment of a holistic rural policy framework. Following on examples from European Union states, the Norwegian rural policy looks to support rural industries, communities, and regions within a mixed public and private sector suite of initiatives. In terms of the public sector, there are overt policies respecting the distribution of state ministry and department offices to rural places to provide additional employment and economic stability (this stands in marked contrast to the BC case, where front-line delivery offices closed and ministerial headquarters in metropolitan Vancouver-Victoria expanded). In terms of public sector supports, there has been extensive investment across the four key infrastructures identified throughout this book, as well as support and coordination for rural trade and rural economic and community development research. In both cases, the Norwegian rural policy is instructive for the key coordinating role that it gives to government. Also important is that this policy is entrenched in legislation.

An example closer to home is the Quebec rural policy. As with the Norwegian example, there is strong recognition of the need for significant and coordinated public and private sector contributions. In support of public sector activity, there is strong economic stimulus and supportive public policy. There has been innovative investment in critical infrastructure. One key example has been the way Quebec supported the extension of a fibre-optic Internet backbone across rural Quebec by connecting key hubs associated with the dispersed Université du Québec campuses. In terms of public sector activity, there is a strong local presence of services (like those described earlier in the case of northern Alberta). There has also been significant re-investment in rural economic and community development research such as found in the Groupe de recherche interdisciplinaire en développement régional de l'Est du Québec at the Université du Québec à Rimouski. Again, Quebec's rural policy is entrenched in legislation, complete with structures for regular dialogue between ministers and rural development interests.

Investment

A vision for development is meaningless without adequate funds and supports allocated for its implementation. A review of the WAC Bennett era identifies that the investment model used to open up the province had three main drivers. First, the government faced a province devoid of adequate infrastructure. The solution to this, spurred by the boom following the Second World War, was significantly enhanced industrial infrastructure through support for large industries and the creation of transportation and communications networks. Second, the government sought to stabilize provincial revenues for program development through an expansion and consolidation of resource revenues, accomplished primarily through Fordist production of commodity resources, particularly in forestry. Finally, the government facilitated investments in the resource sector with the specific objective of creating resource employment and growing rural and small-town economies.

The willingness to invest represents a point of similarity with the lessons drawn from more recent understandings of place-based development. Postproductivist, new regionalist, and community economic development research informs us that we must look to replace a singular commodity focus with a multiplicity of economies and values and potential local and regional assets in order to support rural economies. The passive space economy is just not able to sustain complex rural societies within a global economy. Moreover, researchers are gaining an in-depth understanding of the connection between social and economic development (Shaffer et al. 2006). This connection generates economic advantages, such as enhanced innovation, and is better able to create the social service and amenity environment necessary for attracting and retaining a quality labour force.

Perhaps the most glaring example of the investment shortcomings of the past twenty-five years is our crumbling physical infrastructure. Canadian communities face a (very conservative) $123 billion infrastructure deficit, an experience shared with cities and towns in other industrialized countries (see Table 14; Mirza 2007). Economic and political restructuring over the past twenty-five years, which has witnessed less interventionist senior governments and off-loading of responsibility to municipalities, has, unfortunately, coincided with the end of the lifespan of much of our core infrastructure. Our present foundation of water supply facilities, waste treatment systems, and transportation networks was largely built in the period leading up to the early 1970s.[2] The fiscal and ideological squeeze now means that much of that infrastructure is crumbling under the weight of overuse or unintended use by the demands of the new economy. In the worst-case scenario, the infrastructure deficit threatens the safety of Canadians, something already witnessed by bridge and overpass collapses and the failed integrity of our water systems in certain areas. Outside of these direct impacts, our ability to adapt and update our community infrastructure will influence our ability to compete economically and address many of the pressing environmental and social challenges (e.g., climate change and homelessness) that face our communities.

QUEBEC NATIONAL RURAL POLICY

In 2006, the Quebec government initiated a provincial dialogue designed to support a new National Rural Policy. The policy represents a comprehensive and detailed framework to ensure that Quebec's rural regions develop and thrive in the new economy. We are highlighting specific dynamics of the policy because it encapsulates many of the concepts and practices associated with place-based development. The Quebec Rural Policy also exemplifies a balanced approach to intervention that involves government leadership while recognizing the inherent need for bottom-up direction, commitment, and flexibility.

There are a variety of aspects to the principles/directions and implementation components of the framework that make it particularly useful as a model for place-based policy. The Quebec Rural Policy includes the following:

- a clear understanding of the concept of *rurality*, in terms of recognizing the unique characteristics and diversity of rural settings and rural communities
- a territorial approach to development facilitated by a commitment to the role of local governments in the rural development process
- a long-term approach to the implementation and monitoring of the policy
- an integrated approach to rural development
- an ongoing commitment to participatory processes and evaluation
- flexibility in both fostering rural capacity for development and applying the policy to meet specific local conditions.

An important, but less obvious dimension of the infrastructure deficit is the realization that senior governments have been even less willing to invest in the social infrastructure of communities and regions. Importantly, in the new economy, the social infrastructure will ultimately enable the productive use of physical infrastructure. The retention, and attraction, of people and capital to place is now highly dependent on the quality of life of specific areas – a quality of life influenced by the availability of social and cultural services and opportunities. This is particularly important for rural communities seeking to diversify their economic base. All communities face challenges in addressing the infrastructure gap. However, rural communities face particular challenges. Rural places face additional capacity barriers, such as access to information, limited staff resources, small pools of expertise, and limited financial resources that may place an extra burden on innovative processes to plan for future infrastructure needs. The Federation of Canadian Municipalities (FCM) recognizes the different infrastructure and capacity

The Quebec Rural Policy creates a variety of implementation mechanisms that support active intervention, rather than the apparent redistribution or re-labelling of existing policies, for rural development. It is very much a place-based policy framework seeking to ensure the development of rural communities by relying on their diversity, specific traits, and the ability of rural areas to take the initiative.

The Quebec Rural Policy's approach centres on four strategic directions that correspond to targets that rural communities actively helped to design:

1 Promote the renewal and integration of migrant and immigrant populations.
2 Foster the development of human, cultural, and physical resources.
3 Ensure the survival of rural communities.
4 Maintain a balance between the quality of life, the environment, and economic activities.

Intervention objectives in the policy strengthen the role of elected local government representatives, scale up local government dialogue to "regional" levels, and provide supportive public policy and the fiscal resources to help rural places act on their development plans. With regard to the last point, the Quebec government earmarked $280 million over seven years specifically for implementation (Quebec, Ministère des Affaires Municipales et des Régions 2006).

Table 14

Canada's municipal infrastructure deficit

	Deficit ($ billion)
Water and waste water systems	31.0
Transportation	21.7
Transit	22.8
Waste management	7.7
Community, recreation, cultural, social	40.2

Source: Mirza (2007: 2).

needs of rural and remote communities. In their recommendations, they are calling for a separate infrastructure fund for rural, remote, and northern communities; identifying the need for the integration of policies from different levels of government to avoid a one-size-fits-all approach to rural development, and highlighting the particular need to expand broadband Internet access to rural areas (FCM 2007).

Policy Coordination

Having a vision and the resources to support it without an adequate structure for implementation is counterproductive. Continuing our look back at the WAC Bennett policy era, we find that the government made distinct efforts to coordinate different policies to ensure their compatibility. The impact of this coordinated approach was the facilitation of multiple benefits that ensured the wise allocation of resources for the broadest and longest-term benefit.

Within a place-based economy, a more complex approach to governance replaces the singular ease of government-directed, top-down implementation. Within the rural territory, the partnership approach inherent in governance is particularly necessary because no single stakeholder has the resources or jurisdiction to tackle the multidimensional problems of rural development. Through adequate governance mechanisms, the actions of different governments and agencies may complement each other (Pezzini 2000).

To varying degrees, both top-down and bottom-up policy and programmatic responses that adopt a more place-based approach now exist in northern BC (Halseth et al. 2007). Senior governments, for example, have responded with resource management policy (such as increasing the number of community resource management agreements and select conservation agreements) and have developed a variety of rural and northern trust agreements. Through these trust arrangements, the provincial government has diverted some resource revenues for management by regional bodies.

Similarly, northern BC's rural and small-town places have been organizing through their own economic planning processes and regional networking initiatives to foster a collective voice for change. Our northern research reveals a strong desire to establish an agency to help facilitate regionally based initiatives and coordinate policy dialogue and implementation with senior governments. Such regional agencies have existed in the past; however, they have lacked a strong mandate, management structure, and sanction abilities (MacKinnon 2002). They have lacked the institutional capacity needed to generate the necessary supports to foster meaningful change. To emulate the decisiveness of the WAC Bennett policy era within a more complex governance environment, the mandate and financial security of representative regional institutions must be strong. Failure to provide an adequate foundation for regional institutions will only serve the rhetoric of bottom-up development and empowerment, without attaining significant impact. To guide the specific recommendations that follow this chapter, the next section takes a closer look at some guiding principles (rather than providing an overt structure) for developing appropriate and effective regional institutions.

Building Regional Institutions

The consideration of models for implementing and promoting regional development sets up an interesting dilemma. Based on historical evidence in British Columbia, it is not difficult to imagine that there will be resistance to virtually any type of organizational structure. We must note that no single template will be capable of facilitating development in every region of the province (Savoie 1997). Nevertheless, our research has revealed a willingness in the north to establish a bottom-up mechanism to coordinate and mediate strategic community and economic development investment discussions across the region and with senior levels of government.

Our discussions with participants in community interviews, workshops, and meetings raised and debated the ideas and elements that people felt should guide a regional forum, regardless of the specific model selected to facilitate regional connectivity. From this wide-ranging dialogue, the following seven key principles emerged to guide regional development in northern BC: institutional stability, inclusive representation, responsive governance, clear roles and responsibilities, independent funding, northern location, and complementarity with local action.

Institutional Stability

Given the time and capacity building that economic development requires, participants identified institutional stability as very important for any northern BC development body or forum. This includes a sense of permanence,

REGIONAL DEVELOPMENT MODELS

Successful regional development depends on the existence of an organization with a mandate to coordinate and facilitate development initiatives. Regional development strategies recognize that we *can* influence and change factors like capacity and competitiveness. Having an organization dedicated to regional development increases the likelihood that development will proceed in an organized, transparent, and efficient way – all necessary in an increasingly competitive economic environment.

The Canadian provinces, as well as other countries around the world, offer a large variety of models and programs to promote regional development: ministries, trusts, boards, commissions, regional economic development organizations, different funding programs, etc. The purpose here is to outline some key organizational features attached to different regional development structures.

General Organization

Research and experience point to a variety of organizational necessities that regional development structures must have in order to be successful, including the following:

- a clear vision – almost unanimously, accounts of regional development stress this given that regional development bodies are introducing new approaches and linking different sectors, cultures, and agencies
- a clear mandate
- a clear management structure
- clear goals.

The Oregon Benchmarks (a highly successful regional development program in the United States) offers an excellent example of simple and clear goals to guide their development efforts (Lewis and Lockhart 2001). These include:

- Invest in Oregonians to build a workforce that is measurably the best in the United States by the year 2000, and equal to any in the world by 2010.
- Maintain Oregon's natural environment and uncongested quality of life to attract the people and firms that will drive an advanced economy.
- Create an international orientation in Oregon's business and cultural life that distinguishes Oregonians as unusually adept in global commerce.

Respect for Local Context

Regional development programs cannot be imposed from above (a lesson painfully learned via previous programs in Canada and elsewhere). Policies and programs must respect local knowledge, be mindful of local conditions, and work to involve local people in decision-making and implementation. The Canada-Saskatchewan Northern Development Agreement offers an interesting example of select principles, used to guide the implementation of their regional development objectives (Canada, Ministry of Public Works and Government Services 2002), which stipulate:

- Northern development needs to take a strategic approach.
- Northern problems require northern solutions.
- Northern development can most effectively be promoted through a genuine partnership between the federal and provincial governments, and with First Nations, Metis Nation of Saskatchewan locals in northern Saskatchewan, local government authorities, northern communities, industry, labour, and non-governmental organizations.
- The traditions and cultures of all northerners must be respected.
- In implementing initiatives in support of the goals, efforts will be made to treat all regions of the north equitably.

Organizational Models: Pros and Cons

Two of the most common institutional structures used to manage and implement regional development strategies are to create a specific ministry (e.g., the Ministry for Northern Development and Mines in Ontario) or to create one or more regional development agencies (e.g., the Northern Alberta Development Council). There are a variety of pros and cons attached to both models. Local conditions and resource availability generally dictate which model is to be used:

Ministry

- pros: more resources; direct access to government
- cons: less flexible; distant from regions; extensive structural change and heavy costs; may provide an excuse for other government ministries to pay even less attention to place-based regional development issues.

Regional Development Organization

- pros: greater flexibility; better local integration; cost-effective; degree of independence from political process may lead to better decision-making
- cons: fewer resources; easier to ignore; potentially competitive with other levels of government.

security, and longevity such that the model is robust enough to survive economic cycles and government change. Time is needed to secure experienced institutions and organizations, and providing a long period for the development of regional bodies is one of the key requirements for success.

Inclusive Representation

The people and groups who spoke to us were adamant that membership in any northern BC regional development model must be inclusive and have an equal contribution from local governments and First Nations governments. They argued that regional development must be a forum that includes all of the voices of northern BC. Additionally, further discussion about model options should consider the need to involve representation from at least four subregional advisory bodies (Northeast, Northwest, Central, and Cariboo) and the need to have open access to labour, business, industry, and other community and private sector social and economic interests.

Responsive Governance

The governance model the participants most often suggested involves a small number of board members supported by a small staff. Most participants favour efficiency and responsiveness over a large bureaucracy. Suggestions for the selection of representatives focused on existing institutions (such as the North-Central Local Government Association and the First Nations of northern BC). The participants felt that linkages to the provincial government would be appropriate at the deputy minister level for staff and that some form of reporting access to the provincial legislature should be established through a minister for the board or council itself.

Clear Roles and Responsibilities

People told us that a northern BC regional development model should serve as a voice for the region, that it should provide input into policy and regulation development, and that it should play an advocacy role for the region and its communities. In addition to being a forum for the discussion of strategic development issues affecting the region, people said that it could create a solid base for community and economic development action and be a resource body to which communities could turn for advice on how local plans fit with regional interests. The regional forum model could undertake a series of vision and strategy exercises across the region and perhaps establish a set of northern BC benchmarks to track how the region is responding to change.

Independent Funding

To ensure longevity, people supported the principle that a stable source of funding is required for any northern BC regional development model to remain independent of government or funding agencies. A wide variety of potential funding sources that could be deployed to support a regional discussion model or forum were identified. Key was the resource revenue that the region generates. People felt that core funding should involve both operating funds as well as legacy or endowment funds. They spoke about the need for a commitment of public resources to allow northern BC to move forward in a socially and economically sustainable manner. Finally, there were very clear messages that municipalities, regional districts, band councils, and tribal councils should demonstrate buy-in through nominal financial contributions.

Northern Location

People very clearly supported the notion that any northern BC regional model should be housed in northern BC. While it may have a central office, earlier principles supporting subregional advisory committees suggest a presence throughout the region in order to enhance access, information flows, and accountability. In addition, people supported a presence in Victoria or Vancouver that could act as a liaison with the federal and provincial governments, and they supported an annual meeting in Victoria or Vancouver with government and media in order to reinforce the messages from northern BC.

Complementarity with Local Action

People, businesses, community groups, and agencies across the region spoke clearly about how any regional framework must not usurp local interests or impose a top-down direction. Regional initiatives should be about constructing a shared foundation for regionwide strategic discussions to support local planning processes. Regional development in northern BC should not be about giving up local power; rather, it should be about building communication and collaboration, and developing closer links between a wide range of strategic planning processes and partners.

Conclusion

Mobilizing for change towards a more place-based rural and small-town economy in northern BC means attention to bottom-up processes of creating a community development vision and making the strategic choices to fulfil that vision. Mobilizing for change means reinvigorating top-down supportive public policy and investments. Implementation of a regional approach, however, is challenged by the legacy of past development approaches. Communities developed under, and conditioned by an equity policy regime have clearly had negative experiences with retrenchment and cuts associated with a withdrawal from this approach. As a result, specific communities may be rightly skeptical about regional cooperation and unsure whether it will lead to the value-added promises in the literature or serve as a cover for the further loss of community infrastructure and services.

Complexity is inherent within regional approaches, and lessons for success highlight the extent to which regional strategies reflect the needs and aspirations of regional locales. As the provincial and federal governments work to address ongoing and new sources of uncertainty, instability, competition, and opportunity in northern BC, regional strategies embedded in the dynamics and culture of the north will stand a better chance of long-term success. The voices and ideas captured through our research animate many of the more abstract concepts in the regional development literature and have the potential to lead us to strategies that may help to construct a fully integrated and truly connected north. The purpose of the following chapter is to build on this foundation and offer concrete recommendations for governments, communities, and the business sector.

9 Directions

> I feel pretty good about life. That is not to say that the sad things, the social problems that are still with us and spoil life for my people, don't worry me every hour of the day and night. Those problems should never have happened to us. Drugs and alcohol, and the violence that goes with them, would never have got a foothold in our communities if we had been able to retain our culture. I believe that only a return to our traditions, our language, and the potlatch spirit is going to get us through the bad times, so that we come out as a whole people at the other end. I have a belief that this is the course my people will follow in the future, and that there will be healing and renewal. (Justa Monk, former Carrier Sekani Tribal Chief, in Moran 1994: 190)

As part of an argument for renewal, this chapter looks at directions and actions that can be taken to move northern BC, and by extension the province itself, into a more place-based economy that can be responsive to shifts and opportunities in the global economy. When facing a large challenge, it is important to keep sight of your goals and to execute the small things that over time cumulatively build towards that goal. In this chapter, we look at some of the things that we can focus on in supporting this renewal of northern BC's community and economic foundations. A starting point for renewal includes using a vision of northern BC "in twenty years" as a way to frame actions and opportunities for a host of players in the public and private sectors. This is a common technique in community development processes, to remove the constraints of present barriers (be they institutional, economic, or relational) in order to imagine a better future.

Northern BC "in Twenty Years"

To this point, our discussion has focused largely on the issues and background important for understanding the social and economic change occurring in northern BC. At many points, there were suggestions about ways to initiate new approaches and understandings to re-equip northern BC to be more competitive in the fast-changing global economy. Here we undertake a different form of discussion as we look forward twenty years and create a fictional portrait of northern BC as it could be if the types of actions described in this book were performed.

In describing a possible vision for northern BC in twenty years, we first need to say that the vision is not meant to be prescriptive but, rather, illustrative of the kinds of things that might be imagined and enacted by various community, economic, and policy players to take us to a more competitive and successful position in both local and global economies. Emphasis here is on actions, initiatives, commitments, and purposeful interventions. These actions will prioritize place-based development, aiding in competitiveness and, importantly, making rural and small-town communities vibrant places where people want and choose to live.

In setting a context for northern BC twenty years into the future, the foundational argument for this book is about the increasing importance of place in the global economy. The question posed at the beginning was how to equip northern BC so that its place-based advantages are able to meet the development opportunities and challenges of the global economy on our own terms. The fictional portrait that follows describes how to realize such a vision if we take the small steps that cumulatively lead to significant change and renewal.

Readiness

How might we imagine northern BC in twenty years? To start, we need to be comfortable with a sense that across the different places and regions, we will have different mixes of local economies and populations. This differentiation will stem from the creative reimaging and rebundling of local assets and the ongoing discussion about how they fit with local aspirations.

Northern BC in twenty years is forward-looking and proactive in its attention to economic activities and social investment. Communities, industries, businesses, civil society groups, and local governments are not simply reliant on what they have always done. In many respects, they maintain a level of monitoring and readiness to respond to change and opportunity through an ongoing discourse about local assets and aspirations. From a foundation of awareness and openness, places across northern BC seek constantly to be ready for opportunity and change in the fast-paced global economy.

Relationships

Northern BC in twenty years is a region in which relationships are a central part of our concern and effort. Northern BC is working collectively and cooperatively to position and reposition itself in the global economy. It has forged strong urban-rural ties so that the province speaks with one voice and works as one functional economy.

In 2035, BC communities are organizing the anniversary of the final treaty settlement in the province, illustrating that we have truly moved to a new position in relationships between Aboriginal and non-Aboriginal peoples and communities. We have developed a new sense of cultural and economic sustainability that grounds the whole north in a collective relationship that recognizes people sharing space. The competitive advantage of our youthful population, composed in large measure of young Aboriginal people, is a key economic driver in northern BC's economy – one that is supported with appropriate educational and community development investments.

Services

In 2035, we are celebrating the success of the province's Integrated Service Delivery Initiative. Beginning some twenty years earlier, this initiative sought to deliver new models of service provision that support flexibility and responsiveness. These integrated and flexible models allow local places and regions to create more cost-effective solutions and opportunities. To support the integrated delivery of services, the significant investments initiated long ago by the provincial government into the availability and wise use of technology are now delivering more services to small places than ever before. Coupled with the dissolution of service delivery "sites," the end costs of those technology investments are insignificant against the benefits now being realized.

Technology supports have resulted in many spin-offs. To start, they facilitate the work of our skilled professionals living in isolated locations. Practitioners are able to access specialists for advice and referral. Professionals are able to maintain contact with educational and learning communities so they stay up-to-date on practice developments. Moreover, BC's technology expertise in the delivery of rural and remote services is itself a product now marketed around the world.

One area of special benefit from technology is the provision of health care in small communities across northern BC. People are now "treated" locally as much as possible. Local nurses and physicians are able to send a vast number of tests for analysis electronically – thereby greatly reducing the need for patient travel. While people do still travel for special treatments at tertiary care institutions, they no longer travel for simple or routine tests. This has helped to keep health care costs down, improved patient quality of life, and reduced the time needed for diagnosis. The support for place-embedded services has increased and so has the collective management of a wide range of services.

In 2035, the Northern Health Authority is undertaking a transition from a very successful expansion of services that supported seniors in their own homes to the creation of more extensive senior support and housing services. Supported by the Northern Medical Program, and other northern-focused training initiatives, northern BC is now supplying a large part of their care and service needs through "home grown" professionals. In 2035, BC's health care and social services providers (public, private, and voluntary sectors) are celebrating ten years of the successful "one-care" model of patient (or client) management. Overcoming the challenge of balancing confidentiality with information sharing across care agencies now ensures that few people "fall through the cracks" of our care and support services. This breakthrough has led to a much better coordinated, effective, and lower-cost system.

The reorganization of school districts across northern BC is now old news in 2035. The development of a renewed rural teaching platform means that high-quality teaching is available in all northern communities and that it supports not only the local community and economy, and the professional teaching staff delivering the curriculum, but also provincial goals in developing the workforce needed for the late twenty-first century. Built on earlier models like that found in Port Clements, long gone are the days when schools sat isolated in the middle of school district property – owned, maintained, and administered solely by a single organization. Today, rural schools share space with rural governments, community groups, and service agencies in buildings that are energy efficient and have low operating costs. Professional teaching staff and students alike benefit from the wise application of appropriate high technology tools to deliver curriculum reimagined so that it truly supports our future generation as they prepare for the flexible world they will grow into. Ensuring cultural appropriateness, like that found in the Chalo School, is equally important.

Population Change

In 2035, the demographics of northern BC continue to change. The population pyramid for the north is approaching a rectangular shape, meaning that we have a more balanced population distribution between young and old. Population aging now means that older residents, who have been retained in the region by supportive in-home programs, are now moving in larger numbers than ever before into new seniors' housing.

Attention to local amenities and place-based assets is creating new economic opportunities, and this is attracting in-migrants of all ages to the region. It is proving to be successful in holding the region's youth and, when those youth go off to educational opportunities elsewhere, it is proving to be successful in attracting them back when they want to start their careers and families.

Investments in growing a knowledge economy have been married to investments in lifelong learning such that northern BC supports a globally competitive workforce. An emphasis on continuous capacity development is paying

CHALO SCHOOL: AN EXAMPLE OF INNOVATIVE EDUCATION

A community development approach to renewal is based, in part, on enhancing the capacity of people to respond to opportunities and challenges. This allows individuals, families, communities, and regions to be innovative and flexible as they work through change. The need to support human capacity development is especially important in First Nations communities, where the legacies of colonialism and residential schools have left multiple barriers to education and wellness. A successful and innovative approach to Aboriginal education is found in Fort Nelson at Chalo School.

Fort Nelson First Nation

The Fort Nelson First Nation (FNFN) is located about 7 km south of Fort Nelson in northeastern BC. The FNFN is comprised of Slavey and Cree people. In 1910, they were one of several First Nations bands in the northeast that signed an "adhesion" to Treaty 8. In 1962, they changed their name from the Slavey Indian Band to the Fort Nelson Band (Spencer 2004). Comprised of ten reserves covering nearly 10,000 hectares, the FNFN is in a resource-rich region with tourism, wildlife, forestry, and oil and gas assets.

The mission for the FNFN is to be a strong, healthy, proud, and self-reliant community, made up of strong, healthy, proud, and self-reliant community members (see http://www.treaty8.bc.ca/communities/fortnelson.php). It is to this mission that the work of Chalo School is directed.

Chalo School

Chalo School is an independent Aboriginal school owned and operated by the FNFN. The school follows the BC Ministry of Education curriculum and is fully accredited. At the same time, it maintains independent school status in the province and has been accredited by the First Nations Education Steering Committee.

Chalo School opened for the 1981-1982 school year. It is named to honour Harry "Chalo" Dickie, a long-time proponent of Aboriginal education for the FNFN. Chalo School started as a one-room primary school housed in a portable classroom. A new school structure was completed in 1996 with a library, computer lab, classrooms, gym, and meeting areas. With the expansion into high school programming, a new building recently opened that also accommodates a cultural arts room and a culinary arts program (see http://www.chaloschool.bc.ca/index.html).

The school enrolment is about 200 pupils from preschool to Grade 12, supported by about sixteen teachers and eleven staff. For the Chalo School, it is this notion of "support" that has been critical to their success.

The school has grown and prospered because of strong governance and leadership. Key leadership is provided by a principal who was also a long-time Chalo School teacher. With a focus on effective communication between teachers and parents, and between the school and the community, the principal has supported a school environment marked by caring and mutual respect. In turn, this has created a climate of trust and commitment in which teachers, students, families, and the community are working together towards academic success (Spencer 2004). A five-member Chalo Board of Education meets every two weeks and serves as a critical link between the school and the community. There is a transparency to all decision making that reinforces and affirms this community ownership and support. In fact, it is "Chalo's governance and the sense of community ownership that contributes to its success" (99).

There is a very purposeful attempt to overcome the damage caused by the historical processes of colonization and residential schools. Particular attention is given to children with special learning needs, and ways are found to support the families of these children. Chalo's school atmosphere "exudes trust, love, care, respect, and high expectations. The school feels good to the visitor, more like a home than an institution" (106). The teachers "expect quality work and expect their students to be leaders and models in the community" (107).

It also draws strength from traditional practices. The Morning Circle "is broadly acknowledged as the defining characteristic of Chalo School. The beginning of a new school day is signalled by the sound of soft drum beats beckoning students, staff, and visitors to assemble. This morning exercise was conceived by the principal and is intended to serve as a meaningful ritual for setting the school day on a good footing. It brings unity of purpose and care to the school environment through sharing knowledge and wisdom, and achievements and successes. The Morning Circle models and defines the ethos of respect" (107).

In the curriculum, there is a core emphasis on reading, language, and mathematical skills. There is also a strong emphasis on traditions, Aboriginal languages, and cultural understandings. These are embedded across the curriculum, and FNFN members are employed as language and culture teachers and educational

dividends for local and First Nations governments as well as for the private sector. Innovative, age-connecting mentorship and internship opportunities have been critical to repositioning northern BC in the global economy.

Robust Resource Sector

In 2035, northern BC is home to a robust and competitive suite of natural resource industries. The lumber and pulp and paper economy continues assistants. The language and cultural teachers "employ a medicine wheel model representing the wholeness of life and organize instruction around spiritual, emotional, physical, and intellectual understandings" (114). This attention to language and cultural education begins in the kindergarten classes, and it, too, relies on community and family support.

As Chalo School is not unionized, BC-certified teachers are selected in part for their ability to develop relationships with the school and with the community (Spencer 2004). Teachers expect the best from the students, and the classrooms are personalized, high-energy environments. The teachers communicate "respect and high expectations to the students and accept responsibility for seeking strategies that will support their success" (112). The staff typically have a long tenure at Chalo School, and reported levels of satisfaction among the staff are very high.

In 2003, Chalo School was recognized as one of ten exemplary schools for Aboriginal education in western Canada-Yukon. In 2006, Chalo School was recognized in the House of Commons as a role model for British Columbia and the country (see http://www.chaloschool.bc.ca/index.html). In a report by the Society for the Advancement of Excellence in Education, Chalo School was recognized as a "fabulous school with strong, enthusiastic leadership of long tenure, a history of documenting student academic progress by means of the Canadian test of basic skills, and a history of family and community support and leadership" (Spencer 2004: 99).

The student population is diverse. While most of the children come from the FNFN, it also includes children who come from the neighbouring community of Fort Nelson. The quality of the educational environment attracts these students to the school. Student achievement, as tracked by the Canadian Test of Basic Skills and the BC Foundational Skills Assessment, shows that Chalo School has far fewer students "not meeting expectations" than Aboriginal students across the BC school system. For the FNFN, the school is "fundamental to laying the foundation for a strong, healthy, proud, and independent nation" (117).

because of extensive investments both to create cost-effective and innovative product lines and to make creative use of all waste and previously unexplored chemical, biological, and structural characteristics of our very special trees and forests. Several older pulp mills were long ago converted into bio-refineries such that northern BC now supplies large quantities of green fuels and biochemicals into the global economy. Private sector investments were aggressively supported by public policy targeting research, training, and innovation.

Such changes and the expansion of the forest sector into greater value-added activities has overcome the late-twentieth century trap of trying to compete with low-cost competitors in the provision of basic structural commodity lumber. Finished wood products, for example, fit perfectly into the decorative moulding and trim markets of China and India, and have buffeted the BC lumber industry from the flows of low-cost lumber out of Siberia.

In addition, greater flexibility and access to the forest and other ecosystems now supports a greater range of nontimber forest product activities in our resource sector. These include products consumed for food and medicinal purposes – and some of these have moved well beyond niche activities to become major economic players in the region and in the global economy. Balancing complementary land uses with a more careful social, economic, and cultural evaluation of which types of activities generate the best long-term returns from the province's forest lands has meant an increase in employment and broader support for sustainable economic activities in sensitive ecosystems. The nurturing of the forest ecosystem by small tenure and conservation interests is helping BC address current and future carbon sequestration goals as well as finally turning the corner on environmental remediation after the mountain pine beetle epidemic of 2004-2012.

Drawing on his long experience with the BC, Canadian, and international forest industries, Mike Apsey has argued time and again that a strong research, innovation, and science-technology sector must be "the heartbeat of the Canadian forest sector" (2006: 265). With this focus, the industry can be competitive and successful in the rapidly changing global marketplace. Building from a place-based approach, Apsey submits (283):

> The BC forest should be sustainably managed for a range of values, indeed a wider range than many of us now recognize as inherent to the forest. There are many goods in the woods. Beyond timber, recreation, wildlife, water, and aesthetics, there are nontimber commercial products like mushrooms, Christmas trees and salal. We should consider the contribution the forest makes to the health of the planet by taking carbon from the atmosphere. Perhaps under some future version of the Kyoto Protocol, British Columbia will someday be paid by the world for this essential service. Perhaps too we will levy an economic charge on forest values now provided for free – like the scenic beauty of SuperNatural British Columbia that supports a tourist industry, or the service the forest provides to municipalities by soaking up rainwater so that it can find its way to aquifers and reservoirs instead of running back into the sea.

Important in the diversity of the resource sector has been the expansion of community-based resource control that supports people and local places by reinvesting profits locally. This has been assisted by revisions to community forest regulations that have greatly increased their size while decreasing the regulatory burden. It provides a local tax base necessary to supplement provincially delivered services in urban and rural areas alike. The development of some of these products, and the decision not to develop some other potential products, indicates the value of linking research with traditional ecological knowledge. Protective regulations brought in by the federal and provincial governments have safeguarded this knowledge, and the products, from biological patenting by external multinational corporations so that more benefits and more profits stay in the local economy.

By 2035, northern BC had taken the examples of innovative industrial partnerships with First Nations communities to develop its own models and become a world leader in the cooperative development of communities and commodities. By working together in collaborative and supportive structures, both Aboriginal and non-Aboriginal places are realizing some economies of scale in community and economic development while at the same time protecting their local independence.

The mining industry has flourished in areas where effective and mututally beneficial partnerships with First Nations have expanded the lessons learned through the Tahltan Declaration and through the diamond mining agreements in the Northwest Territories of twenty years ago. Sensitive, appropriate, and environmentally sound approaches allow new mining opportunities with greater certainty and speed in those places where they fit with local and regional aspirations.

In 2035, the energy future of northern BC has been fully realized. Whether in conventional hydro sources, small and independent sources, or a variety of new sources including hydrogen, northern BC is, literally and figuratively, a powerhouse in the "green" North American economy. Importantly, for the region and its communities, the completion of the electrical power grid now gives more options for economic diversification and expansion, and has done away with diesel electric generators.

Global Positioning

In 2035, northern BC continues to reap the benefits of initiatives that organized community-based activities into large marketing coalitions. These coalitions have been termed the twenty-first-century model of co-operatives such that they make large economic players out of the small and independent producers still so important in northern BC. Media coverage from Europe reports how the forest products label "Sustainably Harvested by Northern BC's First Nations" is now the preferred product brand in many European economies. Finally, the provincial government's Global Market Surveillance Initiative is celebrating in 2035 nearly two decades of success in identifying new opportunities and positioning BC's economic responses into a highly fluid and competitive global economy.

TAHLTAN FIRST NATION: THE TAHLTAN DECLARATION

In April of 2003, the Tahltan First Nation held a mining symposium in the northwestern BC community of Dease Lake. The purpose of the symposium was to examine and discuss the relationship between the Tahltan people and mining and mineral activities in the region. The goal was to create a framework to guide the Tahltan in their relationships with the mining industry. One result was the report *Out of Respect: The Tahltan, Mining and the Seven Questions to Sustainability* (Tahltan First Nation and International Institute for Sustainable Development 2004).

The Tahltan First Nation

The Tahltan people live in northwestern BC on a traditional territory that covers more than 93,500 km^2 and is centred on the Stikine River Watershed. Highway 37 cuts through the area, but most of the Tahltan traditional territory is not accessible by road. The three main community sites are at Iskut, Dease Lake, and Telegraph Creek. Dease Lake is the regional service centre and the territory is home to about 1,300 people, of which about 1,000 are members of the Tahltan First Nation.

Most jobs are in the public and service sectors; however, the region is rich in resources. The Tahltan are active in both traditional and market economy activities in construction, mining, fishing, trapping, guiding, forestry, and agriculture. Tahltan traditional territory is also home to three large parks and protected areas: the Spatsizi Plateau Wilderness, the Mount Edziza Provincial Park, and the Stikine River Recreation Area.

Background

The Tahltan First Nation has long experience with mining. For many thousands of years, they traded the highly prized obsidian from Mount Edziza into the continental Aboriginal trade networks. They also traded copper, gold, jade, agate, and precious stones. "Modern" mining activities came to the region in 1861, when gold was discovered on the Stikine River. One result of these pressures and encroachments was the 18 October 1910 Declaration of the Tahltan Tribe which asserted sovereign rights to the lands that had been held intact from time immemorial and called for a treaty to be signed between the Tahltan and the Dominion and British Columbia governments (Tahltan First Nation and International Institute for Sustainable Development 2004: 33).

There has been cooperation as well as conflict in the Tahltan's relationship with mining in their territory. In addition to exploration and geologic survey work in the nineteenth and twentieth centuries, the Tahltan were active in the

Cassiar asbestos mine and the Eskay Creek gold mine. The Tahltan Nation Development Corporation was also active as a subcontractor in maintaining access roads and providing a range of mine services. There have also been blockades of mining activities in cases in which Tahltan people have felt there were potential threats to culturally or environmentally important lands.

Although the Tahltan have been involved with mining and mineral exploration in many different ways over the decades, they have not always realized as many benefits as possible, and yet their land still bears the burdens of these activities. The 2003 symposium marked the beginning of a strategic effort to ensure that mining activity in Tahltan territory creates a net positive benefit for Tahltan people and for their territory.

Mining, Minerals, and Sustainable Development

The 2003 symposium drew on the concept of sustainable development. Specifically, it drew on a global review of mining practices compiled in 2001 by the World Business Council for Sustainable Development and the International Institute for Environment and Development (Tahltan First Nation and International Institute for Sustainable Development 2004: v). This review had led to a general framework for assessing and evaluating mining proposals that came to be known as the Seven Questions to Sustainability (7QS).

The 2003 Tahltan Mining Symposium provided an opportunity to address mining proposals against the 7QS framework and Tahltan needs, concerns, and interests. At the symposium, ten recent initiatives were reviewed.

Seven Questions to Sustainability

As described in the 2003 Tahltan Mining Symposium report, the Seven Questions framework includes the following:

1 *Engagement:* Are engagement processes in place and working effectively?
2 *People:* Will people's well-being be maintained or improved?
3 *Environment:* Is the integrity of the environment assured over the long term?
4 *Economy:* Is the economic viability of the project or operation assured, and will the economy of the community and beyond be better off as a result?
5 *Traditional and nonmarket activities:* Are traditional and nonmarket activities in the community and surrounding area accounted for in a way that is acceptable to the local people?
6 *Institutional arrangements and governance:* Are rules, incentives, programs and capacities in place to address project or operational consequences?
7 *Synthesis and continuous learning:* Does a full synthesis show that the net result will be positive or negative in the long term, and will there be periodic

▶

reassessments? (Tahltan First Nation and International Institute for Sustainable Development 2004: 16).

For each of the seven questions, the analysis matrix includes reference to objectives, indicators, and evaluative metrics.

From the 2003 symposium, the Tahltan created a multifaceted strategy for action that aims to do the following:

1 Send a signal that Tahltan people are supportive of mining and mineral activity on their land under conditions that such activities are "done right" from a Tahltan perspective.
2 Facilitate Tahltan participation in mining and mineral activity – not only through direct and indirect employment, but also in terms of overall management/co-management as well as the broad perspective of seeing a fair distribution (considering all participating interests) of all benefits, costs, and risks.
3 Ensure that the broad range of concerns raised in the *Seven Questions to Sustainability* report are addressed, in particular the health/social/cultural implications of mining/mineral activity that continue to receive inadequate attention. (Tahltan First Nation and International Institute for Sustainable Development 2004: 27)

In 2035, northern BC is remarkable for the breadth of economies working in harmony across the region. Here are some examples: the purposeful expansion of tourism; the innovative activities in energy development; the increasing growth of technology industries; the additional growth and supply of food to regional, national, and continental markets; the growth in some locations of population migrations attracted by local amenities or recreation opportunities; and the expansion in production of many sectors through flexible support for small value-added industries that make use of complementary relationships with existing actors. In all of these, knowledge products generated through innovation in various sectors have become a key export from northern BC.

These types of learning economies are dependent on a sound educational and research infrastructure. Having learned the lessons from knowledge economies like Japan and Finland, BC's long-term investment in schools and postsecondary education has met the goal of producing the best-educated workforce among OECD states. Similar investment in research universities continues to support the basic and applied research that is now a key economic driver in the province.

Across this dynamic economic landscape, different communities are, of course, home to different mixes of economic activities, as fits the creative mixing of local assets and aspirations. Northern BC has sold the cost, quality-of-life, and community advantages of rural and small-town living as part of initiatives to decongest urban cores and reduce corporate costs. In addition to provincial ministry offices, several large corporate R and D, financial management, and similar footloose components have relocated to northern BC. With rising energy costs, northern BC has been able to aggressively plug earlier local economic leakages with more local production.

Resource Trust

In 2035, northern BC is enjoying the benefits of more than a decade of ongoing investment in its resource trust. Working on a modification of the Norwegian model, British Columbia has devoted a small portion of the revenues generated annually from both renewable and nonrenewable resource and industrial streams into a northern BC resource trust. Using only the investment interest income, and focusing on "infrastructure for the future economy," the trust drives extensive infrastructure investments for further re-equipping northern BC to be flexible in the face of constantly shifting global economies. All of these investments are driven by the cooperative development of a long-term regional development vision and strategic approach. The resource trust has become a significant contributor to the economy and the future stability of northern BC's communities.

To realize efficiency in operations, the Northern BC Resource Trust is under the management of the earlier created Northern Development Initiative Trust. The NDI Trust, in addition to expanding its role in managing trust funds, has made two changes now being celebrated in BC and imitated in many Nordic countries. The first was the expansion of its board to include full Aboriginal as well as non-Aboriginal interests. The second has been its evolution from "lending bank" to vision leader. For more than fifteen years, the NDI Trust has managed a Northern Forum so that northern BC has a platform on which to debate its vision and investments for the future.

Renewed Infrastructure

In 2035, northern BC is witnessing the completion of an extensive array of reinvestments in our infrastructure. The four lanes of highways 97 and 16 that were created in an earlier period are now being repaved. The northern Roads to Diversity Initiative by the provincial government is finalizing linkages to create opportunity in formerly isolated resource-dependent towns, and this underscores their successful transition to more diversified and viable economies.

Northern BC is celebrating the next generation of satellite Internet applied through the Northern Communications Advantage Initiative, a joint federal and provincial policy initiative of the early twenty-first century that supports economic, social, community, and cultural development. In 2035, the provincial and federal governments' strategy for small airports has finally come to completion as the last piece of the transportation infrastructure puzzle that now fully allows both people and products to move freely and quickly between the global economies and our northern communities. Collectively, these investments allow northern BC to remain flexible and competitive in the global economy. Collectively, this means that our northern places are ahead of a curve in economic trends and shifts.

Closing

In 2035, northern BC has created a platform for responsiveness. No longer are we simply reacting to positive and negative changes in the global economy. Instead, long-term investments in our human and physical infrastructures build on the notion of being ready for any economic opportunity that comes.

While the above list provides a glimpse at an imagined northern BC, our purpose is simply to suggest that unless we know where we want to go, we will have trouble initiating the coordinated and long-term actions and policies needed to get there. Northern dialogue forums will also unveil numerous opportunities not yet envisioned.

Actions and Opportunities

The last section of this chapter describes a range of actions that can be taken to move northern BC into a more proactive and competitive position. There are suggestions for community, economic, and policy sectors. With a vision of renewal based on flexibility and diversity, these small steps can start us on the pathway out of the staples trap.

For Communities

Some of the key steps for communities across northern BC include moving forward with "readiness." To start, local governments need to ensure they have their own "house in order." This will include attention to minimizing long-term economic costs by employing smart and energy-efficient design, avoiding physical sprawl developments, and managing local infrastructure. It will include attention to reducing long-term operating costs by limiting the distance over which public services are carried and looking for cost savings in energy efficiency.

A second area of readiness involves attention to the "new normal" operating environment identified in UNBC's Community Development Institute's Transition Toolkit (plans, operations, and networks). Arising from the attention to place-based community and economic development will be the need to open dialogues and innovation with regard to local assets and local aspirations. This includes continuing the local dialogue around a community vision and rebundling assets to create new opportunity.

Local governments need to stay the course on supporting the local voluntary sector and community-based organizations. During times of challenge, the well-practised networks and supports of social cohesion and social capital that such groups create are vital to local flexibility and responsiveness. These extend to newer activities such as farmers' markets and local food initiatives. Such supports not only need to be part of routine local government activities but also need to be inculcated within integrated community sustainability plans and official community plans.

Local governments need to maintain a focus on long-term economic and community development. The lessons of the past are far too vibrant for us to ignore the need to pay continual attention to renewing our community and economic foundations. As part of this, local governments need to remain involved with and supportive of initiatives for "scaling up." Working together as regions can bring benefits to all – speaking together with a collective voice can bring a force of weight to policy debates and the marketplace that must be heard.

Local governments need to become partners with both the federal and provincial governments in the development of a robust and comprehensive rural strategy (FCM 2009; Akin 2008). These exist in other jurisdictions, and the components of that strategy document are generally known in the research literatures.

For Regional Districts

Regional districts play a crucial role in new governance since they already provide a meeting place for municipal and rural representatives. In addition to their current tasks, regional districts can play a role in wider regional discussions of assets, aspirations, and innovations in support of community futures.

Regional districts were first envisioned and created to undertake those functions that were more efficiently handled at a collective level. The Community Transition Toolkit of UNBC's Community Development Institute identifies many activities that could be centralized and incorporated into regional district operations. This would provide efficiencies for smaller local governments – such as updating lists of key contacts, local plans and initiatives, and local socio-demographic information.

For the Provincial Government

Because it controls key policy and program "levers," the provincial government must remain a supportive partner in renewal. The continuing value of

THE TRANSITION TOOLKIT: WORKING FRAMEWORK FOR A MORE RESILIENT COMMUNITY

If there is a flood, local governments have disaster plans to follow. When it is time for an election, local governments have a well-practised sequence of actions to follow. From crises to more mundane responsibilities, local governments make effective use of framework plans to help manage orderly and efficient responses. This is especially important for smaller local governments with limited staff time and resources. But what happens when small places encounter the sudden crisis that arises from an (often unexpected) announcement that a large local employer will close? What happens when economic and social concerns build up over time and must be addressed through long-term actions and solutions? Answers to these questions are especially vital in small places with a narrow economic base. Too often, rural and small-town governments meet such questions without a ready framework for action.

The Transition Toolkit was designed in the late spring of 2007 as the Community Development Institute (CDI) at UNBC worked with the District of Mackenzie on a plan to respond effectively to threatened industrial closures. It collected together lessons learned in northern BC and elsewhere about successful strategies for meeting economic and community change. The toolkit served Mackenzie's purposes very well, with the result that the CDI held follow-up training sessions with local governments around northern BC and received external requests from communities eager to use this "economic emergency toolkit."

In partnership with the Omineca Beetle Action Coalition and the Community Transition Branch of the BC Ministry of Community Services, the CDI undertook to update and revise the toolkit in 2008. Key in the revision was identification of the steps needed to make communities more resilient – to make transition planning a normal part of local government business. As a result, the "emergency toolkit" became the Transition Toolkit.

The range of social and economic changes experienced by rural and small-town places means that their local governments must be at the forefront of responding effectively to economic and social change. Part of supporting more resilient communities includes mobilizing strategies, assets, aspirations, resources, and networks to help places overcome challenges and pursue opportunities.

The Transition Toolkit is built around a "generic framework." This is in explicit recognition that community transition must be suited to the unique circumstances and issues of each place. Its purpose is to assist small local governments in their long-term adjustment planning and in their initial reactions to sudden challenges. Attention to community transition is now the "steady state" of rural and small-town local governments.

The Transition Toolkit outlines the following three key areas of "things we need to do" in order to make communities more resilient.

1 Develop a clear *communications strategy* to support a variety of ways to share information, gather input, dispel rumours, and communicate a clear message about the future of the community.
2 *Know what we have and where we stand* in order to assess and take stock of available critical services, the status of plans and strategies to guide community and economic development, and thus determine what services, supports, and strategies are needed to build capacity and position the community so that it is "ready" to pursue new opportunities.
3 Develop and maintain *support and information networks* to connect with other decision makers and to obtain timely and relevant information to inform local decisions.

The Transition Toolkit has a four-stage timeline:

1 short-term "triage"
2 follow-through on early actions
3 development of a sustainable long-term transition plan
4 transition planning made the "new normal" for local government.

During each of these stages in the timeline, all of the action plan components of the framework need attention, including the following:

- support and dialogue circles
- critical services availability
- communications strategy
- stock-taking
- transition supports
- community and economic renewal planning.

Preparation is the key to a successful response. With this generic framework in hand, we urge small local governments to use an upcoming strategic planning session to build their own local version. Strategic scenario planning is common in the business world, and it is useful for local governments. Experience has shown that even where no such crisis develops, attention to the host of issues collected together under this framework can assist small local governments in working towards a more resilient community and local economy.

As we note in the Transition Toolkit: "It is important to remember that crisis from external (industry or corporate) decision making does not mean you have 'done anything wrong.' But it does highlight that you will need to 'get right' your responses within a matter of hours (for the message) and days (for the action plan). In this, preparation and forward planning will better equip the local government response."

For further information, see Halseth et al. (2008a, 2008b, 2008c).

the tourism sector to BC's economy needs to be recognized within the structure of the provincial cabinet. Outside of the run-up to the 2010 Olympics, a well-staffed Ministry of Tourism is required to both coordinate, and argue for, ongoing investments in tourism promotion, coordination, and development. At best, BC experiences "accidental tourism." We need a more serious approach and supportive framework. To visit a part of the world where tourism is a vital part of the national economy is to see a very different approach to supporting tourism and extracting value from this economic sector.

Rural and small-town places eager to undertake economic and community strategy planning need access to critical information at a scale useful to their community context. The provincial government should create a portal that municipalities can use to access the expertise and information of BC Stats. This involves much more than is presently available on the various BC Stats websites – it involves a Crown agency that responds to the needs of communities by answering requests for timely special tabulations of information to meet urgent data needs for making decisions. Such access to information needs to extend across provincial ministries. While respecting issues of confidentiality and information privacy, there is a great deal of information available in various ministries that can be harnessed to support rural and small-town community and economic renewal. A key role for the provincial government is to use its existing tools and information to become a more supportive development instrument. The province's current web data portal is a start, but a more engaged mechanism for meeting community development information needs is required.

A similar coordinating and supporting role for the provincial government is needed in the area of economic competitiveness. As noted earlier in this book, international market surveillance and assessment of the competitive position of BC industries in emergent markets and with emergent products can assist entrepreneurs and local economies. The recently created "WoodSourceBC.com" service that brought many partners (including the province) together to address the long-standing challenge of connecting wood buyers and sellers is an example of the kind of multi-sector partnerships the province should be encouraged.

The provincial government should remain attentive to the five key recommendations of the Northern BC Economic Development Vision and Strategy Project:

1 Settle treaties in a fair and timely fashion.
2 Complete the electrical power grid across the region to facilitate new economic development opportunities in northern BC.
3 Move forward with the next steps in discussions about creating some form of a northern BC regional development council.

4 Move on suggested resource revenue–sharing arrangements with the region's Aboriginal and non-Aboriginal communities.
5 Foster greater cooperative and coordinated policy development within and between all levels of Aboriginal and non-Aboriginal government to support economic and community development across the region.

There has been progress on most of these recommendations, but additional work remains.

The provincial government must follow through with infrastructure investment. Specifically, four-laning Highway 97 and Highway 16 is needed to support the northern transportation corridor and to facilitate economic development through alleviating transportation bottlenecks and reducing transport times. The examples from the Okanagan of the benefit from the Coquihalla Highway investments and across metropolitan Vancouver of the benefits from SkyTrain are evidence of the critical role that transportation, accessibility, and the ease of moving goods and people has for creating economic opportunity.

In tune with current understandings of the competitiveness agenda, there are some crucial areas for new or improved investments. The rise of the "knowledge economy" has a very real regional dimension, and the provincial government needs to continue investments in upgrading education and occupational skills. The provincial government, in particular, must take a leadership role in renewing rural and small-town elementary education. Similarly, the increasing role of voluntary organizations in community and economic renewal requires better and more consistent support. This approach to investments in support of competiveness must extend to services. For three decades, we have needed a more focused "smart" approach to rural and small-town services that takes advantage of technology and synergy (as opposed to the current pattern of services delivered by "silo" ministries). The creation of place-appropriate service delivery will be critical to renewal – especially in the critical services of health care and education.[1]

The provincial government has an opportunity to invest in economic spin-offs through the location of footloose government services in non-metropolitan locations (Akin 2008). Many of these services can include "backroom" processing and management tasks. Many tasks and offices do not need the synergy of access to the deputy minister's office, and locating them in northern BC may offer a way to reduce government costs. The benefits for local and regional development from the location of the BC Lottery Corporation offices in Kamloops is illustrative of the value non-metropolitan locations bring to government functions and the benefits that those functions can generate in terms of direct and indirect economic spin-offs and investments. Such relocations can be cost-effective. The high ranking of Prince George, for example, in KPMG's Competitive Alternatives (2010), demonstrates the advantages of smaller places to business and public sector location decision making.

As stated above, the provincial government must develop a resource trust account for future generations and not spend all of our revenues now.[2] The resource trust should apply to both renewable and nonrenewable resources and associated benefits. In addition, the provincial government should continue to investigate arrangements for sharing resource royalties in order to transform existing beetle action coalitions into regional development trust funds.

Finally, the provincial government needs to change its mindset around two key issues. The first shift concerns the future of rural and small-town places. We know that these places drive the provincial economy; we know that the withdrawal of services has contributed to population losses in small places; and we know that many of these places have also experienced growth. The province must recognize that rural and small-town places are viable and must undertake positive moves to support their continued viability. The second critical change has to do with abandoning the expectation that one-off, short-term programs will change the social and economic development destiny of rural and small-town places. While they may make good routine photo opportunities for politicians, the long-run record of such programs is not one of cumulatively successful investments towards renewal. Instead, we must set forth our vision and work over the long term, and across government areas of responsibility, to realize that vision.

For Individuals

Given that change and uncertainty are central pieces in all economic activities, individuals have a responsibility to equip themselves for new opportunities and for change. This includes attention to issues such as skills upgrading and other educational opportunities. The economy is now a learning economy in which ongoing attention to lifelong learning will be key to personal and business success.

Individuals have a responsibility to manage personal and household debt. In circumstances in which employment opportunities can change dramatically in a very short time, individuals should ensure they are prepared for periods with lower incomes. This means attention to household debt loads, household monthly expenses, and related retirement investments and savings. Lessons from Newfoundland and Labrador and the Maritime provinces following the moratorium on cod fishing are instructive in this case. Studies show that people invested a significant amount of the funding provided to fishermen through programs such as TAGS (The Atlantic Groundfish Strategy) in home renovations. With a long-term view to reducing their housing costs, investments in more energy-efficient heating systems, better insulation, and improved window and door systems end up reducing long-term costs to households.

People need to renew their commitments to their community. Voluntary groups can always use new helpers and skills sets. The growing share of young retirees in northern BC is creating a new pool of experienced people able to support both community development activities and successful population aging.

For Unions

Unions have a successful legacy and long-standing commitment to the welfare and well-being of their memberships. To maintain this role, unions should continue to support in-service training and skills improvement opportunities for their members. Through these investments, members will have a better chance of maintaining employment within a rapidly changing industrial and workplace environment. This is typically an area of union strength, and it needs to be enhanced to keep pace with the education and skills demands of new industries.

Unions should become prepared to provide information and support for workers considering an employee purchase of a production facility. There are many examples across Canada of successful employee purchase arrangements, with the most referenced illustration being the evolution of Tembec within the forest sector from its early beginnings through an employee purchase of a small forest-processing facility. But there are many other examples of this across BC, ranging from larger to smaller firms. Such circumstances may arise more frequently, for example, within the forest sector when major licensees focus on the high volume, low cost production of basic commodities and thus create opportunities for smaller facilities to become niche market producers. Production employees typically have the know-how to make plants run both effectively and efficiently. They will need support in areas of management, development, financial arrangements, and marketing.

Organized labour needs to expand some of the current models of emergency layoff and shutdown responses. When jobs are suddenly lost, the rapid deployment of information about processes, options, and expectations can be very helpful. Already tested by the Steelworkers Union in BC's central interior, this form of emergency support needs to be generalized.

Organized labour needs to be active in discussions about a creative re-bundling of assets and opportunities for small-, medium-, and large-scale innovations. The massive reduction in the number of members in forestry locals in the past twenty-five years means that fighting for the status quo industry should no longer be a focus. Expanding the range of forest timber and nontimber-related products, and the number and range of higher value and more labour intensive industries, needs attention. Flexibility also means developing innovative ways to organize those who now find themselves without the protection or support of collective agreements.

For the Federal Government

In northern BC, the federal government has developed a very effective tool for small business and entrepreneurial development. This tool is the network of Community Futures Development Corporation offices. Each of these offices is managed by an independent community-based board, and thus is responsive to local needs, but they also have a network of managers who can meet regularly to share information and best practices. They are supported by Canadian regional organizations that bring economies of scale to their internal information and education services. The federal government should renew its support for the Community Futures offices. It should strengthen the Community Futures interest in its original and core business of facilitating community development through management and investment advice for existing and new small businesses, including through its small business lending and self-employment programs.

An original Community Futures role in strategic community economic development planning needs to be modified and should move from "leading" to "supporting," commensurate with the argument for a more robust partnership between bottom-up initiatives and top-down supports. This modified role must move forward via a significant federal government base of support for the active participation of Community Futures offices in local and regional community and economic development planning. The skills and expertise in Community Futures offices around business and community economic development are significant and need to be made available within bottom-up debates and strategic-planning efforts. These efforts will occur across a scale from the community to large regions that far exceeds current Community Futures office service areas. Additional funding should be set in place to support and enhance the networking activities of the Community Futures offices and their role in communicating with the emerging regional development organizations across northern BC. A key piece of the community and economic development puzzle, they must be funded properly in order to contribute their full potential.

A second key area of activity for the federal government concerns the need to recognize that the time has come to finally transform Aboriginal Affairs and Northern Development Canada from a management to a capacity-building organization. The recent renaming of Indian and Northern Affairs Canada (INAC) to Aboriginal Affairs and Northern Development (AAND), together with its new vision, is reflective of the impetus for change, but our recommendations go further. The legacy of more than 130 years of federal agency management demands that something different be done to support

Aboriginal peoples across northern BC as they work to improve their social, economic, cultural, and environmental destinies. As part of a transition process, the federal government should consider creating up to four or more agencies within other line departments. In northern BC, however, these agencies would initially work between AAND and the line department, but would soon be incorporated within the existing activities and functioning of those line departments. Budget allocations for these new units would come from existing AAND funding. A transition could include the following:

- All matters related to health and health care issues would be transferred to a new unit that would eventually move into Health Canada.
- All matters related to the provision of social services, employment assistance, training, and related human development issues would be transferred to an interim unit that would eventually become part of Service Canada. There is perhaps no more important issue than human resources development. As more First Nations move to self-government and take responsibility for local delivery of a host of services and activities, there must be commitment to the long-term development and renewal of community capacity and readiness.
- All financial matters related to band administration and governance would be transferred to an interim unit that would eventually be moved into the Department of Finance.

All of these transitions need to be conceptualized and operationalized as part of the capacity building needed in support of moves towards the self-governing future that awaits First Nations after treaty settlement. These changes need to be about more than just creating "four new silos" within government – they need to be about moving towards an assistive platform for community development. The community development case for these changes is built around the need to shift from AAND's legislated responsibility for Indians under the Indian Act mandate to one that is more typically found in line with federal departments where the principle is to provide the national-level supports so that Canadians can realize their own, and their community's, potential. This is a critical shift in orientation. The former keeps us within a world of dependency through a "ward of the state" approach, while the latter can proactively prepare both people and places for the future. The latter also supports our argument for bottom-up initiatives assisted by top-down supports.

Another critical task is to complete the treaty process. We know that this continues to hamper community development among First Nations, business, and economic development across the province, and revenue streams to a number of levels of government. Both the federal and provincial governments have at times slowed the BC Treaty Commission process. This has not helped renewal in northern BC, and both levels of government must resolve to settle this very old obligation.

The federal government needs to support the process of economic development within First Nations communities. This will mean identifying and supporting an independent body to provide financial and investment advice. Many First Nations communities will be too small to undertake all of these exercises on their own. If First Nations within BC are able to come together to advocate for the creation of a First Nations version of a municipal finance authority, then the functions of this organization could be expanded through federal government support to provide economic development advice for communities entering into partnership and joint agreements. The standard business practice of due diligence must be made available with suitable legal and financial expertise at an affordable cost to our First Nations communities. Foundations for this approach already exist through the various First Nations trusts and equity funds, financial advice offices, and Aboriginal business development organizations.

The federal government needs to direct capacity and skills building around self-government to First Nations people and places. While work on treaties progresses, there is a need to accelerate community capacity building in anticipation of the "day after the treaty is signed." First Nations must be equipped for success.

Many of the above items deal with on-reserve First Nations, and the federal government needs to work in partnership with Aboriginal leaders and the provincial government to create a working framework for urban Aboriginal governance and the social and economic development that the urban Aboriginal community needs. The complexity and challenge of this particular task should not be underestimated. But with half or more of the Aboriginal population living off-reserve in urban settings of all sizes, the importance of the task should not be underestimated. The lack of attention to service delivery mechanisms, Elder circles, business development supports, the needs of the Aboriginal middle class, and a host of other matters underscore the need for attention to urban Aboriginal governance.

Finally, the federal government needs to expand its role in the development of infrastructure to ensure a globally competitive Canadian economy. Recent programs such as the Building Canada Plan, the Canada-BC Municipal Rural Infrastructure Fund, and links through the federal/provincial Gas Tax Agreement to processes like integrated community sustainability planning need to be expanded under a strategic approach for investing our limited infrastructure dollars wisely. These investments need to follow the best of the strategic approaches for competitive and adaptive rural economies recommended by groups like the OECD (2006). In this case, a Canadian version of the European Union's LEADER programs may be needed. Reactive

LEADER AND PLACE-BASED POLICY AND SUPPORT

Attention to a "new rural paradigm" includes attention to places instead of sectors and to investments instead of subsidies. The need for flexible place-responsiveness and an integrated approach to rural development means increased attention to at least the following four critical policy areas: (1) transport and communications infrastructure; (2) public service provision; (3) the value of rural natural and cultural amenities; and (4) the promotion of rural enterprise (including the development and financing of small- and medium-sized enterprises).

To support such an approach, the European Union (EU) has deployed a series of LEADER (Liaison Entre Actions de Développement Rural) programs. The LEADER Community Initiative began in 1991 with LEADER I, continued from 1994 to 1999 with LEADER II, and then from 2000 to 2006 with what is known as LEADER+. The LEADER program budget for 2000-2006 was 5,046.5 million Euros. LEADER is a well-known European program that uses an integrated and endogenous approach to foster rural development throughout the EU. The initiative is used in both lagging and leading rural regions and contains three main elements for implementation:

1 defining a specific territory or LEADER area
2 adopting an integrated approach that relies on endogenous actors and resources
3 creating a local action group (LAG).

The LAGs represent the key innovation in the program. The overall strategy for the program is defined (and primarily funded) by the European Commission. National and regional administrations establish subsidiary application norms, while the LAGs are responsible for managing the implementation of the program, developing local action plans, handling the allocation of project funds, and conducting evaluation procedures (OECD 2006). So successful has been the LEADER experiment that following 2006, most EU nations began incorporating the program's approach into their standard policy and planning frameworks for rural development programming (European Commission 2006).

investments in dated, shovel-ready projects do little to advance the future prosperity of northern BC.

For First Nations Governments

First Nations communities have to find a way to work in partnership with adjoining communities so they can scale up together to meet the needs for community and economic development. One model that has operated successfully in the past is that of the Northwest Tribal Treaty Nations. This voluntary grouping included membership from Haida Gwaii across the central interior to the Prince George region. It was able to undertake several successful exercises, including a very good economic development strategy plan, and to support a long-term basis for dialogue and mutual actions.

Wilson and Poelzer (2005: 12-13) argue that:

> As more self-government arrangements are negotiated and begin to function, First Nations will come into even greater contact and collaboration with existing governments at all levels in the provincial Norths, especially local and municipal governments. The need for some form of intergovernmental framework to address the needs of all peoples living in the provincial Norths, therefore, has never been more crucial.

First Nations governments need to work cooperatively across BC to form a senior body that can be responsible for handling the financial needs and services of individual bands. As noted above, a possible role model in this case may be the BC Municipal Finance Authority (MFA). This highly successful organization manages the loans, financing, and budget advice tasks for municipalities across the province. By pooling their financial resources and requests, the MFA is able to attain loans at much lower interest rates than might otherwise be available to individual municipalities. The MFA has also used its expertise in working with small municipalities to invest their funds for best returns and been helpful to local governments with advice and support during times of economic crisis. The success of the MFA is reflected in the fact that its credit rating has in recent years exceeded that of the provincial government. This type of arrangement will be a very critical tool for First Nations as they move into independent governance and small bands will need the financial clout of a larger organization when they seek funding.

First Nations communities, as other communities, need to focus on a hierarchy of investments that should be made to secure the participation of the whole community in potential employment and traditional activity benefits. To start, this involves investment in youth. Such investment includes support of mothers during their pregnancies and during the first two years after the child is born. This support for parenting and child development can build on successful existing programs so that investments yield very real benefits over the long run. Support for the youngest children will need attention to nutrition, health care, and developmental stimulation. Significant investments will then be needed to bring the best and most suited educational tools into the preschool and elementary school years. Models already exist that bring the community into the school and combine the existing curriculum with traditional activities and learning experiences.

The second level in this community development hierarchy involves the notion that children need opportunities to grow up with a solid cultural foundation. Such a cultural foundation is built with the knowledge of Elders. As a result, a second area of investment is with the Elders as they are the holders of such knowledge and are the traditional line for connecting across the generations. Supports for Elders, and support for bringing Elders into a host of learning opportunities, need to be expanded.

If the next generation of children and youth are to grow up within a balance of traditional and market economies and activities, they will need role models in employment and administrative capacities. As a result, a third area of investment is with working-age people so they can be positive role models and contribute in multiple ways to community development.[3]

In short, community development needs to focus on:

- investing in children first
- creating a healthy social and cultural community for children to grow up in by focusing on social development and community infrastructure
- building a local economy with positive role models in which there is attention to job training, investments in the working-age population, and attention to residential school survivors.

One of the critical issues in business competition concerns the scale at which one is able to operate. The timber allocations made by the Ministry of Forests to various First Nations across northern BC over the past couple of years highlights this issue. An opportunity exists for the creation of cooperative forest industry supports to First Nations-organized businesses (such as timber cruising, hauling, and falling), as well as in co-operative marketing streams. By joining a number of small timber allocations together, such a marketing co-op could have a sizeable timber supply that it can guarantee to local, regional, or international purchasers. The larger supply of product means more ability to negotiate favourable terms.

All of these needs are set against a backdrop of one of the most challenging aspects for First Nations government – namely, the structure and requirements associated with AAND election processes. These challenges are rooted in the fact that the federal government has imposed electoral processes modelled on systems of local governance that often do not fit with culturally appropriate and/or relevant governance mechanisms and that often fail to incorporate traditional leadership positions and roles. In many communities, this can lead to a conflicted set of governance structures including the AAND elected chief and council, hereditary chiefs, and traditional mechanisms for making decisions.

A second challenge associated with the imposed AAND local government model concerns the two-year cycle of elections. In this case, it leaves little opportunity for councils to develop stability and to follow through on long-term commitments to community development, economic visioning, human resource development, and a host of other critical capacity-building elements. Instead, elected chiefs and councils are caught in a continual process of election campaigning. This challenge was recognized many years ago in local government across BC as the terms of municipal and regional district councils were extended to three years.

Where First Nations communities have developed a constitutional management framework that is both culturally and place appropriate, it may be possible that AAND election and governance mechanisms can be removed. Such an approach has already been adopted in some communities. For those communities that choose to continue with the AAND process of chief and council elections, the period between elections should be lengthened to provide some additional foundation for stability.

Finally, we need to resolve the governance circumstances of the many Aboriginal people in northern BC who do not live on reserves. This group confronts a different set of opportunities and challenges. As noted above, this will mean working with provincial and federal governments, with Aboriginal leaders, and with the service providers who in many cases are providing de facto on-the-ground governance for some urban Aboriginal people. A framework for urban Aboriginal governance, which recognizes the contributions of the growing urban Aboriginal middle class, must be set in place soon, as the "urban reality" of northern Aboriginal peoples is very real.

For the Northern Development Initiative Trust

One of the critical needs in northern BC is for an organization with the responsibility to look forward to the future. The Northern Development Initiative Trust would be an appropriate agency for this important function. To realize this potential, however, it must become more than just a funding body and a loans agency with a very good rate of return. Instead, the NDI Trust needs to adopt an additional function around leadership in order to capitalize on the unique opportunity that it represents. The NDI Trust must be responsive to a northern vision and strategy and assist in the development of that strategy.

In addition to leadership, there is the question of inclusiveness. As noted many times in this book, a vision for renewal in northern BC must include

Aboriginal and non-Aboriginal voices and interests. Our future will be a collective future in which we share community, social, economic, and environmental concerns. This leadership will involve creating a forum for the voices of northern BC to debate the region's future and the best places to invest in order to to realize that future. In addition to being home to a northern BC dialogue, such leadership will involve representing the voices of northern BC to senior governments and within the national and international marketplace.

For the Northern Health Authority

Health care services are critical in community transition and the renewal of northern BC via a place-based approach to community and economic development. In view of its key role, the Northern Health Authority (NHA) needs to look at innovative uses of technology to:

- keep appropriate services open in all of our northern BC communities
- support care providers in small places
- continue to grow the skills and flexibility of our northern BC health care professionals
- keep seniors healthy and happy in their homes by providing appropriate supports
- reduce the numbers of northerners who need to travel for routine tests, care, and patient consults.

The NHA also needs to take the lead on supporting greater interagency coordination and cooperation. It can help break silos by partnering in new multi-purpose service centres.

For Northern BC Educational Bodies

To address current and future economic and community development needs for northern BC's rural and small-town places, access to leading edge research is not a luxury but an absolute requirement. In the knowledge economy, access to ongoing research will determine how we remain competitive and how we respond to changes that come our way. In this regard, northern BC has a strong foundation on which to build. In both the short and medium term, we must work towards creating a Northern BC Community Research and Development Cluster. Based on our experience and those of other OECD countries, the cluster would need to be a collaborative exercise involving the critical research hub at the University of Northern British Columbia (and its dispersed regional campuses) as well as the close participation of the three northern colleges (the College of New Caledonia, Northwest Community College, and Northern Lights College). There are supplemental opportunities to link with colleges in the Yukon and the Northwest

Territories. The breadth of facilities, staff, and expertise that each could provide in everything from trades training to small business development to a host of research capacities will help address the breadth of needs in northern communities. These institutions bring their expertise in how to connect effectively with other educational organizations such as professional training institutes for trades and the regulatory bodies of the various professions active across northern BC.

A Northern BC Community Research and Development Cluster would need to address a number of functions. The first component involves research work that combines both basic and applied topics and advances knowledge as developed and tested in our northern setting. The second component is information sharing (or knowledge mobilization in the current language of funding agencies). Many of our northern communities are interested in "doing" rather than "studying." Information sharing will therefore have to demonstrate value by effectively translating existing knowledge into usable material for northern communities. The third component involves capacity building, including a range of training and educational courses yet to be determined in targeted locales around emerging issues and expertise. Finally, such a cluster could serve as a repository for the studies, research, and information critical to supporting community development across northern BC. At present, so much of our history, our experience, and even our investments in critical or technical research are lost because of the lack of such a storehouse. With facilities such as the Northern BC Archives at UNBC, the libraries at each of our postsecondary institutions, and the high speed communications network that links these institutions and their facilities, the cluster could provide the basis for a collective memory of northern BC and a critical support for future decision making.

For Northern BC Economic Development Agencies

A number of economic development organizations and agencies already exist across northern BC. In keeping with the notion of scaling up to be viable in the global economy, we need to seriously look at creating a Trade Northern BC organization. Such an organization needs to operate at two levels. The first is to be a marketing venue for the many small entrepreneurs who lack the skills to use new information technologies to reach potential markets. The second level could be to link our large producers in trading consortia who can work together for better access to markets and transportation. There are some existing examples of this collaboration (e.g., the Northern Interior Mining Group of suppliers and services, and the cooperation between several large forestry companies in a new export shipping facility in Richmond), and the need will only increase over time. If we are to truly develop the potential of existing and nascent economic clusters we will need to support cooperation and information sharing to build competitive strength. The collaborative ingredients within economic clusters do not materialize without concerted and supportive effort.

Conclusion

This chapter has reviewed a variety of issues and actions that various actors can adopt in support of a long-term vision and agenda for renewal in northern British Columbia. It opened with a portrait of "northern BC in twenty years." The purpose of this portrait was to demonstrate what could be accomplished – to illustrate what could be possible. The second part of the chapter identified sets of actions that groups, governments, communities, and organizations need to undertake now to move us towards (or backcast from) realizing this vision. Renewal in northern BC is a huge task – especially given that it has been largely neglected for the past thirty years. These sets of actions are by no means exhaustive, but they speak to an ethos that reminds us of the best way to accomplish large and long-term projects: get started on small things, maintain a commitment to the vision, and this will facilitate a cumulative impact towards renewal.

In the following chapter, we present ideas for innovative policy structures and mechanisms that will bring together the various actors identified in this chapter to help co-construct a renewed northern community and economic landscape.

Part 4
Conclusion

10
On Intervention: Constructing a Northern Place

> W.A.C. Bennett was there through the building, the infrastructure building and had great foresight. Think about the energy plan he had – it was unbelievably courageous and clever. And the bridges and roads. To put that kind of money into the hinterland where nobody was living at the time was courageous. (Grace McCarthy, former BC Cabinet Minister, Social Credit Government, 1975-1988, in Plecas 2006: 85).

> Until we get some sense that there is maybe someone else out there who would maybe want to consume that kind of electricity and actually contribute substantially to the construction of it, I think it's prudent for government to say, "Well, why would we build a line up there that's not going anywhere?" (Richard Neufeld, Minister of Energy, Mines and Petroleum Resources, Liberal Government, 2000-2009, in Simpson 2007).

The research on which this book is based traverses a full cycle of economic boom and bust in northern British Columbia. At the start of the formal research period in 2002, the global demand for resources ushered in a period of economic prosperity that spread throughout the entire province. This period of growth was not, for the first time in years, the exclusive experience of the metropolitan regions of the province. Economic growth, employment demand, population increases, and surplus spread throughout the hinterland. In keeping with the boom mentality, this growth was not conceptualized as a cyclical phenomenon, requiring consideration of planning and investment to counterbalance the impacts of the inevitable bust. Rather, a booster-mentality confidence in the vast resource wealth of the province once again impeded significant discussion of the need to build on strengths to mitigate future downturns. There was no vision for structural transition in the economy of the north to establish a more diversified and resilient economic and social base.

In fairness to decision makers presiding over the boom, the general scramble to capitalize on an economic upswing stresses limited capacity for future planning. Local governments often lose staff to the private sector, citizens are swept up in the surge of opportunity, and all stakeholders are simply reacting to change in an effort to maximize economic gain. This was made worse by decades of inattentiveness to "re-equipping" our northern places and economies. Key economic and transportation infrastructure, as well as workplace skills, were not sufficient to extract maximum wealth from the boom. Structural conditions of inherent weakness in the economy were hidden by the surge of capital, and cries of "this boom can't end" stifled reflection and thinking and planning for the future. This cycle has repeated itself to varying degrees a half-dozen times since the early 1980s.

In 2008, over the course of a few brief months, thousands of jobs were lost. The combination of the strong Canadian dollar, the collapse of the US housing market, and ongoing taxes and duties for exports to the United States slammed the BC forest sector. Rising development costs have hit other industries, halting projects and extending the downturn to other resource industries. As the world sunk into economic crisis, the shifting economic climate once again exposed our long-term dependency on commodities. As with other bust periods, there was a growing chorus from industry and businesses for assistance. The federal government responded with a broad but unfocused and unstrategic stimulus package, and the BC government followed suit in a more limited, but still unstrategic way.[1]

For students and followers of the economic history of British Columbia, the above paragraphs could have been written in 1983, or 1992, or 1999. The pattern is largely the same, and the proposed solutions to each bust are equally repetitive: calls for the diversification of product lines, diversification of markets, investments in research and development, replacement of aging capital infrastructure, cutting tax rates, etc. So, if the action-reaction cycle is the same, with only the date changing, what value does this book add (value-added being, of course, a favourite mantra of the diversification efforts for the economy as a whole) to our understanding of the northern economy? How does our research advance the cause for change, such that we are better able to mediate the vagaries of the market and public policy priorities and build more robust and resilient northern communities?

These questions underlie the core purpose of this book, which is to describe the meaning, and reveal the potential, of a place-based approach to development in northern BC. In the increasingly fast-paced and changing global economy, the significance of place-based development is underscored by the fact that competitiveness is now the key to success. To reiterate: if global capital can invest anywhere, why would it invest in your place? The focus of supportive public policy and of local actions must be on equipping our northern places to be competitive in the twenty-first-century global economy.

In addition to guiding our analysis of northern BC, the lens of place contributes an important perspective that does alter the traditional dynamics of the boom-bust patterns that define the northern economy. By adopting a place-oriented approach to our work, we have heard voices in the north calling for change: not bandaid assistance or the same booster tools of economic development, but real systemic change across the economic, social, environmental, and cultural landscape of the north. These voices are questioning the economic imperative of growth that has led to uneven development and growing social pressures, and they are looking for alternatives to the stopgap programs that past policy typically delivered during economic bust periods. People in the north are seeking structural change to the dynamics of the northern economy, mainly, more guidance by the voices and aspirations of northerners than by metropolitan-oriented politicians and distant market forces. Through the lens of place, we have witnessed the emergence of northern BC as a genuine place, growing up from its origins as an economic space, to a region defined by whole communities, rooted peoples and cultures, and a regional identity that may mobilize to foster collective action for development.

The purpose of this chapter is to reflect on and advance core themes discussed throughout this book. We use the concept of intervention as an integrative tool to present various dynamics associated with the essence of place-based development, which we have described throughout as being the following: doing things matters and not doing things has consequences. Place implies intervention to create a multifaceted foundation for development: intervention means actively shaping and investing in places to produce a variety of long-term goals, be they economic, community, environmental, or cultural.

Intervention

Throughout the text, we have drawn comparisons with the WAC Bennett era that governed BC for more than twenty years through a period that is commonly known as the "long boom." While not wishing to romanticize this period (and we have taken lengths to illustrate the weaknesses and negative legacies of the decisions taken during this time), it provides a valuable comparative perspective because of the interventionist approach to development adopted by this conservative-leaning government. The WAC Bennett era informs the present that, even given the dramatic differences in economic situation, when guided by a distinct vision, we have the capacity to influence and shape our development future.

The WAC Bennett era is useful because then, as now, intervention was approached with caution. The period following the Second World War was dramatic for its legacy of public investment, and as noted, Bennett's approach was characterized as intervention if necessary, but not necessarily intervention. This strategy was indirectly supported by a national and international climate of public investment in postwar reconstruction. Supported by Keynesian policy approaches, Western governments were actively engaged in development programs to address regional disparities and uneven development. As such, the investment orientation of the Social Credit party was certainly not contradicting any international economic trend or ideology that would have stigmatized it as a reckless spender or inefficient interferer in market forces.

Over the course of the past thirty years, a number of factors shifted the strategic and perceptual orientation of governments towards development. First, the influence of neoliberalism fundamentally altered the strategic orientation of Western governments. Intervention gained a poor reputation as interference, corrupting the efficiency and flow of "natural" market forces. Similarly, investment in social and economic infrastructure was largely abandoned in favour of tax cuts, deregulation, and the withdrawal of programs and services. In economies such as Canada and BC, successive generations were content to exploit the investments of the postwar generation with little reinvestment of their own – choosing instead the empty rhetoric of "tax cuts." The theoretical underpinnings of early neoliberalism predicted that governments could achieve the reproduction of social and economic development primarily as a by-product of economic growth. The global economic collapse of 2008, and the lack of residual social and economic development strength, has shown these assumptions to be patently false. As McArthur (2010: 3) argues, the "recession of 2008 was for many an unexpected development. It has re-focused attention on the need for government and government policy."

Second, aside from the ideological drivers of the neoliberal agenda, there was a case for the legitimate questioning and assessment of particular development programs. As described in earlier chapters, the narrow economic lens of various regional development programs through the 1980s and 1990s, their reliance on abstract theories such as growth poles, the unquestioned adherence to an export-based theory as a one-way prescription, and the challenges posed by intergovernmental policy coordination produced uncertain results and soured the reputation of intervention. The long-term commitments and integrated approaches that delivered results during the WAC Bennett era were not easily replicated under the conditions of shorter-term cycles (and some would argue attention spans) of other provincial and federal governments.

Finally, the forces of economic and political restructuring brought about significant economic and population decline in rural areas. There are, of course, other drivers of the overall global trend towards urbanization (e.g., amenities, opportunities for dual incomes). However, the experience of decline perpetuated a commonly held policy perception that the deterioration of the rural condition was inevitable and that intervention in this sense was tantamount to propping up failing communities or impeding the progressive flow of labour and other factors of production to more prosperous areas. Such an incorrect perception fails to recognize the very clear hand of policy in these matters – policy that often undercuts local capacity, economic resiliency, and the conditions for potential success. These policy actions include the purposeful withdrawal and closure of rural services by successive federal and provincial governments that have contributed to a recursive process of population and social and economic development loss in rural and small-town places. As a result, the political weight of rural areas declined significantly during this period. The political cost of ignoring the rural vote decreased significantly, fundamentally altering the dynamics of power that previously shaped heartland-hinterland relations.

Ultimately, the combined weight of these forces both caused and simultaneously reinforced the resource bank perception of rural areas that we have critiqued throughout the text. Concerning more recent economic and development trends, we state emphatically that the resource bank approach to provincial development is short-sighted and rural decline is not inevitable. The ideological certainty of a narrow and reductionist view of neoliberalism has waned, and into that breach we are starting to recognize the important role of the state. Our understanding and documentation of the development process – in terms of its complexity, integration, and indicators – has improved. Moreover, rural places themselves have proved to be far more durable than the predictions of urban-based policy makers. In short, the entire pretext that has undermined the foundation of intervention over the past thirty years is reversing. Researchers, development practitioners, and politicians are re-examining roles and questioning theory in favour of seeking to understand rural opportunity in its context, a conceptual transition we interpret as the shift from space economies to place economies.

In the following sections, we outline a variety of the forces and trends associated with the emergence of place as a legitimate rationale for rural intervention: the new economy, rural-urban interdependence, sustainable development, and the continued role of the state in rural and northern development. As the epigraphs at the beginning of this chapter illustrate, we have some distance to travel before we have an approach to rural development that is driven by foresight and courage instead of withdrawal.

The New Economy in the North

Throughout this book, we have discussed various dimensions of the new economy. It is interesting to note that the term "new economy" is not necessarily met with enthusiasm across northern BC. New economy has been associated with a variety of programs or used as rationale in recent years for de-emphasizing the important role of the resource economy in favour of, for example, the "information economy" or other such terms (e.g., high tech economy). Governments, chasing the high tech bubble, raced to implement programs to support the "dot com" industry. While the relevance of these programs in certain areas no doubt played a role in facilitating an awareness of the information economy as a sector of diversification, its relevance across the northern landscape is highly variable. The fact that workers in the high tech economy can choose to live anywhere, does not mean that they will do so. Access to amenities, the networking effects of clustering, availability of communications infrastructure, and access to education are important variables in attracting and retaining high tech businesses and workers and their families. The concern from northern places that are unable to compete in these sectors is that their failure to do so represents yet another reason to ignore their communities or to view their ties to traditional economic sectors as backward and subject to decline.

Our view of the new economy, one that is relevant to the context of the north, is associated with a broader and more integrated understanding of the whole economy. First, we have illustrated how competitive advantage now matters more than comparative advantage, and that territory or place now matters more than economic sector. What this means in real terms to northern communities and regions is that we must seek to understand economies and economic development "in place." This does not entail a discarding of the resource economy, but, rather, a rebundling of traditional assets to better serve both community and economic development. For example, Prince George has been successful in fostering an emerging high-tech sector, but one based on its traditional strengths within the forestry sector. The town is not expecting to compete with the Lower Mainland for the attraction of the video game industry, but, rather, is looking to its traditional assets and seeking diversity based on those niche areas as a technology hub for industrial processing.

Second, we have illustrated how competitiveness within the new economy demands investment. Strategic investments in the place economy do not represent an inefficient form of interference with the market. They do not entail propping up enterprises that have failed to invest properly in their own productivity. Similarly, investment here is not dependent on governments picking winners and losers in the economy – something for which they have shown a particularly poor record over the years. Rather, place-based investment is about maintaining and advancing the broader social and economic infrastructure of communities and regions in order to provide a resilient and flexible foundation for all potential forms of development. Cuts to services and infrastructure here represent a short-term "expenses" approach to viewing rural expenditures that undercuts the framework necessary for thriving within the new economy. Intervention in the place-based economy is necessary for facilitating the multiplier effects of investments in social and economic infrastructure, thereby turning these expenses into a platform for real future development.

From Northern Town to Northern Community

The first wave of intervention in the north was supported by the concept of instant towns. These towns were intimately tied to the surrounding resource base, usually forestry or mining. The model for postwar instant town development, as discussed earlier, was Kitimat. Built with private industry leadership (Alcan), the tenets for success included the separation of industrial from residential land uses, the provision of a high amenity community that would be attractive to a range of family and household types, and the establishment of a suite of local industries to diversify the economy and avoid the problems of single-industry dependence. The first two lessons were well replicated in government-led instant towns such as Mackenzie and Tumbler Ridge. The failure to prebuild economic diversity into all the subsequent instant towns in northern BC both confirmed the resource bank view that successive provincial governments have held of northern BC and created the boom-bust treadmill that has continued to challenge us.

This background provides two important cautions to the enthusiasm of place-based development. First, the development destiny of rural and northern communities is still very much dependent on their geographic reality. Distance and isolation still matter. Place is not an independent variable, but an integrated characteristic within a surrounding territory. Places that are isolated, despite their potential assets, face competitive disadvantages that permeate all social and economic dimensions. These barriers may prove significant to attempts to diversify the local economy or seek innovative solutions to service provision. Second, towns have demonstrated resolve to succeed following boom-bust periods: committees were struck, strategic plans developed, and initiatives mobilized and launched to revitalize the community. As this social response to economic challenge varies from community to community, studies have sought to understand this process of resilience or capacity. Researchers have provided lists of characteristics and indicators, but the reality of what works in one place versus what works in another is perhaps best captured by the phrase: it depends. The robustness of the network of social relations and the capacity of the actors involved are complex and interacting ingredients in the development process. What is certain is that bottom-up activities and plans still need supportive top-down policy supports to assist with economic renewal and diversification.

Over time, northern BC's resource-dependent and instant towns have transformed themselves into complete communities. Certainly, part of this may be because of their strategic location or the vastness and ongoing market competitiveness of their particular commodity. These variables allow communities the time needed to establish complex social and economic roots. However, it is clear in the communities that we have visited throughout the north that many survive for social and economic reasons beyond the single resource they were created to exploit or because of the transportation corridor they inhabit. These communities exist because they have become home to the people who live there – and are, therefore, places worth caring about and working to maintain. The extraordinary volunteer commitments dedicated to community planning and development throughout the north speak to the importance of place. Equally, dedication to home underscores the innovative capacity witnessed throughout the north to devise alternative approaches to service delivery and the provision of amenities in order to maintain a sense of community and ongoing development. Recent efforts to build the service and infrastructure base to support population aging-in-place and create more senior-friendly communities are proof of this trend.

For Aboriginal communities, the recognition and reconciliation of title over traditional territories has the same transformative effect. First Nations are experiencing a period of renewal in their cultures, communities, and economies. Title and treaty processes (or the memoranda of understanding or government-to-government agreements that precede them) have begun to address the attempted cultural annihilation associated with the reserve system and the Indian Act, bringing about cultural revival, associated with the powers of political control and self-determination, and economic revival, associated with territorial resources and monetary compensation. Addressing the development deficiencies of Aboriginal communities will be a long-term process, but one grounded in cultural and economic ties to place. For example, the Northwest Tribal Treaty Nations developed the following eight-part strategic action plan to foster sustainable wealth for First Nations in northern BC (NWTT 2004):

1 Governance – Stable First Nation governance, which creates a secure political environment for business, is required. It will build confidence, attract commitment, and provide security of assets for enterprises.
2 Access to lands and resources – First Nations need to reclaim traditional territories and utilize their resources. The exercise of jurisdiction and utilization of these resources, and the management and utilization of these resources for their own benefit, is essential to economic progress.

3 Planning capacity – Develop, initiate, complete, and implement sound fundamental planning processes. First Nations should move away from short-term and program-dependent activities, and towards being multifunctional and comprehensive.
4 Human resource capacity – Strategies must be implemented that focus on increasing educational attainment, complemented by a broad program of community and economic development at the regional and local levels.
5 Entrepreneurship – Developing and fostering an entrepreneurial community with an entrepreneurial attitude is necessary. It demands the provision of capital and training courses to develop entrepreneurial skills, a supportive environment, effective leadership, sound institutions with integrity, and strong business relations.
6 Business and financial capacity – Strategies to increase expertise and proficiency in financial and business operations are needed, along with an organizational format that is managed with sound business and financial principles and is not based on political criteria.
7 Access to capital – Access to equity capital is essential to strengthening First Nations participation in the economy. There is a need for more capital overall, for a broader scope of financing instruments, including a pool of equity capital, new sources of equity capital, a focused effort to accumulate and retain capital, and a community-based focus to programs.
8 Access to markets – Recognition is needed of key markets outside the north, market demands and prices for products or services, and a clear focus on creating access to markets for the products and services that First Nations plan to develop and produce.

For both the Aboriginal and non-Aboriginal communities of the north, the emerging or reawakened sense of community informs us that the economy, even in its most extreme globalized forms, is not placeless. Many of the arguments presented in this book to promote or defend the concept of place as an instrument of development are grounded in an economic rationale. This is done, in part, to sway the skeptics of intervention and to illustrate the integrated complexity of the development process. However, the evolution of community in the north transcends economic arguments. Intervention for the sake of community, for home, is representative of the values of British Columbians and Canadians to provide quality of life and a fair standard of living to the people engaged in economic activities that serve us all. Everything we are learning about the creative and knowledge economy and the next generation workforce reinforces the value and critical importance of these very features of economic success. The economic argument remains, but the economic renewal of the north is dependent on its communities of place as much, if not more, than its physical resources.

Rural-Urban Interdependence

The messy dynamics associated with arguments concerning the economic dependency of rural areas on urban economies present significant challenges to calls for the economic renewal of northern BC through a heightened threshold of state and private sector intervention. Rural areas across Canada, and throughout the industrialized world, have been adjusting to the postwar demographic realities associated with urbanization. In BC, this has led to the growing population and political weight of the metro Vancouver and Capital regions, continuing and reinforcing the core-periphery dynamics that link urban and rural areas in the province. We have discussed the implications of these dynamics in terms of hiding BC's economic dependence on natural resources (sourced in the hinterland) and leading to a perpetuation of the resource bank model of development for the province. Each of these forces limits the economic diversification potential of the north by binding the region within the confines of the staples trap.

We have illustrated how a continued resource bank model of provincial development is supported by an aging and creaking rural infrastructure. The question, then, is, can we continue to separate economic development for the province as a whole from the dynamics of rural development? If this is both economically feasible and culturally acceptable, then we should not advocate in favour of rural intervention. Our purpose here has been to illustrate the social, economic, and environmental reasons that this is neither economically prudent nor acceptable to the people and the future of BC. As such, the independency between rural and urban areas demands greater attention to rural reinvestment for two main reasons (FCM 2009). First, while urban economies are obviously significant to the economic diversification of the province, the most recent economic boom in BC, still driven by the global demand for resources, illustrates the continuing clear interdependency between rural areas and overall provincial prosperity. Some may feel that the resource economy is hidden to urban populations, politicians, and researchers, but it is hidden in the concrete, the buses and SkyTrain cars, the health care services, and the education facilities of the metropolitan core.

Second, place-based development informs us that we are missing the economic potential of relatively untapped local and regional economies throughout the north. Northerners spoke to us about the "missing 80 percent" of the economy – the community economy – that rarely receives any attention from policy makers or funders, but that is most fundamentally linked with residents and overall community resilience. Investments in the local economy stimulate the local multiplier effect, create local job opportunities, and support residents committed to building more stable long-term communities that offer a greater diversity of services and economic opportunity. This local economy requires the attention of supportive endogenous development policies and internal business retention and expansion programs. To that end, a significant gap exists in the number of northern communities that have community economic development plans and strategies and dedicated institutional resources (like an economic development officer) to coordinate and facilitate local economic activities. Moreover, there is the challenge and opportunity of regionalizing community business ventures to receive economy-of-scale advantages through activities such as sourcing, production, marketing, and transportation to make niche businesses more competitive. Programs like the NDI Trust and the regionally based Community Futures organizations represent positive institutions that can foster contextually sensitive and informed development. They can provide support for the "other" 80 percent of the economy, but they do so through highly variable and relatively small-scale mechanisms. Foresight to support rural and small-town community economic development recognizes that healthy northern economies will contribute to a more robust provincial economy and ease the social and economic costs commonly associated with boom-bust patterns of resource dependency that may exacerbate trends towards uneven development.

Sustainable Development

People across northern BC understand the basic tenets of sustainability and wish to see a revitalization of the north grounded in principles that respect the integration of the community, cultural, economic, and environmental attributes of the province. However, translating the principles of sustainable development into action faces a variety of inherent rural challenges. A first barrier concerns the common rural economic practice of attracting large resource-intensive industries. In colloquial terms, this "smokestack chasing" is a stubbornly consistent if not wholly outdated development strategy that persists, despite research that points to its relative impotence in terms of net gain for community economies (Markey et al. 2005). Sustainability principles within this context may be seen as a threat to traditional rural economies. At best, sustainability is ignored as irrelevant, or at worst, targeted as a distinct threat to community viability and a rural "way of life." At a deeper conceptual level, combinations of the rural idyll and frontierism may hinder the connection between rural lifestyle and the need to adopt more sustainable living practices. People and communities in northern BC do not experience the same pressures of finiteness when compared with their more densely populated urban neighbours. As a result, northern populations may be less likely to adopt sustainable planning practices (Wells 2002).

In addition to the perceived relevance of sustainability in the northern BC setting, the dependence of communities on the resource and public sectors, and the lack of capacity to adjust to change and accommodate additional responsibilities, impacts their ability to incorporate sustainability into community plans. Communities across northern BC may have fewer resources at their disposal, due to the processes of economic and political restructuring, to commit to sustainable development projects. This, however, represents both a significant challenge to and opportunity for these communities. Northern places may accommodate or be stressed by the additional burdens of responsibility demanded by the governance regimes of sustainable development (i.e., greater local participation). Economically, northern BC's communities may plan in more integrated ways to maximize economic advantages, or they may become overwhelmed by the infrastructure deemed necessary to compete and to provide new standards of amenities for local quality of life. Furthermore, the potential cost advantages associated with sustainable forms of infrastructure (e.g., less waste, less energy use) may provide viable solutions for communities to afford infrastructure renewal, providing they are able to make the investments in the first place and construct financing arrangements that allow a longer term to recoup costs. Senior governments can play vital roles in providing programs and leveraging funds to help places overcome specific capacity limitations.

In addition to these community-level impacts, the application of sustainable development at broader scales presents two additional compelling arguments favouring policy, program, and investment intervention in northern BC. First, the province has a responsibility to balance and mediate the impacts of sustainable development across the provincial landscape. As we have illustrated, however, the ecosystem conservation or preservation objectives associated with provincial sustainability have often been imposed on rural areas. Rural places tend to absorb the negative externalities associated with environmental decision making, to the benefit of broader provincial and even global ecological objectives. There is now an opportunity to take advantage of, and support, the important agricultural, local foods, farmers' markets, organic farming, and similar land-based activities and movements common across the north. BC has a long history of area-based management processes designed to achieve environmental objectives through integrated planning (e.g., land and resource management processes); however, the plans are under constant pressure, tend to ignore the most contentious land use issues, and are rife with power imbalances in the debate among competing interests. Given that meeting the demands of sustainable development will be an ongoing process (i.e., a single plan or planning process will not suffice in perpetuity), senior levels of government will continue to have a role to play in coordinating and mediating area-based sustainability objectives. In addition, ensuring that the costs and benefits of these decisions are shared equitably (in terms of impact and compensation) among rural and metropolitan residents remains a government responsibility.

Second, perhaps the greatest test of vision and foresight for northern development in BC will entail the future dependency of urban areas on the accessible resources and food production systems of adjacent rural regions.

Climate change, rising energy costs, and the associated challenges of containing and minimizing greenhouse gas production, will likely have a localizing effect on the economy. Our capacity to import cost-effective resources and foodstuffs from distant, now competitive, regions will diminish. This will increase our reliance on local, nearer, producing regions. Moreover, the modes of production themselves are likely to change, which may have a reversing effect on the amount of labour required to produce agricultural products and extract other types of resources. The transition of the entire system of rural production will require considerable leadership and coordinative capacity from senior governments.

The present uncertainties associated with the localization of the economy (including issues like the timeline of transition, the viability of technological replacement, and costs) represent dynamics of uncertainty that are similar to those that confronted the WAC Bennett government in the 1950s. First, the decision to inject massive amounts of public funds into what were largely considered empty hinterlands required a commitment to a long-term vision and an integrated approach to reaping the benefits of an investment orientation to province building. Similarly, the decision to invest in flexible, resilient, and sustainable forms of development will require a commitment to a long-term vision of renewing the economy. Both periods require the leadership capacity to rise above the fray of dissenting voices and the muddle of indefinite causality – that is, intervention if necessary, but not necessarily intervention. Second, the WAC Bennett government did not "go it alone" in its approach to development. Social Credit policies were consistent with the public investment patterns of other provinces and industrialized nations during the postwar reconstruction boom. BC was then, as it is now even more so, part of the global trading and production system. Decisions to invest in new technologies, sustainable forms of infrastructure, and the conservation and preservation of public land are interdependent with the sustainability decisions of other places – at least in terms of mitigating the short-term displacement costs of shifting the economy onto a more sustainable platform of production and trade. This provides an additional rationale for the intervention of senior governments in advocating and negotiating with trading partners.

State Role in the North

Attention to the role of local actors and the need to accommodate local flexibility sometimes obscures a rationale, indeed a need, for continued involvement by the state in supporting rural and small-town development across northern BC within a global economic context. One of the central lessons we draw from BC's province-building era is that effective rural development must include a partnership between top-down state actors and bottom-up community interests. The continued participation of the state is crucial. This is because it has jurisdictional responsibility over critical public policy levers that can facilitate local and regional change. The state has the mandate to act on a provincial scale and, thus, has responsibility for a wider body of supports and tools to facilitate locally based, bottom-up, rural and small-town development visions based on local assets and aspirations. It is just not practical to talk about new local industry and/or development options without recognizing the provincial policy levers needed to realize them.

In addition to leveraging and facilitating rural development opportunities, the challenges facing the northern hinterland require the scale and coordinating capacity of senior governments. The impacts of the mountain pine beetle epidemic, issues of land use uncertainty tied to the First Nations treaty process, and the search for innovative solutions to service delivery require diverse state roles. These issues are of a structural nature that supersedes the capacity of individual communities, and even the region, to confront them effectively.

The lesson of critical state involvement has not entirely been lost. For example, there has been considerable federal and provincial government investment in the retrofitting of the port of Prince Rupert from a bulk cargo terminal to a container cargo terminal. From the remediation perspective, the decision of the federal government to establish a $1 billion community transition fund is evidence of its willingness to intervene. This recognizes that flexible engagement with the global economy to create local, regional, and national benefits requires significant state interest and investment. However, while piecemeal examples of such state investment do exist, what has not been carried forward from the WAC Bennett era lessons is the need for a long-term and coherent approach to such state partnerships with local initiative. We are not advocating for a return to the 1950s industrial resource model of rural development; however, we are arguing for the lessons that show the value of top-down and bottom-up partnerships working over time within a coherent and supportive public policy framework. Such a framework is necessary for rural development that is appropriate to the new circumstances of the contemporary global economy. The state, simply put, still has a basic and supportive role in equipping rural and small-town places to be responsive and flexible.

Intervention as Investment in Northern BC

Intervention to build resilient and responsive communities in northern BC will require investment. This investment includes direct infrastructure development and enabling funds to support local and regionalist efforts. We have consistently emphasized the developmental benefits associated with the scale and coordinated nature of the investments injected into the hinterland throughout the earlier province-building era. Acknowledging the comparative uncertainty and complexity of that past era with the current

Table 15

Investment options for Northern BC

1950s Resource development policies	2010+ Options
Enhance industrial infrastructure • large industries • communication networks	Build flexible infrastructures • physical • human • community • economic
Stabilize provincial revenues • certainty to invest in other programs • commodity focus	Create new revenue streams • rebundle traditional assets • create clusters of economic innovation
Create resource employment • build town economies • support regions generating BC's wealth	Recreate regional employment • provide a service foundation • exploit competitive assets

times (in order to counter arguments that paint the past as a much simpler period), we do recognize that given current budgetary dynamics and the nature of modern development, the two periods are not interchangeable. As such, we have sought to learn from earlier investment lessons and to infuse them with both a highly contextualized understanding of northern BC and more recent insights into place-based development. Through this synthesis, we can identify strategic opportunities for updating a vision for investment in northern BC (see Table 15).

Our first theme, renovating the industrial infrastructure, requires a holistic and updated understanding of infrastructure itself. Our research identified four areas of flexible infrastructure development needed in northern BC. To reiterate, each represents targets for investment that are designed to revitalize opportunities for long-term, diversified economic development. First, there is a need to renew and extend the region's physical infrastructure. Such investments have been a cornerstone, and to meet the needs of a new economy, this infrastructure needs to be renewed (Harvey 2004). Investments, transportation, communications, and local civic infrastructure act as long-term development assets that pay dividends over decades and generations. Second, human capacity infrastructure concerns education and training, both for youth and for an established workforce seeking to compete in new economic sectors. Human resource development will be a crucial support to regional diversification in a new economy described as flexible and dynamic. Third, there is a very strong need to renew and diversify community capacity. Delivery of health care, education, social services, and support for the social economy and the voluntary sector must be accomplished in ways that recognize rural and small-town realities in order to assist both community and economic development. Fourth, infrastructure renewal must encompass economic and business support and training services including access to capital and business development advice, especially for small and emerging businesses, and supports for the development of a robust suite of social economy businesses (Lukkarinen 2005).

Our second theme involves shifting from a focus on stabilizing provincial revenue to creating new revenue streams. Investments must focus on a rebundling of the traditional assets in the north. Northern BC's economy will continue to depend on its resource strengths, but the province must view and use these resources in different ways in order to create innovative clusters based on knowledge and skills (de Wolf 2002; Goldberg 2004). This represents a reversal of the resource bank approach to provincial growth and fosters opportunities for regional economic diversification through active reinvestment.

Finally, revitalizing regional employment in the north requires an investment orientation that recognizes the critical role played by services in rural communities and demonstrates a more sophisticated understanding of rural competitive advantage. First, given the challenges posed by market-based service delivery models, the provision of services in rural and small-town places faces particular geographic and demographic challenges. However, the narrow parameters on which questions of efficiency are assessed completely miss a deeper understanding of the role of services within small-town economies. In rural and small-town places, the provision of basic social, health, education, and infrastructure services provides a crucial foundation for both day-to-day economic activities and periods of economic adjustment. An investment mindset (in addition to policy coordination) is necessary to realize the leveraging effect generated by such services. Second, before committing to an investment approach, local and extra-local decision makers must wrestle to understand the dynamics of rural competitiveness. Too often, economic strategy reports fail to adequately fit development recommendations into the context of particular rural places. Within the rural context, however, constructing place-based competitiveness can be a challenge (Markey et al. 2006b). The specific dynamics of rural and small-town places (smaller populations and more limited financial and technical capacity) may limit the effectiveness with which rural places are able to respond to the complex and often resource-intensive (e.g., amenity pressures) demands of evolving competitive standards. As a result, rural areas must make investment decisions wisely and capitalize on any potential for regional cooperation in order to compete. This includes reconceptualizing traditional comparative assets like cheap land and access to resources, and capitalizing on rural strengths, such as the existence of strong social networks and a high quality of life. It necessitates proactive and innovative approaches to building consensus for identifying and sharing regional investments. Realizing the investment mentality and facilitating appropriate action requires new ways to frame the roles and responsibilities of all actors.

Co-constructing Northern Renewal

One of the continuing arguments in this book is that effective responsiveness to ongoing social and economic change in today's fast-paced world must involve place-based, bottom-up initiatives that are linked closely with supporting top-down public policy. This recognizes the inherent limits on the ability of senior governments to react to rapid change across diverse regions, as well as the desire and, indeed, the requirement to use local and regional knowledge in finding flexible opportunities within local, regional, national, and global economies that fit with place-based assets and aspirations. Combining the assets of the top down with the bottom up, and reframing the relationships between such actors, defines a co-constructed development reality for northern BC (Bryant 2010). This approach involves the three elements described below:

1. supports and structures for bottom-up strategic planning dialogue
2. supports and structures for coordinating the provincial government's role in the co-creation of supportive top-down public policy
3. a mechanism for facilitating ongoing exchange between the development of bottom-up strategic planning and the co-creation of top-down supportive public policy to ensure they are complementary.

Supports and Structures for Local and Regional Strategic Planning

A critical first element in the bottom-up generation of strategic planning goals and initiatives involves creating a structure for regional dialogue and collaboration. Regional districts may be an option, but in the literature they are generally considered to cover too small an area to be effective. In some cases, nascent structures may already exist – such as beetle action coalitions, trusts, etc. But even where they exist, these bodies must address critical structural issues – specifically by including more equal participation by Aboriginal and rural interests, as well as a mandate that is expanded to recognize and include the recursive and reciprocal relationship between community development and economic development – in order to be effective.

A second key element in creating a local and regional strategic planning structure is that there must be a process for ongoing dialogue with the communities and people. For both local governments and these new regional development bodies, there must be mechanisms for continually reassessing economic and social pressures and opportunities against community aspirations and assets. Failure to do so will create a significant disjuncture between plans and communities – a recipe for delay, wasted investment, and failure.

A third element involves the need to provide support for these new strategic planning bodies. Their key activity of dialogue and communication in support of strategic community and economic development planning takes time and fiscal resources. Our work has shown that the failure of most economic strategies across rural and small-town BC is the direct result of a lack of commitment and investment in both the foundations of the strategy creation process and in the follow through and implementation of suggested initiatives.

For those who argue we already have enough of these bodies, the lessons from around the world are clear. We need to refocus on effective regional collaborating bodies (meaning that some will evolve and some will disappear). We need to be engaged in a continual process of community development and economic development renewal. We have wasted too much money on ineffective responses after crises have arisen, and even a portion of this money would be much better invested in ongoing strategic regional community and economic development planning. Finally, in order to be successful, we need to work bottom-up solutions into the co-creation of supportive public policy.

We need to work to support linkages with existing local and regional government economic and community development organizations, as well as other private, public, and nonprofit supportive agencies. In other words, there are already many groups and organizations doing good work in this area, and their expertise, advice, experience, and networks need to be brought into a participatory and open framework.

Supports and Structures for Provincial Policy Reform

We have learned from other jurisdictions around the world, and from lessons learned from over ineffectively addressing the recurring crises of resource dependence since the early 1980s, that the old way of public policy development and action through line ministries is not suited to the new realities of the global economy. The complexity of change to date demands the use of complex cross-government initiatives, not single "silver bullet" policy solutions. From the European Union to the OECD, policy co-creation in support of place-based community and economic development is now an accepted response and innovative tool for rural development. For BC's provincial government, this means four things with respect to nonmetropolitan development.

First, we need to create a deputy minister's council on nonmetropolitan community and economic renewal to coordinate and facilitate collaboration and engagement. Through this high-level council:

- The policy directions coming from individual ministries are vetted for their cumulative and positive contribution to supporting bottom-up initiatives.
- Any new monies allocated by government will flow down through this council to ensure that they are coordinated, properly oriented, and evaluated for the effectiveness of their investment.
- Ministries, programs, policies, initiatives, and decisions can be held accountable to the goal of renewing rural community and economic foundations so that we can better respond to change.
- Coordination of a place-based approach to fiscally responsible and regionally sustainable policy co-creation can be managed and will happen.

Second, the provincial government must counter its tendency to centralize bureaucratic and decision-making power in offices in the metropolitan Vancouver and Victoria areas. This process has stripped capacity and jobs from rural and small-town places while, at the same time, exacerbating the isolation of urban-based decision makers from intelligence about non-metropolitan BC and its potential and possibilities. The provincial government must decongest its metropolitan Vancouver and Victoria offices and renew its commitment to the rest of the province through the recreation of effective regional offices. Other provincial governments in Canada have been able to maintain a full-service presence in rural and small-town areas, and the use of electronic communications for information exchange and meetings defeats most rationales for continued centralization. An added benefit for government decision making is that regional offices provide opportunities for "on-the-ground" staff experience with the realities of how policies and programs work in rural and small-town places.

This might seem a struggle for current political and bureaucratic managers. BC has, however, a brilliant historical example to draw from in the pursuit of place-based approaches to support, and be supported by, public policy: the BC Forest Service. Not today, but in its proud past, the BC Forest Service was charged with stewarding a provincial resource for sustainable social, economic, and ecological benefits to the province as a whole. Directed by general public policy imperatives, it had regionally embedded offices and managers fully charged with being able to fine-tune programs and initiatives to meet local needs and be suited to BC's landscape of highly diverse ecosystems and communities. We know how to do this, and we know it can be successful.

Third, the province must open portals at senior decision-making levels (political and bureaucratic) to allow for participation by the regional economic and community development bodies in the co-creation of supportive public policy. This will be quite a dramatic shift and challenge. For too long, broad political directives have been a secretive product of overt political "chess play" in BC's highly charged blood-sport arena of provincial party politics. This has not been productive and, instead, has led to a hugely wasteful process of policy reversals, policy false starts, and near ongoing ministerial reorganizations. All of these have consumed precious time and resources over a period of our history (post-1980) during which we could afford neither.

Fourth, the province must continue with efforts to employ its information resources to better serve local initiatives and regional community and economic development strategic-planning initiatives. Suggestions for these types of actions appear throughout this book and can build on recent changes such as the province's 2011 introduction of an Internet-based "data" portal.

Co-creation Platform

The third and the most critical aspect of a new approach to combining bottom-up place-based development with supportive top-down public policy involves the creation of a platform of ongoing dialogue and exchange. Like some of the changes required of the provincial government, this may not be an easy task for those wedded to the idea of powerful premiers managing policy for political gain. However, the evidence of continued collapse after global demand-driven resource booms reminds us that the old approaches do not work.

A new platform involves a managed joint table, extending beyond the proposed deputy minister's council, at which provincial and regional representatives engage in routine and ongoing discussions of challenge and change. Remember that the new global economy means that we must always be preparing for new circumstances, and that the successful thirty-year run of single-focus policy initiatives that British Columbia experienced from 1950 to 1980 will not be repeated. The joint table must both facilitate dialogue as well as commission the background work to support debate on issues as they arise. Clear links exist to other recommendations in this book respecting the provincial government using its capacity to establish mechanisms for ongoing market surveillance and to provide access to the internal data needed for the evaluation of policy and market impacts.

A platform for ongoing dialogue and debate towards the co-creation of supportive public policy will have the following key principles:

- Stability – which requires a funded management secretariat to coordinate and hold the group accountable and on track
- Equality – which requires that the regional body representatives and the senior provincial government representatives (political and bureaucratic) must be committed to an open and equal dialogue about opportunities for improving policy and program support

- Accountability – which requires that the provincial government representatives must have reporting requirements to the legislature and to the provincial deputy ministries roundtable noted above, while the regional body representatives must submit reports on the agenda of local and regional government bodies
- Assessment – which requires that the platform must have access to the review and analytical capacity of the provincial government to continually assess and reassess the broader systemic implications of policy and program suggestions for regional strategic renewal.

A final rejoinder in the discussion of a framework for bottom-up and top-down collaboration in support of community and economic development concerns the private sector – especially large resource development projects. The present system clearly creates significant problems and delays for these investments. Even this sector, and its development project plans, can benefit from the creation of a strategic regional economic and social development approach bolstered with supportive top-down public policy. The foundation of these strategic regional economic and social plans and ideas in robust local and regional dialogue rooted in place-based assets and aspirations can provide early insight and clarity on development possibilities. It can provide a stable and ready organizational framework for project-specific discussions and debate. More than any aspect of the current approach, this framework can deliver a measure of certainty for investment capital.

Conclusion

As witnessed from northern BC, the recent global economic boom and recession illustrate the clear interdependency between the economic success of the north and overall provincial prosperity that defines the BC economy and society. Our purpose here has been to chart a course of future development in what are still referred to as the hinterland regions of the province such that the benefits of future economic upswings are invested wisely in development decisions that may facilitate a more economically diversified and socially sustainable north.

To identify an appropriate approach to hinterland development, we have combined lessons drawn from the WAC Bennett era and adapted them with specific insights offered by literatures investigating the significance of place in social and economic development processes. This synthesis exposes particular gaps in the approach (or lack thereof) to rural and northern development displayed by senior governments in BC since the early 1980s. These gaps exist to such an extent that despite recent booms, northern BC continues to struggle with downward demographic trends, comparatively poor social and economic performance, and an overall sense of uncertainty compounded by an inability to capture and retain resource wealth for foundational development investment.

There are significant external factors that contribute to rural decline. Economic restructuring and the relative power of senior governments within a globalizing world underscore many factors of decline beyond local control. Moreover, rural development is a complex process made increasingly so within a planning environment of multiplicity in values and interests. Designing the right kind of intervention and achieving expected results is a precarious endeavour under even the best circumstances.

From a comparative perspective, however, the postwar era in BC faced similar pressures of complexity and the mobility of capital; nevertheless, a dynamic vision was crafted and supported with real investment. The government of the day understood the vital connection between social and economic development and sought solutions that brought a broader range of benefits to the province.

From a more recent perspective, the ascendancy of place tells us that abandoning communities and regions to the vagaries of the market and yesterday's public policy perspectives is shortsighted. Strategic investments are necessary to establish a foundation on which diversified economic and community development can flourish. This competitive approach requires a transition from the traditional roots of comparative advantage, a shift not currently addressed in BC. The province is not investigating or exploiting the full range of competitive assets found in the north. Significant, and known, opportunities lay dormant for lack of an adequate investment approach to development.

Looking to the past for lessons about development is not about nostalgia. Equally so, looking at the importance of place is not about seeking some form of a rural idyll. Each informs us that there are grounded and tested approaches to hinterland development that may offer viable solutions and opportunities for building a sustainable northern BC.

Conclusion: Renewal for Rural and Small-town Northern BC

> A British Columbia parable:
>
> In the aftermath of the first decade of the twenty-first century, the provincial government and the communities of northern BC worked together on a new program and policy vehicle for renewal. As a partnership, each side contributed – the provincial government with a coordinated set of public policy supports that spanned government and provided real resources to communities; and communities, by working together as a region to mobilize a vision. This new vehicle was built for flexibility and responsiveness – for the drivers knew that the only thing certain about the road ahead was that the forecast said: "Prepare for rapidly changing conditions." Luckily, their new vehicle was equipped to deal specifically with a world defined by constant and fast-paced change.

We started this book with a "British Columbia parable" to highlight that the policy framework guiding community and economic development in the province has run its course. In the 1950s, against the backdrop of the expanding industrial manufacturing economies of the OECD states, which needed raw resource inputs, British Columbia embarked on an industrial resource development policy. This multifaceted, cross-government policy led to thirty years of unbroken economic and community growth and prosperity across the province. However, the useful life for that policy framework has long since passed. The signpost of the early 1980s recession marked a turning point to which we will not return. In the remainder of this book, we focused on sketching the background, foundation, and future directions for a new policy and program vehicle for economic and community renewal in northern BC's rural and small-town places. This chapter seeks to close our arguments in support of that renewed, long-term, place-based, approach to renewal.

This chapter has four sections. The first revisits a made-in-northern-BC vision for future community and economic development. This vision is critical for pointing out where we should go with our policy and program investments. In the years since the vision was outlined, an increasing number of OECD countries have aligned their rural and small-town community and economic development policies to fit with these same elements of vision. To move that vision forward, steps in policy development need to be mindful of the future conditions into which those policies and programs will be working. As such, the second section of this chapter presents some future conditions that will influence our capacity to initiate and sustain renewal. The third section examines the critical components of place that will guide investments in renewal. Finally, we emphasize the need to change our perspective on how we should approach rural and small-town policy and program renewal investments.

Vision for the Future

In arguing for a new approach to rural and small-town community and economic development in northern BC, this book has built on the lessons learned by the people living and working every day in this region. From their collective experience and wisdom comes a strong sense of vision and direction for the future.

The basis of this vision is an appreciation of, and attachment to, the "northern lifestyle." Rural and small-town places across northern BC continue to have an affordable lifestyle and a high quality of life that forms the foundation for their future. These are high-value economic and community development assets. Increasingly, our competitor regions are marketing these lifestyle assets as commodities unto themselves and as ways by which to attract new residents and new economic activities.

The critical element of the northern BC vision is the notion of inclusiveness. Inclusiveness means listening to our diverse voices, coming together as a collective region, and finally, coming to terms with full Aboriginal and non-Aboriginal community involvement in all our key actions and activities. As a result, community and economic development in northern BC is such that it not only creates jobs for northerners, but also respects the people, the environment, and the quality of life that defines the northern lifestyle. In reviewing this, we identified the four critical bottom lines of culture, community, economy, and environment. With an inclusive approach to renewal, all four of these bottom lines are now important to ensuring that we maintain our assets and use them to open possibilities and create new opportunities.

In identifying a strategic direction to move this vision forward, the people of northern BC were equally clear. Economic transition in northern BC is about moving from northern strength to northern strength. It is about moving from a dependence on our industrial resource activities into a diversified economy that is grounded in resource industries, but inclusive of manufacturing and other options. To do this, there is a need to creatively rebundle our community and economic development assets so that they meet the inputs required for twenty-first century economic activities across a host of current and emergent sectors. The rebundling of traditional assets means getting past the jargon of temporary economic development fads. We need to envision clusters as much more than groupings of old industrial infrastructure, and look beneath them for special skills, knowledge, connections to information networks, and connections to global markets to truly exploit the emerging opportunities within traditional sectors and identify new opportunities in other sectors.

Future Conditions

If we are to come together around a new policy and program vehicle for community and economic renewal, we not only keep a sense of vision (for where we want that vehicle to take us), but also a sense of the conditions through which that vehicle will have to operate in both the near and long-term futures. As we look to the suite of future conditions, we wish to highlight two trends that will affect the policy and program development environment.

First, we need to recognize that for close to thirty years, there has been considerable and ongoing social, economic, and political restructuring. Regarding social restructuring, there has been a fundamental transition in what coming generations expect from the work and community life they will be going into. No longer bound by a primary concern over wages and jobs, young people are searching for quality of life, clean environments, and good places where they can raise children and achieve a balance between their work and life spheres. They want to live in places where they can make a difference, every day, on a human and community level, while at the same time remaining "plugged into" the global communications world. We will be in very difficult circumstances if our community and economic development leaders cannot adapt to the new realities of this next generation workforce.

Regarding economic restructuring, the transition from resource industries to service industries is well underway across OECD and other global economies. The good news is that many of our northern BC communities already know how to do this. In Prince George, there has been a long-term recruitment effort to attract service sector economic actors. Included in this initiative has been the expansion of the main campus of the University of Northern British Columbia, considerable growth at the Northern Health Authority's local facilities, and at a host of federal and provincial agencies that have located in this city. As described earlier, communities such as Terrace, Smithers, Valemount, and others have been very good at looking forward to create a platform for success in attracting other sectors and industries to complement, supplement, and work within a circumstance of changing resource industry places. However, at the provincial policy and program level, much of our economic thinking still rests on the resource sector, and large parts of this resource sector are plainly in a "run down of assets" stage of development.[1] The fact that we have not had a new pulp mill built in BC for forty years speaks to our competitiveness in that industry for the next forty. Similarly, the rise of low cost production regions will increasingly displace our market share in low value-added commodities such as dimension lumber.

Regarding political restructuring, in Canada and across all OECD countries, the state has significantly reduced its ability to intervene in the economy, and its willingness to do so. Local governments are left with increasing responsibility and decreasing resources for managing economic diversification. At worst, state governments have transferred responsibility to act while actively undercutting the tools and flexibility for small places to react. Given these trends, it is clear that the future is about new economic sectors that build on, and grow from, the high amenity attributes of our local places.

The above-noted trends have been with us for some time, and it is important to remember that these forces will shape the action needed in policy and programs to create the vehicle for renewal in northern BC. As those policies and programs begin their work, however, there are the immediate challenges of the next decade, which might be characterized as possessing a series of short-term stresses. Key among these stresses will be the response to the continuing global economic recession. This recession has been exacerbated in northern BC since much of our economic product goes to the United States, and its housing market will be slowly responding to nascent economic upswings. The US housing market, in other words, will take a long time to reach its previous levels. More likely to respond in the short term will be the renewal of the Chinese economy and its manufacturing sector's need for mineral products and its rural and urban housing demand for lumber. These two different trajectories of growth will affect both resource industries across northern BC and the provincial budget through resource revenues.

A second short-term stress will be a consequence of the fact that both the federal and provincial governments will need to significantly cut budgets and reduce expenditures to compensate for their failure to anticipate the first year of the global economic recession and their perhaps overexuberant exercises in uni-dimensional economic stimulus programs. Again, this will mean challenges for local places that have to renew infrastructure and undertake other retooling exercises that might normally have involved a senior government partner.

Third, while some communities across northern BC have started to address this issue, we really have not come to grips with the full implications of a rapidly aging population across our rural and small-town communities. There have been some new investments, but our research identifies that a "retirement industry" changes virtually every aspect of civic operations. This will mean significant challenges over the next decade as very large numbers of the workforce, which had originally come for the new jobs of the 1970s, start to retire. These demographic realities mean that we must pay greater attention in the immediate and intermediate future to quality of life and community livability as cornerstones for attracting footloose economic activity and for holding aging populations so that they spend their retirement years (and incomes) as part of the local economy.

What to Build On

This book is about the critical transition from a space-based economy to a place-based economy. Through the 1950s to the 1970s, a space-based approach to regional development exercised notions of comparative advantage to exploit northern BC's abundant resource base and set the stage for BC to become a key raw material supply warehouse for the industrial economies of what would become the OECD countries. The space-based regional development approach was facilitated by critical infrastructure investments and a broad sweep of policy initiatives to support new resource industries and towns. The global commodities downturn during the early 1980s set in place a new trajectory for resource hinterlands and signalled the need to fundamentally rethink that approach. For regional development across northern BC, lessons from the past thirty years show how economic booms now come faster, and the busts follow sooner and go deeper than those we experienced before. To build a more resilient community foundation, we need to shift away from single-resource commodities to economies that mix commodity production with a range of other services, actions, and values in the creation of more complex and resilient economies. Places across northern BC that have shown resilience to commodity cycles have drawn on local amenity assets to underscore new economic opportunities.

A place-based approach to rural development means that the unique attributes and assets of individual communities and regions now underscore and support their attractiveness for particular and appropriate types of activities and investments. The policy and program vehicle for renewal should focus on building a strong community development foundation so that localities can exercise their place-based competitive advantages to hold existing businesses and residents while working to attract new-economy activities and the residents who might accompany and expand these new economies.

Critical to the success of place-based economies has been the emergence of the global economy in which we now find ourselves immersed. As space has become less important to the global movement of capital and goods, small differences between places now are critical elements in the decisions on where industries, and firms, invest. In short, "place" has re-emerged as a fundamental ingredient in the rural economy. Attention in the global economy will be on flexibility and responsiveness. For our rural and small-town places to have and exercise these attributes will require continuous attention to our rural and small-town community and economic development foundations. The new rural and small-town economy for northern BC will require making strategic investments in the physical and social infrastructure of communities – in other words, making investments in place. A coming decade that may become preoccupied with government cuts and fiscal restraint will demand that any investments we make in creating more flexible, resilient community and economic development foundations must be made strategically and must be made on a regional level so as to achieve the greatest and widest benefit for each dollar invested.

Change in Mindset

Through the preceding chapters, we examined a wide range of areas in which a true "change in mindset" is needed for us to break from the repetitive cycles of the past towards a new foundation for community and economic development renewal in northern BC. In closing, we highlight two critical facets of this need for change. The first concerns the need to work regionally. Rural and small-town places have relatively limited capacity to do all of the tasks now required of them in planning for economic and community development futures. Similarly, there has been limited funding available to meet the needs of that renewal. A quick survey across northern BC reveals massive deficits in infrastructure, community capacity, and human capacity. Similarly, we must continue to grow and enhance our ability to talk together as a region to ensure we invest limited funding wisely. We need to be able to work as a region in order to market our collective strengths across the global economy.

An additional item, so necessary for northern BC to become competitive in the global economy, is the need to "scale up." Drawing on examples from around the world, we see that our communities and our economic regions need to work together. Our small businesses need to find ways to work together. For example, our small commodity-producing players such as community forests and First Nations timber allocations, need to find ways to scale up so that they can market collectively, work for better deals in transportation and global commodity exchange, and share skills and knowledge so that the sector can have a stronger competitive bargaining position. The establishment of strategic alliances and knowledge relationships are critical in twenty-first-century regional development success. Technical assistance, shipping and trading issues, marketing and market research, innovation, and research are all areas in which strategic alliances can bring benefit in the form of economic competitiveness.

A second key facet in changing our mindset, and perhaps the most crucial, is to advance and update our understanding of investment. In the 1950s and 1960s, the WAC Bennett government understood that spending on industrial, community, and provincial infrastructure was, in fact, an investment for the long term. Now, some fifty and sixty years later, the province is still reaping the benefits of those investments. Unfortunately, an ethos of public debate in Canada since the early 1980s has eschewed the notion of "investments" in favour of viewing all government spending as "expenses." Too often, spending is seen only against the matrix of being able to pay dividends in the short term. While governments across the country, and in British Columbia, have demonstrated many instances of undertaking long-term investments for the greater public good, this must become more our norm in how we approach community and economic renewal. Investments in the four critical infrastructures identified above to mobilize a more flexible and resilient community and economic development foundation across our northern BC rural and small-town places will pay back the people and economies of BC for the next fifty years and beyond.

Closing

This book is about renewal. It is about imagining a framework and a pathway for renewing the community and economic development foundations of northern BC. This book draws on leading research from British Columbia, Canada, and other OECD countries. In many respects, northern BC has been a leader in the ideas and debates about rural and small-town renewal into the twenty-first century. We hope this book contributes to repositioning how we approach and execute policy and program vehicles for renewal and how our rural and small towns reimagine their futures and undertake activities to realize those futures.

Notes

Chapter 1: Introduction

1 The way that Statistics Canada collects and reports on manufacturing data has always been problematic for understanding the structure of the BC economy. In BC, most of the "manufacturing" products are pulp, paper, dimension lumber, and wood products like oriented strandboard, plywood, etc. – not the types of products that typically come to mind, for most residents, when thinking of manufacturing. The Province of Ontario, as home to Canada's most advanced manufacturing sectors – primarily the auto sector but inclusive of consumer goods sectors as well – has experienced revenue/export declines in resource commodities and in what are more popularly understood as "true" manufactured goods.

2 The expression "strength to strength" paraphrases a comment often used by Ray Bollman of Statistics Canada. A recognized leader in rural and small-town development studies, Bollman often uses the line in his presentations that rural places must find something else to "export" and thus move from "strength to strength."

3 Reference to "4 bottom lines" has become more common in recent years, but the people of northern BC have known about this evaluative matrix for a long time. UNBC's Community Development Institute first enunciated this through its Northern Economic Vision and Strategy Project as early as 2003 (Halseth et al. 2007).

4 There is a considerable literature on social capital, but at its simplest it represents the levels of trust within networks that allow groups to accomplish things. In rural and small-town places struggling to cope with opportunities or challenges, social capital can be a resource drawn on to support local actions. Its companion term, social cohesion, also has a considerable literature and debate associated with it. Again, at its simplest, social cohesion refers to the creation and efficacy of these networks themselves. As a process of community development, social capital and social cohesion are recursive and reinforcing.

5 A recent study by Statistics Canada points out that those rural and small-town places that "were more diversified and had a higher educational attainment at the beginning of the 1980s experienced higher population growth over the following two decades" (Alasia 2010: 16). This reinforces the notion that in a rapidly changing global economy, local diversity and capacity, in its many forms, are critical to success.

Chapter 2: The Development of Northern British Columbia

1 Regional districts, established in BC in the late 1960s, address two key issues in local government. The first was to provide a regional government table at which municipalities and unincorporated rural areas could talk together about joint services needs. The second was to create a local government option for residents in the unincorporated rural areas as they could now vote on a local government official to represent their interests in local matters.

2 A recent report by Statistics Canada also confirmed that rural Canada, in general, is aging faster than urban centres (Dandy and Bollman 2008).

3 Such changes to a mixed economy are well under way in many other former resource hinterland areas of North America. In fact, in the United States, they define the "nonmetropolitan west," where climate, quality of life, retirement migration, availability of services, and affordability of land are significant in supporting rapid growth (Nelson 1999; Nelson and Sewall 2003). It is important to note, however, that along with job losses in traditional resource industries, population growth through new "industries" also creates a set of social, service, and policy challenges for communities and regions.

4 For a more intimate portrait of the impacts that assimilationist policies had on people, please see Bridget Moran's (1994) moving biography of Justa Monk. As a child, Justa lived many of the seasonal rhythms long associated with an economy organized around the fur trade, but his apprehension by white officials to force him into residential school at Lejac changed that life completely. Struggling against a variety of issues, Justa went on to become a respected leader in his own community and a respected voice for Aboriginal interests across northern BC, where he has worked effectively to improve the lives and circumstances of future generations of Aboriginal people.

5 As described McArthur (2010: 2), neoliberalism "increasingly emphasized free trade, deregulation of markets, increased incentives for private wealth creation and capital accumulation through tax reductions and subsidies, and a reduced role for government."

6 A more recent review by de Peuter et al. (2008) of the research and policy literature also supports this notion of a valuable interconnectedness between rural and urban Canada.

7 This use of the terms heartland and hinterland in our discussion, and in Canadian regional science and geography scholarship, is not to be confused with the BC provincial government's announcement in 2003 of a "heartlands strategy" for nonmetropolitan BC (British Columbia 2003a, 2004b). In this case, the policy intent focused on the resource hinterlands of BC. The term "heartlands" in this policy case may have been co-opted from the United States context, where the rural Midwest is often labelled as the "US heartland."

8 The population of Vancouver's census metropolitan area was 2,116,581 in 2006, while the population of Victoria's census metropolitan area was 330,088. The 2006 census population of British Columbia was 4,113,487. A census metropolitan area is defined as a major urban core (with a population of at least 100,000) together with its adjacent municipalities.

9 At its core, two resettlement processes have defined the spatial relationships between Aboriginal and non-Aboriginal communities in BC (e.g., see work by Harris 1997, 2002). Both revolve around the competition for good quality land for settlement. At European contact, BC was a fully occupied and governed territory. A first resettlement process, therefore, involved removing First Nations inhabitants from their traditional territories and placing them onto designated Indian reserves. Given the desire for European settlers to have access to good quality lands, these Indian reserves were often the areas thought to be less desirable. The second process involved the "resettlement" of many former First Nations sites by settler populations. In Prince George, the resettlement process underwent multiple rounds. First, the Lheidli Ténneh were moved onto Indian Reserve No. 1 (a swampy area adjacent to the Fraser and Nechako rivers), and later, when that land became valued by the Grand Trunk Pacific Railway, they were relocated again further up the Fraser River to a new Indian reserve at Shelley (Leonard 1996).

Chapter 3: The Whole Community Approach

1 Bruce (2010) describes a circumstance where general infrastructure, new information technologies, and investments in cultural amenities come together through the case of the new animation sector developing in northeastern New Brunswick. A support base for the technology in combination with local investments in amenities attracts creative economy workers. The goal is to diversify a region that had previously been very reliant on the forest industry and where restructuring within that industry has created difficult times across the region.

2 What we do now has significant consequences for the future. In local government planning, for example, the application of development cost charges shifts infrastructure costs from municipalities onto developers. This shifting has allowed many developers to continue

patterns of urban and suburban sprawl as they argue that there is little cost to local taxpayers. Once built, however, the local tax base funds the long-term maintenance, and replacement, of many extra kilometres of roads, sewage and water lines, snow clearing, etc.

3 Fordism describes an industrial period from the Second World War through to the mid-1970s. Fordism standardizes the production process through mechanization and a rigid, highly specialized labour force that combine to generate high volumes of uniform goods. A social compromise between companies, unions, and an interventionist state maintained the Fordist system. This trilateral agreement produced high levels of productivity, high wages for workers, and the expansion of social welfare policies. The Fordist production regime fostered mass consumption (of the industrial products being generated by the system), thereby leading to a period of relative economic stability and growth (Peet 1997). Post-Fordism, on the other hand, refers to an economic period since the mid-1970s, with highly flexible forms of production, in contrast to Fordist standardized mass production. Post-Fordist flexibility affects the labour force (in terms of the quantity of jobs, the consistency of employment, and labour functions) and business practices (in terms of subcontracting, types of products produced, and the vertical disintegration of larger companies). The proliferation of information technology, the globalization of capital markets and production systems, the decline of unionism, and a less interventionist state represent primary characteristics of post-Fordism (Johnston et al. 2000).

4 As profiled later, two types of regional "governance" organizations that recently emerged in northern BC are worth noting. The first includes the beetle action coalitions. In response to the significant mountain pine beetle (MPB) epidemic in the province's forests, a wide range of community and economic interests in the Cariboo-Chilcotin area came together to develop and present to the provincial government a "home-grown" plan for preparing the region to meet and work through the community, cultural, economic, and environmental impacts. The province supported the Cariboo-Chilcotin Beetle Action Coalition (C-CBAC) from early 2005 with funding to develop a regional action plan. Subsequently, the provincial government supported the founding of the Omineca Beetle Action Coalition and a Southern Interior Beetle Action Coalition. A second example came about as a group of local government economic development officers organized a cooperative dialogue process to help coordinate and achieve synergies in their economic planning initiatives. The 16/97 Economic Alliance (named after the intersection of key provincial highways 16 and 97) has been very effective since 2007-2008 in supporting work on regional cluster and transportation initiatives that benefit the region as a whole and has advanced, in large part, because of the coordinated effort and the collective voice of these communities.

5 Community economic development (CED) emerged through debate as a response to the inadequacies of the mainstream economy. Embedded in alternative and radical frameworks, CED must nevertheless simultaneously function within general market conditions and under the dominant capitalist regime (Lo and Halseth 2009).

6 We need to pay ongoing attention to re-equipping rural and small-town BC to be competitive in the new economy. The recent story of two employees at a suddenly closed forest products plant illustrates this. These two employees, hired right out of high school more than twenty-five years ago, had worked continuously at the plant, earning good wages and benefits. In 2009, the plant was permanently closed. The closure was unexpected. One of those employees had spent considerable time over the years learning a trade and upgrading his skills. He had done this mostly on his own time and with his own financial resources. Very soon after the closure, he was working at another job plying his trade quite successfully. The other employee did not take any upgrading or trades training – content to work within the 1960s economy that described this plant. As a result, the closure has left this second person unemployed and in difficult financial and personal circumstances. Much like northern BC's economy, complacency with resource sector industries built in the 1960s leaves us unable to compete in a new and fast-paced economy.

7 Social cohesion and social capital accrue through the normal functioning of communities. During times of stress, they may be mobilized or "drawn down." If not renewed through routine community processes, social cohesion and social capital can degrade.

8 The challenge of diversifying within existing sectors cannot be underestimated. One of the most commonly citied barriers to forest industry product, market, and firm diversification has been access to timber (Myers 2000). That so much of this timber is allocated to a small number of large forest products companies means that small-scale enterprises have difficulty securing the wood supply for their businesses.

9 BC Transmission Corporation (BCTC) has submitted an Environmental Assessment Certificate Application to the BC Environmental Assessment Office (BCEAO) for the proposed Northwest Transmission Line (NTL) Project. Proposed is a 335 km, 287 kV transmission line between Skeena Substation (near Terrace) and a new substation near Bob Quinn Lake. This new line would provide a secure interconnection point for clean generation projects and provide reliable power to potential industrial developments in the area. The BCEAO screening of the application takes thirty days. Once the BCEAO accepts the application, it posts it on their website, and a review period of up to 180 days begins. During this public comment period, interested parties are encouraged to submit comments and participate in public information sessions before the BCEAO provides a report with its recommendation for government consideration of and decision on the project proceeding. Since 2007, extensive consultation on the NTL has taken place through community information sessions, meetings, responses to information requests, regular public updates and workshops with the Nisga'a Nation, other First Nations, municipalities, regional districts, stakeholder groups, landowners, and interested parties.

Chapter 4: Province Building

1 These impacts have been documented across Canada. Richmond and Ross (2009) describe how environmental dispossession through colonialism negatively affected the health of Aboriginal peoples and limited their chances for economic development. Smylie (2008) also talks about the relocation of the Inuit, the effects of overcrowded housing, and a host of other Indian Act impacts including residential schools and child seizures.

2 The classic Canadian story of this process is about the iron ore mines at the Quebec/Labrador border. Work by John Bradbury and Isabelle St. Martin (1983) on now-closed towns such as Schefferville, Quebec, followed the investment decisions, and the implications of those decisions, of the Iron Ore Company of Canada.

3 Technological constraints within the minerals-processing industry, however, have acted over time to limit the amount of smelting and downstream processing. Many of these processing technologies are under patent and industrial secrecy. Further, the considerable costs involved in developing a technologically complex smelter acted as a damper on the desire of industry to locate in more marginal or unproven territory.

4 This aggressive policy to improve the transportation network very much seems to emulate the federal "roads to resources" program, initiated by Prime Minister Diefenbaker and closed in the 1970s by Prime Minister Trudeau.

5 The need to create such "instant towns" coincident with the development of massive resource industry projects necessitated the creation of a body of legislation that collectively came to be known as the Instant Towns Act. This legislation gave clear management tasks to an interim local government during the town's construction phase and then set the stage for a rapid transition to civic government based on local elections once the workers and their families had moved in. A key element of the Instant Towns Act is to limit the early roles of local governments so that they could not interfere with the resource industry base (Halseth and Sullivan 2002).

Chapter 5: Restructuring and Response

1 As noted in Chapter 4, writers such as Bernsohn (1981), Drushka (1998), and Marchak (1983) have supplied detailed descriptions and insights into the operations of resource industries in the period before 1980.

2 Recent analyis by Edenhoffer (2012) highlights the emergence of a duality in industrial structure in the BC forest sector, consisting of the large commodity players and a "highly dynamic" smaller value-added sector.

3 There are many other movements in the marketplace towards more environmentally friendly products. Most readers will be aware of the publishing phenomenon that is the Harry Potter books written by J.K. Rowling. If you have these paperback books on your child's bookshelf, have a look at the first couple of volumes. By the time the second book appeared in print, Raincoast Books (the publisher in Canada) had made it common practice to advertise on the back cover and on the copyright page that the paperback was "Ancient Forest Friendly" and printed on recycled paper using vegetable-based inks.
4 This type of inventory management structure, adopted across numerous sectors, has especially been refined in the retail sector. Many of the products one sees in stores are still "owned" by the manufacturing company, which is paid only when the product sells.
5 Even when they visit, metropolitan Vancouver- and/or Victoria–based decision makers often follow a troubling pattern of flying up in the morning, and spending several hours in meetings, only to fly home in the afternoon. Many are the stories of northern communities' frustration regarding what they see to be a lack of appreciation of "place" and the opportunities for "place-based" development that northern BC represents.
6 Concerns in the northern Rockies region over the massive impacts of energy development have led to a creative and innovative process for change. To start, the Northern Rockies Regional District and the Town of Fort Nelson merged into a single Northern Rockies Regional Municipality. Then, with the assistance of the Fraser Basin Council and UNBC's Community Development Institute, they engaged in a dialogue process with area First Nations. The result was a Northern Rockies Regional Community Agreement. The first of its kind in BC, the agreement creates a working relationship for seeing that current and future resource development initiatives are undertaken in such a way as to enhance the communities rather than detract from them.
7 It is worth noting that the entire Canadian population is almost equivalent to the population of a single metropolitan region in China. The population of China is about 1,335 million, and of India, about 1,144 million, while all of BC registers at just over 4 million. For BC to make a mark as an effective player in global markets such as China and India, we must work as a single functional unit that draws on all of our strengths and roles.
8 This lack of services to support the work of the Immigrant and Multicultural Services Society is quite remarkable given the general attention to immigration issues. A CBC news story (2009) referring to a new report by the Federation of Canadian Municipalities, which compared the social and economic conditions for immigrants between 2001 and 2006, described how changing patterns of immigration settlement pose new challenges for both small and large communities across Canada. It stated: "large cities are finding it more difficult to meet their labour requirements as more highly skilled and educated immigrants choose to settle in smaller communities," and that "at the same time, an influx of newcomers in smaller communities is placing more demands on municipalities that are already struggling to find services from the limited property tax base." Highlighting the need for additional investments in welcoming services, the CBC report went on to point out that "if we want to come out of this recession with the skilled workforce we need, it's time to coordinate immigration policy and services and provide municipalities with the funding to meet immigrants' needs."

Chapter 6: Struggles in Transition

1 Ramsey (2005) examines some of the arguments for the creation of a Ministry of Northern Affairs in BC. He describes how BC's attention to northern issues has lagged behind other Canadian provinces' and submits that BC's provincial political landscape has significantly hampered long-term efforts at supporting northern issues and nurturing a northern voice in policy and development debates.
2 Towns for Tomorrow, launched in December 2006, is part of the province's effort to address the unique challenges faced by smaller communities in British Columbia with respect to sustainability and meeting their infrastructure needs. A five-year, $71 million program, Towns for Tomorrow provides funding for infrastructure projects that address climate change and contribute to the overall health, sustainability, and livability of communities. Unlike traditional government infrastructure programs that provide matching provincial funding

to up to one-third of the total project costs, Towns for Tomorrow provides up to 80 percent of the funding for approved projects. Under the revised program structure, communities with populations under 5,000 will continue to share costs with the province on an 80/20 basis, with a maximum provincial contribution of $400,000. Communities with populations between 5,000 and 15,000 will share on a 75/25 basis, with a maximum provincial contribution of $375,000.

3 Since 2007, the $40 million Local Motion Program has funded more than 122 projects across British Columbia with the goal of helping local governments create even better places to live, work, and play. Local Motion provides up to 50 percent of eligible projects costs, with a maximum annual contribution of $1 million.

4 The Rural Economic Diversification Initiative of British Columbia (REDI-BC) is a joint initiative between Western Economic Diversification and Community Futures British Columbia to encourage economic diversification in rural communities. From 1 October 2008 to 31 March 2012, REDI-BC will provide $3 million in funding for projects to support regional diversification and promote long-term community economic sustainability, resiliency, and improved economic conditions.

5 One of the most absurd examples our research team has come across involves a plan by a small settlement to extend its community water system to support additional housing developments, community growth, and local economic activity. The community commissioned an engineering study on the feasibility and costs of this water system extension. The engineering company, to their credit, wrote at the beginning of the new report that their findings were very similar to the findings of an engineering report conducted for the same project and idea less than a decade earlier. The turnover of even a few individuals in leadership positions in small local government offices can lead to almost a complete loss of collective memory. In this case, that loss of collective memory cost a good deal of money to be spent on additional engineering feasibility work.

6 The notion of resourcism is found in a variety of research streams. The political scientist Ed Black (1968, 1989) has studied the critical challenge for economic and community transition posed by the embeddedness of corporate and political power in the existing economic structures. In a similar vein, work by House (1999) in Newfoundland shows how, for similar reasons, a provincial bureaucracy and senior decision makers effectively stall efforts at transition and renewal.

7 See Friedmann's (1987) "systems maintenance" versus "systems transforming" development planning choices.

Chapter 7: An Economy of Place

1 Efforts by residents in northern BC to build the University of Northern British Columbia are a significant success story in increasing human capacity investment across the entire region. Some of the university's first significant impacts occurred when young students, born in northern BC, graduated from UNBC, and then moved into teaching positions in the elementary and secondary schools in their home communities. Although the data are limited at present, survey work by the BC University Presidents' Council and, more recently, the Research Universities Council (2010), shows that between 43 and 50 percent of graduates from UNBC live in northern BC, and an additional 18-23 percent live in other areas of nonmetropolitan BC two to five years after graduation.

2 In 1988, three years after Tumbler Ridge residents began to arrive in town, the Women's Resource Society collective was formed. Over time, the organization had a membership that numbered over one hundred. It hosted a variety of women-centred events and provided social networking opportunities. With the 2000 announcement of the Quintette mine closure, the Society established a "Women in Transition Coffeehouse" which held evening events that provided women with the opportunity to share stories and enjoy music, laughter, dessert, and coffee. The goal of the coffeehouse evenings was to help women celebrate friendships and to talk about the changes they were experiencing as the town went through the dramatic social and economic transition. This group later disbanded as organizers left with their families for work elsewhere.

Chapter 8: Mobilizing for Change

1 Kennedy (2005) describes the evolution of a northern development council among interested regional districts beginning in the 1970s and lasting until 1990. The challenge for this earlier, regional district–based, development council was that intense rivalries between communities and regions made it difficult to arrive at a meaningful consensus. Since that time, efforts at regional cooperation have been limited, and the support mechanisms of the North Central Municipal Association (now the North Central Local Government Association) have fluctuated. He points out that the Northwest Corridor Development Corporation has been a successful example of intermunicipal cooperation (including private sector interests) and that the Peace River region, in general, has been able to come together more effectively to motivate regional-level activities and investments.

2 Canada has used up approximately 79 percent of the total service life of its public infrastructure (only 41 percent of infrastructure is between 0-40 years old; 31 percent is 40-80 years old; and 28 percent is 80-100 years old). Infrastructure deterioration accelerates with age (Mirza 2007).

Chapter 9: Directions

1 In a competitive economy, we are also competitive for labour. Gone are the 1950s, when people would go anywhere for a labouring job. The attractiveness of large cities is, in part, related to the wide range of amenities they supply and the diversity of job and career choices. An expression of this attractiveness has been the thesis of Richard Florida's "the creative class." The "next" workforce is an educated one looking for a wide range of values beyond jobs. Key to success in the competitive and knowledge-based global economy is the ability to attract and maintain this next generation workforce – people who can go anywhere they want, and demand what they want, pretty certain that there will be more jobs than there are workers. Research suggests that they want good jobs but also a clean environment, reasonable access to services, safe and healthy places in which to raise families, a balance between work and life activities, and a sense of local community combined with global connectivity. In many ways, these wants have long described rural and small-town places. Attention to enhancing local amenities, services, and global connectivity can cement rural and small-town places as competitive players for the next generation workforce.

2 The impact and importance of the Norwegian Petroleum Fund should be a significant lesson for BC and its own failure to develop a similar form of resource royalties investment fund. As the world plunged into economic crisis through 2008 and 2009, the *New York Times* (Thomas 2009) reported, "The global financial crisis has brought low the economies of just about every country on earth. But not Norway." The writer continued, "In the midst of the worst global downturn since the Depression, Norway's economy grew last year by just under 3 percent. The government enjoys a budget surplus of 11 percent and its ledger is entirely free of debt. By comparison, the United States is expected to chalk up a fiscal deficit this year equal to 12.9 percent of its gross domestic product and push its total debt to 11 trillion dollars, or 65 percent of the size of its economy." As a major oil exporter, "Norway avoided the usual trap that plagues many energy-rich countries. Instead of spending its riches lavishly, it passed legislation ensuring that oil revenue went straight into its sovereign wealth fund. Norway's relative frugality stands in stark contrast to Britain, which spent most of its North Sea oil revenue (and more) during the boom years."

3 One illustration of flexibility and creativity in broad community development projects – that can support multiple outcomes – is a story from Haida Gwaii. The Old Massett Village Council Economic Development Department partnered with Northwest Community College to offer a Culinary Arts Program in the community (McKinley 2009). In just over a year from start-up, the eleven students in the program put on various community dinners in the Old Massett hall. In addition to their classroom work and the community dinners, "they do catering – this summer's Davidson potlatch, for various community service meetings are examples – and they provided regular meals at cost for various community programs – the language nest and the Elders program are examples. It's one of those win-win scenarios, where the students get the work experience they need – a whopping 5,100 [hours] in total

as part of their red seal designation – and community members get to tantalize their taste buds."

Chapter 10: On Intervention

1 One way in which the provincial government enacted stimulus spending in northern BC was to get moving on a promise made two elections earlier to start increasing the length of four-lane traffic on Highway 97 north.

Conclusion

1 PricewaterhouseCoopers' 2008 global forest survey is a sobering analysis of the urgency with which we need to attend to renewal across northern BC. Citing Craig Campbell, a PwC partner, press coverage observed, "Canadian companies had a capital reinvestment ratio of 0.4, well below the 1.0 needed to maintain the current level of activity. 'That means we are not replacing the assets that are being shut down or depreciating,' Campbell said. 'But that's inevitable in British Columbia because of high costs in certain sectors, such as newsprint, which can't compete with countries elsewhere in the world,' Campbell said. In the pulp-and-paper industry, 'it's just a transformation we have to get used to,' Campbell said. 'It's kind of like the restructuring of the steel industry and the shipbuilding industry when it went from Europe to Asia'" (*Vancouver Sun* 2008).

Works Cited

16-97 Economic Alliance. 2007. *Working Together – Expanding Our Economies*. Prince George: Author. http://1697alliance.com/downloads/16-97-Business-Plan-FINAL-Jan22-2007.pdf.

–. 2008. *Industry Cluster Identification and Prioritization Project, Executive Summary*. Prince George: Author. http://1697alliance.com/downloads/Executive%20Summary%2010Jan 2008-finalacknowldge.pdf.

–. 2010. *Northern Interior Mining Group*. Prince George: Author. http://1697alliance.com/projects/northern-interior-mining-group.

Aarsaether, N., and J. Baerenholdt. 2001. Understanding local dynamics and governance in northern regions. In *Transforming the Local: Coping Strategies and Regional Policies*, ed. J. Baerenholdt and N. Aarsaether, 15-42. Copenhagen: Nordic Council of Ministers.

Aarsaether, N., and L. Suopajärvi. 2004. Innovations and institutions in the North. In *Innovations in the Nordic Periphery*, ed. N. Aarsaether, 9-35. Stockholm: Nordregio, Nordic Centre for Spatial Development.

Adams, P. 1992. *Access to the Industrial Tax Base in the North East*. Victoria: Semmens and Adams.

AGRA Earth and Environment. 2000. *Northwest Transportation and Trade Corridor Capability Report: Access, Capacity and Development Guide to One of Canada's Best Kept Trade Secrets*. Vancouver: Northwest Corridor Development.

Akin, D. 2008. Move civil servants to rural areas: Panel. Senate committee wants to shift 10 percent of federal workers to hinterland. *Edmonton Journal*, 18 June, A5.

Alasia, A. 2005. *Skills, Innovation and Growth: Key Issues for Rural and Territorial Development: A Survey of the Literature, 1980-2003*. Ottawa: Statistics Canada.

–. 2010. Population change across Canadian communities, 1981 to 2006: The role of sector restructuring, agglomeration, diversification and human capital. *Rural and Small Town Canada Analysis Bulletin* 8(4): 1-32.

Alasia, A., and E. Magnusson. 2005. Occupational skill level: The divide between rural and urban Canada. *Rural and Small Town Canada Analysis Bulletin* 6(2): 1-30.

Amin, A. 1999. An institutionalist perspective on regional economic development. *International Journal of Urban and Regional Research* 23(2): 365-78.

Amin, A., and N. Thrift. 1994. *Globalization, Institutions and Regional Development in Europe*. Oxford: Oxford University Press.

Angus, C., and B. Griffin. 1996. *We Lived a Life and Then Some: The Life, Death, and Life of a Mining Town*. Toronto: Between the Lines.

Apedaile, P. 2004. The new rural economy. In G. Halseth and R. Halseth, *Building for Success*, 111-36.

Apsey, M. 2006. *What's All This Got to Do with the Price of 2x4s?* Calgary: University of Calgary Press.

Argent, N. 2002. From pillar to post? In search of the post-productivist countryside in Australia. *Australian Geographer* 33(1): 97-114.

Armstrong, J. 2002. BC mayor ends fast over closing of school. *Globe and Mail*, 27 Aug., A5.

Attridge, C., C. Budgen, A. Hilton, J. McDavid, A. Molzahn, and M. Purkis. 1997. The Comox Valley Nursing Centre. *Canadian Nurse* (Feb.): 34-38.

Aucoin, P. 1990. Administrative reform in public management: Paradigms, principles, paradoxes, and pendulums. *Governance* 3(2): 115-37.

–. 1995. *The New Public Management: Canada in Comparative Perspective*. Montreal: Institute for Research on Public Policy.

Australian Government, Department of Transport and Regional Services. 2002. *Stronger Regions, a Stronger Australia*. http://www.dotars.gov.au/regional/statement/contents.htm.

Baldwin, J.R., W.M. Brown, and T. Vinodrai. 2001. *Dynamics of the Canadian Manufacturing Sector in Metropolitan and Rural Regions*. Ottawa: Statistics Canada. Cat. no. 11F0019MIE 2001169.

Bandias, S., and S. Vemuri. 2005. Telecommunications infrastructure facilitating sustainable development of rural and remote communities in Northern Australia. *Telecommunication Policy* 29(2-3): 237-49.

Banks, J., and T. Marsden. 2000. Integrating agri-environment policy, farming systems and rural development: Tir Cymen in Wales. *Sociologica Ruralis* 40(4): 466-80.

Barcus, H. 2004. Urban-rural migration in the USA: An analysis of residential satisfaction. *Regional Studies* 38(6): 643-57.

Barman, J. 1996. *The West beyond the West: A History of British Columbia*. Toronto: University of Toronto Press.

Barnes, T.J. 1996. *Logics of Dislocation: Models, Metaphors, and Meanings of Economic Space*. New York: Guilford.

Barnes, T.J., J. Britton, W. Coffey, W. Edgington, M. Gertler, and G. Norcliffe. 2000. Canadian economic geography at the millennium. *Canadian Geographer* 44(1): 4-24.

Barnes, T.J., and M. Gertler, eds. 1999. *The New Industrial Geography: Regions, Regulation and Institutions*. New York: Routledge.

Barnes, T.J., and R. Hayter. 1994. Economic restructuring, local development and resource towns: Forest communities in coastal British Columbia. *Canadian Journal of Regional Science* 17(3): 289-10.

Barnes, T.J., and R. Hayter, eds. 1997. *Troubles in the Rainforest: British Columbia's Forest Economy in Transition*. Victoria: Western Geographical Press.

Barnes, T.J., R. Hayter, and E. Hay. 2001. Stormy weather: Cyclones, Harold Innis, and Port Alberni, BC. *Environment and Planning A* 33(12): 2127-47.

Barr, C., L. McKewon, K. Davidman, D. McIver, and D. Lasby. 2004. *The Rural Charitable Sector Research Initiative: A Portrait of the Nonprofit and Voluntary Sector in Rural Ontario*. Toronto: Foundation for Rural Living.

Barry and Associates Consulting. 2003. *Stuart Nechako Regional Development Initiative: Final Report – Phase 1*. Vanderhoof, BC: Community Futures Development Corporation of Stuart Nechako.

Baxter, D., and A. Ramlo. 2002. *Resource Dependency: The Spatial Origins of British Columbia's Economic Base*. Vancouver: Urban Futures Institute.

Baxter, D., R. Berlin, and A.Ramlo. 2005. *Regions and Resources: The Foundations of British Columbia's Economic Base*. Vancouver: Urban Futures Institute.

BC Competition Council. 2006. *Enhancing the Competitiveness of British Columbia*. Vancouver: Author.

BC Progress Board. 2002. *Restoring British Columbia's Economic Heartland*. Vancouver: Author.

–. 2004. *Transportation as an Economic Growth Engine: Challenges, Opportunities and Policy Suggestions*. Report prepared by M.A. Goldberg. Vancouver: Author.

–. 2006. *Boosting Incomes, Confronting Demographic Change: BC's Productivity Imperative*. Vancouver: Author.

BC Stats. 2006. *A Guide to the BC Economy and Labour Market*. Victoria: Author.

–. 2008. *Regional District 55: Peace River Statistical Profile*. Victoria: Author.

–. 2009. *Regional District 49: Kitimat-Stikine Statistical Profile*. Victoria: Author.

BC Treaty Commission. 2002. *"Improving the Treaty Process": Report of the Tripartite Working Group*. Vancouver: Author.
–. 2007. *What's the Deal with Treaties? A Lay Person's Guide to Treaty Making in British Columbia*. Vancouver: Author.
–. 2008. *Why Treaties?* Vancouver: Author.
–. 2009. *BC Treaty Commission: Annual Report 2009*. Vancouver: Author. http://www.bctreaty.net/files/pdf_documents/2009_Annual_Report.pdf.
–. 2012. *BC Treaty Commission: Updates*. Vancouver: Author. http://www.bctreaty.net/files/updates.php.
Beattie, M., and R. Annis. 2008. *The Community Collaboration Story: Community Collaboration Project – Empowering and Building Capacity, 2005-2008*. Final Report. Brandon: Rural Development Institute.
Beckley, T. 1995. Community stability and the relationship between economic and social well-being in forest-dependent communities. *Society and Natural Resources* 8(3): 261-66.
Beesley, K., and L. Daborn, eds. 1997. *Proceedings Rural Resources-Rural Development Conference*. Truro: Nova Scotia Agricultural College, Rural Research Centre.
Berman, E., and J. West. 1995. Public-private leadership and the role of non-profit organizations in local government: The case of social services. *Policy Studies Review* 14(1/2): 235-46.
Bernsohn, K. 1981. *Cutting Up the North: The History of the Forest Industry in the Northern Interior*. North Vancouver: Hancock House.
Beshiri, R. 2001. Employment structure in rural and small town Canada: The manufacturing sector. *Rural and Small Town Canada Analysis Bulletin* 2(8): 1-15.
–. 2004. Immigrants in rural Canada: 2001 Update. *Rural and Small Town Canada Analysis Bulletin* 5(4): 1-27.
–. 2010. Manufacturing employment in resource value chains: A rural-urban comparison from 2001 to 2008. *Rural and Small Town Canada Analysis Bulletin* 8(5): 1-34.
Binkley, C.S. 1997. A cross-road in the forest: The path to a sustainable forests sector in British Columbia. In T.J. Barnes and R. Hayter, *Troubles in the Rainforest*, 16-35.
Birkeland, I. 2008. Cultural sustainability: Industrialism, placelessness and the re-animation of place. *Ethics, Place and Evironment* 11(3): 283-97.
Black, E.R. 1968. British Columbia: The politics of exploitation. In *Exploiting Our Economic Potential*, ed. R. Shearer, 23-41. Toronto: Holt, Rinehart, and Winston.
–. 1989. British Columbia: The politics of exploitation. In *A History of British Columbia: Selected Readings*, ed. P. Roy, 129-42. Toronto: Copp Clark Pitman.
Bluestone, B., and B. Harrison. 1982. *The Deindustrialization of America: Plant Closings, Community Abandonment, and the Dismantling of Basic Industry*. New York: Basic Books.
Bollman, R.D. 2007. *Factors Driving Canada's Rural Economy, 1914-2006*. Ottawa: Statistics Canada.
Bollman, R.D., and H.A. Clemenson. 2008. *Structure and Change in Canada's Rural Demography: An Update to 2006 with Provincial Detail*. Ottawa: Statistics Canada.
Bollman, R.D., and M. Prud'homme. 2006. Trends in the prices of rurality. *Rural and Small Town Canada Analysis Bulletin* 6(7): 1-25.
Bonnell, J., N. Irving, and J. Lewis. 1997. *Timber Workers in Transition: An Ethnographic Perspective on Forest Worker Retraining in the Pacific Northwest*. Victoria: Ministry of Environment.
Booth, A.L., and G. Halseth. 2011. Why the public thinks natural resources public participation processes fail: A case study of British Columbia communities. *Land Use Policy* 28(4): 898-906.
Borgen, W. 2000. Developing partnerships to meet clients' needs in changing government organizations: A consultative process. *Journal of Employment Counseling* 37(2): 128-42.
Bowles, P., J. Lytle, and S. Paterson. 2002. *The Weakest Link: Northern British Columbian Local Communities in the Global Forest Products Chain*. Prince George: Northern Land Institute.
Bowles, R.T. 1982. *Little Communities and Big Industries: Studies in the Social Impact of Canadian Resource Extraction*. Toronto: Butterworths.
–. 1992. Single-industry resource communities in Canada's North. In *Rural Sociology in Canada*, ed. D.S. Hay and G.S. Basran, 63-83. Toronto: Oxford University Press.

Bradbury, J.H. 1978. Class structure and class conflict in "instant" resource towns in British Columbia, 1965 to 1972. *BC Studies* 37: 3-18.
–. 1987. British Columbia: Metropolis and hinterland in microcosm. In *Heartland and Hinterland: A Geography of Canada*, ed. L.D. McCann, 400-41. Scarborough, ON: Prentice-Hall.
Bradbury, J.H., and I. St. Martin. 1983. Winding down in a Quebec mining town: A case study of Schefferville. *Canadian Geographer* 27(2): 128-44.
Bradford, N. 2003. Public-private partnership? Shifting paradigms of economic governance in Ontario. *Canadian Journal of Political Science* 36(5): 1005-33.
–. 2005. *Place-Based Public Policy: Towards a New Urban and Community Agenda for Canada*. Ottawa: Canadian Policy Research Networks.
Bradshaw, B. 2003. Questioning the credibility and capacity of community-based resource management. *Canadian Geographer* 47(2): 137-50.
British Columbia. 1943. *Interim Report of the Post-War Rehabilitation Council*. Victoria: Queen's Printer, The Council.
–. 1981. *Letters Patent – Tumbler Ridge*. Victoria: Queen's Printer, Ministry of Municipal Affairs.
–. 1998. *British Columbia Municipal Act (consolidated)*. Victoria: Queen's Printer, Ministry of Municipal Affairs.
–. 2003a. *B.C. Heartlands Economic Strategy: A Plan to Revitalize Our Entire Province*. Victoria: Government of BC.
–. 2003b. *Forestry Revitalization Plan*. Victoria: Queen's Printer, Ministry of Forests.
–. 2003c. *Report of the BC Climate Change Economic Impacts Panel*. Victoria: Queen's Printer, Ministry of Water, Land and Air Protection and Ministry of Energy and Mines.
–. 2004a. *Northern Development Initiative Trust Act*. Victoria: Queen's Printer. http://www.bclaws.ca/EPLibraries/bclaws_new/document/ID/freeside/00_04069_01.
–. 2004b. *Rebuilding the Heartlands: What We've Accomplished Together*. Victoria: Government of BC.
–. 2006. *Preparing for Climate Change*. Victoria: Queen's Printer, Ministry of Forests and Range.
–. 2007a. *Mountain Pine Beetle Action Plan: Annual Progress Report 2006, 2007*. Victoria: Queen's Printer, Ministry of Forests and Range.
–. 2007b. *New Relationship*. Victoria: Government of BC. http://www.newrelationship.gov.bc.ca/shared/downloads/new_relationship.pdf.
–. Ministry of Aboriginal Relations and Reconciliation. 2010. *First Peoples' Language Map of B.C.* Victoria: Queen's Printer, Ministry of Aboriginal Relations and Reconciliation. http://maps.fphlcc.ca/.
–. Ministry of Community, Aboriginal and Women's Services. 2005. *Memorandum of Understanding between the Province and the Region*. Victoria: Queen's Printer, Ministry of Community, Aboriginal and Women's Services.
–. Ministry of Forests and Range. 2009. *Generating More Value from Our Forests*. Victoria: Queen's Printer, Ministry of Forests and Range.
–. Northern and Rural Health Task Force. 1995. *Report of the Northern and Rural Health Task Force*. Victoria: Queen's Printer, Ministry of Health and Ministry Responsible for Seniors.
–. Provincial Health Officer. 2009. *Provincial Health Officer's Report 2007: Pathways to Health and Healing*. Victoria: Ministry of Healthy Living and Sport.
Bruce, D. 2001. *The Role of Small Businesses and Cooperative Businesses in Community Economic Development*. Montreal: Canadian Rural Revitalization Foundation.
–. 2010. Nurturing the animation sector in a peripheral economic region: The case of Miramichi, New Brunswick. In G. Halseth, S. Markey, and D. Bruce, *The Next Rural Economics*, 128-41.
Bruce, D., and G. Halseth. 2001. *The Long-Run Role of Institutions in Fostering Community Economic Development: A Comparison of Leading and Lagging Rural Communities*. Montreal: Canadian Rural Revitalization Foundation.
Bruce, D., P. Jordan, and G. Halseth. 1999. The role of voluntary organizations in rural Canada: Impacts of changing availability of operational and program funding. In B. Reimer, *Voluntary Organizations*, 2.1-2.52.

Bruce, D., and G. Lister, eds. 2001. *Rising Tide: Community Development Tools, Models and Processes*. Sackville, NB: Rural and Small Town Programme, Mount Allison University.
Brunet, R. 1998. Woodmen, spare those trees! Ending clearcutting of old-growth forest could position MacBlo for a quick sale. *British Columbia Report* 9(37): 19.
Bryant, C. 1995. The role of local actors in transforming the urban fringe. *Journal of Rural Studies* 11(3): 255-67.
–. 2010. Co-constructing rural communities in the 21st century: Challenges for central governments and the research community in working effectively with local and regional actors. In G. Halseth, S. Markey, and D. Bruce, *The Next Rural Economics,* 142-54.
Bulkeley, H. 2006. Urban sustainability: Learning from best practice? *Environment and Planning A* 38(6): 1029-44.
Bulkley Valley Economic Development Office. 2010. *Bulkley Valley Economic Development Initiative*. Smithers: BVEDO.
Burke Wood, P., and D.A. Rossiter. 2011. Unstable properties: British Columbia, Aboriginal title, and the "new relationship." *Canadian Geographer* 55(4): 407-25.
Burnley, C., C. Matthews, and S. McKenzie. 2005. Devolution of services to children and families: The experience of NPOs in Nanaimo, British Columbia, Canada. *Voluntas International Journal of Voluntary and Nonprofit Organizations* 16(1): 69-87.
Butler, R.W. 1980. The concept of a tourist area cycle evolution: Implications for management of resources. *Canadian Geographer* 24(1): 5-12.
Caffyn, A., and M. Dahlström. 2005. Urban-rural interdependencies: Joining up policy in practice. *Regional Studies* 39(3): 283-29.
Canada. Department of Justice. 2007. *Canada Health Act*. Ottawa: Queen's Printer.
–. Indian and Northern Affairs Canada. 2004. *Sustainable Development Strategy 2004-2006: On the Right Path Together – A Sustainable Future for First Nations, Inuit and Northern Communities*. Ottawa: Queen's Printer, Minister of Public Works and Government Services.
–. Industry Canada. 2003. *Innovative Communities in Canada: A Workshop on Best Practices*. Winnipeg: Queen's Printer, Innovation Policy Branch.
–. 2004. *Making a Difference: Contributing to the Quality of Life of Canadians 2003*. Ottawa: Queen's Printer.
–. Infrastructure Canada. 2009. *Canada's Economic Action Plan: Immediate Action to Build Infrastructure*. Ottawa: Queen's Printer. http://www.buildingcanada-chantierscanada.gc.ca/index-eng.html.
–. Ministry of Public Works and Government Services. 2002. *Saskatchewan Northern Development Accord*. Ottawa: Queen's Printer.
–. Secretary of State for Rural Development. 2002. *Fact-Finding Visit to the United States, France, Belgium, Finland and Norway. Summary Report*. Ottawa: Queen's Printer.
–. Senate Standing Committee on Agriculture and Forestry. 2003. *Climate Change: We Are at Risk*. Ottawa: Queen's Printer.
Canada NewsWire. 1999. *Weyerhaeuser Company to Acquire MacMillan Bloedel Limited*. 21 June, 1.
–. 2003. *Canfor Corporation Announces the Sale of BC Chemicals Division*. 29 July, 1.
Canada West Foundation. 2001. *Building the New West: A Framework for Regional Economic Prosperity*. Calgary: Author.
–. 2008. *Economic Development Issues for Rural Communities in the Four Western Provinces: 2010-2015-2020*. Vancouver: Community Futures Pan West.
Canadian Airports Council. 2006. *Consolidated Review of Small Airport Viability Studies*. Ottawa: Author.
Canadian Chamber of Commerce. 2011. *The Business Case for Investing in Canada's Remote Communities*. Ottawa: Author.
Canfor. 2003. Canfor announces sawmill closures. News Release, 23 Jan. Vancouver: Canfor.
–. 2009. Canfor fact sheet. Vancouver: Canfor. http://www.canfor.com/.
Careless, J.M. 1989. *Frontier and Metropolis: Regions, Cities, and Identities in Canada before 1914*. Toronto: University of Toronto Press.
Cariboo-Chilcotin Beetle Action Coalition (CCBAC). 2005. *Cariboo-Chilcotin Beetle Action: 2005-2006 Business Plan*. Williams Lake, BC: Author. http://c-cbac.com/Documents/aboutus/C-CBACBusiness%20PlanJuly27.pdf.

–. 2008. *Cariboo-Chilcotin Mountain Pine Beetle Mitigation Strategy: Living on the Edge of Climate Change – Executive Summary*. Williams Lake, BC: Author.

Castellano, M.B., L. Archibald, and M. DeGagné. 2008. *From Truth to Reconciliation: Transforming the Legacy of Residential Schools*. Ottawa: Aboriginal Healing Foundation.

Cater, J., and T. Jones. 1989. *Social Geography: An Introduction to Contemporary Issues*. New York: Edward Arnold.

CBC News. 2002a. Closure of B.C. legal aid offices will hurt communities, say legal workers. http://www.cbc.ca/stories/2002/08/16/bc_legalaid020816.

–. 2002b. Towns told to pay up to keep courthouses. http://vancouver.cbc.ca/template/servlet/View?filename+bc_courts020815.

–. 2009. Municipalities struggle to cope with influx of immigrants. 19 March 2009. http://www.cbc.ca/canada/story/2009/03/19/immigrants-municipalities-ottawa.html.

Christensen, P., N. McIntyre, and L. Pikholz. 2002. *Bridging Community and Economic Development*. Cleveland, OH: Shorebank Enterprise Group.

City Spaces. 2008. *Community Economic Development Study from Boomtown to Sustainable Town*. Smithers: Economic Development Committee, Town of Smithers.

Clapp, A. 1998. The resource cycle in forestry and fishing. *Canadian Geographer* 42(2): 129-44.

Clark, G., P. Feldman, and M.S. Gertler, eds. 2000. *The Oxford Handbook of Economic Geography*. Oxford: Oxford University Press.

Coles, T. 2006. Enigma variations? The TALC, marketing models and descendents of the product life cycle. In *The Tourism Area Life Cycle,* vol. 2, ed. R.W. Butler, 49-66. Clevedon, UK: Channel View Publications.

Community Futures British Columbia. 2011. *History of Community Futures in British Columbia*. Vancouver. http://www.communityfutures.ca/uploads/CFHistory_handout_col_final2.pdf.

Conference Board of Canada. 2007. *How Canada Performs*. Ottawa: Author.

–. 2011. *Northern Assets: Transportation Infrastructure in Remote Communities*. Ottawa: Author.

Cooke, P., and K. Morgan. 1998. *The Associational Economy: Firms, Regions, and Innovation*. New York: Oxford University Press.

Counsel on BC Aboriginal Economic Development. 2002. *A New Way of Doing Business: A Vision for Aboriginal Economic Development in British Columbia*. Vancouver: Author.

Dale, A., C. Ling, and L. Newman. 2008. Does place matter? Sustainable communtiy development in three Canadian communities. *Ethics, Place and Environment* 11(3): 267-81.

Dandy, K., and R.D. Bollman. 2008. Seniors in rural Canada. *Rural and Small Town Canada Analysis Bulletin* 7(8): 1-56.

Davidson, D.J., T. Williamson, and J.R. Parkins. 2003. Understanding climate change risk and vulnerability in northern forest-based communities. *Canadian Journal of Forest Research* 33: 2252-61.

Davis, H.C., and T.A. Hutton. 1989. The two economies of British Columbia. *BC Studies* 82: 3-15.

Dawe, S. 2004. Placing trust and trusting place: Creating competitive advantage in peripheral rural areas. In G. Halseth and R. Halseth, *Building for Success,* 223-50.

de Peuter, J.C., A. Macdonald, M. Sorensen, and M. Bernard. 2008. *Urban-Rural Interdependencies: Annotated Bibliography*. Edmonton: City-Region Studies Centre, University of Alberta.

de Scally, F., and C. Turchak. 1998. Some environmental aspects and impacts of rapid population growth in the Okanagan Valley, British Columbia, Canada. *Salzburger Geographische Arbeiten* 32(65): 43-63.

de Souza, A. 1990. *A Geography of World Economy*. New York: Macmillan.

de Wolf, J. 2002. *Growth Drivers in British Columbia*. Vancouver: BC Progress Board.

Devuyst, D., and L. Hens. 2000. Introducing and measuring sustainable development initiatives by local authorities in Canada and Flanders (Belgium): A comparative study. *Environment, Development and Sustainability* 2(2): 81-105.

Doloreux, D., L. Hommen, and C. Edquist. 2004. Nordic regional innovation systems: An analysis of the region of East Gothia, Sweden. *Canadian Journal of Regional Science* 27(1): 1-26.

Donaldson, D., and A. Docherty. 2004. *Community Development in the Upper Skeena: Death Feasts and Transformative Change*. Ottawa: Caledon Institute of Social Policy.
Douglas, D.1999. The new rural region: Consciousness, collaboration and new challenges and opportunities for innovative practice. In W. Ramp et al., *Health in Rural Settings*, 39-60.
–. 2003. *Towards More Effective Rural Economic Development in Ontario*. Guelph, ON: School of Environmental Design and Rural Development, University of Guelph.
–. 2005. The restructuring of local government in rural regions: A rural development perspective. *Journal of Rural Studies* 21(2): 231-46.
Douglas, D., ed. 2010. *Rural Planning and Development in Canada*. Toronto: Nelson Education.
Drabenstott, M., and K.H. Sheaff. 2002a. A new generation of rural policy: More lessons from abroad. *Main Street Economist* (Sept.): 1-4.
–. 2002b. The new power of regions: A policy focus for rural America. *Main Street Economist* (June): 1-6.
Drache, D. 1976. Rediscovering Canadian political economy. *Journal of Canadian Studies* 11(3): 3-18.
Drushka, K. 1998. *Tie Hackers to Timber Harvesters: The History of Logging in British Columbia's Interior*. Madeira Park, BC: Harbour Publishing.
Duffy, D., L. Hallgren, Z. Parker, R. Penrose, and M. Roseland. 1998. *Improving the Shared Decision-Making Model: An Evaluation of Public Participation in Land and Resource Management Planning (LRMP) in British Columbia*, vol. 1. Burnaby, BC: Department of Geography and the School of Resource and Environmental Management, Simon Fraser University.
du Plessis, V., R. Beshiri, R. Bollman, and H. Clemenson. 2004. Definitions of rural. In G. Halseth and R. Halseth, *Building for Success*, 51-80.
Dupuy, R., F. Mayer, and R. Morissette. 2000. *Rural Youth: Stayers, Leavers, and Return Migrants*. Report submitted to the Rural Secretariat of Agriculture and Agri-Food Canada and to the Atlantic Canada Opportunities Agency. Ottawa: Statistics Canada.
Edenhoffer, K. 2012. Recession, restructuring, and routine: The case of BC's forest industries, 1980-2008. Ph.D. thesis, Department of Geography, Simon Fraser University.
Edgington, D. 2004. British Columbia and its regional economies: An overview of research issues. *Canadian Journal of Regional Science* 27(3): 303-16.
Essex, S.J., A.W. Gilg, R.B. Yarwood, J. Smithers, and R. Wilson, eds. 2005. *Rural Change and Sustainability: Agriculture, the Environment and Communities*. Oxfordshire: CABI.
European Commission. 2006. *The Leader Approach: A Basic Guide*. Luxembourg: Office for Official Publications of the European Communities.
Evenden, L.J., ed. 1978. *Vancouver: Western Metropolis*. Victoria: University of Victoria.
Fairbairn, B. 1998. *A Preliminary History of Rural Development Policy and Programmes in Canada, 1945-1995*. Saskatoon: NRE Program, University of Saskatchewan.
Federation of Canadian Municipalities (FCM). 2007. *Losing Ground: Canada's Cities and Communities at the Tipping Point*. Ottawa: Author.
–. 2009. *Wake-Up Call: The National Vision and Voice We Need for Rural Canada: The Federal Role in Rural Sustainability*. Ottawa: Author.
Ference Weiker. 2002. *The Impact of Community Futures in Western Canada: Final report*. Vancouver: Western Economic Development Canada.
–. 2003. *Promoting Innovation and Commercialization in Rural BC*. Vancouver: Ference Weiker and Co.
Filion, P. 1998. Potential and limitations of community economic development: Individual initiative and collective action in a post-Fordist context. *Environment and Planning A* 30(6): 1101-23.
First Nations Summit. 2005. *Backgrounder: "A New Relationship"– Implementation of Supreme Court of Canada Decisions*.
Fisher, R. 1992. *Contact and Conflict: Indian-European Relations in British Columbia, 1774-1890*. 2nd ed. Vancouver: UBC Press.
Fitchen, J. 1991. *Endangered Spaces, Enduring Places: Change, Identity, and Survival in Rural America*. Boulder, CO: Westview.
Florida, R. 1995. Towards the learning region. *Futures* 27(5): 527-36.

–. 2002. *The Rise of the Creative Class and How It's Transforming Work, Leisure, Community and Everyday Life*. New York: Basic Books.
Florida, R., C. Mellander, and K. Stolarick. 2010. Talent, technology, and tolerance in Canadian regional development. *Canadian Geographer* 54(3): 277-304.
Forrex. 2006. *BC's Mountain Pine Beetle Epidemic: The Future of Communities and Ecosystems*. Kamloops, BC: Author.
Foster, H. 2002. *Litigation and the BC Treaty Process*. Vancouver: BC Treaty Commission.
Frame, T.M., T. Gunton, and J.C. Day. 2004. The role of collaboration in environmental management: An evaluation of land and resource planning in British Columbia. *Journal of Environmental Planning and Management* 47(1): 59-82.
Freshwater, D. 2003. Will manufacturing remain the pillar of rural development? In OECD, *The Future of Rural Policy: From Sectoral to Place-Based Policies in Rural Areas*, 99-124. Paris: OECD.
Friedmann, J. 1987. *Planning in the Public Domain: From Knowledge to Action*. Princeton, NJ: Princeton University Press.
Fuller, T. 1994. Sustainable rural communities in the arena society. In *Towards Sustainable Rural Communities*, ed. J.M. Bryden, 133-39. Guelph, ON: School of Rural Planning and Development, University of Guelph.
Furuseth, O. 1998. Service provision and social deprivation. In *The Geography of Rural Change*, ed. B. Ilbery, 233-56. Essex, UK: Longman.
Gamu, J.K. 2008. Y they matter: recruitment and retention of Generation Y. *Public Sector Digest* (Dec.): 22-26.
G.E. Bridges and Robinson Consulting. 2005. *Northwest BC Mining Projects: Socio Economic Impact Assessment*. Victoria: Ministry of Small Business and Economic Development.
GE Canada's Remote Communities Initiative. 2011. *Towards a Remote Communities Investment Strategy for Canada*. Mississauga, ON: Remote Communities Initiative.
Gibson, C., M. McKean, and E. Ostrom. 2000. *People and Forests: Communities, Institutions, and Governance*. Cambridge, MA: MIT Press.
Gill, A.M. 1984. Resource towns in British Columbia: The development of Tumbler Ridge. In *Geographic Perspectives on the Provincial Norths*, ed. M.E. Johnston, 134-50. Thunder Bay, ON: Centre for Northern Studies, Lakehead University.
–. 1991. An evaluation of socially responsive planning in a new resource town. *Social Indicators Research* 24(2): 177-204.
–. 2002. Respecting context in northern resource town planning: The case of Tumbler Ridge. *Western Geography* 12: 113-29.
Gill, A.M., and G. Smith. 1985. Residents' evaluative structures of northern Manitoba mining communities. *Canadian Geographer* 29(1): 17-29.
Goebel, J.M., C. Fox, and K.U. Wolniakowski. 2004. *The Role of Rural Communities in Biodiversity Conservation and the Transition to Sustainability: Practical Experiences from the Pacific Northwest United States*. Amsterdam: IOS Press.
Goldberg, M.A. 2004. *Regional Economic Development in British Columbia: Innovation and Renewal for BC's Two Economies*. Vancouver: Centre for Urban Economics and Real Estate.
Greenwood, R., C. Pike, and W. Kearley 2011. *A Commitment to Place: The Social Foundations of Innovation in Newfoundland and Labrador*. St. John's, NL: Harris Centre.
Gregory, D., R. Johnston, G. Pratt, M. Watts, and S. Whatmore. 2009. *The Dictionary of Human Geography*. Malden MA: Blackwell.
Gunton, T. 1997. Forestry land use and public policy in British Columbia: The dynamics of change. In T.J. Barnes and R. Hayter, *Troubles in the Rainforest*, 65-74.
–. 2003. Natural resources and regional development: An assessment of dependency and comparative advantage paradigms. *Economic Geography* 79(1): 67-94.
Guy, S., and S. Marvin. 1999. Understanding sustainable cities: Competing urban futures. *European Urban and Regional Studies* 6(3): 268-75.
Hak, G. 2007. *Capital and Labour in the British Columbia Forest Industry, 1934-74*. Vancouver: UBC Press.
Hallin, L. 2008. Steady growth in 2007 despite slowdown in goods sector. *Business Indicators* (April): 1-8.

Halseth G. 1999a. Resource town employment: Perceptions in small town British Columbia. *Tijdschrift voor Economische en Sociale Geografie* 90(2): 196-210.
–. 1999b. "We came for the work": Situating employment migration in B.C.'s small, resource-based communities. *Canadian Geographer* 43(4): 363-81.
–. 2004. Attracting growth "back" to an amenity rich fringe: Rural-urban fringe dynamics around Metropolitan Vancouver, Canada. *Canadian Journal of Regional Science* 26(2/3): 297-318.
–. 2005. Resource town transition: Debates after closure. In S.J. Essex et al., *Rural Change and Sustainability,* 326-42.
–. 2010. Understanding and transforming a staples economy: Place-based development in northern BC, Canada. In G. Halseth, S. Markey, and D. Bruce, *The Next Rural Economics,* 251-62.
Halseth, G., and A. Booth. 2003. What works well; what needs improvement: Lessons in public consultation from British Columbia's resource planning processes. *Local Environment* 8(4): 437-55.
Halseth, G., and R. Halseth, eds. 2004. *Building for Success: Explorations of Rural Community and Rural Development.* Brandon, MB: Rural Development Institute, Brandon University.
Halseth, G., S. Killam, and D. Manson. 2008a. *Transition Toolkit: Working Framework for a More Resilient Community.* Updated Version. Oct. Prince George: UNBC Community Development Institute. http://www.unbc.ca/assets/cdi/toolkit/mackenzie__transition_toolkit_ed._1_oct._20_2008.pdf.
–. 2008b. Working framework for economic emergencies for smaller municipalities - Part I. *Municipal World* 118(3): 35-39.
–. 2008c. Working framework for economic emergencies for smaller municipalities - Part II. *Municipal World* 118(4): 35-38.
Halseth, G., D. Manson, S. Markey, L. Lax, and O. Buttar. 2007. The connected North: Findings from the Northern BC Economic Vision and Strategy Project. *Journal of Rural and Community Development* 2(1): 1-27.
Halseth, G., S. Markey, and D. Bruce, eds. 2010. *The Next Rural Economies: Constructing Rural Place in a Global Economy.* Oxfordshire: CABI.
Halseth, G., and L. Ryser. 2001. *Tumbler Ridge Community Transition Survey 2001: Socio-Economic Profile Report.* Prince George: Geography Program, UNBC.
–. 2004a. Gender at work and gender at home: The mediating role of the household economy in northern British Columbia's resource dependent towns. In *The Structure and Dynamics of Rural Territories: Geographic Perspectives,* ed. D. Ramsey and C. Bryant, 162-93. Brandon, MB: Rural Development Institute, Brandon University.
–. 2004b. *Service Provision in Rural and Small Town Canada: A Cross-Canada Summary Report.* Montreal: Canadian Rural Revitalization Foundation.
–. 2006. *Service Provision in Rural and Small Town Canada: A Cross-Canada Summary Report.* Montreal: Canadian Rural Revitalization Foundation.
Halseth, G., L. Ryser, and L. Sullivan. 2003. Service provision as part of resource town transition planning: A case from northern British Columbia. In *Opportunities and Actions in the New Rural Economy,* ed. D. Bruce and G. Lister, 29-56. Sackville, NB: Rural and Small Town Programme, Mount Allison University.
Halseth, G., D. Straussfogel, S. Parsons, and A. Wishart. 2004. Regional economic shifts in BC: Speculation from recent demographic evidence. *Canadian Journal of Regional Science* 27: 317-52.
Halseth, G., and L. Sullivan. 1999. Report on the new rural economy: Government funding of community based organizations, Mackenzie and Tumbler Ridge, British Columbia. In B. Reimer, *Voluntary Organizations,* 4.37-4.61.
–. 2002. *Building Community in an Instant Town: A Social Geography of Mackenzie and Tumbler Ridge, British Columbia.* Prince George: UNBC Press.
Halseth, G., and A. Williams. 1999. Guthrie House: A rural community organizing for wellness. *Health and Place* 5(1): 27-44.
Hanlon, N., and G. Halseth. 2005. The greying of resource communities in northern British Columbia: Implications for health care delivery in already under-serviced communities. *Canadian Geographer* 49: 1-24.

Hanlon, N., and M. Rosenberg. 1998. Not-so-new public management and the denial of geography: Ontario health-care reform in the 1990s. *Environment and Planning C: Government and Policy* 16(5): 559-72.

Harris, R.C. 1997. *The Resettlement of British Columbia: Essays on Colonialism and Geographical Change*. Vancouver: UBC Press.

–. 2002. *Making Native Space: Colonialism, Resistance, and Reserves in British Columbia*. Vancouver: UBC Press.

Harris, [R.]C., and R. Galois. 1994. Recalibrating society: The population geography of British Columbia in 1881. *Canadian Geographer* 38(1): 37-53.

Harris, R.C., and G.J. Matthews, eds. 1987. *Historical Atlas of Canada*, vol. 1: *From the Beginning to 1800*. Toronto: University of Toronto Press.

Harvey, R.G. 2004. *Head On! Collisions of Egos, Ethics, and Politics in B.C.'s Transportation History*. Surrey, BC: Heritage House.

Hayter, R. 1979. Labour supply and resource-based manufacturing in isolated communities: The experience of pulp and paper mills in north-central British Columbia. *Geoforum* 10(2): 163-77.

–. 1982. Truncation, the international firm and regional policy. *Area* 14(14): 277-82.

–. 1997. High-performance organizations and employment flexibility: A case of in situ change at the Powell River paper mill, 1980-1994. *Canadian Geographer* 41(1): 26-40.

–. 2000. *Flexible Crossroads: The Restructuring of British Columbia's Forest Economy*. Vancouver: UBC Press.

–. 2003. "The War in the Woods": Post-Fordist restructuring, globalization and the contested remapping of British Columbia's forest economy. *Annals of the Association of American Geographers* 93(3): 706-29.

–. 2004. The contested restructuring qua remapping of BC's forest economy: Reflections on the crossroads and war in the woods metaphors. *Canadian Journal of Regional Science* 27(3): 395-414.

Hayter, R., and T.J. Barnes. 1990. Innis' staple theory, exports, and recession: British Columbia, 1981-1986. *Economic Geography* 66(2): 156-73.

–. 1997a. The restructuring of British Columbia's coastal forest sector: Flexibility perspectives. In T.J. Barnes and R. Hayter, *Troubles in the Rainforest*, 181-203.

–. 1997b. Troubles in the rainforest: British Columbia's forest economy in transition. In Barnes and Hayter, *Troubles in the Rainforest*, 1-11.

Henderson, J., and N. Novack. 2003. Building new competitive advantages for the 21st century. *Main Street Economist* (Jan.): 1-4.

Herbert-Cheshire, L., and V. Higgins. 2004. From risky to responsible: Expert knowledge and the governing community-led rural development. *Journal of Rural Studies* 20(3): 289-302.

Hessing, M., and M. Howlett. 1997. *Canadian Natural Resource and Environmental Policy*. Vancouver: UBC Press.

Himelfarb, A. 1976. *The Social Characteristics of One-Industry Towns in Canada: A Background Report*. Ottawa: Royal Commission on Corporate Concentration.

Hirczak, M., M. Moalla, A. Mollard, B. Pecqueur, M. Rambonilaza, and D. Vollet. 2008. From the basket of goods to a more general model of territorialized complex goods: Concepts, analysis grid and questions. *Canadian Journal of Regional Science / Revue canadienne des sciences régionales* 31(2): 241-60.

Hodgson, G.M. 1998. The approach of institutional economics. *Journal of Economic Literature* 36: 166-92.

Hoekstra, G. 2002. Ferry cuts blasted. *Prince George Citizen*, 11 Oct., 1.

–. 2008. Mackenzie demands help. *Prince George Citizen*, 24 May, 1.

Hood, P. 1991. A public management for all seasons? *Public Administration* 69(1): 3-19.

Hope, M. 2001. Town that wouldn't take a tumble: Huge real-estate sale brings new life to B.C. community. *Calgary Herald*, 16 June, HS04.

Horne, G. 2004. *British Columbia's Heartland at the Dawn of the 21st Century: 2001 Economic Dependencies and Impact Ratios for 63 Local Areas*. Victoria: Ministry of Management Services.

Horne, G., and B. Penner. 1992. *British Columbia Community Employment Dependencies*. Victoria: Planning and Statistics Division and Ministry of Finance and Corporate Relations.

House, J.D. 1999. *Against the Tide: Battling for Economic Renewal in Newfoundland and Labrador.* Toronto: University of Toronto Press.
Hudson, R. 2005. Region and place: Devolved regional government and regional economic success? *Progress in Human Geography* 29(5): 618-25.
Hunter, J., and C. McInnes. 2000. Miller powerless to stop death of Tumbler Ridge: Minister said he was blindsided by Teck's decision to close mine. *Vancouver Sun,* 2 March, D1.
Hutton, T. 1997. Vancouver as a control centre for British Columbia's resource hinterland: Aspects of linkage and divergence in a provincial staple economy. In T.J. Barnes and R. Hayter, *Troubles in the Rainforest,* 233-62.
–. 2002. *British Columbia at the Crossroads.* Vancouver: BC Progress Board.
Huxham, C., and S. Vangen. 1996. Working together: Key themes in the management of relationships between public and non-profit organizations. *International Journal of Public Sector Management* 9(7): 5-17.
Innis, H.A. 1933. *Problems of Staple Production in Canada.* Toronto: Ryerson Press.
–. 1950. *Empire and Communications.* Toronto: University of Toronto Press.
– (edited by Mary Q. Innis). 1956. *Essays in Canadian Economic History.* Toronto: University of Toronto Press.
Isaksen, A. 2001. Globalisation: A challenge for local industrial policy. *Canadian Journal of Regional Science* 24(1): 101-20.
Iyer, S., M. Kitson, and B. Toh. 2005. Social capital, economic growth and regional development. *Regional Studies* 39(8): 1015-40.
James, A.M. 1999. Closing rural hospitals in Saskatchewan: On the road to wellness? *Social Science and Medicine* 49: 1021-34.
Jentsch, B., and M. Shucksmith, eds. 2004. *Young People in Rural Areas of Europe.* Aldershot: Ashgate.
Johnson, J., and R. Rasker. 1995. The role of economic and quality of life values in rural business location. *Journal of Rural Studies* 11(4): 405-16.
Jones, M. 2001. The rise of the region state in economic governance: "Partnerships for Prosperity" or new scales of state power? *Environment and Planning A* 33(7): 1185-1211.
Joseph, A., and P. Bantock. 1984. Rural accessibility of general practitioners: The case of Bruce and Grey counties, Ontario, 1901-1981. *Canadian Geographer* 28(3): 226-39.
Kearney, B., G. Boyle, and J. Walsh. 1994. *EU LEADER I in Ireland: Evaluation and Recommendations.* Dublin: Department of Agriculture, Food and Forestry.
Keast, R., M. Mandell, K. Brown, and G. Woolcock. 2004. Network structures: Working differently and changing expectations. *Public Administration Review* 64(3): 363-71.
Kedgley, G. 2009. Lessons from the development of northeast coal in British Columbia. Prince George: Community Development Institute, UNBC.
Kennedy, W.D. 2005. Local government in northern British Columbia: Competing or cooperating? *Northern Review* 25/26: 50-58.
Kitson, M., R. Martin, and P. Tyler. 2004. Regional competitiveness: An elusive yet key concept. *Regional Studies* 38(9): 991-99.
Kjos, J. 2002. *Rural Roads in the North Peace: Driving British Columbia's Economy.* Fort St. John: North Peace Economic Development Commission.
Konkin, J., D. Howe, and T. Soles. 2004. SRPC policy paper on regionalization, spring 2004. *Canadian Journal of Rural Medicine* 9(4): 257-59.
Korsching, P., S. El-Ghamrini, and G. Peter. 2001. Rural telephone companies: Offering technology innovations to enhance the economic development of communities. *Technology and Society* 23: 79-91.
KPMG, 1996. *The Benefits and Costs of Treaty Settlement in British Columbia.* Vancouver: Author.
–. 2010. *Competitive Alternatives: KPMG's Guide to International Business Location.* Toronto: Author.
Kraybill, D., and M. Kilkenny. 2003. Economic rationales for and against place-based policies? Paper presented at Agricultural and Applied Economics Association and Rural Sociological Society Annual Meeting, Montreal, 27-30 July.
Kresl, P.K. 1995. The determinants of urban competitiveness: A survey. In *North American Cities and the Global Economy,* ed. G. Gappert and P.K. Kresl, 45-68. Thousand Oaks, CA: Sage.

Kunin, R. 2003. *Maximizing 2010 Employment and Skills Opportunities*. Vancouver: 2010 Winter Games Human Resources Planning Committee.

Lane, E. 2000. *New Public Management*. London: Routledge.

Larsen, L., S. Harlan, B. Bolin, E. Hackett, D. Hope, A. Kirby, A. Nelson, T. Rex, and S. Wolf. 2004. Bonding and bridging: Understanding the relationship between social capital and civic action. *Journal of Planning Education and Research* 24(1): 64-77.

Larson, S. 2004. Place identity in a resource-dependent area of northern British Columbia. *Annals of the Association of American Geographers* 94(4): 944-60.

Lawlor, A. 2002. B.C. heritage site to go private. *Globe and Mail*, 7 Aug. http://www.globeandmail.com/servlet/ArticleNews/front/RTGAM/20020807/.

Lax, L., J. Backhouse, and P. Bowles. 2001. *The Northern Development Commission: One Model for Supporting Community Economic Development in Northern British Columbia*. Prince George: UNBC.

Laxer, G. 1989. *Open for Business*. Toronto: Oxford University Press.

Leach, B., and A. Winson. 1999. Rural retreat: The social impact of restructuring in three Ontario communities. In *Restructuring Societies*, ed. D.B. Knight and A.E. Joseph, 83-104. Ottawa: Carleton University Press.

LeBlanc, S., S. LeBlanc, and C. von Schilling. 2003. *Labour Market Partnership for Trades in North-Central British Columbia: Discussion Document*. Report prepared for the Labour Market Partnership for Trades Steering Committee. Ottawa: Human Resources Development Canada.

Lee, M. 2003. *Bleeding the Hinterland: A Regional Analysis of BC's Tax and Spending Cuts*. Vancouver: Canadian Centre for Policy Alternatives.

Leonard, F. 1996. *A Thousand Blunders: The Grand Trunk Pacific Railway and Northern British Columbia*. Vancouver: UBC Press.

Leroy, A. 1997. *Les activités de service: Une chance pour les économies rurales? Vers de nouvelles logiques de développement rural*. Paris: L'Harmattan.

Lesky, S., E. O'Sullivan, and B. Goodman. 2001. Local public–non-profit partnerships: Getting better results. *Policy and Practice* (Sept.): 28-32.

Lewis, M., and S. Lockhart. 2001. The Oregon Benchmarks: Oregonians are getting results from this approach to governance – Can we too? *Making Waves* 12(2): 4-12.

Little, B. 2002. B.C.'s decades of genteel decline. *Globe and Mail*, 20 April, B1, B4.

Liu, L., J. Hader, B. Brossart, R. White, and S. Lewis. 2001. Impact of rural hospital closures in Saskatchewan, Canada. *Social Science and Medicine* 52(12): 1793-1804.

Lo, J., and G. Halseth. 2009. The practice of principles: An examination of CED groups in Vancouver, BC. *Community Development Journal* 44(1): 80-110.

Loppie Reading, C., and F. Wien. 2009. *Health Inequalities and Social Determinants of Aboriginal Peoples' Health*. Prince George: National Collaborating Centre for Aboriginal Health.

Louden, P. 1973. *The Town That Got Lost: A Story of Anyox, British Columbia*. Sidney, BC: Gray's Publishing.

Lovering, J. 1999. Theory led by policy: The inadequacies of the "new regionalism." *International Journal of Urban and Regional Research* 23: 379-85.

Lowndes, V. 2004. Getting on or getting by? Women, social capital and political participation. *British Journal of Politics and International Relations* 6(1): 45-64.

Lucas, R.A. 1971. *Minetown, Milltown, Railtown: Life in Canadian Communities of Single Industry*. Toronto: University of Toronto Press.

Lukkarinen, M. 2005. Community development, local economic development and the social economy. *Community Development Journal* 40(4): 419-24.

Mackenzie, S., and G. Norcliffe. 1997. Restructuring in the Canadian newsprint industry. *Canadian Geographer* 31(1): 2-6.

MacKinnon, D. 2002. Rural governance and local involvement: Assessing state-community relations in the Scottish Highlands. *Journal of Rural Studies* 18(3): 307-24.

MacKinnon, D., A. Cumbers, and K. Chapman. 2002. Learning, innovation and regional development: A critical appraisal of recent debates. *Progress in Human Geography* 26(3): 293-311.

Mackintosh, W.A. 1991. Economic factors in Canadian history. In *Approaches to Canadian Economic History*, ed. W.T. Easterbrook and M.H. Watkins, 1-15. Toronto: McClelland and Stewart.

MacLeod, G. 2001a. New regionalism reconsidered: Globalization and the remaking of political economic space. *International Journal of Urban and Regional Research* 25(4): 804-29.

–. 2001b. Beyond soft institutionalism: Accumulation, regulation, and their geographical fixes. *Environment and Planning A* 33(7): 1145-67.

Malecki, E. 2004. Jockeying for position: What it means and why it matters to regional development policy when places compete. *Regional Studies* 38(9): 1101-20.

Marchak, P. 1983. *Green Gold: The Forest Industry in British Columbia*. Vancouver: UBC Press.

–. 1995. *Logging the Globe*. Montreal and Kingston: McGill-Queen's University Press.

Marchak, P., S. Aycock, and D. Herbert. 1999. *Falldown: Forest Policy in British Columbia*. Vancouver: David Suzuki Foundation and Ecotrust Canada.

Markey, S. 2003. Facing uncertainty: Building local development institutions in rural British Columbia. Doctoral Dissertation, Department of Geography, Simon Fraser University.

–. 2005. Building local development institutions in the hinterland: A regulationist perspective from British Columbia, Canada. *International Journal of Urban and Regional Research* 29(2): 358-74.

Markey, S., G. Halseth, and D. Manson. 2006a. *From Planning to Action: Reconciling Community Development Strategies with Regional Assets and Infrastructure: A Report on Re-orienting to Readiness and Overcoming Barriers to Implementation in the Northwest Region of British Columbia*. Prince George: Community Development Institute, UNBC.

–. 2006b. The struggle to compete: From comparative to competitive advantage in northern British Columbia. *International Planning Studies* 11(1): 19-39.

–. 2007. The (dis)connected North: Persistent regionalism in northern British Columbia. *Canadian Journal of Regional Science* 30(1): 57-78.

–. 2008a. Challenging the inevitability of rural decline: Advancing the policy of place in northern British Columbia. *Journal of Rural Studies* 24(4): 409-21.

–. 2008b. Closing the implementation gap: A framework for incorporating the context of place in economic development planning. *Local Environment* 13(4): 337-51.

Markey, S., J.T. Pierce, K. Vodden, and M. Roseland. 2005. *Second Growth: Community Economic Development in Rural BC*. Vancouver: UBC Press.

Marsden, T., and J. Murdoch. 1998. Editorial: The shifting nature of rural governance and community participation. *Journal of Rural Studies* 14(1): 1-4.

Marsden, T., E. Eklund, and A. Franklin. 2004. Rural mobilization as rural development: Exploring the impacts of new regionalism in Wales and Finland. *International Planning Studies* 9(2-3): 79-100.

Marsden, T., P. Lowe, and S. Whatmore, eds. 1990. *Rural Restructuring: Global Processes and Their Responses*. London: David Fulton.

Marsden, T., and R. Sonnino. 2008. Rural development and the regional state: Denying multifunctional agriculture in the UK. *Journal of Rural Studies* 24(4): 422-31.

Marshall, J. 1999. Voluntary activity and the state: Commentary and review of the literature relating to the role and impact of government involvement in rural communities in Canada. In B. Reimer, *Voluntary Organizations,* 1.1-1.36.

Martin, S. 1998. The forest and the trees: Tom Stephen's bold vision for BC forests – No more clear-cuts, privatized woodlands, challenges his industry to think differently. *Report on Business Magazine* 15(6): 60.

Mascarenhas, M., and R. Scarce. 2004. "The intention was good": Legitimacy, consensus-based decision making, and the case of forest planning in British Columbia, Canada. *Society and Natural Resources* 17(1): 17-38.

Massey, D. 1984. Introduction: Geography matters. In *Geography Matters! A Reader*, ed. D. Massey and J. Allen, 1-11. Cambridge: Cambridge University Press.

–. 1995. *Spatial Divisions of Labour*. London: Macmillan.

Masuda, J., and T. Garvin. 2008. Whose heartland? The politics of place in a rural-urban interface. *Journal of Rural Studies* 24(1): 112-23.

Mather, A., G. Hill, and M. Nijnik. 2006. Post-productivism and rural land use: Cul de sac or challenge for theorization? *Journal of Rural Studies* 22(9): 441-55.

McArthur, D. 2010. *Looking Forward: The BC Economy at a Crossroads*. A background discussion paper commissioned by the Leader of the British Columbia New Democrat Official Opposition. Vancouver: Simon Fraser University. http://www.ourprovinceourfuture.bc.ca/discussion-paper.

McCann, L.D., ed. 1987. *Heartland and Hinterland: A Geography of Canada*. 2nd ed. Scarborough, ON: Prentice-Hall.

McDonald, C., and J. Warburton. 2003. Stability and change in nonprofit organizations: The volunteer contribution. *Voluntas: International Journal of Voluntary and Nonprofit Organizations* 14(4): 381-99.

McGillivray, B. 2005. *Geography of British Columbia: People and Landscapes in Transition*. 2nd ed. Vancouver: UBC Press.

McInnes, C. 1995. Prince George: Re-inventing the university. *Globe and Mail*, 8 April, D3.

McKinley, J. 2009. International dinners wows Old Massett. *QCI Observer*. http://www.qciobserver.com/Article.aspx?Id=4192.

McMahon, F. 2003. Rural development: An oxymoron. *Time Magazine* (Canadian Edition), 13 Oct. 62(15): 59.

Meinhard, A., and M. Foster. 2003. Differences in the response of women's voluntary organizations to shifts in Canadian public policy. *Nonprofit and Voluntary Sector Quarterly* 32(3): 366-96.

Milbourne, L., S. Macrae, and M. Maguire. 2003. Collaborative solutions or new policy problems: Exploring multi-agency partnerships in education and health work. *Journal of Education Policy* 18(1): 19-35.

Mirza, S. 2007. *Danger Ahead: The Coming Collapse of Canada's Municipal Infrastructure*. Ottawa: Federation of Canadian Municipalities.

Mitchell, D. 1983. *WAC Bennett and the Rise of British Columbia*. Vancouver: Douglas and MacIntyre.

Mitchell, T.L., and D.T. Maracle. 2005. Healing the generations: Post-traumatic stress and the health status of Aboriginal populations in Canada. *Journal of Aboriginal Health* (March): 14-23.

Moran, B. 1994. *Justa: A First Nations Leader*. Vancouver: Arsenal Pulp Press.

Morey, C. 2008. Speaking notes at Horn River Symposium, Fort Nelson, BC, 21 Sept.

Morford, S., and R. Kahlke, eds. 2004. *Communities and Natural Resources in Transition: Linking Social Science, Decision Makers, and Practitioners for a Sustainable Future*. Kamloops: Forrex-Forest Research Extension Partnership.

Morrison, H.T. 2006. Pursuing rural sustainability at the regional level: Key lessons from the literature on institutions, integration, and the environment. *Journal of Planning Literature* 21(2): 143-52.

Mulkey, S., and D. Murphy. 2002. *Survey of Capacity Building Initiatives for Rural Economic Development in North America*. Nelson, BC: Columbia Basin Trust.

Munro, J.M. 2004. Policies to induce structural change in the British Columbia economy. *Canadian Journal of Regional Science* 27(3): 447-69.

Murdoch, J., and S. Abram. 1998. Defining the limits of community governance. *Journal of Rural Studies* 14(1): 41-50.

Myers, H. 2000. *Final Report to Forest Renewal BC Research Program: Experiences of Small-Scale Forest-Based Enterprises in Northern British Columbia*. Victoria: Science Council of British Columbia.

Natcher, D., S. Haley, G. Kofinas, and W. Parker. 2003. *Effective Local Institutions for Collective Action in Arctic Communities: Workshop Summary*. Anchorage, AL: Institute for Social and Economic Research, University of Alaska.

National Collaborating Centre for Aboriginal Health. 2009/2010a. *Economic Development as a Social Determinant of First Nations, Inuit and Métis Health*. Prince George, BC: National Collaborating Centre for Aboriginal Health.

–. 2009/2010b. *Poverty as a Social Determinant of First Nations, Inuit, and Métis Health*. Prince George: National Collaborating Centre for Aboriginal Health.

National Post. 2003. Duke Energy gets go-ahead for pipeline extension, 7 Jan., FP2.

Neil, C., A. Tykkläinen, and J. Bradbury. 1992. *Coping with Closure: An International Comparison of Mine Town Experiences*. New York: Routledge.
Nelles, H.V. 2005. *The Politics of Development: Forests, Mines and Hydro-electric Power in Ontario, 1849-1941*. 2nd ed. Montreal and Kingston: McGill-Queen's University Press.
Nelson, H., K. Niquidet, and I. Vertinsky. 2006. *Assessing the Socioeconomic Impact of Tenure Changes in British Columbia*. Vancouver: BC Forum on Forest Economics and Policy.
Nelson, P. 1999. Quality of life, nontraditional income, and economic growth: New development opportunities for the rural west. *Rural Development Perspectives* 14(2): 38-43.
Nelson, P., and A. Sewall. 2003. Regional comparisons of metropolitan and nonmetropolitan migration in the 1970s and 1980s: Age and place implications. *Professional Geographer* 55(1): 83-99.
Nelson, R., and R. MacKinnon. 2004. The peripheries of British Columbia: Patterns of migration and economic structure, 1976-2002. *Canadian Journal of Regional Science* 27(3): 353-94.
Nicol, S. 2003. *Northeast BC Oil and Gas Sector Employment Analysis*. Fort St. John: North Peace Economic Development Commission.
Nolin, C., K. McCallum, and A. Zehtab-Martin. 2009. *Regionalization BC 2008: Regionalization and Rural Immigration in British Columbia*. Vancouver: Metropolis British Columbia, Centre of Excellence for Research on Immigration and Diversity, University of British Columbia.
North, D., and D. Smallbone. 2000. The innovativeness and growth of rural SMEs during the 1990s. *Regional Studies* 34(2): 145-57.
Northern Alberta Development Council. 2002. *Analysis of Container Use in the Alberta and British Columbia Peace Region: Terms of Reference*. Peace River, AB: Northern Alberta Development Council.
Northern Development Initiative (NDI) Trust. Homepage. http://northerndevelopment.bc.ca/.
–. n.d. *Strategic Plan 2006-2008*. Prince George: Northern Trust.
–. 2009. *Northern Economic Summit A Resounding Success!* Prince George: Author. http://northerndevelopment.bc.ca/news/43/57/Northern-Economic-Summit-A-Resounding-Success.
Northern Priorities. 2002. *2002 Symposium on Northern Transportation Issues, Conclusions, and Recommendations*. Prince George: Northern Priorities.
Northwest Tribal Treaty Nations. 2004. *Working Together to Create Sustainable Wealth*. Terrace, BC: Author.
Notzke, C. 1994. *Aboriginal People and Natural Resources in Canada*. Toronto: York University Publications.
Nutter, R., and M. McKnight. 1994. Scope and characteristics of CED: Summary, policy implications and research needs. In *Community Economic Development: Perspectives on Research and Policy*, ed. B. Galloway and J. Hudson, 92-96. Toronto: Thompson Educational.
O'Brien, P., A. Pike, and J. Tomaney. 2004. Devolution, the governance of regional development and the Trades Union Congress in the northeast region of England. *Geoforum* 35: 59-68.
OECD. 2005. *The Measurement of Scientific and Technological Activities: Guidelines for Collecting and Interpreting Innovation Data – Oslo Manual*. 3rd ed. Paris: Author.
–. 2006. *The New Rural Paradigm: Policies and Governance*. Paris: Author.
Omineca Beetle Action Coalition (OBAC). 2007. http://www.ominecacoalition.ca/who-we-are.htm.
–. 2009. *OBAC Diversification and Implementation Plan*. Prince George: Author.
Osborne, D., and T. Gaebler. 1993. *Reinventing Government*. New York: Plume.
Osborne, S., and N. Flynn. 1997. Managing the innovative capacity of voluntary and non-profit organizations in the provision of public services. *Public Money and Management* (Oct.-Dec.): 31-39.
Osborne, S., and K. McLaughlin. 2002. A new public management in context. In *New Public Management: Current Trends and Future Prospects*, ed. K. McLaughlin, S. Osborne, and E. Ferlie, 7-14. London: Routledge.
O'Toole, K., and N. Burdess. 2004. New community governance in small rural towns: The Australian experience. *Journal of Rural Studies* 20(4): 433-43.

Ostry, A. 1999. The links between industrial, community, and ecological sustainability: A forest case study. *Ecosystem Health* 5(3): 193-203.

Parkins, J. 2008. The metagovernance of climate change: Institutional adaptation to the mountain pine beetle epidemic in British Columbia. *Journal of Rural and Community Development* 3(2): 7-26.

Partridge, M. 2006. *Geography of American Poverty: Is There a Need for Place-Based Policies?* Kalamazoo, MI: W.E. Upjohn Institute for Employment Research.

Patchell, J. 1996. Kaleidoscope economies: The process of cooperation, competition, and control in regional economic development. *Annals of the Association of American Geographers* 86(3): 481-506.

Peet, R. 1997. *Theories of Development*. New York: Guilford.

Peters, E.J. 2000. Aboriginal people and Canadian Geography: A review of the recent literature. *Canadian Geographer* 44(1): 44-55.

Petroleum Human Resources Council of Canada. 2003. *Strategic Human Resources Study of the Upstream Petroleum Industry: The Decade Ahead*. Calgary: Author.

Pezzini, M. 2000. *Rural Policy Lessons: From OECD Countries*. Kansas City, MO: Federal Reserve Bank of Kansas City.

–. 2001. Rural policy lessons from OECD countries. *International Regional Science Review* 24(1): 134-45.

Pierce, J.T. 1992. Progress and the biosphere: The dialectics of sustainable development. *Canadian Geographer* 36(4): 306-20.

Pierce, J.T., and A. Dale, eds. 1999. *Communities, Development and Sustainability across Canada*. Vancouver: UBC Press.

Plecas, B. 2006. *Bill Bennett: A Mandarin's View*. Vancouver: Douglas and MacIntyre.

Polèse, M. 1999. From regional development to local development: On the life, death, and rebirth(?) of regional science as a policy relevant science. *Canadian Journal of Regional Science* 22(3): 299-314.

Porteous, D.J. 1970. Gold River: An instant town in British Columbia. *Geography* 55(3): 317-22.

–. 1987. Single enterprise communities. In *British Columbia: Its Resources and People*, ed. C.N. Forward, 383-99. Victoria: University of Victoria.

Porter, M. 2000. Location, competition, and economic development: Local clusters in a global economy. *Economic Development Quarterly* 14(1): 15-34.

–. 2004. *Competitiveness in Rural US Regions: Learning and Research Agenda*. Boston, MA: Institute for Strategy and Competitiveness, Harvard Business School.

Potapchuk, W., J. Crocker, and W. Schechter. 1997. Building community with social capital: Chits and chums or chats with change. *National Civic Review* 86(2): 129-39.

Price Waterhouse. 1990. *Economic Value of Uncertainty Associated with Native Land Claims in British Columbia*. http://www.bctreaty.net/files/issues_financial.php.

PricewaterhouseCoopers. 2009. *Financial and Economic Impacts of Treaty Settlements in BC*. Vancouver: Author.

Prince George Citizen. 2004. Permit issued for coal mine near Chetwynd, 11 Sept., 3.

Putnam, R. 2000. *Bowling Alone: The Collapse and Revival of American Community*. New York: Simon and Schuster.

Québec. Ministère des Affaires Municipales et des Régions. 2006. *National Policy on Rurality: A Source of Strength for Quebec*. Quebec: Government of Quebec.

Ramírez, R. 2001. A model for rural and remote information and communication technologies: A Canadian exploration. *Telecommunications Policy* 25(5): 315-30.

Ramp, W., J. Kulig, I. Townshend, and V. McGowan, eds. 1999. *Health in Rural Settings: Contexts for Action*. Lethbridge, AB: University of Lethbridge.

Ramsey, P. 2005. Some thoughts on a Northern Ministry for British Columbia. *Northern Review* 25/26: 59-70.

Randall, J.E., and G. Ironside. 1996. Communities on the edge: An economic geography of resource-dependent communities in Canada. *Canadian Geographer* 40(1): 17-35.

Reed, M.G. 2003a. Marginality and gender at work in forestry communities in British Columbia, Canada. *Journal of Rural Studies* 19(3): 373-89.

–. 2003b. *Taking Stands: Gender and the Sustainability of Rural Communities.* Vancouver: UBC Press.
Reed, M., and A. Gill. 1997. Tourism, recreational, and amenity values in land allocation: An analysis of institutional arrangements in the postproductivist era. *Environment and Planning A* 29(1): 2019-40.
Reimer, B. 2002. A sample frame for rural Canada: Design and evaluation. *Regional Studies* 36(8): 845-59.
–. 2006. The rural context of community development in Canada. *Journal of Rural and Community Development* 1(2): 155-75.
–. 2009. *Key Findings from 20 Years of Canadian Rural Research.* Vancouver: Real Estate Foundation of BC.
Reimer, B., ed. 1999. *Voluntary Organizations in Rural Canada: Final Report.* Montreal: Canadian Rural Restructuring Foundation.
Reimer, B., and S. Markey. 2008. *Place-Based Policy: A Rural Perspective.* Report prepared for Human Resources and Social Development Canada. Montreal: Concordia University.
Rennie, B., and G. Halseth. 1998. Employment in Prince George. In *Prince George: A Social Geography of B.C's "Northern Capital,"* ed. G. Halseth and R. Halseth, 45-66. Prince George: UNBC Press.
Research Universities Council of BC. 2010. *Baccalaureate Graduates Survey (2006 Survey of 2004 Graduates; 2005 Survey of 2000 Graduates; 2004 Survey of 2002 Graduates).* Victoria: Author. http://www.rucbc.ca/content/view/33/31/.
Richmond, C.A., and N. A. Ross. 2009. The determinants of First Nation and Inuit health: A critical population health approach. *Health and Place* 15(2): 403-11.
Robinson, E.L. 2007. The cross-cultural collaboration of the community forest. MA Thesis, UNBC.
Romanow, R. 2002. *Building on Values: The Future of Health Care in Canada – Final Report.* Commission on the Future of Health Care in Canada. Ottawa: Health Canada.
Rosenfeld, S.A., and K.H. Sheaff. 2002. Can regional colleges make a difference in rural America? *Main Street Economist* (May): 1-4.
Rothwell, N. 2010. Standing firm: Rural business enterprises in Canada. *Rural and Small Town Canada Analysis Bulletin* 8(3). http://www.statcan.gc.ca/pub/21-006-x/21-006-x2008003-eng.htm.
Royal Commission on Aboriginal Peoples. 1996a. *People to People, Nation to Nation: Highlights from the Report of the Royal Commission on Aboriginal Peoples.* http://www.ainc-inac.gc.ca/ap/pubs/rpt/rpt-eng.asp.
–. 1996b. *Report of the Royal Commission on Aboriginal Peoples.* 5 vols. Ottawa: Indian and Northern Affairs Canada. http://www.collectionscanada.gc.ca/webarchives/20071124125216/http://www.ainc-inac.gc.ca/ch/rcap/sg/sg1_e.html.
Rural Secretariat. 2001. *Enhancing the Quality of Life for Rural Canadians: Annual Report to Parliament.* Ottawa: Author.
Rye, J. 2006. Heading for the cities? Gender and lifestyle patterns in rural youths' residential preferences. *Norsk Geografisk Tiddskrift – Norwegian Journal of Geography* 60(3): 199-20.
Sasaki, H., I. Saito, A. Tabayashi, and T. Morimoto, eds. 1996. *Geographical Perspectives on Sustainable Rural Systems: Conference Proceedings.* Tsukuba, Japan: Kaisei Publications.
Saunders, R. 2004. *Passion and Commitment under Stress: Human Resource Issues in Canada's Non-profit Sector – A Synthesis Report.* Ottawa: Canadian Policy Research Networks.
Savoie, D. 1992. *Regional Economic Development: Canada's Search for Solutions.* Toronto: University of Toronto Press.
–. 1997. *Rethinking Canada's Regional Development Policy: An Atlantic Perspective.* Ottawa: Canadian Institute for Research on Regional Development.
Schrier, D. 2007. *BC's Commodity Exports Are Still Largely Forest-Based.* Victoria: BC Stats.
Schuller, T. 2001. The complementary roles of human and social capital. *ISUMA* (Spring): 18-24.
Scott, A.J. 1998. *Regions and the World Economy.* Oxford: Oxford University Press.
–. 2000. Economic geography: The great half-century. In G. Clark et al., *Oxford Handbook of Economic Geography,* 18-44.

–. 2009. Jobs or amenities? Destination choices of migrant engineers in the USA. *Papers in Regional Science* 89(1): 43-63.
Scott, M. 2004. Building institutional capacity in rural Northern Ireland: The role of partnership governance in the LEADER II programme. *Journal of Rural Studies* 20(1): 49-59.
Shaffer, R., S. Deller, and D. Marcouiller. 2006. Rethinking community economic development. *Economic Development Quarterly* 20(1): 59-74.
Simpson, S. 2007. Collapse of Galore mine project leaves transmission line in limbo. *Vancouver Sun*, 28 Nov. http://www.canada.com/vancouversun/news/business/story.html?id=12ec5fd0-604c-4758-83d6-6859792efdf8.
Skeena Native Development Society. 2003a. *Labour Market Census*. http://www.snds.bc.ca/lmc.htm.
–. 2003b. *Masters in Our Own House: The Path to Prosperity – Report of the Think Tank on First Nations Wealth Creation*. Terrace, BC: Author.
Smylie, J. 2008. The health of Aboriginal peoples. In *Social Determinants of Health: Canadian Perspectives*, 2nd ed., ed. D. Raphael, 281-301. Toronto: Canadian Scholars' Press.
Southern Interior Beetle Action Coalition (SIBAC). 2011. http://sibacs.com/.
Spencer, K. 2004. Chalo School. In *Sharing Our Success: Ten Case Studies in Aboriginal Schooling*, ed. D. Bell, 97-119. Kelowna, BC: Society for the Advancement of Excellence in Education.
Stabler, J., and M.R. Olfert. 1992. *Restructuring Rural Saskatchewan: The Challenge of the 1990s*. Regina, SK: Canadian Plains Research Centre, University of Regina.
Statistics Canada. 1981. *Census of Canada*. Ottawa: Author.
–. 1991. *Census of Canada*. Ottawa: Author.
–. 2001. *Census of Canada*. Ottawa: Author.
–. 2003. Rural economic diversification: A community and regional approach. *Rural and Small Town Canada Analysis Bulletin* 4(7): 1-16. Ottawa: Author.
–. 2006. *Census of Canada*. Ottawa: Author.
Stein, C.S. 1952. Planning objectives. Kitimat, BC: District of Kitimat, reprinted in *Kitimat Townsite 1962 Report*.
Stohr, W., and F. Taylor. 1981. *Development from Above or Below?* Toronto: Wiley.
Storper, M. 1997. *The Regional World: Territorial Development in a Global Economy*. New York: Guilford.
–. 1999. The resurgence of regional economics: Ten years later. In T.J. Barnes and M. Gertler, *The New Industrial Geography*, 23-53.
Sullivan, L.M. 2002. The geography of community crisis: A case of Tumbler Ridge, BC. MA Thesis, UNBC.
Swanson, L. 1990. Rethinking assumptions about farm and community. In *American Rural Communities*, ed. A. Luloff and L. Swanson, 19-33. Boulder, CO: Westview.
Swyngedouw, E. 2000. Elite power, global forces, and the political economy of "glocal" development. In G. Clark et al., *Oxford Handbook of Economic Geography*, 541-58.
Synergy Management Group. 2003. *The Regional Net Wealth Balance Sheet: Economic Modeling (Regional Inflow and Outflow of Funds for the Central Coast Regional District)*. Victoria: Ministry of Sustainable Resource Management.
Tahltan First Nation and International Institute for Sustainable Development. 2004. *Out of Respect: The Tahltan, Mining, and the Seven Questions to Sustainability*. Winnipeg: Author.
Tang, S.Y., and A.J. Browne. 2008. "Race" matters: Racialization and egalitarian discourses involving Aboriginal people in the Canadian health care context. *Ethnicity and Health* 13(2): 109-27.
Teitelbaum, S., and B. Reimer. 2002. *The Social Economy in Rural Canada: Exploring Research Options*. http://nre.concordia.ca/nre_reports.htm.
Tennant, P. 1990. *Aboriginal Peoples and Politics: The Indian Land Question in British Columbia, 1849-1989*. Vancouver: UBC Press.
Terluin, I. 2003. Differences in economic development in rural regions or advanced countries: An overview and critical analysis of theories. *Journal of Rural Studies* 19(3): 327-44.
Terrace Standard. 2005. Northern hydro line needed for development, 7 Sept., 1.
Thomas, L., Jr. 2009. Thriving Norway provides an economics lesson. *New York Times*. 14 May. http://www.nytimes.com/2009/05/14/business/global/14frugal.html.

Thornton, G. 1999. *Financial and Economic Analysis of Treaty Settlements in British Columbia*. Victoria: Grant Thornton Management Consultants.
Tindal, R., and S. Nobes-Tindal. 2004. *Local Government in Canada*, 6th ed. Scarborough, ON: Nelson/Thompson.
Tomblin, S. 1990. W.A.C. Bennett and province-building in British Columbia. *BC Studies* 85: 45-61.
Torjman, S., and E. Leviten-Reid. 2003. *Innovation and CED: What They Can Learn from Each Other*. Ottawa: Caledon Institute of Social Policy.
Troughton, M. 1999. Redefining "rural" for the twenty-first century. In W. Ramp et al., *Health in Rural Settings*, 21-38.
–. 2005. Fordism rampant: The model and reality, as applied to production, processing and distribution in the North American agro-food system. In S.J. Essex et al., *Rural Change and Sustainability*, 13-27.
Tumbler Ridge Community Connections. 2000. Tumbler Ridge – in for the long haul, 15 March, 1.
Tumbler Ridge, District of. 2003. *Official Community Plan*. http://www.district.tumbler-ridge.bc.ca/econ.html.
Tumbler Ridge News. 2004. Western Canada Coal open house, 9 June, 1.
Tumbler Ridge Revitalization Task Force. 2000. *Terms of Reference: Structure of the Tumbler Ridge Revitalization Task Force*. Tumbler Ridge, BC: District of Tumbler Ridge.
Tumbler Ridge Tattler. 1984a. Price hikes held off, 14 May, 2.
–. 1984b. Price a question, 9 Jan., 1.
Turok, I. 2004. Cities, regions and competitiveness. *Regional Studies* 38(9): 1069-83.
Union of BC Municipalities. 2004. *Proposal for Sharing Resource Revenues with Local Governments*. Victoria: Author.
University of Northern British Columbia (UNBC). 2003. *Building for the Future of Health Care in Northern B.C.* Prince George: UNBC Northern Medical Program Community Action Group.
Usher, P.J. 2003. Environment, race and nation reconsidered: Reflections on Aboriginal land claims in Canada. *Canadian Geographer* 47(4): 365-82.
Valemount, Village of. 2004. *Valemount 2020 Vision: Implementation Strategy*. Prepared by Brent Harley and Associates, and Western Management Consultants, for the Village of Valemount. Valemount, BC: Author.
Valley Sentinel. 1992a. The last mail train, 7 April, 2.
–. 1992b. Shortage of nurses forces cutbacks at D and T, 11 Feb., 3.
–. 1994. After hours service at Valemount Health Centre remains suspended, 12 April, 1.
–. 1995. VIA passenger service reduced, 4 May, 3.
–. 1996a. Employment Offices close, 31 Jan., 6.
–. 1996b. McBride loses government agents, 27 Nov., 3.
–. 1996c. Forestry Office loses a quarter of its staff, 11 Dec., 5.
Vancouver Sun. 2001. Tumbler Ridge coal feasible, study says, 1 Feb., D3.
–. 2008. "Not a good year" for Canadian Forestry, 24 July 2008. http://www.canada.com/story_print.html?id=2f1352c7-7d31-441f-8cbb-c6595c08858c&sponsor=.
Wall, E., G. Ferrazzi, and F. Schryer. 1998. Getting the goods on social capital. *Rural Sociology* 63(2): 300-22.
Wallis, A. 1998. Social capital and community building: Part two. *National Civic Review* 87(4): 317-36.
Walter, G.R. 1997. Staples, regional growth and community sustainability. In T.J. Barnes and R. Hayter, *Troubles in the Rainforest*, 287-303.
Watkins, M. 1981. The staple theory revisited. In *Culture, Communication, and Dependency: The Tradition of H.A. Innis*, ed. W.H. Melody, L. Salter, and P. Heyer, 53-71. Norwood, NJ: Ablex.
–. 1982. The Innis tradition in Canadian political economy. *Canadian Journal of Political Science and Social Theory* 6(1-2): 12-34.
Wells, B. 2002. *Smart Growth at the Frontier: Strategies and Resources for Rural Communities*. Washington, DC: Northeast-Midwest Institute.

Welsh Development Agency. 2002. *Competing with the World: Best Practices in Regional Economic Development*. Treforest, Wales: Author.

West Fraser Timber. 2007. *Annual Report*. Vancouver: Author.

Wien, F. 2009. *The State of the First Nations Economy and the Struggle to Make Poverty History*. Ottawa: Assembly of First Nations.

Williston, E., and B. Keller. 1997. *Forests, Power, and Policy: The Legacy of Ray Williston*. Prince George: Caitlin Press.

Wilson, G. 2004. The Australian *Landcare* movement: Towards "post-productivist" rural governance? *Journal of Rural Studies* 20(4): 461-84.

Wilson, G.N., and G. Poelzer. 2005. Still forgotten? The politics and communities of the provincial Norths. *Northern Review* 25/26: 11-16.

Wilson, J. 1997. Implementing forest policy change in British Columbia: Comparing the experiences of the NDP governments of 1972-75 and 1991-?. In T.J Barnes, and R. Hayter, *Troubles in the Rainforest,* 75-98.

Windley, P. 1983. Community services in small rural towns: Patterns of use by older residents. *Gerontologist* 23(2): 180-84.

Woods, M. 1998. Advocating rurality? The repositioning of rural local government. *Journal of Rural Studies* 14(1): 13-26.

–. 2007. Engaging the global countryside: Globalization, hybridity and the reconstitution of rural place. *Progress in Human Geography* 31(4): 485-507.

Young, N. 2008. Radical neoliberalism in British Columbia: Remaking rural geographies. *Canadian Journal of Sociology* 33(1): 1-36.

Young, N., and R. Matthews. 2007. Resource economies and neoliberal experimentation: The reform of industry and community in rural British Columbia. *Area* 39(2): 176-85.

Zahner, S. 2005. Local public health system partnerships. *Public Health Reports* 120(1): 76-83.

Index

f = figure, n = note, t = table

Printed and bound in Canada by Friesens
Set in Stone by Artegraphica Design Co. Ltd.
Copy editor: Kate Baltais
Proofreader: Dianne Tiefensee
Cartographer: Eric Leinberger